POLICING AND URBAN SOCIETY IN EIGHTEENTH-CENTURY PARIS

Policing and urban society in eighteenth-century Paris

Edited by

PASCAL BASTIEN

Published by Liverpool University Press on behalf of
© 2024 Voltaire Foundation, University of Oxford
ISBN: 978 1 83553 676 6
eISBN: 978 1 83553 677 3
ePUB: 978 1 83553 678 0

Oxford University Studies in the Enlightenment 2024:08
ISSN 2634-8047 (Print)
ISSN 2634-8055 (Online)

Voltaire Foundation
99 Banbury Road
Oxford OX2 6JX, UK
www.voltaire.ox.ac.uk

A catalogue record for this book is available from the British Library

The correct style for citing this book is
Pascal Bastien, ed., *Policing and urban society in
eighteenth-century Paris*
Oxford University Studies in the Enlightenment
(Liverpool, Liverpool University Press, 2024)

Cover illustration: Anonymous, Scène de rue, engraving, around 1732.
Musée Carnavalet, Paris. CC0 Paris Musées / Musée Carnavalet

Oxford University Studies in the Enlightenment

POLICING AND URBAN SOCIETY IN EIGHTEENTH-CENTURY PARIS

In the eighteenth century, as the forms, practices and spaces of urban sociability emerged and took shape (for instance in salons, clubs, theatres, public places and promenades), police forces and policing practices were undergoing far-reaching changes, which occurred at different rates, in different ways and with varying degrees of intensity. Prompted by recent works examining the dynamics of communal living and social regulations at the time of the Enlightenment, this volume explores the transformations of urban sociability through the prism of police reform – not through direct convergences, but in the articulation of communal issues and the possible meeting or tensions between the processes that are more closely linked than previously thought.

Policing and urban society in eighteenth-century Paris connects several different expressions of sociability with the practices of police administration to investigate the stakes, innovations and relationships that disrupted and moulded the institutional and social frameworks of Enlightenment Paris.

Contents

III. The people of Paris: negotiating and resisting authority

List of figures and tables

To Daniel Roche (1935-2023)

Acknowledgements

This project was initiated at a workshop held in spring 2018 at the Institute for Advanced Studies in Paris. The hospitality we were given at the time enabled the whole team to debate and reflect in the best possible conditions. It was the starting point of a long-term collaboration that continues to this day.

This book owes a great deal to Nicole Charley, who translated the texts of the French contributors into English. Her discussions with the authors ensured that the translation was as faithful as possible to the French context and historiography.

The financial support of the Groupe de recherche en histoire des sociabilités (GRHS) was essential to the realisation of this project, and we are very grateful for it.

Finally, this book is indebted to the teaching, advice and friendship of Daniel Roche, who passed away in 2023. His insights have nourished ours, and his work lives on in our own.

Introduction: policing urban community, solidarity and sociability in eighteenth-century Paris

Pascal Bastien

Université du Québec à Montréal, GRHS, IHMC

To characterise Paris in the eighteenth century, we could probably come up with a dozen or so well-established formulas, strong and effective archetypes that are, *a priori*, undisputed and that, each in its own way, allow us to encompass a city of 650,000 inhabitants in a single idea.

Capital of the Enlightenment.

Capital of politeness and elegance.

Capital of philosophy.

But also a capital of insurrection, if not revolution.

And, above all, a capital of enforcement, repression and even despotism.

In the eighteenth century, Paris was a hub for people and goods, a world of salons and cafés, the headquarters of the Republic of Letters. At the same time, it was the abyss into which the naive and the ambitious were swallowed up, the cesspool where misery bubbled, the arena where anger roared. And it was the place where the police had been invented: this modern, omnipresent police force whose agents watched over and supervised, filleted writers, threw beggars in jail and maintained moral and social order at the point of their swords. For a long time, historiography has seen eighteenth-century Paris as all of these things, to varying degrees. But beyond these fragments of truth, it was also something else entirely.

Order and disorder in the city

At its core, a city is simply a means of controlling people and spaces. Cities allow for the running of courts, the collection of taxes, the provision of sanitation services, the supervision of food supply, the curtailing of begging, the development of trade and a close watch over morality.[1] However, the methods, conditions and built environments that encouraged *le vivre-ensemble* (the art of harmonious cohabitation) were also central preoccupations of city officials. Though models of sociability aplenty circulated in the eighteenth century, each city devised its own particular brand – worldly or informal, scholarly or plebeian, conservative or subversive – according to its own social, political, professional, confessional and territorial specificities, excluding or including individuals to varying degrees.[2] How did the police regulate, monitor, administer – and help fashion – the urban environment and social relationships in Paris?

Civitas (in Latin) and *polis* (in Greek) refer to our modern concept of 'city'. *Civitas* – from which we derive 'civilisation' and 'citizenship' – and *polis* – from which we derive 'politeness', 'politics' and the 'police' as the administration of the city – constitute two legacies from which the history of the city, of any city, takes its meaning. More than a space and its infrastructures, it is a population conceived through a territory; sociability imagined through a form of citizenship; political communities envisaged through social and spatial proximities.

The aim of this book is to examine this tension: how did the Paris police regulate, monitor and administer the urban space of the city and the social relations that were played out and constructed within it? What was, in the age of Enlightenment, the relationship between

---

1. Alan Williams, 'The police and public welfare in eighteenth-century Paris', *Social science quarterly* 56:3 (1975), p.398-409; Martin Raeff, *The Well-ordered police state: social and institutional change in the Germanies and Russia, 1600-1800* (London, 1983); David G. Barrie, *Police in the age of improvement: police development and the civic tradition in Scotland, 1775-1865* (Cullompton, 2008); F. M. Dosworth, 'The idea of police in eighteenth-century England: discipline, reformation, superintendance, c. 1780-1800', *Journal of the history of ideas* 69:4 (2008), p.583-604; Marco Cicchini, *La Police de la République: l'ordre public à Genève au XVIIIᵉ siècle* (Rennes, 2012); *Cameralism in practice: state administration and economy in early modern Europe*, ed. Marten Seppel and Keith Tribe (Cambridge, 2017).

2. Brian Cowan, 'In public: collectivities and polities', in *A Cultural history of emotion in the Baroque and Enlightenment age (1600-1800)*, ed. Claire Walker *et al.* (London, 2019), p.155-72.

the police and the people of Paris? Was policing a constraint, or a public service?

These questions are rooted in a banality: the city is a place of promiscuity. A promiscuity that sometimes protects, sometimes threatens. Neighbourhoods are both intrusive and protective, based on administrative boundaries, religious interactions, voluntary associations and groups of political influence centred around a prominent figure. In fact, the neighbourhood can be understood on the scale of a parish, a district, a block, a street or even a building.[3] A neighbourhood is an inhabited space; it lives and it breathes with the people who navigate its every nook and cranny – and Paris was a jumble of neighbourhoods that stood cheek by jowl. So, too, was Paris sociability a pell-mell juxtaposition of associations, frictions, solidarities and oppositions.[4] How did the interplay between inclusion and exclusion take shape in such a world, where spatial proximity and social proximity did not necessarily equate? Spaces sometimes worked to blur the lines of status, and periods of migration could rapidly make neighbours out of strangers.[5] These closely intertwined networks – woven, unravelled and woven anew – harmonised individual interests, strengthened social ties, forged business relationships, publicly aired or settled conflicts, exploited neighbourhood solidarity, and mediated the interactions between inhabitants and city authorities.[6] Like

3. *Voisiner: mutations urbaines et construction de la cité du Moyen Age à nos jours*, ed. Laurent Besse *et al.* (Tours, 2018); David Garrioch, *Neighbourhood and community in Paris, 1740-1790* (Cambridge, 1986); Alain Cabantous, 'Le quartier, espace vécu à l'époque moderne', *Histoire, économie et société* 13:3 (1994), p.427-39; Maurizio Gribaudi, *Paris ville ouvrière: une histoire occultée, 1789-1848* (Paris, 2014).

4. Daniel Roche, *The People of Paris: an essay in popular culture in the 18th century* (1981; Berkeley, CA, 1987), and David Garrioch, *The Making of revolutionary Paris* (Berkeley, CA, 2002).

5. *La Ville promise: mobilité et accueil à Paris (fin XVIIᵉ-début XIXᵉ siècle)*, ed. Daniel Roche (Paris, 2000); Olivier Zeller, 'Espace privé, espace public et cohabitation: Lyon à l'époque moderne', in *La Société des voisins: partager un habitat collectif*, ed. Bernard Haumont and Alain Morel (Paris, 2005), p.187-207; Marc Vacher, 'Au bonheur de voisiner: sociabilités et solidarités dans les immeubles lyonnais au XVIIIᵉ siècle', in *Etranges voisins: altérité et relations de proximité dans la ville depuis le XVIIIᵉ siècle*, ed. Judith Rainhorn and Didier Terrier (Rennes, 2010), p.67-93; Suzanne Rau, *Raüme der Stadt: eine Geschichte Lyons 1300-1800* (Frankfurt, 2014).

6. *Etre Parisien*, ed. Claude Gauvard and Jean-Louis Robert (Paris, 2004); *Notre-Dame et l'Hôtel de Ville: incarner Paris du Moyen Age à nos jours*, ed. Isabelle Backouche, Boris Bove *et al.* (Paris, 2016); *La Ville est à nous! Aménagement*

any capital of the Enlightenment (London, Vienna, Amsterdam or Geneva), but in its own way, Paris allows us to examine the contacts, frictions, solidarities and resistances that occured, at ground level, between all the players who made up the city.

At the crossroads of a social and urban history of the people of Paris in the eighteenth century, our aim in this book is to examine the links, tensions and breakdowns of trust between the people of the capital and one of the most important institutions responsible for supervising them, the Parisian police. What bonds were formed, what tensions were generated, what trust was breached between the people of the French capital and one of the foremost institutions charged with their supervision? Historians have recently come to question the idea that urban order and social regulations were maintained – and contained – by a vast yet efficient royal bureaucracy, the long arm of the police and justice system vigilantly watching for signs of disorder in the capital, primed to punish. If this had been true, the whole century would have seemed one constant, irreconcilable conflict between the people's right to happiness and the protection of traditional hierarchies provided by the authorities. To be sure, those pressures did exist. Yet urban sociability was part and parcel of the city's political economy; *le vivre-ensemble* was not achieved *in opposition* to a people whose every gesture was bridled, but *collectively*, by means of constant negotiation.

The nine contributions in this book, rounded off by Marco Cicchini's brilliant conclusion in a rich comparative assessment, reconstruct, chronologically and thematically, *from below* and *from above*, the social history of a capital city, and the political history of Parisians without authority. It is, we believe, a new history of Paris in the eighteenth century that we offer here. This volume aims to expand the notion of sociability to encompass the broad range of informal, variable, everyday interactions. Through a shift in viewpoint, Paris is repositioned from simple backdrop to central figure in our understanding of the social interactions that distinguished eighteenth-century life. It is the city, the public places, the streets that provide the critical link between policing and urban society. The authors have sought to move beyond the well-lit spaces

urbain et mobilisations sociales depuis le Moyen Age, ed. Isabelle Backouche, Nicolas Lyon-Caen *et al.* (Paris, 2018); *Paris et ses peuples au XVIIIe siècle*, ed. Pascal Bastien and Simon Macdonald (Paris, 2020).

in the historiography of sociability (theatres,[7] salons[8] and cafés[9]) to concentrate instead on sociable *practices*. Police regulations can be seen as a form of sociability, albeit one that is imposed. In a certain sense, the police records themselves, on which a large part of this research is based, were part and parcel of the construction of social interactions, sociability and solidarity. Each contribution probes the various touch points between the people and the police, naturally passing through different spaces, yet the focus remains the intersection between social practices and methods of control. This book explores the transformations in eighteenth-century urban sociability through the prism of police reform – not where the two converge directly, but in their symbiotic relationship, each fuelling the other. Something unique was born of their unlikely partnership.

What is the *police*?

Despite the numerous works devoted to the history of the Parisian police in the seventeenth and eighteenth centuries, from volumes by Alan Williams and Marc Chassaigne[10] to the more recent research of Vincent Milliot and Nicolas Vidoni,[11] the 'police system' still retains a number of grey areas. Each of the essays in this book seeks to dispel some of them. In fact, around an institution – the Chambre de police du Châtelet de Paris – that was fairly firmly anchored in the body of government, constellations of agents worked for the city and the state, for social and urban order, sometimes attached to the Paris police force, sometimes not; sometimes acting under its authority

7. Jeffrey S. Ravel, *The Contested parterre: public theater and French political culture, 1680-1791* (Ithaca, NY, 1999).
8. Antoine Lilti, *The World of the salons: sociability and worldliness in eighteenth-century Paris* (2005; Oxford, 2015); and Steven D. Kale, *French salons: high society and political sociability from the Old Regime to the Revolution of 1848* (Baltimore, MD, 2004).
9. Brian Cowan, 'English coffeehouses and French salons: rethinking Habermas, gender and sociability in early modern French and British historiography', in *Making space public in early modern Europe: performance, geography, privacy*, ed. Angela Vanhaelen and Joseph P. Ward (London, 2013), p.41-53; Thierry Rigogne, 'Readers and reading in cafés, 1660-1800', *French historical studies* 41:3 (2018), p.473-94.
10. Alan Williams, *The Police of Paris, 1718-1789* (Baton Rouge, LA, 1979); Marc Chassaigne, *La Lieutenance générale de police de Paris* (1906; Paris, 1975).
11. Vincent Milliot, *'L'Admirable Police': tenir Paris au siècle des Lumières* (Ceyzérieu, 2016); Nicolas Vidoni, *La Police des Lumières, XVIIᵉ-XVIIIᵉ siècles* (Paris, 2018).

or protection, sometimes not. Everything was far from settled in 1667, with the edict establishing the Lieutenance générale de police. Historians have long considered – almost taken for granted – the year 1667 as a definitive shift, from the old world of communities and neighbourhoods to a new world of centralised authorities and supervision. However, as we will see, the old world never completely disappeared, especially in the minds of the people; nor was the new world the caricature that accounts from the last decade of the *Ancien Régime* would have us believe.

Between 1667 and 1789, the way in which law and order was maintained in the capital changed rapidly. The most obvious change was undoubtedly the increase in the power of the royal government over the city, which at the same time eroded the powers of local authorities such as the municipality and seigneurial and ecclesiastical jurisdictions. This gradual concentration of power led to changes in the way the various agents responsible for maintaining order and security operated. This led to changes in the principles and methods of social control in the city. The various reform movements can be characterised by three trends: the territorialisation of policing forces (i.e. 'the division of space into units of territory that are sufficiently well calibrated to be properly administered');[12] a move towards the specialisation and professionalisation of the agents responsible for policing;[13] and greater attention to written procedures and their formalisation.[14]

12. Vincent Milliot, 'Réformer les polices urbaines au siècle des Lumières: le révélateur de la mobilité', *Crime, histoire & sociétés* 10:1 (2006), p.25-50 (38). Translations are my own unless otherwise noted. See also Alan Williams, 'The police and the administration of eighteenth-century Paris', *Journal of urban history* 4:2 (1978), p.157-82; Brigitte Marin, 'Administrations policières, réformes et découpages territoriaux (XVIIᵉ-XIXᵉ siècle)', *Mélanges de l'Ecole française de Rome: Italie et Méditerranée* 115:2 (2003), p.745-50; Milliot, *'L'Admirable Police'*; Vidoni, *La Police des Lumières*.

13. Steven Laurence Kaplan, 'Note sur les commissaires de police de Paris au XVIIIᵉ siècle', *Revue d'histoire moderne et contemporaine* 28:4 (1981), p.669-86; Milliot, *'L'Admirable Police'*.

14. Vincent Denis, 'Quand la police a le goût de l'archive: réflexions sur les archives de la police de Paris au XVIIIᵉ siècle', in *Pratiques d'archives à l'époque moderne: Europe, mondes coloniaux*, ed. Maria-Pia Donato and Anne Saada (Paris, 2019), p.183-203; Marie-Elisabeth Jacquet, 'Vie et mort d'un dépôt d'archives: les archives de la Bastille dans les années 1780', *Circé. Histoire, savoirs, sociétés* 16:1 (2022), http://www.revue-circe.uvsq.fr/vie-et-mort-dun-depot-darchives-les-ar-chives-de-la-bastille-dans-les-annees-1780/ (last accessed on 16 January 2024).

In eighteenth-century Paris, the exercise of power influenced all urban functions and practices. The legal territories were defined by the ordinances, laws and regulations issued by the King's Council or Parliament, which defined the extent and limits of the respective powers of the Châtelet (royal provost) and the Bureau de la ville (municipal administration) in the capital. At the end of the seventeenth century, the definition of these territories was based on an amalgam formed, on the one hand, by ancient legislation on the powers of the Prévôté des marchands dating back to Charles VI and, on the other hand, by a recent creation, the Lieutenance générale de police, which, at the heart of the Châtelet, involved a redistribution of powers between the urban authorities. If the responsibilities devolved to the new magistrate were partly at the expense of other institutions, however, the terms of this legislation were in many respects rather vague, and did not always explicitly distinguish the boundaries of the jurisdictions or the limits of each party's powers. Every contribution in this volume focuses on and analyses the muted tensions, and head-on confrontations, between a Lieutenance générale de police seeking to structure and centralise a system for bringing order to the capital, and authorities and populations whose autonomy and capacity to act are being reorganised and redefined, sometimes with complicity, sometimes with a little more resistance. Between the all-too-smooth image of a capital governed by police despotism, and the jumble and apparent confusion of the jurisdictions that the archives first present to us, this book seeks to reconcile the objective of rationality and efficiency of the police administration, and the more or less harsh frictions of practice on the ground.

Before the creation of the Lieutenance générale, policing duties in Paris had been shared between two competing institutions: the Prévôté des marchands and the Châtelet royal courts. The first relied on minor municipal officers serving within the city's sixteen quarters.[15] The latter allocated authority in civil and criminal matters to the *lieutenant civil* and the *lieutenant criminel*. The *lieutenant civil* had monopoly of everyday policing activities. The Paris Parlement had oversight of the municipality and the Châtelet courts, and mediated any jurisdictional conflicts – and there were indeed many – between them.

In the second half of the seventeenth century, the Parlement would combine the offices of the *prévôt des marchands* and the *lieutenant civil*,

---

15. Robert Descimon and Jean Nagle, 'Les quartiers de Paris du Moyen Age au XVIIIe siècle', *Annales. Economies, sociétés, civilisations* 34:5 (1979), p.956-83.

establishing a sort of municipal government that included magistrates, petty officers, *échevins* (aldermen) and simple bourgeois notables.[16] Police ordinances relayed the work of this hybrid police force. Town criers recited the new (or renewed) orders in public squares or outside churches, and posters were plastered on city walls. The ordinances published rules about vagrancy,[17] street maintenance,[18] fire prevention,[19] food supply[20] and urban traffic flow.[21] Police ordinances were evidently prescriptive (and inevitably preceded by a preamble declaiming their merits), but they also relied on the people's tacit consent, a certain trust that Parisians, mindful of public order and the common good, would naturally adopt the new regulations.[22] Parish assemblies, corporations and local communities were the regulatory bodies that cemented social relationships for the common good. Police oversight could afford to be more lax, less proactive, since these other bodies helped regulate behaviour within communities. While various authorities might be responsible for cleaning and security within a community, surveillance was a responsibility everyone shared.

The edict of 1667 redefined the powers of the civil and criminal lieutenants of the Châtelet, entrusting a single entity, the lieutenant of police, with ensuring public order and maintaining an abundant supply of food to the capital.[23] The scope of police responsibilities

16. Mathieu Marraud, *De la ville à l'Etat: la bourgeoisie parisienne XVIIᵉ-XVIIIᵉ siècle* (Paris, 2009); Nicolas Lyon-Caen and Mathieu Marraud, 'Multiplicité et unité communautaire à Paris: appartenances professionnelles et carrières civiques, XVIIᵉ-XVIIIᵉ siècles', *Histoire urbaine* 40:2 (2014), p.19-35.

17. Christian Romon, 'Mendiants et policiers à Paris au XVIIIᵉ siècle', *Histoire, économie et société* 1:2 (1982), p.259-95.

18. Nicolas Lyon-Caen and Raphaël Morera, 'Naissance, réorganisation ou formalisation d'un système d'information? La propreté des rues de Paris, XVIᵉ-XVIIIᵉ siècles', *Flux* 1-2:111-12 (2018), p.44-56.

19. David Garrioch, 'Why didn't Paris burn in the seventeenth and eighteenth centuries?', *French historical studies* 42:1 (2019), p.35-64.

20. Reynald Abad, *Le Grand Marché: l'approvisionnement alimentaire de Paris sous l'Ancien Régime* (Paris, 2002).

21. Annik Pardailhé-Galabrun, 'Les déplacements des Parisiens dans la ville aux XVIIᵉ et XVIIIᵉ siècles: un essai de problématique', *Histoire, économie et société* 2 (1983), p.205-53.

22. Garrioch, *Neighbourhood and community in Paris*; Nicolas Lyon-Caen and Raphaël Morera, *A vos poubelles citoyens! Environnement urbain, salubrité publique et investissement civique (Paris, XVIᵉ-XVIIIᵉ siècle)* (Ceyzérieu, 2020).

23. It is often difficult to distinguish between royal, police and judicial functions during this period, particularly since the various responsibilities were frequently grouped together and carried out by the same people. Some illuminating

was relatively clearly defined even if the jurisdictions of court, armed forces and police forces were not. The lieutenant general of police and the officers under his authority were the newest contenders in the race to keep one of the largest and most populous capitals in Europe running smoothly. They exercised authority over public safety and morality,[24] religion,[25] food supply,[26] health and hygiene, and kept watch over public opinion,[27] the printing industry,[28] public markets[29] and how these latter were organised. The Châtelet now had its own lower court where the lieutenant general of police himself sat in judgement. This new administration answered directly to the Conseil du roi (King's Council). In the ten years following its establishment, operations were restructured and streamlined at a pace that alarmed many observers. The administrative map of the capital was being redesigned. What had previously come under the authority of the parishes, local notables and trade communities was allocated to the administration of the lieutenant general. Historians have attempted to describe the transition from the sociability of notables in the late seventeenth century to the centralised *citadinité*, or urban identity, of the eighteenth century, which saw the dissolution of local consultative bodies and the Bureau de la ville's waning influence, as the state used its new police instrument to expand its own sway.[30] In the first half of

---

observations on this issue can be found in Marguerite Boulet-Sautel, 'Police et administration en France à la fin de l'Ancien Régime: observations terminologiques', in *Histoire comparée de l'administration (IVᵉ-XVIIIᵉ siècles)*, ed. Werner Paravicini and Karl Ferdinand Werner (Munich, 1980), p.47-51; Paolo Napoli, *Naissance de la police moderne: pouvoirs, normes, société* (Paris, 2003).

24. Erica-Marie Benabou, *La Prostitution et la police des mœurs au XVIIIᵉ siècle* (Paris, 1987).

25. Pierre Chaunu *et al.*, *Le Basculement religieux de Paris au XVIIIᵉ siècle* (Paris, 1998); David Garrioch, *The Huguenots of Paris and the coming of religious freedom, 1685-1789* (Cambridge, 2014).

26. Abad, *Le Grand Marché*.

27. Lisa Jane Graham, *If the king only knew: seditious speech in the reign of Louis XV* (Charlottesville, VA, 2000); Robert Darnton, *Poetry and the police: communication networks in eighteenth-century Paris* (Cambridge, 2010).

28. Robert Darnton, *Pirating and publishing: the book trade in the age of Enlightenment* (Oxford, 2021).

29. Abad, *Le Grand Marché*; Elisabeth Rochon, 'Le marché aux chevaux de Paris (1662-1789): un espace, des usages, une police', doctoral dissertation, Université du Québec à Montréal and Université Paris 1, Panthéon-Sorbonne, 2023.

30. Thomas M. Luckett, 'Hunting for spies and whores: a Parisian riot on the eve of the French Revolution', *Past and present* 156 (1997), p.116-43; Laurence Croq, 'La municipalité parisienne à l'épreuve des absolutismes: démantèlement

the eighteenth century, the relationship of the commissaires with local communities similarly shifted from one of neighbourly proximity to a compartmentalisation of specialised skills. The edict lists a wide range of matters over which the police lieutenant's jurisdiction extends, but the (deliberately?) vague nature of these legal texts obviously opens the door to multiple interpretations. Briefs submitted to Parliament when a dispute arose revealed divergent, even contradictory, interpretations of the texts that still governed their powers at the end of the eighteenth century. In addition to the sometimes blurred lines drawn between their jurisdictions by royal legislation, the Châtelet and the Bureau de la ville, but also the Généralité, the Chambre des bâtiments, the *enclos* (Saint-Martin-des-Champs, Le Temple, etc.) and sometimes even the Church, themselves drew lines through their claims, which more often than not aimed to increase the territory under their authority. We can then understand the crucial importance of producing archives and building a 'state memory' capable of classifying precedents, ensuring legitimacy based on the written word, and transferring and organising the knowledge of officers, who made it their property, to the institution they were to serve, in the name of the common good.

What is *policing*?

Even after 1667, the police were not alone in policing Paris. Although the Lieutenance générale de police had a strong presence in the capital and, certainly more than other institutions in the city, had direct access to the king's ear, the administration and the protection of urban order were shared. The contributions in this volume explore the different players involved in policing: the men of the Lieutenance générale were undoubtedly the most visible, but they were not the only forces on the ground. The common good was everyone's business.

The Enlightenment fully embraced the issue of urban security. The Lieutenance générale de police divided and organised its central services into specialised offices, themselves subdivided into different departments. All of these departments – foreigners,[31] usury and

---

d'une structure politique et création d'une administration (1660-1789)', in *Le Prince, la ville et le bourgeois (XIVᵉ-XVIIIᵉ siècles)*, ed. Laurence Croq (Paris, 2004), p.175-201.

31. Romon, 'Mendiants et policiers'; *Police et migrants: France, 1667-1959*, ed. Marie-Claude Blanc-Chaléard *et al.* (Rennes, 2001); Vincent Denis et Vincent

pawnbroking,[32] the supervision of inns and garrisons,[33] bookshops,[34] begging,[35] the horse trade,[36] the recruitment and payment of wet-nurses,[37] putting the unemployed to work,[38] morality and theatre – required manpower that was carefully chosen by the *lieutenant général*: forty-eight commissioners and around twenty inspectors, stationed throughout the twenty police quarters into which the capital had been divided at the beginning of the century.

The duties of the commissaires at the Châtelet have already been described elsewhere and will be recalled only briefly here.[39] Judicial officers with very wide-ranging duties, the commissaires performed civil functions (they affixed seals, heard and settled accounts, and oversaw the sharing and payment of damages), criminal functions (they received complaints, carried out investigations, drew up reports and questioned defendants) and police functions (they were responsible for ensuring public safety, warning of imminent dangers and enforcing laws concerning the police and public order). The forty-eight Châtelet commissioners were divided between the capital's police quarters, with two or three commissioners per quarter. Familiar faces on the streets, they knew and arbitrated a considerable number of cases that were not necessarily brought elsewhere. In the same way, it is

---

Milliot, 'Police et identification dans la France des Lumières', *Genèses* 54 (2004), p.4-27.

32. Guillaume Pastureau, 'L'argent secours sous l'Ancien Régime: le cas du Mont-de-Piété', in *Argent, commerce et échange sous l'Ancien Régime*, ed. Anne-Sophie Fournier-Plamondon and Andrée-Anne Plourde (Paris, 2016), p.27-45.

33. Daniel Roche, 'Le cabaret parisien et les manières de vivre du peuple', in *Habiter la ville, XVe-XXe siècle*, ed. Maurice Garden and Yves Lequin (Lyon, 1984), p.233-51.

34. *La Police des métiers du livre à Paris au siècle des Lumières*, ed. Jean-Dominique Mellot *et al.* (Paris, 2017).

35. Romon, 'Mendiants et policiers à Paris au XVIIIe siècle'; Laurence Fontaine, *Vivre pauvre: quelques enseignements tirés de l'Europe des Lumières* (Paris, 2022).

36. Rochon, 'Le marché aux chevaux de Paris'.

37. Clyde Plumauzille, 'L'allaitement nourricier des petits Parisiens: naissance d'un service public au XVIIIe siècle', in *Paris et ses peuples au XVIIIe siècle*, ed. P. Bastien and S. Macdonald, p.39-48.

38. Lisa DiCaprio, *The Origins of the welfare state: women, work, and the French Revolution* (Champaign, IL, 2007).

39. David Garrioch, 'The people of Paris and their police in the eighteenth century: reflections on the introduction of a "modern" police force', *European history quarterly* 24 (1994), p.511-35; Kaplan, 'Note sur les commissaires de police de Paris au XVIIIe siècle'.

no longer surprising to find a variety of colleagues from different institutions working alongside them, or even traders, engineers, doctors and other experts lending a hand in conflict resolution. A stolen object, a market brawl, an abandoned child, a sick horse, an overcrowded cemetery, a nurse with unhealthy breasts: policing was a collective mission. As evidence of their varied daily activities, their records contain a mixture of minutes, guard reports, interrogations, information, and various accounts and transcripts. The formalisation of records and the creation of a 'paper memory' were among the many inventions produced by the transformation of the police institution up until the Revolution. Statistics, forms, cartography: the administration adapted its methods to ensure the effectiveness of its social improvement projects. The police were very much in the spirit of the Enlightenment, rational, utilitarian and confident that progress would continue to be shaped by mankind. They saw themselves as guardians of the general interest. They had to protect Paris and its people through surveillance, prevention, benevolence often, constraint sometimes.

As for the inspectors, they embodied the new modern police force, zealous and efficient, focused on maintaining order and policing public spaces, with particular attention paid to certain groups deemed dangerous or at risk, such as beggars and foreigners. The very specific world of the 'king's orders', denounced on the eve of the Revolution but popular until then with families anxious to stifle the scandals of a dissipated relative, was under their control since it was the inspectors who delivered the *lettres de cachet* and led the unfortunate to prison.[40] Now, while security was the domain of the inspectors, who were responsible for ensuring public order, it also involved the citizens themselves, who participated in the establishment of public order, particularly when it came to domestic violence or heated disputes between neighbours. In other words, residents coproduced public order and supported – often requested – the active presence of the police. The police apparatus was no mere vertical hierarchy; it was more pyramidal in structure, its base a network of resources the police could turn to for information or to ease tensions in the population:

40. Graham, *If the king only knew*; Robert Darnton, *The Devil in the holy water, or the Art of slander from Louis XIV to Napoleon* (Philadelphia, PA, 2010); Goulven Kerien, *Pour l'honneur des familles: les enfermements par lettres de cachet à Paris au XVIIIᵉ siècle* (Ceyzérieu, 2023).

innkeepers,[41] lodging-house owners,[42] shopkeepers and masters of workshops,[43] priests,[44] and second-hand clothes dealers.[45] Naturally, some spaces were more difficult to regulate, and trusted allies in short supply. Yet, in places such as gaming circles,[46] or under shop galleries where prostitutes more or less openly solicited their clients,[47] tolerance was the general policy, and surprising collaborative relationships developed. In this way, domestic servants and female brothel keepers found themselves in the employ of the police. The requirement that commissaires should reside in their assigned neighbourhoods,[48] and the strategic distribution of inspectors' offices[49] and of guard posts along coordinated patrol routes,[50] contributed to a more visible police presence and generally quick response times. Commissaires typically resided in the same quarter for ten, fifteen or even twenty years; the most competent among them gained a reputation for trust and wisdom with the inhabitants under their supervision,[51] and they used their discretionary powers in a spirit of benevolence that was generally well received. Inspectors did not have the same role and functions, but also recognised that tolerance, not repression, was generally key to keeping the peace. Mediation was the core feature of

41. Thomas Brennan, *Public drinking and popular culture in eighteenth-century Paris* (Princeton, NJ, 1988).

42. Roche, *La Ville promise.*

43. Arlette Farge, *Fragile lives: violence, power, and solidarity in eighteenth-century Paris* (1986; Cambridge, 1993).

44. Jean-Yves Grenier, 'Temps de travail et fêtes religieuses au XVIIIᵉ siècle', *Revue historique* 663 (2012), p.609-41.

45. Daniel Roche, *The Culture of clothing: dress and fashion in the Ancien Régime* (1989; Cambridge, 1997).

46. Francis Freundlich, *Le Monde du jeu à Paris, 1715-1800* (Paris, 1995).

47. Benabou, *La Prostitution et la police des mœurs.*

48. Vincent Milliot, 'Saisir l'espace urbain: mobilité des commissaires et contrôle des quartiers de police à Paris au XVIIIᵉ siècle', *Revue d'histoire moderne et contemporaine* 50:1 (2003), p.54-80.

49. Rachel Couture, '"Inspirer la crainte, le respect et l'amour du public": les inspecteurs de police parisiens, 1740-1789', doctoral dissertation, Université du Québec à Montréal and Université de Caen Basse-Normandie, 2013.

50. Jean Chagniot, 'Le guet et la garde de Paris à la fin de l'Ancien Régime', *Revue d'histoire moderne et contemporaine* 20:1 (1973), p.58-71, and 'Le problème du maintien de l'ordre à Paris au XVIIIᵉ siècle', *Bulletin de la Société d'histoire moderne et contemporaine* 8 (1974), p.32-45.

51. Justine Berlière, *Policer Paris au siècle des Lumières: les commissaires du quartier du Louvre dans la seconde moitié du XVIIIᵉ siècle* (Paris, 2012).

public order in the capital.[52] This form of collaborative social control remained well rooted throughout the century despite the lieutenant general's efforts to centralise activities. Yet it did not completely stem acts of insubordination.

Policing Parisians

As far back as 1981,[53] Daniel Roche refused to see the people of Paris only in terms of the alienation imposed by the state, the Church and the economic structures of a society in the throes of transformation. This was not to deny the difficult life of the working classes, of course, but to emphasise the necessary complicity that could exist between the institutions and the people. He therefore invited his readers to explore the relationships that existed between *policing the city* and *inhabiting the city*. Throughout his career, he believed in a social history that focused not exclusively on the marginalised but, much more broadly, on the capital's most diverse populations, small-scale workers, domestic servants, shopkeepers and transient workers. Extending his intuition that all social history is total history, this book offers a new reading of the police experience in the eighteenth century through a dozen specific cases that capture distinct and varied places, times, agents and social or political problems.

***

The first three essays begin at the end of the seventeenth century, demonstrating how *spaces* took centre stage in the contest between authorities and the inexorable push of social, economic and political dynamics at play. First, Laurence Croq introduces the corps of *commissaires du Châtelet*: she identifies the social and ideological positions of its members at the turn of the eighteenth century, before following their political and religious involvement in their neighbourhoods and

---

52. Forged in the 1970s, the concept of *citadinité* makes it possible to read local belonging and its rights without any legal formalisation, since it refers, in a slightly different way from the notions of citizenship and even bourgeoisie, to the complex relationships existing between social actors and urban objects, which emerge in particular through the demands made by residents' collectives. Croq, 'La municipalité parisienne à l'épreuve des absolutismes'; Julien Puget, 'From public garden to public city: the controversy over the housing project at the Palais-Royal in 1781', *French history* 31:2 (2017), p.174-93.
53. Roche, *The People of Paris*.

the community right up to the threshold of the Revolution. What kind of notables, what kind of honourable people were the commissioners of the Lieutenance générale de police? It is with this first contribution that these public-service officers, who were the pillars of the police apparatus in the eighteenth century, take shape with greater precision, as they served a neighbourhood rather than particular interests, a common good and a common space rather than a private life. Julie Allard and Christine Métayer then turn their attention to public places as areas of transit, and thus as spaces of tension, power play and rivalries. Legalities and legitimacies clashed, and it was sometimes the officers, sometimes the merchants and residents, who laid claim to the market's boundaries, and sometimes even imposed them: here, below these lines, the city is ours! In her contribution, Julie Allard stops off at the place de Grève, in front of the Paris Hôtel de ville. A great observatory of the tensions that existed between the municipal and the police administration, the place de Grève became the arena for all kinds of demands, to the point where it gave rise to a rival commissioner, the *huissier-commissaire* of the Hôtel de ville, who sought to curb the centralisation of powers initiated by the crown for the benefit of the lieutenant general. In the next essay, Christine Métayer's study of the Marché-Neuf, where goods and merchandise were exchanged and where women merchants stood out in the arena, also brings to light a power struggle based on space. Who can occupy the market space and, above all, who has the authority to decide? The power struggles between the city authorities and the *lieutenant général de police* are at the heart of the tensions in the Marché-Neuf, and it is not clear whether either side succeeded in imposing its will on residents, shoppers and merchants.

What does policing mean? As the *lieutenant général de police* did not limit himself to imprisoning beggars and thieves, policing was not carried out exclusively by the police officers of the Châtelet. Administering, supervising, monitoring and containing were all shared responsibilities, and we therefore need to look beyond the commissioners, inspectors and guards in order to understand policing in the eighteenth century less in terms of competition than in terms of complementarity. The essays in part II examine the diversity of those who policed the city. Going beyond the black legend of the *lieutenant général*'s army of shadows, Vincent Milliot offers the first in-depth study of police surveillance agents in the eighteenth century. To what extent did police work rely on this knowledge of whispers and secrets? This essay looks at how these infamous police auxiliaries were recruited, how they were paid and how effective they were. Next, David Garrioch opens the question of surveillance and repression to religious sociability, at a time when secular communities were able to meet and contravene royal ordinances strictly governing devotional practices. To what extent were devotional practices considered police matters? Why did they require formal and organised supervision? In the following contribution, Jeffrey Ravel focuses on the regulations governing the production and circulation of playing cards (from which the monarchy derived substantial tax revenues), tracing the strategies used by Parisians, *régisseurs*, inspectors and commissioners to regulate without prohibiting, with the aim of negotiating to the satisfaction of all parties. This second part focuses above all on the kind of compromise that the police agents and Parisians were able to reach when both parties found common ground.

As we know, the people of Paris and public opinion in the eighteenth century were not blocks of clay that could be moulded to suit the king's whims. We also know that it is not possible to write history from below, to study the history of the working classes, simply through their acts of resistance. Paris could certainly be angry, but that was not all it was. It is as *citizens* that Parisians are captured in part III, which explores how social order was a matter of consultation, transaction, rhetoric of course and politics most certainly. The last three essays round off our study by assessing Parisians' difficult relationship with the police who were charged with protecting the moral and social order of the city. They examine the divisions, alliances and rivalries that impacted the relationship between police practices and urban sociability. Through the eyes of the police inspectors and by examining the mechanics of the *lettre de cachet* for which they were responsible, Lisa Jane Graham shows how, in the second half of the eighteenth century, the supervision of debauchery and so-called illegitimate sexual practices became an increasingly tense issue between the police and the public. Initially auxiliaries of families who sought to suppress a scandal by enlisting the support of the king and his personal justice, the police inspectors came under fire, with the hunt for debauchery becoming, in the eyes of Parisians, one of the many illustrations of arbitrariness and police despotism. What were the legitimate missions of an Enlightenment police force? Through another issue of morality and decency in the public space, Bruno Belhoste examines one of the many debates on public health in Paris, by analysing the police and political controversy surrounding animal magnetism and mesmerism. A public affair that went far beyond the restricted circles of aristocrats and doctors, the mesmerism trial was played out in the street, on the theatre stage and in the press, in an astonishing game of communication in which the police sought, on the orders of the government, to shape the perceptions of the capital's public. In the following essay, looking at the new police institution set up by the Revolution, Vincent Denis uses episodes of the fraternal banquets in Paris in the early days of the Republic to understand how the maintenance of order and police supervision, reviled throughout the last decade of the *Ancien Régime*, became a major civic issue in the revolutionary democratic laboratory. Can an elected citizen police force be effective, or even simply blind and fair, as the ideal of justice would have it?

Sociabilities were at the heart of the cities of the Enlightenment. They were the driving force behind enlightened debates, emancipation claims and the fight against inequality. The police, by the same token, was an essential component of the Enlightenment state, not in opposition to sociability, but in coordination, or negotiation, with it. Yet the police force of eighteenth-century Parisian sociability was not the only experiment, nor the most successful laboratory, of the Enlightenment way of living together. Marco Cicchini concludes our volume with an original look at the policing of urban sociability by presenting the case of Geneva, which sheds light on the limits, expectations, similarities and specificities of the Parisian example. Although Geneva was Protestant while Paris was Catholic, the shared heritage of Roman law in the fields of justice and politics offers a more enlightening, and undoubtedly more unusual, counterpoint than the Paris–London comparison to which historiography has accustomed us. The Geneva revolution of 1782 also allows us to finely question the teleological reading to which Paris at the end of the eighteenth century so often lends itself.

By presenting the paradoxes but also the logics of the parallel and intertwined development of the police institution and civil society, this book offers an original, concrete and embodied analysis of the Parisian players and police practices that traversed a century shaken by novelty and tradition, community and centralisation, the efficiency of the authorities and the discovery of citizenship.

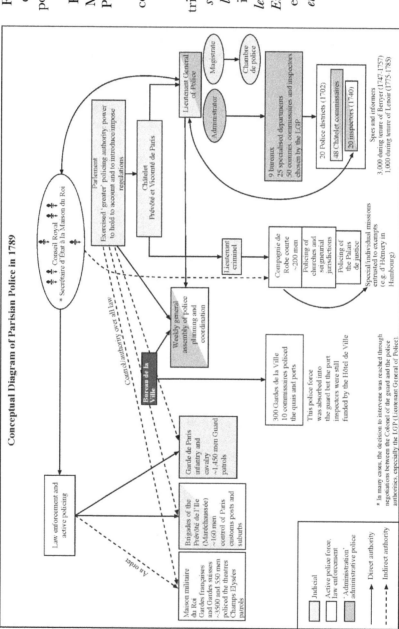

Figure 1: Conceptual diagram of Parisian police in 1789. Source: Steven Laurence Kaplan and Vincent Milliot, 'La police de Paris, une "révolution permanente"? Du commissaire Lemaire au lieutenant de police Lenoir, les tribulations du *Mémoire sur l'administration de la police* (1770-1792)', in *Réformer la police: les mémoires policiers en Europe au XVIIIe siècle*, ed. Catherine Denys *et al.* (Rennes, 2009), p.69-115 (113-15).

Preliminary comments on the Paris police in the eighteenth century

In his 'Mémoire sur l'administration de la police', Commissaire Lemaire was prone to depict the Parisian police system in oversimplified terms. Figure 1 is intended to illustrate its true complexity and uniqueness. The commissaire essentially focused on the forces which reported directly to the lieutenant general of police, the magistrate of the Châtelet, or to his offices. Yet Lemaire underestimated or entirely passed over the roles of the Parlement and of its *procureur général*, and over the formal mechanisms of cooperation between the municipality, the Parlement and the lieutenant general, such as the general assembly of the police. He equally disregarded the role of the armed forces in enforcing the law, which was not always a repressive, heavy-handed form of enforcement.

The police system established in Paris existed in no other French municipality. In other cities, the urban magistrates were inclined to jealously defend their policing powers. The Parisian system was defined by the strict control the royal government exercised over it, through the authority theoretically entrusted to the Secretary of State in charge of the royal household. In the capital, the police was attached to the king's personal household, not to the 'state' in an abstract sense. The 'police system' emerged as a distinctly *Ancien Régime* mixture of inherited roles built up over time and of new functions and practices, of traditional agents of the law and new types of 'police officers', such as inspectors and spies.

All this took place against a backdrop of rapid transformations in Parisian society during the eighteenth century. In a curious paradox, the new, unconventional missions and methods harmonised somehow with highly conventional and traditional forms of governance.

It is here that the limitations of a diagram such as the one in Figure 1 are revealed as, inevitably, it can provide only a static snapshot of the situation on the eve of the Revolution.

It gives an incomplete picture of the shock waves that spread through the Parisian police as Colbert's 1667 reform was implemented. This 'reform' had repercussions which extended beyond the mere creation of the Lieutenance générale de police, which is often perceived, *pars pro toto*, as its sum total. It was more a sequence of measures taken over time, periodically accelerated by the personalities and political orientations of certain lieutenants general who, moreover, did not work in a vacuum, but depended heavily on their teams. Internal power dynamics evolved in the course of this process as police practices and attitudes were regularly challenged and debated. The rapport between the police and the population, and societal expectations with regard to the police, also shifted.

The second limitation consists in imposing too institutional an interpretation on the system. Figure 1 artificially perpetuates a rigid notion of policing. However, those within the Parisian system saw a police in constant evolution, and an approach to law enforcement endlessly stripped down and reinvented. The force made use of numerous 'auxiliaries' who do not appear on the diagram (though Lemaire mentions some of them in his text): *jurés* (officials) and masters of corporations, second-hand sellers of all sorts, lodging-house owners and innkeepers, masters of the *académies de jeu*, female brothel keepers, postmasters and even nursemaids.

The third limitation of Figure 1 is that it does not demonstrate the complex territorialisation of the diverse forces, in constant flux. For instance, Châtelet commissaires also intervened in the suburbs and infringed local jurisdictions. The Prévôté de l'Ile, whose primary mandate was to patrol the suburbs, did not concentrate on surveillance of the customs posts until the 1780s, after the construction of the Ferme générale's tax wall. Similarly, the Prévôté intervened in Paris proper on certain missions, such as for the surveillance of the 'sodomites' in the Tuileries garden, or policing during the Réveillon riots of April 1789.

While tables have certain pedagogical virtues, they are also misleading because they can never reflect the practices and evolution of the institutions they seek to present.

The descriptions given in Table 2 are succinct and do not cover all the responsibilities of each bureau. Some of them administered vast areas (Bureau de sûreté), while others had more limited responsibilities (Bureau des nourrices). It also seems clear that the prerogatives and missions of certain bureaux overlapped, making it very problematic to compartmentalise responsibilities. In addition, many bureaux were

Table 1: The lieutenants general of police of Paris (1667-1789)

1667-1697	Gabriel Nicolas de La Reynie (1625-1709)
1697-1718	Marc René de Voyer de Paulmy, marquis d'Argenson (1652-1721)
1718-1720	Louis Charles de Machaut d'Arnouville (1667-1750)
1720	Marc Pierre de Voyer de Paulmy, comte d'Argenson (1696-1764)
1720-1722	Gabriel Taschereau de Baudry (1673-1755)
1722-1724	Marc Pierre de Voyer de Paulmy, comte d'Argenson (1696-1764)
1724-1725	Nicolas Ravot d'Ombreval (1680-1729)
1725-1739	René Hérault (1691-1740)
1739-1747	Claude Henry Feydeau de Marville (1705-1787)
1747-1757	Nicolas René Berryer (1703-1762)
1757-1759	Henri Léonard Jean-Baptiste Bertin (1720-1792)
1759-1774	Antoine de Sartine (1729-1801)
1774-1775	Jean Charles Pierre Lenoir (1732-1807)
1775-1776	Joseph d'Albert (1721-1790)
1776-1785	Jean Charles Pierre Lenoir (1732-1807)
1785-1789	Louis Thiroux de Crosne (1736-1794)

broken down into more specialised 'departments': Alan Williams counted twenty-five in 1789. It turns out that these departments (poultry or cattle markets, gambling, foreigners, prostitutes, sodomites, beggars, etc.) were entrusted more to inspectors, because of their expertise, than to a bureau as such.

The way these bureaux were set up remains unclear, although it is known that their number increased between the tenures of Berryer, Sartine and Lenoir. Created under Berryer, a Bureau des dépôts ou archives de la police, with its various registers of suspects and convicts, may have seen its prerogatives and officers integrated elsewhere under Sartine. It was also under Sartine that a bureau specifically dedicated to the horse trade was created, but it was not officially part of the bureaux of the administration of the Lieutenance générale de police: the responsibility was entrusted to the Guillote family (father and sons), but it did not form part of the official organisation structure. Table 2 should therefore be used with caution, as each bureau was a laboratory in itself.

Table 2: The police bureaux in 1789

Bureau de cabinet: issued *lettres de cachet* (royal arrest warrants) and received complaints, reports and any other correspondence addressed to the lieutenant general of police.

Bureau de ravitaillement: responsible for food supply and cleaning in the capital. Markets, fairs, water pumps and hospitals were under its administration. The reports of the Garde de Paris were filed in this bureau.

Bureau de sûreté: located at the Châtelet; the inspectors based there heard complaints from the public free of charge. They also conducted certain special investigations.

Bureau des prisons et des maisons de force: managed the prisons and other detention centres with the exception of state prisons (Bastille, Vincennes). This bureau was also responsible for visiting the Chambre syndicale and booksellers to discuss all matters relating to censorship of books and theatre.

Bureau des arts et manufactures: dealt with the corporations, commerce, import/export permits and manufactories of Paris. It also supervised the security of the quarries and ensured order at the lottery draws.

Bureau des nourrices *or* **recommandaresses:** supervised the recruitment and payment of wet-nurses.

Bureau du contentieux: oversaw the collection of revenues, pensions, annuities and all other forms of monies owed, in Paris and elsewhere, upon request.

Bureau de filature: responsible for providing indigent women with spinning work at home and, more widely, organised assistance to the poor.

The organisation of official bureaux within the structure of the Lieutenance générale de police stems from the need to provide the new specialities with essential administrative support and to ensure the best possible conservation and centralisation of the mass of information collected.

Figure 2: The ports and markets of eighteenth-century Paris. Map design: Julien Puget, Groupe de recherche en histoire des sociabilités (GRHS), Université du Québec à Montréal. Sources: Paul Rouet, 'Îlots en 1791 (plan de Verniquet)', ALPAGE, Paris (2015); *Atlas de la Révolution française*, vol.11, ed. Serge Bonin and Claude Langlois (Paris, 2000), p.46.

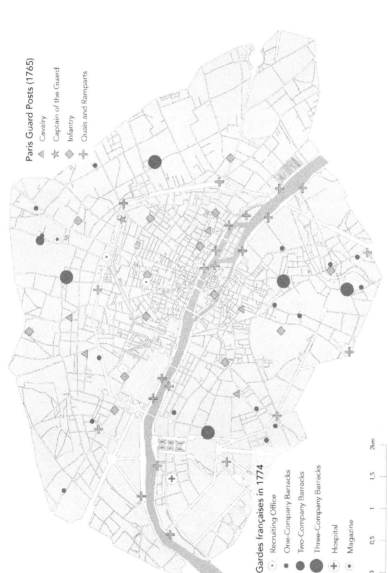

Figure 3: Royal and municipal guards in eighteenth-century Paris. Map design: Julien Puget, Groupe de recherche en histoire des sociabilités (GRHS), Université du Québec à Montréal. Sources: Paul Rouet, 'Îlots en 1791 (plan de Verniquet)', ALPAGE, Paris (2015); Jean Chagniot, *Paris et l'armée au XVIIIᵉ siècle: étude politique et sociale* (Paris, 1985).

Paris Guard Posts (1765)
- △ Cavalry
- ★ Captain of the Guard
- ◇ Infantry
- ✛ Quais and Ramparts

Gardes françaises in 1774
- ⊙ Recruiting Office
- • One-Company Barracks
- ● Two-Company Barracks
- ● Three-Company Barracks
- ✚ Hospital
- ⊙ Magazine

0   0,5   1   1,5   2km

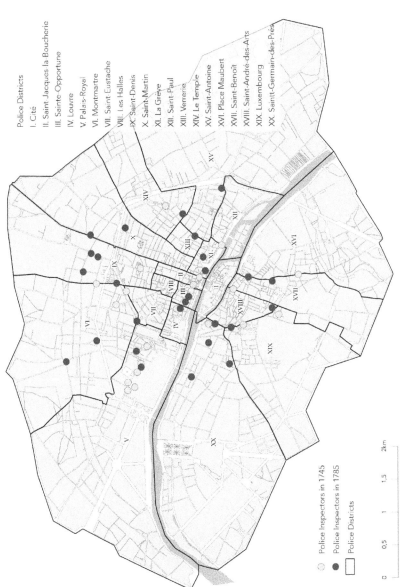

Figure 4: Residence of police inspectors (1745 and 1765). Map design: Julien Puget, Groupe de recherche en histoire des sociabilités (GRHS), Université du Québec à Montréal. Sources: Paul Rouet, 'Îlots en 1791 (plan de Verniquet)', ALPAGE, Paris (2015); Rachel Couture, "Inspirer la crainte, le respect et l'amour du public": les inspecteurs de police parisiens, 1740-1789', doctoral dissertation, Université du Québec à Montréal and Université de Caen Basse-Normandie, 2013.

Police Districts
I. Cité
II. Saint Jacques la Boucherie
III. Sainte-Opportune
IV. Louvre
V. Palais-Royal
VI. Montmartre
VII. Saint Eustache
VIII. Les Halles
IX. Saint-Denis
X. Saint-Martin
XI. La Grève
XII. Saint-Paul
XIII. Verrerie
XIV. Le Temple
XV. Saint-Antoine
XVI. Place Maubert
XVII. Saint-Benoît
XVIII. Saint-André-des-Arts
XIX. Luxembourg
XX. Saint-Germain-des-Prés

Police Inspectors in 1745
Police Inspectors in 1785
Police Districts

0   0,5   1   1,5   2km

Figure 5: Arrests for prostitution and solicitation (1765, 1766, 1770). Map design: Julien Puget, Groupe de recherche en histoire des sociabilités (GRHS), Université du Québec à Montréal. Sources: Paul Rouet, 'Îlots en 1791 (plan de Verniquet)', ALPAGE, Paris (2015); Eliane Hensinger, 'La prostitution et la police des mœurs au XVIIIᵉ siècle à Paris', *Mappemonde* 2 (1988), p.40-44.

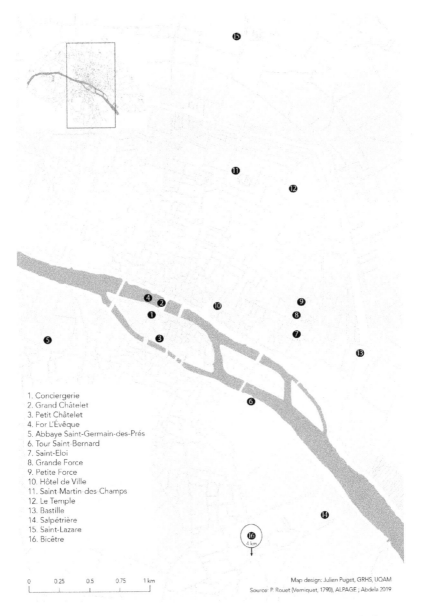

1. Conciergerie
2. Grand Châtelet
3. Petit Châtelet
4. For L'Évêque
5. Abbaye Saint-Germain-des-Prés
6. Tour Saint-Bernard
7. Saint-Eloi
8. Grande Force
9. Petite Force
10. Hôtel de Ville
11. Saint-Martin-des-Champs
12. Le Temple
13. Bastille
14. Salpétrière
15. Saint-Lazare
16. Bicêtre

0   0.25   0.5   0.75   1 km

Map design: Julien Puget, GRHS, UQAM
Source: P. Rouet (Verniquet, 1790), ALPAGE ; Abdela 2019

Figure 6: The prisons of eighteenth-century Paris. Map design: Julien Puget, Groupe de recherche en histoire des sociabilités (GRHS), Université du Québec à Montréal. Sources: Paul Rouet, 'Ilots en 1791 (plan de Verniquet)', ALPAGE, Paris (2015); Sophie Abdela, *La Prison parisienne au XVIIIe siècle: formes et réformes* (Ceyzérieu, 2019).

I

Occupying space: conflict and competition

The Châtelet commissaires in eighteenth-century Paris: bourgeois or policemen?

LAURENCE CROQ

Université Paris Nanterre, IDHE.S

Translated by Nicole Charley

On 17 February, Commissaire Regnard, his clerk Vanneroux and several archers paid a visit to a young clergyman named de Rougemont, who was tutor to Regnard's children. It is said that, upon seeing de Rougemont exit his place of residence, Regnard was unable to hold back his tears. For alas, he is commissaire at a time when one's title often supersedes one's moral obligations. Regnard claimed to have been unaware that he was to apprehend this young man in particular; certainly, the man's clerk was not ignorant of the matter. Whatever the case may be, he acquiesced (as was his custom) to the inequitable expedition.[1]

Commissaire Louis Pierre Regnard was a familiar figure to readers of the *Nouvelles ecclésiastiques*,[2] a weekly underground Paris newspaper that circulated widely amongst dissidents of *Unigenitus*, a bull Pope Clement XI had issued on 8 September 1713 at the behest of Louis XIV. Throughout the 1730s and 1740s, the paper portrayed Regnard as one who readily executed the orders of his king and his *lieutenant de police*, arresting men and women hostile to the bull, brutalising priests and female ecclesiastics who opposed the papal edict and lay members who sympathised, to one degree or another, with the Jansenist cause.[3] His zealousness had earned him

---

1. *Nouvelles ecclésiastiques* (31 March 1731), p.61.
2. *Une Aventure de presse clandestine au siècle des Lumières (1713-1803)*, ed. Monique Cottret and Valérie Guittienne-Murger (Paris, 2016).
3. Nicolas Lyon-Caen, *La Boîte à Perrette: le jansénisme parisien au XVIIIᵉ siècle* (Paris, 2010).

the sobriquet 'Commissaire of the Constitution' (another name for the bull).

The citation opening this article briefly touches on Regnard's conflicting private and professional personas: he was both the son and the brother of Châtelet commissaires, but was also a Parisian bourgeois. For years he resided on the rue Saint-Julien-le-Pauvre, regularly attending services in the parish church of Saint-Séverin, and had even been honoured with a family pew in gratitude for services rendered.[4] The anecdote in the *Nouvelles ecclésiastiques* underscores the delicate balance the forty-eight commissaires of the Châtelet struck with Parisian society: they were accepted members of Parisian sociability yet still somehow interlopers. They shared friendly, neighbourly relations with other Parisians – and so were part of the fold – but were the 'outsiders' who descended on an assembly of 'convulsionaries' or assailed a tavern where members of a confraternity were meeting.[5] Another arrest one Sunday in June 1732 – this time of 'M. Bernard, a "wealthy bourgeois" from the parish of Saint-Paul' – further illustrates their ambiguous status. Bernard and other fellow parishioners had just left the church following curé Gueret's announcement of the upcoming feast of Saint Monique. 'Stopped just outside the main portal, they were conversing peaceably about events when they were verbally set upon by Commissaire [Nicolas] Labbé and an ecclesiastic by the name of Olivier, who reproached them for having brought scandal upon the parish with their rebellion and threatened them with unpleasantness.' 'The old commissaire, Bernard's neighbour', later provided the *lieutenant de police* with a *mémoire* in which he accused Bernard of committing multiple improprieties instead: Bernard had allegedly not only made an appalling racket when exiting the church, he had visited Saint-Médard and 'claimed that the application of earth from the tomb of M. de Pâris had cured a lesion on his face [...] And not

---

4. Laurence Croq and Nicolas Lyon-Caen, 'La notabilité parisienne entre la police et la ville: des définitions aux usages sociaux et politiques au XVIIIᵉ siècle', in *La Notabilité urbaine Xᵉ-XVIIIᵉ siècles*, ed. Laurence Jean-Marie (Caen, 2007), p.125-57.

5. Catherine Maire, *Les Convulsionnaires de Saint-Médard: miracles, convulsions et prophéties à Paris au XVIIIᵉ siècle* (Paris, 1985); David Garrioch, *Neighbourhood and community in Paris, 1740-1790* (Cambridge, 1986); and, by the same author, 'Les confréries religieuses, espace d'autonomie laïque à Paris au XVIIIᵉ siècle', in *La Religion vécue: les laïcs dans l'Europe moderne*, ed. Laurence Croq and David Garrioch (Rennes, 2013), p.143-63.

least,' the commissaire reported, 'at four o'clock one evening, in the café and in the Célestins convent, [Bernard] had spoken against the authorities, saying Commissaire Labbé should be beaten with a stick.'[6] Labbé was an elderly man at the time; he had been in office since 1679 and overseen the Saint-Antoine quarter since 1715. In this situation, however, he had made use of his professional persona for private interests; in doing so, he had violated the most basic tenet of all rural and urban dwellers: 'good neighbourliness'.[7]

Historians might well ponder how Châtelet commissaires managed to reconcile their dual allegiances. How did their duty as officers of the law square with their membership of the bourgeoisie? Were they able to integrate into society? On what level? What was unique to their experience?

In the legal sense of the term, the designation *bourgeoisie* defined individuals who possessed a private residence and had been residing in Paris for at least a year and a day. In this essay, we will be using the notion in its broader sense to denote Parisians occupying a family dwelling comprising a suite of rooms and employing at least one servant. These bourgeois were generally tenants of their abode, but they often had access to a cellar where they could stock their casks of wine. Such residences, with the exception of those for doctors, differed from noble residences in that they had no carriage entrance or stable, nor indeed horses or the personnel to maintain them. While the value of each member or profession in this bourgeoisie was not systematically correlated with that of their commercial assets nor even with that of their office or fortune, there was nonetheless a strict hierarchy in operation. Merchants simply thought themselves superior to artisans, lawyers to *procureurs*, Châtelet commissaires to *inspecteurs de police*, and so on. Within each community, the general principle of equality was the rule, but members could garner added social value through co-option – election by community members to positions of leadership such as merchant *gardes*, *consuls* and *juges consuls* (judges in commercial courts), *bâtonniers de l'ordre des avocats*, *greffiers receveurs* and *syndics* of the Châtelet commissaires. Communities also fiercely fought over urban power centres, especially the *échevinages* (the municipal magistrature) and the parish *fabriques* (councils), to which membership was equally attained through election. In this 'universe

---

6.   *Nouvelles ecclésiastiques* (6 June 1732), p.109.
7.   Marc Vacher, *Voisins, voisines, voisinage: les cultures du face-à-face à Lyon à la veille de la Révolution* (Lyon, 2007).

of notability',[8] the purchase of an office was unnecessary in theory, though it provided a leg up to aspirants. For example, it was possible for a Paris-born bourgeois who did not already have an office to rise to *échevin* (alderman), but fully half of elected aldermen were also men who had previously acquired the office of city or local councillor – worth 8000 to 10,000 *livres* in the 1680s, and at least 20,000 *livres* under Louis XVI. The vast majority of aldermen were elected from amongst the elite of a minority of professional communities, the Six Corps merchant guilds (mercers, drapers, grocer-apothecaries, goldsmith-jewellers, furriers and hosiers), the *notaires* and the *avocats au Parlement*. Châtelet commissaires had disappeared from the ranks of aldermen by the 1680s, though they could once again be counted amongst those members after 1760.[9] Churchwardens were appointed from the same social milieux as aldermen but, depending on the neighbourhood quarter, might also be members of the corporation of court clerks and *procureurs*. Others were minor financial officeholders and, in the less populous parishes of the Cité, even artisans. But after 1690, Châtelet commissaires could no longer aspire to be church-wardens.[10] The consuls and churchwardens who were able to rise through the ranks on their social credit were, until the 1740s, local notables such as aldermen. For Châtelet commissaires, notability was therefore out of reach.

Yet many Paris notables and a greater minority of other bourgeois supported Jansenism, sharing the same devotion to the Jansenist deacon François de Pâris, and were in favour of the Parlement.[11] They all held parochial Catholicism in considerable regard: the administration of sacraments and regular religious observances such

8. Laurence Croq, 'Essai pour la construction de la notabilité comme paradigme socio-politique', in *La Notabilité urbaine Xe-XVIIIe siècles*, ed. L. Jean-Marie, p.23-38.

9. Laurence Croq, 'Des "bourgeois de Paris" à la bourgeoisie parisienne (XVIIe-XVIIIe siècles)', in *Les Histoires de Paris (XVIe-XVIIIe siècle)*, ed. Thierry Belleguic and Laurent Turcot, 2 vols (Paris, 2012), vol.1, p.269-83.

10. Laurence Croq and Nicolas Lyon-Caen, 'Le rang et la fonction: les marguilliers des fabriques parisiennes à l'époque moderne', in *La Paroisse urbaine: du Moyen Age à nos jours*, ed. Anne Bonzon *et al.* (Paris, 2014), p.199-244.

11. Nicolas Lyon-Caen, 'Un "saint de nouvelle fabrique": le diacre Pâris (1690-1727), le jansénisme et la bonneterie parisienne', *Annales. Histoire, sciences sociales* 65 (2010), p.613-42.

as burials and funeral services for middle-class men and women generally took place in parish churches.[12]

A small minority of nobles and bourgeois in the capital nonetheless accepted *Unigenitus* and the pro-constitutional clergy, though they were harshly critical of the Parlement and unhappy with what they considered judicial despotism. This group was powerful, but its ideological disparities were a weak point; aside from a common hostility towards the Parlement, they shared little common ground, either politically or religiously. Some were partisans of enlightened despotism, others favoured the decentralisation of power. The Jansenists painted them as Jesuit supporters, but they were bound by no devotional ties despite the Church's efforts to promote devotion to the Sacred Heart and Jeanne de Chantal. Some were even Voltaireans. But the shift in the institutional configuration – from numerous institutions serving the king and his subjects towards exclusive service to a centralised power – together with mounting political and religious tensions, served to numerically strengthen that minority. Consequently, after the 1740s, the Hôtel de ville was integrated into the monarchical domain. Caught up in this evolution were the *prévôts des marchands* and aldermen who, now royalists, withdrew from the sphere of notability: the majority of potential aldermen felt little loyalty towards the system of corporations and wielded limited influence over their peers.[13]

The Maupeou reforms (1771-1774) revealed still other partisans of centralised power: after the Paris Parlement, the Grand Conseil and the Cour des aides were dissolved, the chancellor created new councillors' offices to compensate for the exiled magistrates who now refused to sit.[14] Some of the lawyers – the *avocats rentrants* – did return and swore oaths to the new Parlement.[15] The hundred newly minted offices of

12. David Garrioch, *The Formation of the Parisian bourgeoisie, 1690-1830* (Cambridge, MA, and London, 1996); Lyon-Caen, *La Boîte à Perrette*; Laurence Croq, 'Les édiles, les notables et le pouvoir royal à Paris, histoire de ruptures (XVIIᵉ-XVIIIᵉ siècles)', in *Le Pouvoir municipal en France de la fin du Moyen Age à 1789*, ed. Philippe Hamon and Catherine Laurent (Rennes, 2012), p.223-50.

13. Laurence Croq, 'La municipalité parisienne à l'épreuve des absolutismes: démantèlement d'une structure politique et création d'une administration (1660-1789)', in *Le Prince, la ville et le bourgeois (XIVᵉ-XVIIIᵉ siècles)*, ed. Laurence Croq (Paris, 2004), p.175-201; Croq, 'Les édiles, les notables et le pouvoir royal'.

14. Durand Echeverria, *The Maupeou Revolution: a study in the history of libertarian France, 1770-1774* (Bâton Rouge, LA, 1985).

15. David A. Bell, *Lawyers and citizens: the making of a political elite in Old Regime France* (New York and Oxford, 1994).

avocat du Parlement, which replaced *procureurs* in the Parlement and Grand Conseil, found willing recipients. In 1774, Louis XVI ascended the throne, restoring the sovereign courts from which Maupeou's magistrates were excluded and regrouped under the Grand Conseil. Yet this victory was only partial for the parliamentary faction; some of the advocates of reform were retained (in the Châtelet, for example) or reassigned to anti-parliamentary or provincial institutions. Though Jansenism was beginning to flag, the rift dividing the politicised elites into two camps persisted. The Intendance de la Généralité de Paris enjoyed an increasing number of prerogatives and, its staff swelling, expanded its fiscal powers at the expense of parish inhabitants and the Cour des aides.[16] The authority of the Lieutenance générale de police increased in a similar manner to the detriment of the *trésoriers de France*[17] and the Six Corps merchant guilds.[18] In other words, though the modest consortium of royalists lacked ideological cohesion and had no seat of power equivalent to that of the Parlement or the structures of notability, its members occupied increasingly important positions in the city.[19]

In which of these two camps did the commissaires belong? By virtue of their role, the police were part of the royalist minority and – like the parish clergy – were expected to ensure the bourgeoisie complied with the *Unigenitus* bull. After the 1740s, the alderman community, comprised of some forty members, also joined their ranks: these were not only former and current aldermen, but also prospective candidates who already held the title of *quartinier* or city councillor, or were known to have used their status as bourgeois in their bid for a position. Such similarities between the aldermen and police communities suggest further comparisons may be drawn.

This essay will focus on three questions. First, I will discuss the economic, social and ideological positions of Châtelet commissaires

---

16. Mireille Touzery, *L'Invention de l'impôt sur le revenu: la taille tarifée 1715-1789* (Paris, 1994).

17. Thomas Le Roux, 'Les effondrements de carrières de Paris: la grande réforme des années 1770', *French historical studies* 36 (2013), p.205-37.

18. Mathieu Marraud, 'Le cérémonial urbain à Paris au XVIIIᵉ siècle: représentation et négociation politique', in *Les Histoires de Paris*, ed. T. Belleguic and L. Turcot, vol.1, p.245-67.

19. Laurence Croq, 'Les années 80 de Siméon-Prosper Hardy: de la mémoire des offenses au triomphe des vaincus', in Siméon-Prosper Hardy, *Mes loisirs, ou Journal d'événemens tels qu'ils parviennent à ma connoissance (1753-1789)*, ed. Pascal Bastien *et al.*, 11 vols (Paris, 2012-2024), vol.8: *1783-1785* (2022), p.1-27.

and where they fit along the divide between the general population and Parisian notables. Next, I will examine elements from the commissaires' private and professional lives to discern to what forms of political or spiritual engagement they subscribed. Finally, I will look at ways commissaires integrated into the new institutions of sociability, the Freemasons, and the Association de bienfaisance judiciaire.

Singular bourgeois

In the eighteenth century, the social status of Châtelet commissaires improved in important and measurable ways. We know that, for commissaires, the value of offices fluctuated greatly – between 1660 and 1680, it varied from 25,000 to 35,000 *livres*, dropping by the beginning of the eighteenth century to between 15,000 and 20,000 *livres*.[20] Over the course of the eighteenth century, the price climbed from 40,000 *livres* (around 1740) to some 100,000 *livres* (according to Lenoir himself) at the start of the Revolution. The latter amount is also corroborated in Jean Thomas Defresne's marriage contract, which valued his commissaire's office at 92,000 *livres*, in addition to which he paid 7000 *livres* for reception into the Compagnie des commissaires.[21] Clearly, despite the Jansenist crisis, the office was still an attractive one, though it was still nowhere near as costly as a notaire's office.[22]

Did this trend have an impact on their fortunes, social status or marriage alliances? Were nuptially inclined commissaires truly more prosperous towards the end of the eighteenth century, or did the cost of acquiring an office mean being burdened with substantial debt? Furthermore, could commissaires expect favourable alliances with wealthy or well-established families?

Regrettably, there is insufficient data on commissaire marriage alliances to indicate an evolution in outcomes. In truth, the growth

---

20. Steven Laurence Kaplan, 'Note sur les commissaires de police de Paris au XVIIIᵉ siècle', *Revue d'histoire moderne et contemporaine* 28:4 (1981), p.669-86.
21. Paris, Archives nationales (AN), MC, XXVI 755, 11 February 1787, marriage of Defresne-Serreau.
22. Robert Descimon, 'Les auxiliaires de justice du Châtelet de Paris: aperçus sur l'économie du monde des offices ministériels (XVIᵉ-XVIIIᵉ siècle)', in *Entre justice et justiciables: les auxiliaires de la justice du Moyen Age au XXᵉ siècle*, ed. Claire Dolan (Quebec City, 2005), p.301-25.

of their social credit allowed commissaires and notaries alike to begin family life with a personal fortune far inferior to the value of their office; for example, police agents possessed no more than 20,000 to 30,000 *livres* when they wed. The rise in the number of dowers promised to widows, common in the bourgeoisie,[23] shows that the families of potential brides gambled on the commissaires' ability to reimburse the cost of their offices, and more generally on the growth of their fortunes.

Table 3: The financial situations of Châtelet commissaires
upon marriage
(L: *livre tournois*; CC: *commissaire au Châtelet*)

Year	Identity of commissaire and spouse	Contribution of groom	Dowry	Community share	Dower
1714	Louis Pierre Regnard – Gabrielle Thérèse Dorey	50,650 L, including an office valued at 30,000 L	12,000 L (gift of uncles and aunts)	4000 L	Annuity of 300 or 400 L
1719	Claude Sautel – Edmée Fetont veuve Jacques Goudin (CC)			no community	Annuity of 500 L
1725	Sébastien Paul Delafosse – Marie Pocquelin	At least 16,000 L	unknown	8000 L	Annuity of 500 L
1764	Michel Pierre Guyot – Marie Catherine Rouen	31,000 L (office financed by an annuity of 1200 L bought with 24,000 L)	50,000 L	10,000 L	Annuity of 1200 L

23. Mathieu Marraud, 'Communauté conjugale et communauté politique: les usages de la coutume de Paris dans la bourgeoisie corporative, XVIIe-XVIIIe siècles', *Revue d'histoire moderne et contemporaine* 58 (2011), p.96-119.

Year	Identity of commissaire and spouse	Contribution of groom	Dowry	Community share	Dower
1769	Jean Marcelin Serreau – Marie Victoire Le Roux	Office of commissaire Annuity of 1987 L interest from the Manufacture royale des glaces Annuity of 127 L 14,000 L in movable property and cash		8000 L	Annuity of 1200 L
1771	Mathieu Vanglenne – Anne Catherine Dumaige	28,560 L, but owed the entire value of his office of commissaire	30,000 L plus an annuity of 268 L	8000 L	Annuity of 600 or 800 L
1787	Defresne – Serreau	17,321 L	At least 8000 L	10,000 L	Annuity of 1000 or 1200 L

As we see in Table 3, there was no significant increase in the material prosperity of Châtelet commissaires. Had their social backgrounds and geographical origins changed in some way since the beginning of the century? This question is far from frivolous, as an analysis of their social position would allow comparisons with that of the parish clergy. In the aftermath of *Unigenitus*, archbishops deliberately purged undesirables from their clerical ranks – mostly local notables and men from good bourgeois families in Paris – making room to enlist more obedient priests who were loyal to the papal bull. The replacements hailed mainly from the provinces but were also children of devout (or else conformist) petit bourgeois in Paris.[24] Were commissaires subject to similar discriminatory recruitment methods? There are two cases

24. Laurence Croq, 'L'entrée en religion, entre choix familial et vocation: l'exemple des fils de la bourgeoisie parisienne au XVIIIᵉ siècle', in *L'Eglise des laïcs, XVIᵉ-XXᵉ siècle*, ed. Ariane Boltanski and Marie-Lucie Copete (Madrid, 2021), p.117-35.

in which they were denied the right to incorporate, but it does not seem to have been for ideological reasons.[25]

Table 4 shows that, in the eighteenth century, commissaires did indeed come from a wide variety of social backgrounds. The Six Corps continued to figure strongly in the ranks of commissaires over the century, making up roughly a quarter of their numbers. Until the 1760s, the police recruited heavily amongst the petit bourgeois – Pierre Chenon *père* was one of this milieu's most exemplary commissaires[26] – after which more prominent bourgeois officeholders, such as *procureurs* and *greffiers*, began to favour the occupation, the scions of suburban and provincial notable families also joining their ranks. In general, with increasing social elevation came relative embourgeoisement, confirming Lenoir's late eighteenth-century assertions that Châtelet commissaires were 'of higher quality' than at the beginning of the century. Unlike the clergy, however, commissaires did not seem to hail increasingly from the provinces or from the lower classes.

The multigenerational vocational dynasties prevalent under Louis XIV, such as in the Regnard and Daminois families, became an irregular occurrence in the eighteenth century. Older generations would now beget the next through marriage alliances: Jean-Baptiste Dorival became Charles Daniel Delafosse's son-in-law and Hugues Philippe Duchesne that of Commissaire André Defacq, Romain Armand Legretz married Adélaïde Catherine Crespy, and so on.

Were commissaires likely to rise to the ranks of the bourgeois elite? It was indeed possible, for some. Commissaires Michel Pierre Guyot and Dorival, both in office since 1756, were elected *échevins bourgeois* in 1777 and 1786 respectively; Mathieu Vanglenne, who had taken office in 1770, became a city councillor in 1778 and was elected alderman sometime around 1796. Guyot and Vanglenne were from Six Corps merchant families. Guyot's father had been a *grand-garde* of the furrier guild and a *consul*, though it seems the position of church-warden had escaped him, both in Saint-Germain-l'Auxerrois and in Saint-Sulpice. Guyot's younger brother was a *grand notable* – rare in Paris towards the end of the *Ancien Régime* – a *grand-garde* of the furrier guild and a *juge consul*; in 1784, he was the third of six candidates of

---

25. Vincent Milliot, *Un Policier des Lumières, suivi de Mémoires de J. C. P. Lenoir, ancien lieutenant général de police de Paris, écrits en pays étrangers dans les années 1790 et suivantes* (Seyssel, 2011), p.127 and 226-27 (Commissaire Antoine Tilloy).

26. Justine Berlière, *Policer Paris au siècle des Lumières: les commissaires du quartier du Louvre dans la seconde moitié du XVIIIᵉ siècle* (Paris, 2012).

Table 4: Occupation and place of residence of the fathers of forty-one Châtelet commissaires (p: *procureur*; P: in Parlement; C: in Châtelet; bdp: *bourgeois de Paris*; mt: merchant)

Year appointed	Châtelet commissaires	Six Corps merchants, notaires and notables	Other merchant occupations and artisans (occupations excluded from aldermanship)	Procureurs, huissiers, greffiers	Bourgeois de Paris and salaried workers	Non-Parisians
1690-1729 (8 cases)	Louis Hiérôme Daminois, Louis Pierre Regnard, Pierre Regnard	Sébastien Paul Delafosse, Pierre Glou	Nicolas Emmanuel Parisot (*boucher privilégié*)	Claude Sautel (*huissier* P)	Louis Anne Jourdan de La Salle (musician)	
1730-1749 (7 cases)	Charles Daniel Delafosse[1]		Thomas Mouricault (wine seller)	François Simon Chastelus (pC)	Guillaume Louis Delafleutrie (bdp), Guillaume Boniface Dupré (bdp), Pierre Chenon (bdp), Hubert Mutel (*chef de fourrière* for the duchesse d'Orléans)	

1.　The brothers Sébastien Paul and Charles Daniel Delafosse were commissaires from 1722 to 1733 and from 1733 to 1760 respectively. They were the sons of jewellery merchants.

Year appointed	Châtelet commissaires	Six Corps merchants, notaires and notables	Other merchant occupations and artisans (occupations excluded from aldermanship)	Procureurs, huissiers, greffiers	Bourgeois de Paris and salaried workers	Non-Parisians
1750-1769 (15 cases)		Jean Graillard de Graville, Jean Marcelin Serreau, Michel Pierre Guyot, Amable Pierre Touvenot (alderman notaire)	Jean Thomas Defresne (mt bdp), Jean-Baptiste Charles Lemaire (mt bdp), Boullanger (wig maker), Claude Robert Coquelin (hatter), Antoine Alexis Belle (painter and contrôleur des rentes)	Jean-Baptiste Dorival (pP), Jérôme Abraham Porquet (pP), René Regnard de Barentin (pC)	Pierre Charles Duruisseau (commis du Garde-Meuble de la couronne), François Jean Sirebeau (inspecteur des Eaux et fontaines publiques)	Louis Joseph Laumonier (alderman from Lille)

Year appointed	Châtelet commissaires	Six Corps merchants, notaires and notables	Other merchant occupations and artisans (occupations excluded from aldermanship)	Procureurs, huissiers, greffiers	Bourgeois de Paris and salaried workers	Non-Parisians
1770–1789 (11 cases)	Marie Joseph Chenon	Mathieu Vanglenne, Pierre Louis Foucault, Noël Louis Gillet, Augustin Charles Pierre	Pierre Nicolas Eustache Landelle (wine seller), Jacques Marie Stanislas Berton (bookseller)	Claude Denis Le Seigneur (*greffier* P), André Nicolas Marie Alix (pC), Antoine Nicolas Gueullette (initially pP, subsequently *greffier de l'officialité*)		Pierre François Simonneau (tanner and leather merchant from Etampes)[2]
Total: 41	4	11	9	8	7	2

2. Simonneau was brother to the *lieutenant particulier civil* au bailliage in Etampes and to Jacques Guillaume Simonneau (1740, Etampes–1792, Etampes), a tanner, leather merchant and mayor of Etampes. He was massacred in 1791.

the Six Corps guilds to occupy the post of *député du commerce* and, in 1786, he was elected alderman. Vanglenne was the youngest brother in a family of ordinary mercers.[27] Jean-Baptiste Dorival came from a family which had produced a dozen *procureurs au Parlement* over three generations.[28]

Was the prospect of being elevated to the nobility sufficient incentive to purchase an office of commissaire?[29] Since the position of alderman granted the legal status of nobility, it is tempting to consider the possibility – Cadot's rise is an oft-cited example supporting this hypothesis, along with others such as Commissaire Michel, who in 1787 became *audiencier en la Chancellerie*. In truth, similar instances were exceptions rather than the rule. The office of *commissaire au Châtelet* did not confer nobility, nor did it provide the capital necessary to enable the acquisition of a noble title. Unlike notaires and the occasional Parlement *procureurs*, commissaires never sold their office to purchase another, such as *commissaire des guerres* or *secrétaire du roi*, even in provincial chancelleries. The majority of Châtelet commissaires who sold their offices seem to have ceased their activities entirely. This may have been because of financial difficulties (as was the case for Gillet) or physical incapacity (the bookseller Hardy reports it was the reason behind Boullanger's retirement).[30] The social trajectories of commissaire offspring, male and female children alike, lend support to the notion that integration into the nobility was as unnecessary as it was uncommon. Genuine embourgeoisement typically accompanied an increase in prosperity, but Châtelet commissaires could never hope to become true members of the nobility.

The following section discusses whether the values and professional practices of commissaires also evolved, and, as their socio-economic conditions improved, whether the increasing gap between commissaires and the working-class population affected their capacity to mediate conflicts.[31]

27. Paris, AN, MC, XLVI 438, 29 August 1771, marriage of Vanglenne-Dumaige. Vanglenne would become *greffier de la Compagnie des commissaires* in 1788, and *receveur* (treasurer) in 1789.
28. Guyot was *greffier de la Compagnie des commissaires* in 1777, receveur in 1778, *syndic* in 1780-1781 and 1786-1788; Dorival was elected syndic in 1779-80.
29. Milliot, *Un Policier des Lumières*.
30. Hardy, *Mes loisirs*, ed. P. Bastien *et al.*, vol.7: *1781-1782* (2019), p.215-16, 6 July 1781.
31. Garrioch, *Neighbourhood and community in Paris*.

"To win over the love and respect of the people"

Châtelet commissaires executed the orders of the king and the *lieutenant général de police* with a mix of preventive and repressive measures, alternating between their roles as judge and officer of the peace. In the course of their official duties in Paris and the surrounding region, they crossed paths with men and women from the lower and middle classes – more rarely from the nobility – in a variety of settings. Parisian men and women alike sought assistance from their commissaires on any number of occasions. For example, until the 1740s, commissaires presided over local meetings to elect lamp lighters.[32] They were summoned to supervise shrine processions down the Sainte-Geneviève mountain.[33] They might equally be called upon to conduct investigations following requests for separation of property, affix the seals on the homes of the deceased with outstanding debts to several creditors or who left behind children under the age of majority, and accompany the juries and guards of corporations in their internal police operations, validating any seizures that were made.[34]

The *lieutenants de police* strongly encouraged officers to 'espouse uncompensated police duties in preference to the more lucrative activities of the contentious jurisdiction', with varying degrees of success.[35] Some commissaires still responded more promptly to the needs of nobles and bourgeois than to those of the common people. Such was the case with Commissaire Louis Hiérôme Daminois, whose career spanned six decades (1690-1752; he died in 1759 at the age of ninety-five). From the 1730s to the 1750s, Daminois, who lived in the parish of Saint-Germain-l'Auxerrois and was responsible for the Palais-Royal quarter, regularly rubbed elbows with the local notables, sharing their ideology. He became a churchwarden in the parish of Sainte-Opportune and, in 1721, married his daughter off to Jean Martin Sandrin, a wealthy mercer who would be elected *garde* in 1729. In 1744, Daminois was tasked with convening a meeting of notables in his quarter to debate how to re-establish the tax for lanterns and removal of refuse. He approved the list of potential meeting participants his collaborator, Jean Olivier Boutray (a mercer

32. Auguste-Philippe Herlaut, 'L'éclairage des rues à Paris de la fin du XVIIᵉ au XVIIIᵉ siècle', *Paris et Ile-de-France: mémoire* 43 (1916), p.130-240.
33. Edouard Pinet, *La Compagnie des porteurs de la châsse de sainte Geneviève, 1525-1902* (Paris, 1903), p.174-76.
34. Milliot, *Un Policier des Lumières.*
35. Milliot, *Un Policier des Lumières.*

and *quartinier*) had prepared, asserting 'those same names would have readily appeared' in any list he made. Daminois's intimate familiarity with the bourgeoisie was in concert with traditional perceptions of his profession: when, in November 1749, two petitioners allegedly went to his home to make a complaint, Daminois's clerk 'had reportedly told the two that, since "they had little money to expend, their complaint would consequently be futile"'.[36] Records of his practice in 1745 confirm there was little sign of activity – only fifty-six causes were registered[37] – and advance age and frequent absences do not completely account for his idleness. Like many other commissaires, Daminois simply disdained tasks which were not profitable, preferring to service the needs of his peers. Commissaire Cadot, in office from 1731 to 1764, acted in much the same way.[38] There is doubtless a kernel of truth in this image of greedy commissaires, yet a form of social selection is what mainly dictated their pecuniary considerations. Daminois and Cadot served the social elite, not commoners, in defiance of the advances in police practices Commissaires Chenon (both father and son) epitomised. The ideal of Enlightenment police serving all social milieux independently of potential material gains took root gradually and not at all uniformly.

Nonetheless, the municipal government would increasingly share the new values, and this served to strengthen the ties between the Châtelet and the office of the *prévôt des marchands*. Support for the privileges of the *bourgeois de Paris*, their fiscal exemptions in particular, disappeared from the municipal agenda. In future the city, like the Châtelet, would make efforts to satisfy the needs of the public as a whole and not merely the social elite. To avoid increases in housing costs and unemployment amongst its water carriers, the municipality refused to connect buildings to a water supply network. It also kept watch over wood supplies to limit the impact on Parisian budgets. At the same time, however, as absolutism tightened its stranglehold, negotiations between central authorities and the bourgeois also declined, which in turn meant fewer local meetings. The experiment in 1744 with local assembly meetings was not repeated. Thereafter, Châtelet commissaires would appoint lamp lighters directly, and the community would only occasionally participate in ensuring police

36. Croq and Lyon-Caen, 'La notabilité parisienne entre la police et la ville', p.136.
37. Isabelle Vandenkoornhuyse-Davet, 'Policer Paris par la lumière (1667-1769)', MA dissertation, Université Paris Nanterre, 2018.
38. Milliot, *Un Policier des Lumières*.

functions. Municipal authorities began to disregard the expertise of residents, planning projects with the aid of scholars and technicians instead. The Prévôté des marchands ceased to be one of the centres of power for notables, and its commissaires became members of an institution which, like the Châtelet, was in service to the king and to the people.[39]

In a sense, the commissaires' embourgeoisement was counter-balanced by their evolving values and professional practices. They retained their power of mediation, and their occupation did not undermine their ability to establish communal roots or develop neighbourly relations. Since, on average, commissaires remained in the same quarter for twelve years, they had ample time to form strong ties with residents. Around 1775, Hardy even admitted receiving some of the news items he recorded in his journal from his landlord, Commissaire Convers-Desormeaux, who was responsible for the place Maubert quarter.[40] In an era when *quartiniers* only rarely resided in the quarter they represented, and when the bourgeoisie restricted their relations with the common people in their community in favour of developing ties with the capital,[41] commissaires were therefore reassuringly solid, familiar mainstays. They were well-known and recognised within the limits of the quarter they supervised – their authority was sometimes ridiculed, but, in general, they commanded respect. True, commissaires were more aggressive towards common men and women than towards bourgeois,[42] but they undoubtedly inspired confidence more often than fear. Most knew how to 'win over the love and respect of the people', as Hardy so elegantly observed.[43] As a result, though predominantly bourgeois, they were increasingly well accepted by their fellow inhabitants.

Political sympathies and spiritual aspirations

Did commissaires come to resemble aldermen as a result of their favourable integration? What of their personal, political and spiritual

---

39. Croq, 'Essai pour la construction de la notabilité'; Croq, 'Les édiles, les notables et le pouvoir royal'.
40. Vincent Milliot, *'L'Admirable police': tenir Paris au siècle des Lumières* (Ceyzérieu, 2016).
41. Garrioch, *Neighbourhood and community in Paris*.
42. Nicolas Vidoni, 'Une "police des Lumières"? La "violence" des agents de police à Paris au milieu du XVIIIᵉ siècle', *Rives méditerranéennes* 40 (2011), p.43-66.
43. Hardy, *Mes loisirs*, vol.7, p.216.

ideologies? Commissaires were required to be discrete with regards to their political leanings; as a result, business was conducted on neutral ground. Close friends and family were also expected to be circumspect.

Maupeou's reforms did not seem to particularly engage the commissaires apart from François Simon Chastelus, who later became *lieutenant particulier au Châtelet* and an Hôtel-Dieu administrator. The impact on the alderman community is more readily apparent: among some of the noteworthy *rentrants* were two former aldermen, Etienne René Viel and Antoine Gaspard Boucher d'Argis, and future alderman Henri Isaac Estienne. Estienne led the *avocats rentrants* and *avocats du Parlement* to swear their oaths before the new *premier président au Parlement*, Bertier de Sauvigny.[44] In August 1773, he was also elected *échevin bourgeois*. The newly revamped Châtelet recruited the son of Boucher d'Argis as a councillor. The former *conseiller de la Cour des aides*, Mathias Bernard Goudin, became the new Parlement *magistrat* in addition to his position as *conseiller de ville de cour souveraine* which he had held since 1769. Moreover, Chancellor Maupeou chose two former aldermen to administrate the Hôpital général: Olivier Clément Vieillard, also an erstwhile grocer who later acquired the office of *payeur des rentes*, and Alexandre Claude Basly, who had been *avocat aux conseils* before becoming comptroller of the Chambre des comptes. Vieillard and Basly diligently attended Hôpital meetings with Archbishop Christophe de Beaumont and Bertier de Sauvigny, the first president of the new Parlement. In January 1774, when it seemed the judicial reforms were there to stay, Estienne arranged a successful match for his son with the daughter of a former mercer and newly appointed *auditeur des reçus des officiers de la Chambre des comptes*. The contract was signed in the presence of some high-ranking 'witnesses', their attendance giving a symbolic nod of approval to the alliance: the maréchal de Brissac (the governor of Paris), the *corps de ville*, the duchesse de Chevreuse, the duc de Luynes and Miromesnil, the former *premier président au Parlement* in Normandy.[45] However, when Louis XVI ascended the throne, there was a partial return to the old order. The Hôpital général's office of administration was completely restructured, and Vieillard and Basly were dismissed. But, in 1777, Lenoir made them administrators of the Mont-de-Piété, also

44. *Journal historique* (12 November 1771), p.232-33.
45. Paris, AN, MC, XCVII 480, 16 January 1774, marriage contract of Estienne-Barraud.

appointing Louis Etienne Framboisier de Beaunay, former *subdélégué de l'intendance* in Rouen, to the position of *directeur général* – and thereby firmly entrenching the Mont-de-Piété in the royalist camp. Populating institutions with men from the administrative *intendances* was a way of increasingly bringing them into the royalist fold. New recruits further benefited by obtaining an office in the city government: in the 1770s, Ethis de Corny, secretary of the *intendance* in Franche-Comté, acquired the offices of *avocat* and *procureur du roi et de la ville*; shortly after, François Joseph Veytard, a former *subdélégué de l'intendance* in Flanders, became *greffier en chef* of the Prévôté des marchands.

Commissaires, however, seem relatively nonpartisan. An analysis of their family ties supports the impression of a group situated midway between the royalist and parliamentary camps. Commissaires who took office before 1780 were only distantly related to Maupeou's coterie: Commissaire Fremyn's son-in-law, Jean-Baptiste Dorival, had three first cousins amongst his few royalist relations. In the opposing faction was Charles Convers-Desormeaux's brother, imprisoned in the Bastille 'for having distributed pamphlets hostile to the chancellor in the Palais-Royal'.[46] The commissaires recruited in the 1780s appear to have more royalist inclinations. Jacques Marie Stanislas Pierre Berton, for example, was the son of a bookseller and a 'devout follower of the Molinist party'.[47] In 1784, Commissaire Augustin Charles Pierre married the sister of two former *avocats du Parlement* (the brothers Colmet de Santerre); in 1816, at the age of seventy-five, he reclaimed his post of *commissaire de police*, amid a 'wave of ultraroyalist nominations'.[48] Commissaire André Nicolas Marie Alix was the brother of André Marie Alix, a former *secrétaire en chef de l'intendance* in Flanders under Lefebvre de Caumartin, whom he followed to Paris in 1778, acceding to the post of *prévôt des marchands*. Compared to the aldermen, there were only a handful of commissaire *subdélégués* who were raised from the bourgeoisie of the Paris region: examples include Louis Le Compte (*subdélégué* of Arpajon and father-in-law to Denis Delavoiepierre, a grocer and future *échevin*) and Alexis Edme Sprote

46. Frédéric Barbier *et al.*, *Dictionnaire des imprimeurs, libraires et gens du livre à Paris (1701-1789)* (Geneva, 2007), p.530.

47. Barbier *et al.*, *Dictionnaire des imprimeurs*, p.217-18.

48. Vincent Denis, 'Les commissaires de police de la chute de la monarchie à la Restauration', in *Le Commissaire de police au XIXᵉ siècle*, ed. Dominique Kalifa and Pierre Karila-Cohen (Paris, 2008), p.27-40.

(a *subdélégué* of Gonesse and the son of mercer and alderman Louis Dominique Sprote).

Amongst this tangled web of alliances, we find the names of some who were of a less neutral bent than their fellow commissaires, as well as signs of stronger political involvement in the 1760s. In 1769, for example, Commissaire Jean Marcelin Serreau, though the son of a mercer, brought only six witnesses to his marriage. Among the family members present were Serreau's brother-in-law, the Châtelet *procureur* Louis Regnard de Barentin (brother to Commissaire René Regnard de Barentin) – in 1763, the Regnards' father, Armand, had taken in an ex-Jesuit (likely a nephew). Serreau was also friends with lawyer Jean Honoré Delaborde, one of the four men who, in 1771, rallied colleagues in support of Maupeou's reform. Delaborde was friends with Commissaire Guyot and Alderman Marie Nicolas Pigeon. Serreau's betrothed, a notaire's daughter, brought three friends to the ceremony, one of whom was René Gaultier Du Breuil,[49] an *avocat rentrant* and also Pigeon's friend. Furthermore, one of Serreau's nieces would marry Commissaire Thomas Desfresne, Delavoiepierre's cousin – and a friend of Antoine Marcel de Bruges, a Châtelet *procureur* who became a member of the Association de bienfaisance judiciaire. Defresne's wife was cousin to Jacques Mathurin Colombeau, another of the four leading the charge in support for Maupeou's reforms; Mme Defresne was also friends with César Chaillon, *procureur* in the Grand Conseil. Meanwhile, Mattieu Vanglenne, whom we saw earlier, was himself friends with Marie Gabrielle Sophie Sprote, Louis Dominique Sprote's daughter. The Sprotes had ties to Mme de Moysan, the *supérieure* of the Hôpital général (Archbishop Christophe de Beaumont had imposed this nomination in 1749; de Moysan's first marriage had been to master dyer Claude Meriel). Vanglenne had his own marriage contract signed by Mme de Moysan's daughter-in-law, Marie Victoire Rouveau (widow of Pierre Meriel, former officer of the Hôtel des Invalides), and two granddaughters, Félicité Madeleine and Marie Blanche Meriel.[50] Commissaire Guyot was friends with Sieur Lecuyer, the *sous-économe* of the Hôpital général who, incidentally, frequently took his meals with one of de Moysan's nieces.[51] The link

49. Paris, AN, MC, LXV 365, 22 November 1769, marriage contract of Jean Marcelin Serreau and Marie Victoire Le Roux.
50. Henry Légier-Desgranges, *Du jansénisme à la Révolution: Mme de Moysan et l'extravagante affaire de l'Hôpital général, 1749-1758* (Paris, 1954).
51. Hardy, *Mes loisirs*, vol.8, p.452-53, 31 January and 2 February 1785.

between Commissaire Guyot and the Hôpital général is perhaps indirect, but was common enough. Commissaire Regnard de Barentin had similar affiliations: after selling his office in 1773, he became an *économe* at Scipion, a division of the Hôpital général, and was still in this position in 1789.

The bonds between these anti-Jansenists and certain individuals connected to the Hôpital général is intriguing. Were the ties merely political, or should we interpret them in terms of more socio-spiritual inclinations? Nicolas Lyon-Caen has demonstrated in his research that the Jansenists had established and retained control of charitable committees in a number of parishes, giving alms (with few exceptions) only to the wretched poor (*pauvres honteux*) who were well established in the parish, and excluding the migrant poor from such assistance.[52] Anti-Jansenists valued alternative forms of charity set in a different venue: the hospital. In principle, hospitals were open to all – none more so than the Hôpital général, which welcomed the infirm, the mentally ill, orphans, prostitutes, beggars and the elderly, regardless of their place of origin or where they lived. Social selection was not completely absent, as most of the elderly and the mentally ill (or their families) were required to pay a stipend in exchange for their care. Yet, here again, we find the opposition between two notions of public service, one open to the greater population, one restricted to the elite.

Châtelet commissaires were not inevitably hostile to Jansenists. Lyon-Caen has shown that, in 1744, 'the commissaires readily chose' at least twenty people 'whose religious allegiances were of public notoriety', such as the hosier merchant Jacques Lesourd, as members of the consultative assemblies of the quarter.[53] Family members echoed their commissaires' moderate stance in both deed and manner. In December 1731, for example, *lieutenant de police* Herault struck up a conversation on the miracles that had occurred at the tomb of François de Pâris because he had learned that Commissaire Divot's wife had visited the cemetery in Saint-Médard. But otherwise, no close relative of a commissaire or an alderman ever advertised belief in the miracles of the Jansenist saint by recording it in Louis-Basile Carré de Montgeron's book – when Jourdan de La Salle acknowledged his

---

52. Nicolas Lyon-Caen, 'Territoire paroissial et investissement notabiliaire: Marc-Etienne Quatremère et les limites de Saint-Germain-l'Auxerrois', *Hypothèses* 9 (2005), special issue: *L'Appropriation du territoire par les communautés*, ed. Nicolas Lyon-Caen, p.79-88; Lyon-Caen, *La Boîte à Perrette*.
53. Croq and Lyon-Caen, 'La notabilité parisienne entre la police et la ville', p.143.

wife's miracle, he was a Châtelet *greffier* and no longer *commissaire*. Apart from Pierre Jacques Coucicault, who commissioned a statue of Pâris, aldermen also shrank from public confessions.[54]

Were there *dévots* amongst the *commissaires*? According to the *Nouvelles ecclésiastiques*, Regnard claimed to be a *bon chrétien*, and swore 'he would let himself be rent to shreds for religion'.[55] The Jansenist newspaper might have mocked Regnard's aspirations of martyrdom, but never cast doubt on his piety, and, in his will, Regnard requested he be interred in the Saint-Séverin cemetery, a humble resting place favoured by the devout. What especially singles out the commissaires and their families is the request for extra masses and *bouts de l'an* (masses commemorating the first year following the death of loved ones) and the printing of *billets d'invitation* (announcements for services) in convents, while bourgeois convention dictated that each and every stage of religious life should be entrusted to one's parish church. Others shared this penchant for convents, such as artisans, *auxiliaires de la justice, procureurs* and *greffiers* – namely, those who were most often excluded from parish administrative positions.

Châtelet *commissaires* account for twenty-one of the twenty-three extra and death anniversary masses celebrated in monastic spaces. In comparison, six death anniversary masses were celebrated for aldermen family members – but four of them were for individuals who belonged to both *commissaire* and aldermanic circles. Of the two others, one was given in 1732 at the Carmelite convent of the place Maubert for the wife of the lawyer and future alderman Nicolas Daniel Phelippes de La Marnière; the second was offered in 1782 at the Barnabite convent for alderman Hubert Cheval de Saint-Hilaire's sister, Marie Marguerite, who had married Jean Marc Antoine Ecosse, a goldsmithing merchant, *grand garde* of his corporation, *contrôleur des rentes* and former churchwarden of Saint-Barthélémy.

The list of convents in Table 5 further suggests divergences in the spiritual preferences of Châtelet *commissaires* and aldermen. It also underscores that, contrary to Jansenist claims, the *dévots* of Paris were rarely connected to the Jesuits. The convents were geographically dispersed, a general reflection of the *dévots'* own fragmented community, as, in the eighteenth century, they had neither spatial nor spiritual centre. It had not always been this way: at the close of the seventeenth century, their spiritual locus had likely been the Couvent

54. Lyon-Caen, *La Boîte à Perrette*, p.221.
55. *Nouvelles ecclésiastiques* (6 December 1737), p.194-95.

Table 5: Extra masses and death anniversary masses for Châtelet commissaires and their kin celebrated in convents[1]
(p: *procureur*; P: in Parlement; C: in Châtelet; mt: merchant; w.: widow; m.: married)

Name of commissaire concerned (dates in office)	Deceased for whom the death anniversary mass was celebrated and relationship to the Châtelet commissaire	Parish burial ground (date of burial)	Convent or priory where extra masses or death anniversary were celebrated
Joseph Aubert (1708-1749)	Himself	? (1749)	*Chanoines* of Sainte-Croix-de-la-Bretonnerie
François Spire Chastelus, *commissaire au Châtelet* (1737-1762), *lieutenant particulier* (C) and administrator of the Hôtel-Dieu (1771-1774)	His mother, Marie Madeleine Boulduc m. François Spire Chastelus (pC)	Saint-Jacques-de-la-Boucherie (1738)	*Pères de la doctrine chrétienne* of Saint-Julien-des-Ménétriers, rue Saint-Martin
Nicolas Philippe Cléret (1725-1749)	His brother, Nicolas Philippe Cléret (notaire)	Saint-Sauveur (1737)	Augustines of Saint-Magloire, rue Saint-Denis

1. Sources: Paris, AN, AD/XXc/96, Joseph Aubert, Françoise Nereau widow of Pierre Baudoyn; AD/XXc/97, Marie Madeleine Boulduc wife of François Spire Chastelus, Nicolas Philippe Cleret, Claude Robert Coquelin; AD/XXc/98, Dorival, Marie Anne Armet widow of M. Duval, Julien Etienne Divot; AD/XXc/99, Marie Madeleine Bouillerot widow of Joseph Fremyn; AD/XXc/100, Pierre Guyot; AD/XXc/101, Marie Marguerite Didelot widow of Jean Emmanuel Porquet and wife of Nicolas Horry; Suzanne Anne Briard wife of Jean Hubert; AD/XXc/103, René Le Comte, Marie Anne Chevenot wife of Nicolas François Lucas; AD/XXc/104, Malice de Troncières; AD/XXc/105, Charles Jacques Etienne Parent, Denis Rouen; AD/XXc/106, André Estienne Serreau, Jean-Baptiste Joseph Thierry, Elisabeth Lagneau widow of François Touvenot. NB: the catalogue of the Archives nationales (Caran) includes a total of 213 'services' and *bouts de l'an* celebrated in parishes and in convents (AD/XXC/96-AD/XXC/107).

Name of commissaire concerned (dates in office)	Deceased for whom the death anniversary mass was celebrated and relationship to the Châtelet commissaire	Parish burial ground (date of burial)	Convent or priory where extra masses or death anniversary were celebrated
Claude Robert Coquelin (1762-1773)	His father, Robert François Coquelin (mt hatter)	Saint-Germain-en-Laye (1763)	Priory of Saint-Denis-de-la-Chartre
Claude Robert Coquelin (1762-1773)	Himself	Saint-Nicolas-des-Champs (1773)	Priory of Saint-Denis-de-la-Chartre
Charles Germain de Courcy (1723-1756)	His mother-in-law, Marie Anne Armet w. of M. Duval	Saint-Eustache (1734)	*Augustins déchaussés*, place des Victoires
Julien Etienne Divot (1720-1730)	Himself	Saint-Jean-en-Grève (1736)	Carmes-Billettes
Jean-Baptiste Dorival (1756-1789)	His uncle Jean-Baptiste Dorival (pP and father-in-law of Etienne René Viel)	Saint-Landry (1768)	Grands-Augustins
Guy Michel Dudoigt (1738-1766)	His mother-in-law, Marie Marguerite Didelot w. of Jean Emmanuel Porquet (pP); m. Nicolas Horry (pP)	Saint-Séverin (1763)	Carmes-Billettes
Joseph Fremyn (1711-1741)	His widow, Marie Madeleine Bouillerot	Saint-Etienne-du-Mont (1773)	*Carmes de la place Maubert*

Name of commissaire concerned (dates in office)	Deceased for whom the death anniversary mass was celebrated and relationship to the Châtelet commissaire	Parish burial ground (date of burial)	Convent or priory where extra masses or death anniversary were celebrated
Michel Martin Grimperel (1730-1774)	His uncle, Malice de Troncières	? (1735)	*Augustins déchaussés*, place des Victoires
Michel Pierre Guyot (1756-1790), alderman (1777)	His father, Pierre Guyot (mt furrier, *grand garde*, consul; also father of an alderman)	Saint-Sulpice (1766)	Grands-Augustins
Michel Pierre Guyot (1756-1790), alderman (1777)	His father-in-law, Denis Rouen (mt manufacturer; also father of Denis André Rouen, *notaire échevin*)	Saint-Laurent (1776)	Grands-Augustins
Jean Hubert (1707-1771)	His second wife, Suzanne Anne Briard	Saint-Sulpice (1778)	*Augustins de la Reine Marguerite*
Antoine Jean-Baptiste Leblond (1779-1791)	His aunt, Marie Anne Chevenot m. Nicolas François Lucas	? (1784)	*Augustins déchaussés*, place des Victoires
René Lecomte (1718-1757)	Himself	Saint-Sulpice (1760)	*Cordeliers du Grand Couvent*
Jacques Léonard Ledroit (1730-1738)	His mother-in-law, Françoise Nereau w. of Pierre Baudoyn (*avocat au P*)	Saint-Etienne-du-Mont (1733)	*Carmes de la place Maubert*

Name of commissaire concerned (dates in office)	Deceased for whom the death anniversary mass was celebrated and relationship to the Châtelet commissaire	Parish burial ground (date of burial)	Convent or priory where extra masses or death anniversary were celebrated
Charles Jacques Etienne Parent (1723-1750)	Himself	Saint-André-des-Arts (1750)	*Augustins réformés du faubourg Saint-Germain*
Jérôme Abraham Porquet (1761-1764, later *receveur des émoluments du sceau*, 1767)	His mother, Marie Marguerite Didelot w. of Jean Emmanuel Porquet (pP); m. Nicolas Horry (pP)	Saint-Séverin (1763)	Carmes-Billettes
Jérôme Jean Remy (1730-1757)	His mother, Marie Catherine Thomas m. Jean Remy (*huissier ordinaire du roi en sa Chambre des comptes*)	? (1753)	Ave-Maria
Jean Marcelin Serreau (1761-1789)	His father, André Etienne Serreau (mt mercer)	Saint-Sauveur (1763)	Saint-Martin-des-Champs
Jean-Baptiste Joseph Thierry (1756-1776)	Himself	Saint-Louis-en-l'Ile (1776)	Carmes-Billettes
Amable Pierre Touvenot (1762-1772)	His mother, Elisabeth Lagneau w. of François Touvenot (notaire and *échevin bourgeois*)	Saint-Laurent (1768)	*Pères de la doctrine chrétienne* of Saint-Julien-des-Ménétriers

des Grands-Augustins, which housed the archives and the meetings of the Order of the Saint-Esprit and was one of the auxiliary sites of monarchic sacrality after Notre-Dame and Saint-Denis. The Archives nationales house several announcements of services for commissaires celebrated at the convent between 1678 (de Barry) and 1708 (Regnault). The commissaires may also have shared a confraternity there with other Châtelet and Parlement officers. Records from 1764 show that the Grands-Augustins had harboured a confraternity and that 'sieurs Voyer, Maillart, Quinson// Coquelin, Luton et Cleret' of the 'sindicat' had commissioned artwork for it that year.[56] It is possible the record refers to Charles François Cleret (an honorary commissaire) and Claude Robert Coquelin (commissaire since 1762). In any event, for roughly a dozen years, the Grands-Augustins convent was the spiritual seat of 'royalist' bourgeois members of the Dorival, Viel and Guyot families.

Some of the details regarding the children of aldermen, notables and commissaires who entered religion contribute further to our comparison of the spiritual inclinations of these professionals. Before 1730, the sons of commissaires and aldermen alike were predominantly secular priests; Louis Hiérôme Daminois's son remained a diocesan priest of Troyes probably due to his too close affiliation with the Jansenists; the son of Commissaire Aubert was a canon of Saint-Thomas-du-Louvre (1730); both of Jean Hubert's sons were priests, and one became the spiritual director of the Ecole militaire. To my knowledge, after 1730, no son of an alderman or commissaire entered religion. The two communities are instead distinguished by the destinies of their daughters. Commissaire families seem to have been particularly drawn to the biblical figure of Martha (who symbolised an active life). In 1742, Commissaire Blanchard's daughter, Catherine Louise Blanchard, entered the convent of the Dames hospitalières de la Roquette, bringing with her a dowry of 6000 *livres*; this convent is also where Commissaire Legretz's sister died in 1782. In the aldermanic community, I have found only one cloistered nun: Marguerite Thérèse Cheval, a professed nun of the congregation of Notre-Dame. Commissaires and aldermen, like the majority of Parisian bourgeois, appear to have been reluctant to let their children enter religion, likely tending towards anticlericalism.

56. José Lothe and Agnès Virole, *Images de confréries parisiennes: catalogue des images de confréries (Paris et Ile-de-France) de la collection de M. Louis Ferrand* (Paris, 1992), p.108.

In the second half of the eighteenth century, it is spiritual inclination, not social origin or political engagements, that seemingly sets the families of commissaires apart. Convents and hospitals appear to be two important guiding stars in their lives. A preference for forms of institutional sociability such as Masonic lodges and the Association de bienfaisance judiciaire confirms the preponderance of spiritual engagement over political involvement.

Institutional sociability

New configurations of institutional sociability indeed characterised the second half of the eighteenth century. These organisations were either spiritually aligned, such as confraternities and Masonic lodges, or politically oriented, like the Association de bienfaisance judiciaire.

Freemasonry was different from traditional forms of sociability in that it welcomed waged workers, the young and merchants who were not part of the Six Corps. It offered those who were excluded from urban power centres, like the commissaires (see Table 4), a space in which to meet and dialogue, both locally and with people living in other cities or even other countries, and likely paved the way for their access to revolutionary citizenship.[57]

Sixteen commissaires were members of a total of ten lodges, with membership mainly concentrated in Les Amis intimes (5), Saint-Etienne de la vraie et parfaite amitié (3) and Le Zèle (2). Did the other members of these lodges have particular religious or political inclinations? Commissaires might have rubbed shoulders with the occasional antiparliamentarian, but, as the latter were members of disparate lodges and evidently circulated from one to the other, it was rare to chance upon more than two or three at a time. Grandin, a member of Le Zèle in 1788, was the commissaire most likely to be found in the company of antiparliamentarians such as Ambroise Falconnet (1742-1817), a former lawyer who, according to Hardy, 'had frequently worked for the interim Parlement'.[58] Others antiparliamentarians include Antoine Louis Michel Judde de Neuville and Antoine Edouard Le Gras de Saint-Germain (both *conseillers au Châtelet* who had taken office under Maupeou), Etienne Louis Desroches (a former *avocat au Parlement*), and François Joseph Colin, a former Châtelet

---

57. Pierre-Yves Beaurepaire, *L'Autre et le frère: l'étranger et la franc-maçonnerie en France au XVIII* siècle* (Paris, 1998).

58. Hardy, *Mes loisirs*, vol.8, p.689-90, 17 December 1785.

Table 6: Châtelet commissaires who were Freemasons of the Grande Loge de France between 1760 and 1795 and electors in their section in 1791[1]

Name (date of birth-death) Years in function as commissaire	Elective positions held by commissaires in the fraternity[2]	Lodge attended (years attended)	Electors in 1791: rank / total number in each section (section name)	Members of the Association de bienfaisance judicaire
Nicolas François Boin 1782-1791	0	Les Amis intimes (1785-1789)	22 / 26 (Théâtre-Français)	*
Adrien Louis Carré (1752-?) 1776-1791	0	Le Zèle (1783-1787)	18 / 27 (Palais-Royal)	
Achille Charles Danzel 1785-1791	0	Les Amis intimes (1786)		
Pierre Jean Duchauffour (1735-1812) 1780-1791	0	Saint-Nicolas-de-la-Parfaite-Egalité (1784)	2 / 9 (Henri-IV)	
André Duchesne 1786-1791	0	Les Amis intimes (1786)		
Bernard Louis Philippe Fontaine 1758-1791	*Greffier* (1778), *receveur* (1779), *syndic* (1781-1784)	Saint-Alphonse des amis parfaits de la vertu (1784-1786)		

1. Source: Alain Le Bihan, *Francs-maçons et ateliers parisiens de la Grande Loge de France au XVIIIe siècle (1760-1795)* (Paris, 1973).
2. Many thanks to Vincent Milliot for sharing his list of the duties performed by the Châtelet commissaires in their corporations.

Name (date of birth-death) Years in function as commissaire	Elective positions held by commissaires in the fraternity[2]	Lodge attended (years attended)	Electors in 1791: rank / total number in each section (section name)	Members of the Association de bienfaisance judicaire
Pierre Louis Foucault (1743-before 1788) 1774-1783	0	Saint-Etienne de la vraie et parfaite amitié (1779-1783)		
Noël Louis Gillet (c.1745-1821) 1774-1787	0	Saint-Etienne de la vraie et parfaite amitié (1778-1781)		
Jean Jacques Grandin 1782-1791	0	Le Zele (1785-1788)	15 / 15 (Arcis)	*
Jean Vincent Gruter Des Rosiers 1783-1791	Syndic (1790-1791)	Saint-Etienne de la vraie et parfaite amitié (1786-1790)		
Claude Nicolas Lebas 1787-1791	0	Les Amis intimes (1788) + La Constance (1788)		
Louis Alexandre Charles Leroux 1785-1791	0	Les Amis intimes (n.d.)		
Gabriel Lucotte de Champemont 1783-1791	0	Les Frères initiés (1787-1791)	1 / 20 (Louvre)	

Name (date of birth-death) Years in function as commissaire	Elective positions held by commissaires in the fraternity[2]	Lodge attended (years attended)	Electors in 1791: rank / total number in each section (section name)	Members of the Association de bienfaisance judicaire
Jean Odent (1749-?) 1777-1791	0	Sainte-Sophie (1785-1788)	12 / 26 (Théâtre-Français)	
Jean Marcelin Serreau 1761-1789	*Greffier* (1782), *receveur* (1783), *syndic* (1785-1789)	L'Amitié (1775)		
Pierre François Simonneau (1744-?) 1769-1791	*Greffier* (1787)	David (1773-1774)	5 / 25 (Ponceau)	

procureur and also a member of the Association de bienfaisance judiciaire.

Did commissaires join the Freemasons out of personal interest or professional initiative? Lenoir would have us believe it was he who encouraged their requests for membership: 'The police were well informed of what went on during these supposedly secret assemblies and inside these purportedly secret lodges. Several police officers who had been admitted as Freemasons compiled reports for me, and their reports, true or false, commonly only contained details of receptions, mystifying stories and, most often, amorous entanglements.'[59]

Freemason membership developed over two distinct periods. The first wave of membership follows Lenoir's arrival at the head of the Paris police force in 1774. Three of the four who first joined in the 1770s were sons of Six Corps merchants: Serreau, the son of a mercer from the Saint-Sauveur parish; Foucault, whose father had also become a mercer before going bankrupt and becoming a commissaire and *huissier audiencier au Bureau de la ville*; and lastly Gillet, the son of one of the last *grands notables* in Paris (a grocer-apothecary who became an alderman in 1751, consul in 1757, and *juge consul* in 1773). Until 1785, members were affiliated to different lodges and membership was staggered throughout the entire period. Simonneau was admitted to the David lodge around 1773, and Serreau's acceptance to L'Amitié followed shortly after in 1775; Gillet and Foucault became members of Saint-Etienne de la vraie et parfaite amitié nearly concomitantly (1778/1779), but they were no longer members when Gruter Des Rosiers joined in 1786. In the period following Lenoir's disgrace in 1785, membership increased and was sometimes concentrated in the same lodges. For example, from 1785 until the Revolution, the Amis intimes lodge welcomed five young Châtelet commissaires who had all taken office in the 1780s.

How did other Freemason members view the commissaires? Were they considered interlopers and, as such, to be mistrusted? Or did the commissaires' participation in Freemasonry help sanction their elevation to the Parisian bourgeoisie? The election results from between 1789 and 1791 give some indication as to how they were perceived. No commissaire was elected deputy of the Third Estate to the Estates General during this period, but some became *juges de paix* or electors of their section. In 1791, the bourgeois designated twelve

59. Jean Charles Pierre Lenoir, *Mémoires*, in Milliot, *Un Policier des Lumières*, p.1018.

Table 7: Freemason alderman and bourgeois candidates for aldermanship of the Grande Loge de France from 1760 to 1795[1]

(cw: churchwarden; mt: merchant; p: *procureur*)

Name (date of birth-death)	Profession and offices held	Lodge attended	Electors in 1790: rank / total number in each section (name of section)
Claude Bougier (1727-1784)	(mt) mercer of plain-weave and fine cotton fabrics; *contrôleur du grenier à sel de Paris* (1756-1779); *garde* (1764); *consul* (1773); *quartinier* (1761-1779); bearer of the shrine of Sainte-Geneviève (1752-1778); *failli* (1778); (cw) Saint-Leu-Saint-Gilles (1762)	Saint-Pierre des vrais frères (1776-1781)	
Denis Delavoie-pierre (1729-?)	(mt) grocer; *consul* (1778); first of six Six Corps candidates for the office of *député du commerce* (1784); elected *échevin bourgeois* (1785); administrator, Grand Bureau des pauvres and Hôpital des Petites-Maisons; bearer of the shrine of Sainte-Geneviève (1756-Revolution); (cw) Saint-Eustache (1775)	La Concorde (1777-1785)	11 / 17 (Mauconseil)
Nicolas-Jean Mercier (1730-1804)	(mt) mercer; elected *échevin bourgeois* in 1783; (cw) Saint-Germain-l'Auxerrois (1779)	Henri-IV (1774-1780) and L'Amitié (1775)	12 / 12 (rue de Bondy)

1. Source: Le Bihan, *Francs-maçons et ateliers.*

Name (date of birth-death)	Profession and offices held	Lodge attended	Electors in 1790: rank / total number in each section (name of section)
Parfait Duparc (1737-1829)	(p) Chambre des comptes (1770-Revolution); city councillor (1778-Revolution)	L'Aménité (1784-1788) and La Modération (1787)	
François Regnaud (1743-?)	Banker expeditionary for the Roman *curia* (1769-Revolution); *échevin notable de la ville de Paris* (may have been elected in 1793)	Saint-Etienne de la vraie et parfaite amitié (1779-1786)	

commissaires electors, including seven who were Freemasons. Perhaps Freemason commissaires inspired more trust in their neighbours.

The enthusiasm the commissaires showed for Freemasonry, however, contrasts sharply with the aldermanic disregard for the institution. Only five aldermen became Freemasons: three merchants, one *procureur* in the Chambre des comptes and one banker expeditionary for the Roman *curia* (see Table 7). Six members of the Six Corps were amongst the first Freemasons: three who joined in the 1770s were merchants (also sons of Six Corps merchants), two were members of the confraternity of the bearers of the shrine of Sainte-Geneviève. The last, a *procureur*, was the son-in-law of a hosier whose death would cut short his ambitions of becoming an alderman. The only common link between the lodges of the commissaires and those of the aldermen was François Regnaud – who, along with Gruter Des Rosiers, was a member of Saint-Etienne de la vraie et parfaite amitié – but he had no family ties to the merchant community.

The aldermen also lagged behind the commissaires in the 1789-1791 elections. In 1791, only five became electors, all from the Right Bank. Two of them, Delavoiepierre and Mercier, were Freemasons. The others were Guyot, a furrier (and Commissaire Guyot's brother), Etienne René Viel, a lawyer (and Commissaire Dorival's first cousin), and Pierre Guillaume Agasse, a city councillor.

There were therefore three times as many commissaires as aldermen in Freemasonry and twice as many among the electors of 1791.[60] The same difference of one to two was found in the Association de bienfaisance judiciaire.[61] For commissaires, it seems, membership of spiritual organisations was far more attractive than political engagement. André Jean Boucher d'Argis, the son of an alderman, created the association in 1787 with the consent of the government, though the very existence of the association was a critique – albeit implicit – of the Paris Parlement. Boucher d'Argis's aim had been to provide a centralised forum in support of the unjustly accused, thereby preventing judicial errors. The inequity of a great many judicial decisions was not a new concern; Voltaire had touched

---

60. Ferdinand Dreyfus, 'L'Association de bienfaisance judiciaire (1787-1791)', *La Révolution française* 46 (1904), p.385-411; Witold Wolodkiewicz, 'L'Association de bienfaisance judiciaire: les philosophes des Lumières à la veille de la Révolution', *Revue historique de droit français et étranger* 68 (1990), p.363-74.

61. Dreyfus, 'L'Association de bienfaisance judiciaire'; Wolodkiewicz, 'L'Association de bienfaisance judiciaire'.

on the subject in the 1760s, and lawyers of the *causes célèbres* further developed the notion in the 1770s.[62] Yet the inherent antiparliamentary political implications, while undeniable, have not often been a focus of study for historians. Some 30 of the 200 association members were former partisans of the Maupeou reform. Commissaires such as Grandin, Boin, Dubois and Ninnin would therefore have rubbed shoulders in 1771 with *avocats rentrants, procureurs* who had acquired the office of *avocat du parlement*, and eminent personalities such as Jacques de Flesselles (*intendant* of Lyon and *premier président du conseil supérieur* of Lyon at the time) and Bertier de Sauvigny (son of the *intendant* of Paris and *premier président* of the Maupeou Parlement). Ninnin's presence in such royalist company is astonishing in light of his protests against Lenoir's methods, his 'brutal, undisguised hierarchical confrontations' with other commissaires, and the control he exerted over their careers.[63] Grandin and Boin, also Freemasons, were the Châtelet commissaires who appear to have most easily assimilated into the Parisian structures of institutional sociability during Louis XVI's reign.

For commissaires, Freemasonry therefore seems to have been the key to social integration, while personal spiritual motivation may have been a greater motivation than any professional reasons for joining. Did membership in the Association de bienfaisance judiciaire reinforce their civic identity? This seems far from likely – the rankings in their respective elections suggest that, while the affiliation did not disgrace them, it undermined their credit in the eyes of the bourgeoisie: Boin was elected in twenty-second position (out of twenty-six) in the section of the Théâtre-Français, and Grandin came in last out of fifteen positions in the Arcis section.

In sum, commissaires clearly preferred the social diversity on offer in the hospitals, Masonic lodges and Association de bienfaisance judiciaire, unlike aldermen. Commissaires eschewed such diversity and were more inclined to spiritual engagements outside of the parish venue, remaining firmly entrenched halfway between the pro- and anti-Jansenist camps.

---

62. Sarah Maza, *Private lives and public affairs: the causes célèbres of prerevolutionary France* (Berkeley, CA, 1993).
63. Laurence Croq, 'Pour ou contre les parlements: genèse des engagements révolutionnaires des bourgeois parisiens', in *Les Pratiques politiques dans les villes françaises d'Ancien Régime: communauté, citoyenneté et localité*, ed. Claire Dolan (Rennes, 2018), p.183-206.

Throughout the Enlightenment, Châtelet commissaires were bourgeois. Their identities, if not their duties, were territorially circumscribed, and they were familiar figures in their quarter. Some continued to serve the needs of the elites, but most came to value serving the people, working together with the municipality. These combined factors compensated for the growing social gap between the commissaires and the common people. As a result, commissaires generally managed to reconcile the dual responsibilities of their profession, serving both the king and his people.

Commissaires were generally excluded from institutions of notability. In the second half of the eighteenth century, they chose increasingly traditional forms of participation (such as *échevinage*) as well as membership in modern organisations (the Freemasons and the Association de bienfaisance judiciaire). Political involvement was not a gateway into their world; in most cases they kept to the middle of the road in terms of political and religious beliefs, though some of the commissaires recruited after the 1760s manifested political sympathies tending more towards the royalist camp. This orientation remained discreet, however. Unlike the new *bulliste* clergy and the Maupeou magistrates, commissaires were never seen as 'intruders'.

The details we have gleaned on commissaires' private cultural practices are far more significant. They had distinctive values and spiritual practices, which generally occurred outside of parish spaces. They were devout, but neither clashed with the Jansenists nor aligned with the Jesuits. They nurtured their spiritual lives in convents (particularly in the Grands-Augustins) or in Masonic lodges, investing deeply in hospitals, especially in the Hôpital général, as cities in which the poor could find both moral and economic refuge.

A space shared, a space contested: policing the place de Grève

JULIE ALLARD

Université du Québec à Montréal

Translated by Nicole Charley

The place de Grève sat across from the île de la Cité, perched on the Right Bank of the Seine virtually in the heart of Paris. It provided a link between river and city, and regulated the constant flux of people and merchandise flowing from one to the other. Passengers travelling by barge and arriving in the capital via the port Saint-Paul could hire a cab there to continue their voyage on dry land, or else ask a boatman to ferry them over to the port Saint-Landry on the Left Bank. As it was also not far from the *croisée de Paris*, the Grève was a focal point from which to gain access to the main thoroughfares of the capital. And though the Grève's centrality might have seemed natural enough when one glanced at a map of the city, it was a historic construction, a man-made feature, a result of the concentration of events which occurred there, of the functions it fulfilled, and of their superimposition in this one space.

As a consequence of this centrality, the place de Grève was also a jurisdictional nerve centre, a shared territory, but one in which the agents charged with maintaining law and order crossed paths with rivals whose authority they disputed. The creation of the office of lieutenant of police in 1667 signalled the progressive centralisation of the royal government's powers on the urban environment, but by no means were municipal powers, duties and functions suppressed. Until the very end of the eighteenth century, city and Châtelet agents alike kept daily vigil in the Grève. Their encounters were neither trivial nor inconsequential. In this essay, the concept of *territoriality* will be used to consider the interactions of each player in the Grève, and what this meant for the evolution of policing in the city. Robert Sack defined 'territoriality' as 'the attempt to affect, influence, or control actions and interactions (of people, things, and relationships) by asserting and attempting to enforce control over a geographic area'.[1] In a given territory, 'the players are not in confrontation with each other; they play their part, they act and interact. In so doing they seek to cement relations, solidify roles, gain leverage, exert control over one another, set limits and allowances, and exercise the freedom to move about as they please.'[2] Such encounters are inscribed within a time and space. They leave their mark and affect each player, transforming their relationships with social and physical spaces.

From the second half of the seventeenth century to the end of the *Ancien Régime*, the Grève was contested terrain for the Bureau de la ville and the Châtelet. Until the end of the eighteenth century, the boundaries of their respective jurisdictions, or the Châtelet's simple recognition of the city's jurisdiction, were the subjects of heated debate. The legal territories defined by ordinances and regulations were somewhat vague, giving rise to a multitude of possible interpretations. The disputes stemmed in part from the resulting confusion in which, naturally, all parties looked to maintain or increase their influence in the city. Divergent interpretations were revised or corrected when jurisdictional conflicts between city and Châtelet officers arose. The judicial *mémoires* they drafted during this period reveal the extent to which territory was at the heart of the disputes. The issue had not yet been resolved by the end of the eighteenth century, and the city held fast to its territorial claims. Jurisdictional disputes are indicators of the reasoning behind individual claims, but they are limited in that they only partially reveal the territorial strategies of the interested parties. To provide a properly documented narrative of their activities, we must dig deeper, enquire further, cross-correlate the archives these professionals left behind. The city archives reveal that the Bureau continued to exercise its jurisdiction throughout the period, even with respect to policing and criminal justice, the two domains most bitterly disputed by the Châtelet after 1770. True, the area in which the Bureau intervened – the Grève, which essentially corresponded to the port, the *quais*, and the grounds of the Hôtel de ville – was limited in comparison with the Châtelet's territory. Nonetheless, despite differences, the two competing jurisdictions developed similar forms of intervention and strategies for appropriating communal spaces.

1. Robert D. Sack, 'Human territoriality: a theory', *Annals of the Association of American Geographers* 73:1 (1983), p.55-74 (55).
2. Claude Raffestin, *Pour une géographie du pouvoir* (Paris, 1980), p.141.

Marking territory

Conflicts of jurisdiction are a veritable gold mine for historians: when individuals converge around a specific issue, the result is frequently an upsurge in the production of written documentation. Indeed, both parties availed themselves of sundry *mémoires*, petitions, regulations, ordinances and supporting documents to defend the rights and prerogatives each deemed their own. These documents are a precious source of information and details which help to hone our understanding of competing interests and of differences in representation.[3] One such opportunity is the 1770 enquiry into the frenzied crush at the entry to the place Louis-XV, which had occurred during public celebrations of the dauphin's union with Marie-Antoinette. The accident had claimed the lives of 132 people and profoundly marked public opinion. The people had expected the court's enquiry to identify those responsible for the tragedy.[4] Officers from both the city and the Châtelet were summoned to clarify which spaces they policed jointly, and on which occasions, as well as to elucidate how they concerted their efforts in such cases. Each presented a *mémoire* detailing their respective positions.[5] Their answers contain several indications as to how they conceptualised their respective territories, and more importantly, how they viewed the Grève.

3. Among the multitude of jurisdictional disputes which punctuated the seventeenth and eighteenth centuries and left their mark on relations between the Bureau de la ville and the Châtelet, many have already been studied with respect to understanding food supply to the capital or the regulation of river traffic, among other topics. See for example Reynald Abad, *Le Grand Marché: l'approvisionnement alimentaire de Paris sous l'Ancien Régime* (Paris, 2002); Isabelle Backouche, *La Trace du fleuve: la Seine et Paris (1750-1850)* (Paris, 2000), p.141-75; see also the series of articles published by Jean-Lucien Gay, still relevant today: 'L'administration de la capitale entre 1770 et 1789: la tutelle de la royauté et ses limites', *Mémoires de la Fédération des sociétés historiques et archéologiques de Paris et de l'Ile-de-France* 8:12 (1956-1961), p.299-370.
4. Vincent Milliot, 'La police parisienne dans la tourmente: la bousculade de la rue Royale et ses retombées (Paris, 30 mai 1770)', in *Una storia di rigore e di passione: saggi per Livio Antonielli*, ed. Stefano Levati and Simona Mori (Milan, 2018), p.317-40.
5. Paris, Bibliothèque nationale de France (BnF), Fonds Joly de Fleury (JF) 2541, 'Mémoire des officiers de police du Châtelet', f.2-15; 'Observations des officiers du Bureau de la ville pour servir de réponse au mémoire présenté à la cour par les officiers de police du Châtelet', f.16-36 (an additional copy is conserved in the city records, Paris, Archives nationales (AN), H 1873, f.586bis-603).

Jurisdiction was, inevitably, a fundamental issue in the dispute opposing the two institutions. Both *mémoires* open with an examination of this subject. The Châtelet argued that it had 'sole responsibility for administering the police' and that 'its jurisdiction encompassed the entire city and extended to all its inhabitants.' Though the officers of the Châtelet acknowledged that the Bureau de la ville also exercised jurisdiction in the capital, they refused to recognise any territory assigned to it. In their eyes, the edict of 1700 designated the Bureau a *ratione materiae* jurisdiction, restricted legally – and uniquely – to ensuring that navigation on the river remained unobstructed and that the riverbanks remained clear of anything which might impair their use or damage the *quais*. The *mémoire* accordingly denounced the city's pretence that, 'under the pretext that policing the river, the riverbanks, and the *quais* was of [the city's] jurisdiction, it also claimed the right to inspect and punish all who would provoke quarrels or trouble the good peace which must reign.'[6] Naturally, the city vigorously rebutted. First, it pointed out, only the Parlement might claim sole responsibility for the administration of the police, the city and its inhabitants. Accordingly, it refuted the assertion that the Bureau de la ville was merely a *ratione materiae* jurisdiction, invoking as proof that the institution pre-dated the Châtelet and 'had formerly been the tribunal for Parisians in matters of commerce and of policing'. Next, it claimed, its territory extended, 'outside of Paris, to the tributaries, their ports of loading and timber-floating; and within Paris, to the river, ports, *quais*, banks, ramparts, city gates, fortifications, sewers, and fountains'. Moreover, the Bureau specified, the city exercised jurisdiction on all which concerned the supply of goods via the waterways and was responsible for all which had a bearing on 'the preservation of inhabitants, order, security and public peace' on the rivers and in the ports. Lastly, the establishment of several bodies of officers reporting directly to the Hôtel de ville, required to give accounts of disturbances, and of a guard 'to keep watch, day and night, over the aforementioned peace and order, at the city's expense', should be taken as further proof that its territorial claims were legitimate.[7]

The two *mémoires* express astonishingly divergent interpretations of the same text. The Châtelet favoured a restrictive interpretation of the edict, limiting the Bureau's authority to the points specified

6.	Paris, BnF, JF 2541, f.2*v*-3*r*.
7.	Paris, AN, H 1873, f.587.

in the text. This is unsurprising, given that the Châtelet did not acknowledge this jurisdiction's territory. The Bureau's argument was that its jurisdiction (and territorial authority) preceded the Châtelet's, and that its powers and authority equally pre-dated the edict of 1667, though they were not mentioned in the document.[8] The Bureau maintained that, though the edict of 1700 drew distinctions between certain key points of authority, it could compete in all other points.

The *mémoires* identify the place de Grève as a space where the Châtelet and the city worked jointly to maintain law and order. But, according to the former, policing the Grève was primarily its responsibility; the Bureau de la ville's competence extended exclusively to public celebrations. What's more, the Châtelet affirmed, on such occasions, the city's policing authority was of necessity confined to the inspection of scaffolding along the riverbanks or in the square itself. Bureau officers were not authorised to interfere in other matters. Furthermore, the Châtelet continued, the city's meddling on the place and port de Grève had resulted in their intervention in more than one quarrel. Among other grievances, the Châtelet officers denounced that certain city *huissiers* 'were informed of the brawls which happened inside the cabaret of the Petit Jardinet near the pont Royal as well as those along the port'.[9]

The Châtelet would have had the city's authority whittled away to next to nothing, while the city obviously claimed a territory which was far more extensive. The Bureau de la ville declared that it had always held complete authority over the Grève, quite apart from public celebrations. If the Bureau recognised that its territory had been progressively curtailed, it nonetheless maintained that 'the greater part of the Grève was still subject to its jurisdiction on days relating to the *étape au vin*'.[10] As for policing activities during public celebrations, the

8.   In a parallel dispute opposing the Bureau with the officers of the Maîtrise des eaux et forêts (the Department of Waters and Forests), the Bureau used the *Dissertation sur l'origine de l'Hôtel de ville* (this chapter had opened the grand treatise written by Félibien and Lobineau, the *Histoire de Paris*, to affirm that its jurisdiction 'was neither a concession nor a foundation of [the king]; its origin went back to time immemorial'. Paris, AN, H 1968, *Mémoire pour le substitut de M. le procureur général au Bureau de la ville, défendeur, contre les officiers de la Maîtrise des eaux & forêts de Paris, intervenants & demandeurs* (Paris, Lottin l'aîné, 1773), p.7.

9.   Paris, BnF, JF 2541, f.5*v*.

10. Paris, AN, H 1873, f.589. Charles VI's ordinance had transferred the sale of wine to the Grève. At the beginning of the eighteenth century, a portion of sales

municipal officers upheld that the proclamation of 1700 did *not* restrict them to merely inspecting scaffolding. In fact, it had not curtailed their authority in any way, but had merely rendered a decision on a dispute between the city and the Châtelet. Consequently, their intervention in quarrels on boats, in the ports and on the *quais* was both justified and legitimate; in contrast, acts such as nightly patrols by Châtelet commissaires to these sectors were an intrusion on their own territory. And, if the city took care to learn of the brawls which occurred in the cabarets or inside other places of business established along the ports, well, there was just cause. It nonetheless reserved the right to intervene on tavern terraces, particularly those in the port au Blé. The city's contentions are indicative of how it perceived its territory in and around the Grève. It is important to remember that, in 1770, the quai Pelletier still bordered on the place de Grève at the rue de la Tannerie. In the direction of the port au Blé, there was no building or structure to mark the limits of where the city ended and the river began. Perhaps there were markings in the paving extending from the edge of the footways, which ended at the *quais*, but nothing interrupted the surface of the port as it sloped gently from the houses along the rue de la Mortellerie down towards the Seine. Many of the tavern owners and beer merchants, the city officers had remarked, were located on the ground floor, and 'set their tables, benches and awnings out in front, blocking the port and the street'.[11] These items were particularly inconvenient at times of flooding when space was at a premium. The edict of 1700 had authorised the Bureau de la ville to control the flow of traffic in the ports and on the *quais*, and the city judged that its territory, linked as it was to the river and its vagaries, extended to the outer walls of the surrounding houses.

One strategy the Bureau had considered, in its quest to have its jurisdiction respected, was to mark the lines of its territory on the pavement. At the beginning of the eighteenth century, a demarcation in the paving did divide territories with respect to the removal of refuse and the cleaning of public streets. The Châtelet lieutenant of police was responsible for cleaning the narrow strip of ground along the rue de la Mortellerie, and the task was supervised by the *commissaire ancien* of the quarter. The city assumed control of the place and port de Grève, 'from where the rope cordons off the paving in the port

---

still took place on the place de l'Etape. Henri Sauval, *Histoire et recherches des antiquités de la ville de Paris*, vol.1 (Paris, C. Moette, 1724), p.655.

11. Paris, AN, H 1873, f.592r.

subject to the Hôtel de ville, to the paved area of the Châtelet'.[12] The line had initially been traced to define the responsibilities and costs relative to the paving, maintenance and cleaning of public streets for both the municipal and royal governments. It is entirely possible that the city also used this line to mark the borders of its own jurisdiction.

A similar example from the end of the eighteenth century reveals how the municipality still considered that its authority was defined by a territory with identifiable boundaries which were stamped into the urban fabric. The little stalls and stands set up along the *quais*, in the streets and in the public places of the capital were notorious for obstructing passageways. The government felt it had become a genuine problem. Both the lieutenant general of police and the Bureau de la ville would have taken great pleasure in seeing them go. While they may well have agreed on the objective, they continued to quarrel over the right to legislate on the matter in locations throughout the city. While the police lieutenant contended that he exercised the same authority over the *quais* as he did in the rest of the city, the Bureau argued that it alone had the competence to safeguard routes used in maritime navigation. The Bureau suggested installing boundary markers at a distance of six feet from the parapets, which, 'by invariably designating its territory, would procure for those on foot, as much as for the watercraft being towed, a free and secure route, and would prevent damage to the *quai* and parapet walls'. The document equally alludes to the existence of paving stones which delineated the walkways and the towpaths, for which the Bureau would also be responsible. The role of the *auxiliaires de justice* would at last be valorised, and it was decided 'thereafter that, to prevent similar difficulties from occurring, [the Bureau] would solicit the necessary orders from the *commandant de la garde* of Paris to ensure the effectiveness of their ordinance; and the *commandant* would be strictly prohibited from allowing the implementation of orders which might be carried out in future by the Tribunal de la police'.[13] Were the boundary stones erected? I have as yet found no indication that they were.

12. Paris, AN, H 1934, petition filed by the *commis préposés à l'enlèvement des boues* (street cleaners), 1726. For more on the pavings subject to the jurisdiction of the Hôtel de ville, see Le Cler Du Brillet, *Continuation du Traité de la police*, vol.4: *De la voirie* (Paris, Chez Jean-François Hérissant, 1738), p.176-77.
13. Paris, AN, H 1958, 19 June 1787. The conflict surrounding the prohibition on stands is discussed in Backouche, *La Trace du fleuve*, p.155-59.

Two years later, the Bureau issued an ordinance which plainly indicates that the conflict between the two institutions had not been resolved. Indeed, the ordinance of 3 March 1789 enjoined 'all workmen, boatmen and merchants plying their trade on the river and in the ports, and all others, without exception' to communicate to an *huissier-commissaire* of the Bureau de la ville 'all thefts and offences [...] as well as knowledge of any act contrary to lawful behaviour and to the security of merchandise, whether on the boats, on embankments, in the ports, and in all other locations where the Bureau's jurisdiction prevailed'; the city forbade 'that similar declarations be submitted to officers outside of the city's jurisdiction'. The ordinance targeted Châtelet commissaires in particular, and was issued in reaction to their condemnation of a man named Etienne, accused of stealing timber from a ship moored in the port Saint-Paul. Commissaire Picard Desmarets, who administered the Grève quarter, had heard the case, but the city considered that responsibility for the affair should have fallen to the Bureau.[14]

With the legislation often unclear as to the competences and prerogatives of each, and constant territorial disputes, we are hard pressed to unravel daily events in this stretch of land. And of course, though this conflict resulted in such a wealth of documentation, there is much that is not divulged. Details which did not serve the interests of one or another of the defending parties naturally tended to be glossed over. By the same token, both likely found it useful to highlight transgressions which were, perhaps, not so frequent. It will come as no surprise, therefore, that there is little trace of potential collaborations between the actors, or much evidence of occasions where the other's territory was unreservedly acknowledged.

Occupied territories

Historians who have closely studied the Grève are familiar with its disputed legal territories. The archives and jurisdictional conflicts arbitrated by Parlement remain the principal sources of information on relations between the Châtelet and the Bureau de la ville. What emerges from these documents is the image of a municipality constantly on the defensive and in need of the Parlement's protection against

---

14. Paris, AN, H 1960, item 86, 'Ordonnance pour conduire les délinquans sur les ports et la rivière chés un commissaire de la Ville et non chés des officiers des autres juridictions', 3 March 1789.

the office of the lieutenant general of police, which bit by bit eroded the city's authority. It is indeed an accurate image: the imbalance of powers was not only real, but tilted increasingly in favour of the lieutenant general.[15] The Châtelet officers accentuated the inequality through ploys to extend its authority and a tendency to downplay the role of other institutions in the capital.[16] Yet, despite the frequent disputes, little is known of the habitual policing and judicial activities in localities such as the Grève, where officers from both the city and the Châtelet crossed paths on a daily basis. Historians have yet to fully exploit the documents which those in charge of maintaining law and order in these territories produced. No meaningful comparison of policing and judicial practices in the two institutions has thus far seen the light of day.

We are well acquainted with the functioning of the Châtelet, which reported to the Parlement alone. It was the most important civil and penal court of first instance in the kingdom, and was commonly equated with a superior court because of its influence and its prestige.[17] The Châtelet employed a considerable workforce, and business was brisk. The perception was that the staff were more competent there, and the justice rendered was of higher quality.

But, with the exception of Pauline Valade's recent study on celebrations in eighteenth-century Paris,[18] scholars have failed to leverage the judicial archives of the Bureau de la ville, and the functioning of this jurisdiction is still poorly understood. This lack

15. Laurence Croq, 'La municipalité parisienne à l'épreuve des absolutismes: démantèlement d'une structure politique et création d'une administration (1660-1789)', in *Le Prince, la ville et le bourgeois (XIVᵉ-XVIIIᵉ siècles)*, ed. Laurence Croq (Paris, 2004), p.175-201 (193).

16. Reynald Abad, 'Les luttes entre les juridictions pour le contrôle de la police de l'approvisionnement à Paris sous le règne de Louis XIV', Mélanges de l'Ecole française de Rome 112:2 (2000), p.655-67 (665-66). Jean Chagniot has highlighted the role of military officers in policing; Jean Chagniot, *Paris et l'armée au XVIIIᵉ siècle: étude politique et sociale* (Paris, 1985).

17. Paolo Piasenza, *Polizia e città: strategie d'ordine, conflitti e rivolte a Parigi tra sei et settecento* (Bologna, 1990), p.72.

18. Pauline Valade, *Le Goût de la joie:* réjouissances monarchiques et joie publique à Paris au XVIIIᵉ siècle (Ceyzérieu, 2021). From a different perspective, Mathieu Marraud's work provides a good understanding of the family and institutional workings of the Bureau de la ville, how it functioned and the people who administered it. Mathieu Marraud, *De la ville à l'Etat: la bourgeoisie parisienne, XVIIᵉ-XVIIIᵉ siècle* (Paris, 2009) and *Le Pouvoir marchand: corps et corporatisme à Paris sous l'Ancien Régime* (Ceyzérieu, 2021).

of interest is no doubt partly due to the Bureau's subaltern status;
in addition to being a lower court, the municipal tribunal was also
a special court, and could only hear cases it had been expressly
assigned.[19] Arlette Farge and André Zysberg's study is emblematic in
this regard: though they identified the Grève and the banks of the
Seine as two of the principal theatres of violence, it was uniquely
through the perspective of the Châtelet archives.[20] Yet we know that
the Bureau heard cases at first instance: between merchants in matters
of commerce, between boatsmen and bridgemasters, and legal action
regarding the dyeing and laundering trades. Municipal magistrates
also heard proceedings pertaining to the maintenance of bridges,
water sources, fountains, *quais*, main thoroughfares and fortifications,
the administration of hospitals, the municipality's domain, and the
service des rentes of the Hôtel de ville. It judged criminal offences
committed by merchants pertaining to goods, and by police officers
while in the performance of their duties. Lastly, it heard disputes
between boatsmen as well as cases of theft committed on watercraft or
in the ports. When disputes involved spirits and other strong liquors,
civil and criminal appeals alike were brought before the Parlement de
Paris or the Cour des aides. But, in the end, the Bureau held only low
justice (jurisdiction of petty offences) and therefore could only impose
fines.[21]

However, many details remain obscured, especially with regard
to the powers the Bureau truly exercised, and to their breadth.
For example, in his presentation of the jurisdiction of the *prévôt des*

19. These are the reasons Henri Gerbaud and Michèle Bimbenet-Privat give;
    for them, there is a sharp contrast between the special courts of Paris, which
    include the Bureau de la ville, and the ordinary courts of the Châtelet.
    See Centre historique des Archives nationales, *Châtelet de Paris:* répertoire
    numérique de la série Y, vol.1: *Les Chambres Y 1 à 10718 et 18603 à 18800*
    (Paris, 1993), p.26. The jurisconsult Claude-Joseph Ferrière concurred with this
    interpretation, indicating that 'the *prévôt des marchands* and the aldermen are
    in no way ordinary judges, but are simply cloven from the order of ordinary
    judges; and in consequence they have been established to pass judgement in
    certain disputes and in no others, for which this competence has been accorded
    them'; Claude-Joseph Ferrière, *Dictionnaire de droit et de pratique*, 2 vols (Paris,
    Chez Brunet, 1749), vol.1, p.687. As we have seen, the city claimed broader
    judicial powers and the question of territory was at the heart of its claims.
20. Arlette Farge and André Zysberg, 'Les théâtres de la violence à Paris au XVIIIe
    siècle', *Annales. Economie, sociétés, civilisations* 34:5 (1979), p.984-1015 (990).
21. Michel Antoine *et al.*, *Guide des recherches dans les fonds judiciaires de l'Ancien
    Régime* (Paris, 1958), p.315-21.

marchands and *échevins* (aldermen), the jurisconsult Claude-Joseph Ferrière indicates that 'many hold that their jurisdiction in criminal matters is limited to imposing fines and to *contraintes par corps*; but they do not possess what we call *jus gladii*.'[22] Despite this, the Bureau pronounced no fewer than twenty-three sentences carrying corporal punishment between 1675 and 1785.[23] In almost every case, the penalty was imposed for theft of merchandise in the ports or on the boats. The most frequent primary punishment was the *carcan* (pillory), to which a combination of other punishments such as flogging, branding or banishment were generally added. Certain crimes were nonetheless more severely penalised, and it seems that the Bureau occasionally pronounced capital punishments. In 1675, it sentenced Louis Merry to hanging for violence against guards, though he was subsequently reprieved. Merry's accomplice was sentenced to give an *amende honorable* before the doors of the Hôtel de ville and in the port, as well as to serve a five-year term in the galleys. The sentences were appealed, but the Parlement upheld the punishments.[24] Most of the sentences of corporal punishment were rendered before the middle of the eighteenth century. Nonetheless, in 1785, the Parlement twice upheld the Bureau's sentence of flogging, which indicates that such punishments, while infrequent, were still possible towards the end of the eighteenth century. Furthermore, there is no indication in the upheld decisions that the sentences rendered were done so by incompetent judges. On the contrary, before turning the accused over to the city magistrates charged with carrying out the judgements, the Parlement often endorsed the sentences the Bureau imposed.[25] But if the jurisconsults were close-lipped about the powers the municipality exercised, this does not dispense the historian from scrutinising the practices of this tribunal. There was almost always a gap between

---

22. Ferrière, *Dictionnaire de droit*, vol.1, p.687.
23. Of these, it seems only two sentences were not appealed in the Parlement. In both cases, the accused were convicted of theft in the ports and sentenced to the *carcan* (pillory). Paris, AN, Z1[h] 599, 28 September and 2 October 1725. This data was obtained through sampling the city's criminal archives and the trial transcripts of the Parlement at ten-year intervals.
24. Paris, AN, X2[b] 788, 6 May 1675.
25. Paris, AN, X2[b] 787, 19 September 1675; X2[b] 788, 20 March and 6 May 1675; X2[b] 849, 13 April 1685; X2[b] 851, 28 August 1685; X2[b] 956, 1 June 1725; X2[b] 976, 29 March 1735; Z1[h] 611, 11 July 1749; X2[b] 1078, 5 October and 21 December 1785; Z1[h] 594, 12 January 1703; Z1[h] 599, 28 September and 2 October 1725; Z1[h] 605, 5 March 1735.

the legislation and its actual application, particularly when the laws were unclear. This lack of congruence offered the city some latitude in defining the rules of its everyday practice.

The city and Châtelet officers who worked the Grève consigned at least part of their daily actions in written accounts which now form voluminous archives. Two sets of documents from these collections were retained for my comparison of their practices: the minutes of the Châtelet commissaires and the criminal proceedings of the Bureau de la ville. These documents capture the actions of both active law-enforcement agents and the local population, and allow us to uncover how the space was used. They record the scores of unlawful acts which were brought to the attention of the authorities, though only a part were ever fully prosecuted.

There is no series of documents in the archives of the Bureau de la ville equivalent to the minutes of the Châtelet commissaires, though the agents of both jurisdictions performed, at least in part, policing and judicial functions alike. The Revolution caused such a sundering of the municipality's archives that, today, they are spread across several series in the Archives nationales. However, their current filing system groups the documents thematically, not under the names of the officers who produced them.[26] The records pertaining to criminal proceedings conserved in the city archives were the main focus of this research. There is comparably less material here than in the civil archives, but the recourse to written documentation was methodical. And, though the records are now incomplete, they provide precious context to the incidents brought to the attention of the municipal magistrates. They also include complaints procedures, reports of the city guards, formal statements, interrogation records and documents related to investigations. Together, they form a whole on a par with the minutes of the Châtelet commissaires. Though the collection does not reflect the activity of the municipal tribunal in its entirety, it does impart valuable details on the city's exercise of its criminal jurisdiction, a main bone of contention with the Châtelet.

To allow for a comparison of the two jurisdictions, parallel surveys were conducted of the minutes of the Châtelet commissaires posted to

---

26. For example, the documents conserved in the sub-series H2 and K of the Archives nationales record an important portion of the policing activities of the Bureau, while the subseries Z1ʰ contain the papers of the city's former jurisdiction. These archives document complementary aspects of the activities of the Bureau and its auxiliaries.

the Grève[27] and of the Bureau's criminal proceedings.[28] In both cases, the data was collected from every tenth year beginning in 1675 and ending in 1785. I retained only the documents relative to incidents occurring in the place and port de Grève and in the immediate surroundings, such as the Hôtel de ville and the houses, boutiques, taverns and streets adjacent to the Grève, when they are mentioned. Nearly 300 incidents were identified, some 100 in the city archives and roughly twice as many in the minutes of the Châtelet commissaires (see Table 8).

Table 8: Incidents in the Châtelet and Bureau de la ville's criminal proceedings

Year	Châtelet	Bureau de la ville	Total
1675	0	18	18
1685	0	20	20
1695	22	7	29
1705	15	2	17
1715	22	1	23
1725	11	7	18
1735	9	3	12
1745	11	15	26
1755	28	10	38
1765	28	15	43
1775	14	0	14
1785	28	8	36
Total	188	106	294

Source: Archives nationales

Châtelet commissaires have a disproportionally greater share of the cases, due in part to the wide diversity of circumstances for which they were summoned in the course of their duties. The minutes of

27. Paris, AN, Y 13031, 13043, 13053, 13061, 13073, 13441[b], 13442, 13633, 14814, 14824, 14835, 15044[a], 15093, 15094, 15330, 15341, 15354, 15355, minutes of the Châtelet commissaires, decennial survey from 1675 to 1785.
28. Paris, AN, Z1[h] 576, 583, 591, 594, 597, 599, 605, 609, 615, 622, 632, 638, 639, sentences and criminal proceedings, decennial survey from 1675 to 1785.

the civil, criminal and police magistrates reflect this heterogeneity. The proceedings registered by the city officers specifically concern criminal cases; the documents analysed here reveal only a part of the policing and judicial activities of the Bureau.

Grouping the cases by type makes it easier to understand the imbalance (see Table 9).

Table 9: Cases handled by each jurisdiction according to category

Category	Châtelet		Bureau de la ville	
	Number of cases	% of total cases (rounded)	Number of cases	% of total cases (rounded)
Verbal assaults and acts of violence	81	43	57	54
Theft	17	9	33	31
Roadways	33	18	1	1
Policing of the trades	15	8	3	3
Disputes between landlords and tenants	10	5	0	0
Begging and vagrancy	10	5	1	1
Sudden death	9	5	3	3
Disciplining of moral conduct	4	2	2	2
Military police	3	2	0	0
Other	6	3	6	6
Total	188	100%	106	100%

Source: Archives nationales

We see that 85 per cent of cases prosecuted by the Bureau de la ville involved petty crime. In more than half of the cases, the municipal magistrates acted as mediators in disputes which turned sour following traded insults and exchanged blows. In 1675, for example, Jacques Robert filed a complaint with the Bureau against the veuve Itant. Robert accused the woman of abusing him verbally in the port de

Grève as he was bringing timber to a bourgeoise. Itant had allegedly been unhappy that the bourgeoise had overlooked her son in favour of Robert for carting the goods. She had 'screeched that [Robert] was a thief and a scoundrel; he did nothing but steal from everyone, and had spent 400 *livres* to learn to become an executioner's assistant. He was fit for nothing but wiping a horse's arse.'[29] At times, situations escalated, causing injuries which required the skills of a surgeon.[30] No charges for murder were discovered for the period studied, however. Nearly a third of the cases brought before the Bureau's criminal court involved theft, petty theft in most cases: Marie Lenfant and Elizabeth Trehée were arrested in the port for stealing three to four *boisseaux* (roughly two litres) of wheat, which they had concealed in their aprons; Nicolas Louis Larivière was seized for having cut a length of cable from a barrel cart; Loup Savard was apprehended for having bagged two logs of wood.[31] On rare occasions, however, the theft of items of greater value required the attention of the magistrates. Such was the case in 1685, when the merchant Jacques Collet filed a report with the Bureau for the loss of a small chest containing '300 *livres*, several personal effects, and important documents'.[32] It was also before the Bureau that the sieur Cauchy presented himself upon realising that a bag, containing 1200 *livres* destined for the Hôtel de ville's dividend payments, had disappeared.[33]

Table 9 shows that the activities of the Châtelet commissaires were more diversified than those of the city magistrates. Arbitrating crimes of petty delinquency also occupied a significant portion of their time, but the number of incidents which concerned theft (9 per cent) and verbal abuse or acts of violence (43 per cent) is proportionally lower. Commissaires often administered to the roadways as well (18 per cent), whether inspecting the cabs parked on the Grève, enforcing regulations concerning cart traffic or responding in the event of an accident.[34] The Bureau heard disputes between boatsmen, dyers, launderers and merchants of spirits, but, for all intents and

---

29. Paris, AN, Z1^h 583, 27 August 1685.
30. Paris, AN, Z1^h 576, 21 January 1675.
31. Paris, AN, Z1^h 576, 24 January and 30 December 1675; Z1^h 599, 26 July 1725; Z1^h 639, 6 August 1785.
32. Paris, AN, Z1^h 583, 28 March 1685.
33. Paris, AN, Z1^h 639, 29 October 1785.
34. Though the absence of this category in the archives of the Bureau de la ville's criminal proceedings does not signify that the magistrates did not hear cases concerning roadways, especially in the ports and on the *quais*. They were

purposes, it was the Châtelet that judged the matters relating to the policing of the trades.[35] Accordingly, the *jurés* (the officials of the corporations) sometimes required that commissaires visit the boutiques to ensure compliance with the regulations, or the offices of trade corporations to settle disputes between members.[36] Commissaires were also responsible for establishing and overseeing *jurés* for the inspection of hay, and accompanying them when they visited the ports and places where this merchandise was sold, including in the Grève. These officers were also more likely to be called upon in the event of sudden death or a drowning, to control begging, or to discipline moral conduct. Lastly, disputes between landlords and their tenants, as well as those which concerned the military police, were brought before the Châtelet commissaires.

The sources used in this study are difficult to quantify because of their diversity. The documents themselves are disparate and their content highly subjective. Just as each case studied here is unique, and thus resists classification into the different subject categories, grouping them according to the location of the incidents is equally challenging. The people of the time decried the Grève as small, irregular and disorderly. It lay open to the Seine and was nestled between a contrastingly tall *quai* and the gently sloping shoreline which extended to the port au Blé. The words contemporaries used to orient themselves are indeed evocative of this open and irregular configuration; they continually, often interchangeably, referred to the *place, quai* and *port* of the Grève. Pinpointing each action and position is a challenge; the spaces stretching between the quai Pelletier and the pont Marie seem almost fluid. Events played out over time and space, protagonists shifted about, and quarrels which had started on the port might well have progressed to a neighbouring alleyway or tavern. To help define the territories in which the city and Châtelet officers intervened, I have indexed the principal sites identified in the accounts. The results are not absolute, but they give us useful indications as to the territorial limits of the two jurisdictions (see Table 10).

---

nonetheless more often resolved during the hearings and therefore do not appear in the sample studied here.

35. Steven Laurence Kaplan, 'Réflexions sur la police du monde du travail, 1700-1815', *Revue historique* 529 (1979), p.17-77.

36. At the start of the eighteenth century, at least fifteen trade corporations had offices situated around the place de Grève or in the immediate vicinity. Charles Tilly, *The Contentious French* (Cambridge, MA, 1986), p.45.

Table 10: Location of Châtelet or Bureau de la ville intervention

Category	Châtelet		Bureau de la ville	
	Number of cases	% of total cases (rounded)	Number of cases	% of total cases (rounded)
Quais, port de Grève and boats	58	31	89	84
Place de Grève	43	23	7	7
Adjacent streets	36	19	1	1
Houses, taverns and shops	48	26	1	1
Hôtel de ville	1	1	6	6
Other	2	1	2	2
Total	188	100%	106	100%

Source: Archives nationales

We observe that 84 per cent of the cases the city magistrates handled occurred on the *quais*, the port de Grève, or the boats moored in port. The Hôtel de ville appears to be the near-exclusive territory of the Bureau, though few incidents took place there between 1675 and 1785. The boundaries of the municipality, as the judicial decisions defined them, were therefore narrowly circumscribed by the waterway, which was shared with the Châtelet, and the enclosed grounds of the Hôtel de ville. The territory of the Châtelet encroached on the city's territory though extended far beyond, since the commissaires maintained a proportional presence along the Seine corridor and in the Grève, the adjacent streets and the neighbouring buildings. The data did not reveal any concrete modifications to territory or to the types of incidents each jurisdiction handled between the turn of the seventeenth and the end of the eighteenth centuries. There were notable differences in the methods the city chose to exercise control over the territory it claimed. Yet the borders between the territories seem to have remained stable as both institutions evolved towards a standardisation of their practices.

Two transformations will be examined next: the evolution in the relationship between the Bureau and auxiliary armed forces; and the gradual institution of an intermediary, the *huissier-commissaire de la ville*, the counterpart of the Châtelet commissaire.

Auxiliary armed forces

City and Châtelet magistrates both relied on armed forces to control the territories over which they claimed to have jurisdiction, to bring offenders before them and to assist in the enforcement of their decisions. From the last quarter of the seventeenth century to the end of the following century, relations between the jurisdictions and their auxiliary forces evolved as much as the practices and composition of the units which patrolled the territory. As Paolo Piasenza has shown, these changes were part of a larger mutation in the Parisian police which occurred at the turn of the eighteenth century.[37] In 1667, the centralisation of power in the hands of the lieutenant of police marked the beginning of a transformation in the principles and methods of law enforcement which were perceptible in the capital as early as the reign of Marc René de Voyer d'Argenson (1697-1718). As a hallmark of this evolution, increased security measures, provided by policing specialists, supplanted the police advisory bodies such as the assemblies of bourgeois and magistrates. Piasenza claims that, before the eighteenth century, the use of armed forces to resolve exceptional circumstances was not the norm – it was merely one approach among others to adopt when traditional social alliances failed to maintain order. Once policing was seen as the domain of specialists, there was every incentive to systematically deploy professional forces in the city as a means to enforce order.[38] The more pragmatic approach inaugurated in 1667 not only governed the changes in policing for Châtelet officers, it equally affected how other actors responsible for law enforcement functioned within the territory.

The 1720s and 1730s saw definite changes in the surveillance of the Grève. Companies of commissioned, professional armed forces were established as first responders. These would take on the bulk of the watch duties, maintaining more diligent patrols and an uninterrupted service. At the beginning of the eighteenth century, however, and despite the fledgling attempts at centralisation, several different agents still actively policed the capital and assisted the magistrates. These agents exercised their powers in territories which overlapped, and collaborated on occasion, but their activities were not directed from a central body. Their interventions were irregular – most surveillance

---

37. Piasenza, *Polizia e città*.
38. Piasenza, *Polizia e città*, p.81-82; Vincent Milliot, *'L'Admirable Police': tenir Paris au siècle des Lumières* (Ceyzérieu, 2016).

was carried out at night, and there was insufficient manpower to thoroughly patrol each sector – and, in times of crises, bourgeois and tradesmen were often called upon to lend a hand.

Towards the beginning of the eighteenth century, two different troops of armed men were tasked with maintaining order in the city. The first, the Guet royal, was already an age-old institution. It was under the command of a *chevalier du guet*, who reported to the Châtelet, and at the time comprised 139 archers excluding officers. In this body, all appointments were hereditary offices, most held by men who had no prior military experience.[39] Until the beginning of the eighteenth century, the Guet kept watch solely at night. In 1666, a second troop, the Garde de Paris, joined the first in patrolling the city streets. It was initially composed of nine brigades on horseback. By the eighteenth century, their numbers had progressively increased, and they had added companies of infantry. The Garde was an irregular company of commissioned men recruited mainly from amongst former soldiers who were well schooled in the use of firearms. At its head was a *commandant de la garde* who reported directly to the lieutenant general of police.[40] But, as we see in Table 11, neither the Guet nor the Garde intervened much in the Grève towards the turn of the seventeenth century: out of 107 incidents reported between 1675 and 1715, they had only responded to three.

Table 11: Interventions of auxiliary armed forces in the Grève, 1675-1715

Year	Garde de Paris and Guet royal	Garde de la ville	Night Watch	Total number of cases brought before the courts
1675	0	0	2	18
1685	2	2	2	20
1695	0	1	0	29
1705	0	0	0	17
1715	1	0	1	23
Total	3	3	5	107

Source: Archives nationales

39. Chagniot, *Paris et l'armée*, p.98.
40. In 1733, following the death of the *chevalier du guet* Choppin, the *commandant de la garde* suspended the nomination of a successor and himself took command of the company. The eighteenth century saw the decline of the Guet which, as it transitioned from hereditary to commissioned appointments, was progressively absorbed into the Garde de Paris. Chagniot, *Paris et l'armée*, p.95-105.

The Garde de Paris intervened twice in brawls, one in the Grève and the other in a neighbouring street, and brought the perpetrators to a Châtelet commissaire.[41] On another occasion, it assisted the Garde de la ville in the apprehension of a thief.[42]

The municipality also maintained its own troop, the Garde de la ville. This was a body of 280 guards, excluding officers, arranged in three companies, one each of archers, crossbowmen and arquebusiers.[43] This city guard recruited from the bourgeois, but they were clearly a military corps, not a municipal militia: their positions were permanent, they received pay, wore uniforms and were required to discharge regular, though not onerous, duties. The city guards had been officeholders since 1690, which brought certain advantages; they often practised another trade on the side to supplement their income. The regiment was commanded by a colonel, and was never convened in full except for special ceremonial occasions.[44]

Until the first quarter of the eighteenth century, the city guard had participated in patrolling the Grève and had provided armed assistance to city officers when theft was committed in the ports.[45] On 9 October 1685, a verbal order from the Bureau sent François de Lamourette, a sergeant in the city guard, and Louis Noël, a *bourgeois de Paris*, to the port to apprehend two men named Pinton and Etienne Lassault, whom the Bureau and the Parlement had already found guilty of theft and sentenced to banishment.[46] The two seem not to have respected their punishment: 'Each night without fail since their arrest, abetted by several vagabonds [...] they had prowled in a punt along the river for boats laden with goods, to see what they could steal.'[47] Lassault was apprehended on the corner of the rue de la Tannerie in the place de Grève, but resisted arrest. Lamourette

---

41. Paris, AN, Y 13043, 31 October 1695; Paris, AN, Y 13061, 19 December 1715.
42. Paris, AN, Z1ʰ 583, 9 October 1685.
43. In 1770, the corps was restructured to include a unit of fusiliers, bringing the number of companies to four, though this did not correspond to an increase in the number of guards. Paris, AN, H 1873, f.439-42.
44. For more on the Garde de la ville, see Chagniot, *Paris et l'armée*, p.85-94.
45. Paris, AN, Z1ʰ 583, 25 October 1685; AN, Z1ʰ 594, 18 October 1702. Around 1745, the Garde de la ville abandoned the surveillance of the ports. It was nonetheless still responsible for security in the Hôtel de ville, and after 1727 kept a permanent detachment on duty there. Paris, AN, H 1857, f.235v-37r.
46. Paris, AN, X2ᵇ 851, 28 August 1685. This judgement sentenced Pinton and Lassault to flogging, branding, the *carcan* and a five-year banishment. The sentence was executed in front of the Hôtel de ville on the place de Grève.
47. Paris, AN, Z1ʰ 583, 9 October 1685.

insisted he would not have successfully detained the man 'without the assistance of a squad of Guet under command of a sergeant named Sainte-Claire, and of M. Le Chevallier of the Guet, who had all come to his aid upon noticing the violent ruckus the aforementioned Lassault had raised.' In most cases, however, the missions assigned to the city guard were expeditious and involved no more than a few dozen men.[48]

Until the 1720s, the guarding of merchandise stored in the docks or on boats was entrusted to the Night Watch. Little is known of these petty officers, who reported to the Hôtel de ville. When historians mention them at all, most often it is to point out their ineffectiveness. And, indeed, such judgements are often echoes of the main criticisms contemporaries themselves levelled at the Watch. The edict of 1672 stipulated that the Night Watch should personally perform their duties and that they were accountable for the goods they guarded.[49] But, until the end of the seventeenth century, their numbers were few. In 1696, a petition presented to the Bureau de la ville mentions that, at the time, there were nine Night Watch guards in charge of the wine and grain port in the Grève.[50] Their total workforce was significantly expanded at the beginning of the eighteenth century, and, by 1704, their numbers had increased from 31 to 160 guards for the entire city.[51] The guards of the Night Watch possessed hereditary offices and formed a community with the obligation of pooling the moneys earned from a tariff set by the Conseil. Unlike the other officers patrolling the city, who in addition to their salary could collect a percentage of the fines from criminal procedures and arrests, the income a Night Watch guard earned was derived essentially from the volume of goods transiting through the ports.

The reports of the Night Watch guards and the testimonies they gave during investigations provide some additional details. Though the 1672 edict stipulated that the guards should discharge their duties

---

48. On occasion, more were required to respond during exceptional events. They were called upon in particular during the Flour War (the *Guerre des farines*) of 1775: 150 city guards were assigned to keep watch over sacks of flour warehoused in the port de Grève. Paris, AN, H 1876, f.127-29*v*.

49. Paris, AN, H 1914, edict of December 1672, ch.4, article 7.

50. Paris, AN, Z1ʰ 449, 7 September 1696.

51. Paris, BnF, Manuscrits français (MS fr.) 21699, f.113-14 and 126; Paris, BnF, F-23617 (721), 'Edit [...] portant création de 20 offices de controlleurs-commissaires jurez gardes de nuit, par augmentation à ceux créez par édit [...] de mars 1704', July 1704.

in person, it seems that the use of replacements was tolerated: in one statement relating to the arrest of an individual suspected of stealing wood from the port, the Night Watch officer identified was the widow Perdigeon; the name of her replacement was not mentioned, however.[52] The Watch also coordinated their response to 'crises': following a surge in incidents of theft, for example, they enlisted the help of civilians to organise systematic surveillance of the territory. On 6 February 1685,

> having ascertained that a small number of individuals had, in the preceding few days, slashed open sacks of wheat in the grain port and made off with the contents, the [Night Watch] posted guards at several points in the said port, accompanied by a man named Pierre Drouin, all the better to keep watch and to surprise those who were committing the act of thievery.

It was Drouin himself, a *bourgeois de Paris*, who caught Philippe Besnard as he made off with a small sack of wheat concealed under his justaucorps. The detainee was then escorted to the prison in the Hôtel de ville by Drouin and Guedois, a Night Watch guard.[53] The guards' arrest record was the primary evidence in the proceedings leading to the Bureau de la ville's judgement, which the Parlement would uphold

52. Paris, AN, Z1ʰ 583, 14 March 1685. Clearly, the integrity of replacements was occasionally questioned. In 1675, Pierre Petit, one of the night guards who worked the port au Bois et charbon, filed a complaint with the Bureau denouncing 'certain individuals whom the guards of the port au Grain et vin had proposed to keep watch on the docks', and who night after night pilfered wood from the merchants and lit fires to keep warm. Paris, AN, Z1ʰ 576, 23 December 1675.

53. Paris, AN, Z1ʰ 583, 6 February 1685. In another case, a cloth-button maker and a *gagne-deniers* lent their support to the night guards. Paris, AN, Z1ʰ 576, 5 and 13 February 1675. For more on the participation of bourgeois and tradespeople in policing the city, see Paolo Piasenza, 'Juges, lieutenants de police et bourgeois à Paris aux XVIIᵉ et XVIIIᵉ siècles', *Annales. Histoire, sciences sociales* 45:5 (1990), p.1189-1215. In the seventeenth and eighteenth centuries, the Hôtel de ville's prison, nicknamed *charbonnière*, was located on the ground floor of the Hôpital du Saint-Esprit. Luc-Vincent Thiéry, *Le Voyageur à Paris, extrait du Guide des amateurs & des étrangers voyageurs à Paris*, vol.2 (Paris, Chez Gattey, 1790), p.38. According to the inventories, it was not built to house many prisoners, nor did they stay long. Georges Bastien, 'Les prisons de l'Hôtel de ville (1515-1794)', *Seine et Paris: bulletin d'information de l'Association générale des administrateurs de la Préfecture de la Seine* 72 (1974), p.1-15.

on 13 April. The accused was sentenced to the pillory on the port au Blé of the Grève before serving a one-year banishment.[54]

As we have seen, around the beginning of the eighteenth century, the Châtelet and city jurisdictions both collaborated with various agents charged with patrolling the urban environment. Yet, despite signs of the professionalisation of auxiliary forces, particularly in the establishment of commissioned guards, patrolling the Grève remained mainly in the hands of a scant few guards who were officeholders. They supplemented their numbers with bourgeois and tradespeople as the situation required, but their response was patchy at best. In the 1720s and 1730s, a series of measures finally brought lasting changes to the organisation and practices of the active police force in the Grève. These measures coincided with a period in which the bankruptcy of Law and the grain crisis of 1725 sparked riots in the capital, and in which there was palpable concern over criminality in the city.[55] The principal result was the replacement of the Night Watch officers with a company of commissioned guards dedicated specifically to the surveillance of ports and *quais*, who could ensure more regular, thorough and professional patrols of the territory. The newly commissioned force was modelled after the other companies of the Garde de Paris and shared in its command. After 1725, both the municipality and the Châtelet considered it the principal auxiliary policing and judicial force in the Grève.

The new model evolved after much trial and error. In the years between 1720 and 1740, the service procedures of the auxiliary armed forces were frequently revised. By order of the Conseil on 5 September 1719, the offices of the Night Watch appointed to the Hôtel de ville were abolished and a new Garde de nuit sur les ports et les quais was established. Initially comprised of 225 men appointed by the Bureau, the company was itself reorganised in 1724 and its workforce reduced to 180 men. The regiment was patterned after the companies of the Garde de Paris and led by Commandant Louis Duval. The guards were armed, wore uniforms and followed a military chain of command. Though they were not required to maintain army discipline, they did evolve over the course of the

54. Paris, AN, X2^b 849, 13 April 1685.
55. Steven Laurence Kaplan, 'The Paris Bread Riot of 1725', *French historical studies* 14:1 (1985), p.23-56; and Patrice Peveri, '"Cette ville était alors comme un bois...": criminalité et opinion publique à Paris dans les années qui précèdent l'affaire Cartouche (1715-1721)', *Crime, histoire & sociétés* 1:2 (1997), p.51-73.

eighteenth century into a more disciplined and military unit.[56] In 1730, following representations made to the king, the Night Watch was re-established and until 1736 shared in the surveillance of the territory. In 1731, a new order of the Conseil dissolved the squads of the Garde des ports et des quais created in 1724, establishing in their stead a new company of 154 men funded by the Royal Treasury. For a short period of time, a hybridised form of surveillance was organised in the ports, with squads of the Garde des ports only patrolling the ports at night to ensure public safety, but taking no part in the surveillance of goods, still entrusted to the Night Watch. In 1736, the Night Watch definitively renounced this duty, leaving it to the Garde des ports.[57] Additional guards and squads were subsequently added at the city's expense.[58] In 1775, the king and the city both had a share in financing the company, which then numbered 298 men.

Two guardhouses, one in the Grève,[59] the other in the port au Blé, accommodated the company squads, who worked in alternating twenty-four-hour shifts. While on duty, the guards formed two groups: one stayed at the guardhouse while the other went on rounds. A few sentinels arrayed throughout the port ensured a tight watch over the territory and alerted the rest of the squad as the need arose. A guard was posted at the quai Pelletier to prevent the theft of warehoused goods through the grates on the arches of the *quai* or hauled over the parapet with a rope.[60] Others were positioned in the place aux Canons, the ports au Blé and au Foin, the place aux Veaux and,

---

56. Chagniot, *Paris et l'armée*, p.515-18.
57. The offices of the Night Watch were nevertheless maintained.
58. More were added in 1736 and posted to the île des Cygnes and to the ramparts; others, in 1764, to the newly built boat dock. The changes and additions to the company are described in *Précis historique de la Compagnie des gardes des ports et des remparts*, in the collections of the Bibliothèque de l'Arsenal (Ars.), Paris, Archives de la Bastille (MS Bastille), 10282. See also Chagniot, *Paris et l'armée*, p.127-35. Despite their brief revival between 1730 and 1736, the Night Watch do not appear in the consulted documents after 1715.
59. In 1731, the city rented a house located on the corner of the rue de la Mortellerie in the place de Grève to set up a guardhouse. Paris, AN, Q1 1246, 17 November 1731, lease agreements for the house known as *la maison des chats*. The guardhouse seems to have stayed put until the end of the eighteenth century. It figures in a 1753 painting by Nicolas-Jean-Baptiste Raguenet, *L'Hôtel de ville et la place de Grève*.
60. Paris, AN, H 1934, 18 February 1726, deliberation to position a guard in front of the quai Pelletier.

during feast days, the place de Grève.[61] Their daily tasks consisted mainly of putting an end to brawls and rowdiness, pursuing thieves and arresting beggars, prostitutes, unlicensed sellers or anyone acting suspiciously. During the day, they made sure the streets were clear and that shops were closed on Sundays and feast days. At night, they verified that alleys and houses were well secured. They could also arrest soldiers recruiting without permission, and new recruits who refused to leave with the recruiting officer after they had enlisted.[62] According to a historical treatise written by Jean-François de Bar in 1775, 'the reports of all things pertaining to the jurisdiction of the Bureau de la ville were delivered to the *procureur du roi* of that jurisdiction, and the sergeants had the *huissiers-commissaires* of the Bureau record any offences'.[63] At all times, the guards in the ports, *quais* and ramparts had to harmonise their activities with those of the other companies under the *commandant de la garde*.

Though discipline and the assigned tasks differed little from company to company, it seems that the command of the Compagnie des ports, quais et remparts was hotly disputed. The municipality repeatedly claimed authority over this armed regiment as it was indispensable to asserting its territory. Consequently, the Bureau strived to keep the Compagnie des ports, quais et remparts distinct from the other companies of the guard. Towards the end of the eighteenth century, the city's interference became a thorn in Dubois's side. In 1777, he requested that the minister grant him definitive command of the regiment and remove the Bureau's authority to issue orders.[64] The Bureau replied with its own complaints against Dubois,[65] denouncing the attempt to absorb the company into the Garde de Paris. It claimed that serving the ports, *quais* and ramparts required special expertise which the other companies lacked, and protested againt the commandant's inconsiderate dispatching of officers. What the city truly sought was the separation of the Garde des ports, quais et remparts from the Garde de Paris so it could maintain its own policing rights in that sector. According to the Bureau, the policing

61. Paris, AN, Y 13061, 12 January 1715; Z1ʰ 599, 11 and 23 May 1725; Z1ʰ 615, 24 November 1755; Z1ʰ 622, 25 March and 3 April 1765; Z1ʰ 638, 15 January 1785.
62. Chagniot, *Paris et l'armée*, p.132-33.
63. Paris, Ars., MS Bastille, 10282.
64. Paris, AN, H 1877, f.189*r*-90*v*.
65. Paris, AN, H 1877, f.191*v*-98*v*.

of this territory was its responsibility; the *commandant de la garde* exercised his authority by delegation only. Furthermore, they argued, it was the city coffers which funded the troop's wages. In the end, the Bureau was not the loser in this tug of war with the commandant; the municipal records indicate that Dubois's proposed reform of the Garde des ports, quais et remparts was never followed up.

The Bureau's desire for a separate Garde des ports, quais et remparts who reported to the *lieutenant de police*, also under its own authority, was not based on a simple hypothetical. In a *mémoire* presented in 1770, the Bureau complained that, due to the prejudice it suffered as a result of the 1700 ruling, the only defendants brought before them were those the Garde des ports, quais et remparts had arrested.[66] This claim can be confirmed through a comparison of the cases in the city and Châtelet commissaire archives. Table 12 quantifies the cases the companies of the Garde de Paris brought before the Châtelet and the Bureau de la ville between 1725 and 1785.

Table 12: Interventions of the various companies of the
Garde de Paris

	Châtelet		Bureau de la ville	
Year	Garde des ports, quais et remparts	Garde de Paris and Guet royal	Garde des ports, quais et remparts	Garde de Paris and Guet royal
1675	0	0	0	0
1685	0	0	0	0
1695	0	1	0	0
1705	0	0	0	0
1715	0	1	0	0
1725	3	3	7	0
1735	0	0	1	0
1745	2	0	10	0
1755	24	2	10	0
1765	15	9	15	0
1775	0	9	0	0
1785	5	1	7	0
Total	49	26	50	0

Source: Archives nationales

66. Paris, AN, H 1873, f.596r.

Here, we see that the Garde des ports et des quais brought an equal number of cases before the Châtelet commissaires and the Bureau de la ville. In practice, it was the responsibility of the company sergeants to sort through each case and redirect the accused to the appropriate jurisdiction. There are nonetheless signs that magistrates regularly pressured sergeants during the triage, looking to increase their ascendancy over the guards and, thus, their authority over the territory. In a record of deliberations dated 10 April 1725, the Bureau de la ville mentioned the arrest of a 'Swiss native stealing wood from a timber storage yard belonging to Dame Poupardin, between the hours of nine and ten at night', which had occurred a few days earlier. The record states that the accused was first taken to the prison in the Hôtel de ville by Jacques Guignard, a sergeant in the company stationed in the ports. Meanwhile, the *lieutenant criminel* took charge of the case. He had the accused brought to the Châtelet prisons instead, 'and tried to have Guignard brought there as well, as he kept insisting the Swiss man be imprisoned in the Hôtel de ville'.[67] The Bureau demanded the accused be transferred back to its own cells as soon as it had been informed of this new development. The incident attests to the role the auxiliary armed forces played, in part, in the jurisdiction's bid to control the territory and exercise its power. From the city's perspective, it proved that the support of the Garde des ports et des quais was all the more crucial. The cases reported by the Garde de Paris and the Guet royal were all brought before a Châtelet commissaire; not one case made it to the Bureau. While it was true that the Paris guards more often brought those they had arrested in the houses, taverns and streets adjacent to the Grève before the Châtelet commissaires, the data shows that these companies also intervened in the ports and on the *quais*, and the suspects they arrested there were brought before a Châtelet magistrate as well.[68] At times, the commissaires themselves called upon the Garde de Paris to escort accused detainees who had been brought before them by the Garde des ports et des quais to the Châtelet.[69] Unlike the city magistrates, who could rely only upon the Garde des ports, quais et remparts to enforce their jurisdiction, the

---

67. Paris, AN, H 1934, Bureau ruling, 10 April 1725.
68. Paris, AN, Y 13073, 7 June 1725; Y 14814, 17 July and 30 December 1765; Y 14824, 16 January, 1 March and 24 August 1775.
69. See for example Paris, AN, Y 15355, 17 and 20 June, 7 September, 31 October and 22 November 1755.

minutes of the Châtelet commissaires reveal that the latter had a more diverse network of auxiliaries at their disposal.[70]

Nevertheless, the data also reveals that the relations between magistrates of both jurisdictions and the auxiliary armed forces grew more normalised over the course of the second half of the century. The changes to the detention procedures of the Hôtel de ville around 1765 are evidence of this transformation. Before this, it had not been necessary for a sergeant of the guard to appear before an officer of the city to imprison an accused. In most cases, the guard report submitted to the *procureur du roi et de la ville* served as a record of proceedings and as the initial procedural document. As an example, on 24 November 1755, around ten o'clock at night, a guard sent to the Grève to monitor the fireworks celebrating the birth of the comte de Provence arrested Marie Madeleine Monsieur, whom he had seen making off with 'a small, brand-new trestle presumably belonging to the pyrotechnicians'. In light of the 'ungodly hour', the woman was imprisoned in the Hôtel de ville and the trestle left with the jailer. As was often the case, her stay in the city prisons was to be brief, and she was released two days later. Her judgement was handed down following the reading of the guard's report and of the accused's statement by an alderman; the guard made no request that a municipal officer draw up a report or an order for detention.[71] Until 1765, it seems, all companies with a presence in the Grève (Night Watch, Garde de la ville, Garde des ports, quais et remparts) were authorised to imprison perpetrators in the Hôtel de ville without needing to have a *huissier-commissaire* first draw up a report. After this date, anyone accused identified in the procedural reports appeared before a municipal officer.[72] This corresponds to the time period J. Chagniot had also identified in his work. Châtelet directives for detention were apparently regularly contravened in the

---

70. As might be expected, the city guards escorted those they had arrested to the Bureau. Châtelet commissaires could also count on the support of other agents, particularly the police inspectors and *observateurs*, the archers of the Hôpital général and the *lieutenants de robe courte*.

71. Paris, AN, Z1ʰ 615, 24 and 26 November 1755.

72. Yet even before 1765, the guards were familiar with the procedure, since, theoretically at least, they were to bring the detainees they had arrested before a Châtelet commissaire. This is only speculation, but the apparent absence of a detention procedure at the Bureau and the proximity of the city's prisons may have prompted some guards to bring certain cases to the city rather than to the Châtelet.

first half of the eighteenth century, and there are multiple examples of sergeants and brigadiers who imprisoned individuals they had arrested despite the Châtelet commissaire's recommendations to the contrary. Chagniot concluded that 'the detention procedure was not conclusively defined until it was laid out in article 3 of the Royal Declaration of 12 July 1765, which Sartine explained in a letter to the police commissaires on 7 September.'[73] The declaration specified that mandated officers and non-commissioned officers of the Garde de Paris were not authorised to put offenders in prison without a written order from a Châtelet commissaire. The city's deliberation records have left no trace of the instructions modifying the detention procedures in 1765. Nonetheless, the change in procedure must have been recent given how the sergeants of the Garde insisted that they had escorted their perpetrator to prison 'on the orders' of the *huissier-commissaire*. One city officer even stated in a report that the sergeant 'had refused to take responsibility for their imprisonment in the Hôtel de ville de Paris without advising us first'.[74] This insistence on following procedures, which would subsequently wane in the *huissiers-commissaires*, does suggest that the rule was a new one. Towards the very end of the century, the procedure seems to have tightened slightly more, and, in 1785, the guards were still routinely indicating that a *huissier-commissaire* had handed them an order authorising them to proceed with detention, though this type of document had never been mentioned in 1765.

In the seventeenth and eighteenth centuries, the Châtelet and the Bureau de la ville were forced to rely in part on auxiliary armed forces to physically exercise their authority in the territory. During this period, the composition and methods of the teams patrolling the city evolved to ensure a more careful, constant and coordinated watch. Associations between the magistrates and armed auxiliaries were not always exclusive; for example, the Garde des ports, quais et remparts collaborated with both the municipality and the Châtelet. As we have seen, relations between this company and the rival jurisdictions could in themselves be points of contention for the magistrates. Nevertheless, an analysis of the relationships between the courts and their auxiliaries reveals that practices were gradually standardised in the second half of the eighteenth century. At the Bureau de la ville, this transformation resulted in a more transparent and bureaucratic

73. Chagniot, *Paris et l'armée*, p.69.
74. Paris, AN, Z1[h] 622, 5 August 1765.

hierarchy within the Garde des ports, quais et remparts, and in the introduction of an intermediary, the *huissier-commissaire de police*.

From huissier-audiencier *to* commissaire de police de l'Hôtel de ville

The appearance of a handful of *huissiers-commissaires* in the Hôtel de ville towards the end of the seventeenth century, along with the increasing number of tasks entrusted to them, is undoubtedly one of the most notable changes in how the Bureau exercised its jurisdiction. Within the space of a century, these officers would come to play the role of intermediary between the Bureau and those brought before the court. The evolution in public perception is evidence of their changing role: originally designated *huissiers-audienciers*, over the course of the second half of the eighteenth century they were increasingly recognised as *commissaires de police*, on a par in a number of respects with the Châtelet commissaires. The latter are familiar figures, but the *huissiers-commissaires de police* remain a mystery in many regards.

The office of *huissier-audiencier* of the Hôtel de ville had already been well established by the end of the seventeenth century.[75] There were ten officers in all; they formed a corps and shared in a common purse.[76] They had two main functions: inspecting the ports and assisting the Bureau. Each day, two were dispatched to report on the crimes detected in the ports. The *huissiers* assigned to the Bureau were required to arrive at their quarters in the Hôtel de ville by eight o'clock daily to receive their assignments and to issue summonses.[77] They were the only officers authorised to serve or execute formal acts relating to matters awaiting decision in the municipal courts. Six of the *huissiers* were assigned to calibrate and mark the measuring cups used to retail goods. The other four ensured that traffic on the Seine tributaries flowed freely. In 1681, all of the *huissier* positions

---

75. In 1415, the Grande Ordonnance of Charles VI reinstated the *huissiers*, then named *sergents du parloir aux bourgeois*, to their former positions after having suspended municipal privileges at the end of the fourteenth century. See 'Lettres de Charles VI, portant règlement pour la jurisdiction des prévôt des marchands & échevins de la ville de Paris', no.512-30, in Louis-Guillaume Vilevault and Louis-Georges de Bréquigny, *Ordonnances des rois de France de la troisième race*, vol.10 (Paris, Imprimerie royale, 1763), p.320-23.
76. Paris, AN, K 986, statutes passed by the *huissiers-sergents* to establish a common purse and to defend their common interests, 1661.
77. Paris, AN, H 1914, edict of 1672, ch.33, articles 2-4.

became hereditary offices. In exchange for their purchase, office-holders retained possession of their rights and prerogatives without limitations to remuneration.[78] In 1690, six offices of *commissaire de police* were created. They were merged with the office of *huissier-audiencier* to 'enforce the ordinances and regulations of the Hôtel de ville and draft reports of the crimes, abuses and disorderly conduct which may transpire in the ports and on the *quais*'. The newly minted *huissiers-commissaires* were then assigned to defined territories.[79] That same year, a second edict increased their number to ten.[80] The *huissiers-audienciers* collectively borrowed the sum required to purchase the ten offices – 9000 *livres* – from various private individuals.[81]

We know little of how these officers were recruited or trained. At least one seems to have previously been a soldier. In a complaint the *huissier-commissaire* Decombes brought against a man named La Sablonnière, he states that he knew the latter 'from before, when in the king's army'.[82] The orders they issued, however, indicate there was a certain degree of professionalisation, which suggests an evolution in their recruitment practices. In 1690, when the offices of *commissaire de police* were created, they were filled by the *huissiers-audienciers* already in office. The conditions for obtaining an office were not very difficult to fulfil, however. For the recruitment of *huissiers*, the prerequisites were threefold: literacy, a minimum age of twenty-five, and the inscription of their signature and initials in the registers of the *greffiers*.[83] While a *huissier* might have a legal background, it was not a requirement.[84] In 1702, the *huissier-commissaire* Nicolas Itier pointed out that he had drafted a report 'with the assistance of a man named Duliege [one of

78. Paris, AN, AD XVI 10, edict of the king, on the establishment of titles of office, for the officers having previously formed the corps of the Hôtel de ville de Paris, July 1681.
79. Paris, AN, AD XVI 10, edict of the king, on the establishment of various offices under the authority of the Hôtel de ville, May 1690.
80. Paris, BnF, JF, 2541, edict of the king, on the adjoining of the office of the lieutenancy under the authority of the jurisdiction of the city, to the corps of the *conseillers* and *quartiniers*, and on the creation of four offices of *commissaire de la police*, August 1690, f.49r-55v.
81. Paris, AN, Z1ʰ 409, 22 August 1731.
82. Paris, AN, H 13043, 1 August 1695.
83. Jean-Pierre Royer, *Histoire de la justice en France* (Paris, 1996), p.146.
84. Anne-Claire Claudel, 'L'intermédiaire entre la justice et les justiciables: l'huissier de justice dans le duché de Lorraine et de Bar au XVIIIᵉ siècle', in *Entre justice et justiciables: les auxiliaires de la justice du Moyen Age au XXᵉ siècle*, ed. Claire Dolan (Sainte-Foy, 2005), p.227-44 (228).

the city archers] and of Thomas de Farnucynez, a legal practitioner in Paris'.[85] Over the years, *huissiers-commissaires* became practitioners in their own right. At least, the style of the formal documents they drafted suggests a certain familiarity with the law. Though they were not authorised to sit in judgement, as were the Châtelet commissaires, the tasks they were delegated required a minimum of legal training. The title of *maître* they were granted in proceedings and in the *Almanach royal*, which announced their nomination from the 1740s onwards, is a further suggestion of such an education.

Huissiers-commissaires neither enjoyed the autonomy of the Châtelet commissaires, nor assumed the same responsibilities. Their wages were also far inferior. The city's financial statements contain valuable information on the earnings of *huissiers-commissaires*, and are especially useful for the second half of the eighteenth century. When first created in 1690, the office provided an annual income of 4000 *livres*. It was reduced to 1800 *livres* in 1720, and remained at that level until the end of the century. It is interesting to note that the wages of *huissiers-commissaires* were reduced at precisely the same moment as the offices of *inspecteurs sur les ports*, with significantly higher wages, were created.[86] *Huissiers-commissaires* could also claim various fees and entitlements, as well as a third of the proceeds from fines imposed by the Bureau. In 1786, this amounted to roughly 2735 *livres*.[87] It is nonetheless difficult to precisely evaluate what a *huissier-commissaire* might have hoped to earn in the exercise of his duties. The dispersal of their papers complicates the assessment of the duties they performed and what remuneration they received in return. It is also difficult to estimate

85. Paris, AN, Z1ʰ 594, 18 October 1702.
86. Backouche, *La Trace du fleuve*.
87. The sums collected by the community of ten *huissiers-commissaires* are itemised as follows: 1800 *livres* in wages, 106 *livres* 10 *sols* for fees relating to the calibration of measuring cups, 101 *livres* for inspections of the embankments, 160 *livres* as an allowance for small fees, and close to 568 *livres* from fine collection. We are fortunate to have one of the first records for this period detailing what percentage fine collection contributed to revenue in the community. In 1786, eager to regulate the recovery of fines, the Bureau gave this task to the *huissier-commissaire* Coutans (Paris, AN, H 1957, 13 January 1786). The first inventory covers a period of approximately eighteen months (October 1785-March 1787). It indicates that the Bureau imposed a little more than 4100 *livres* in fines, of which only 1700 *livres* was received. A third of this sum was yielded to Coutans, who was *syndic* of the *huissiers-commissaires* at the time, and then deposited in the common purse.

the sums they received as honoraria, which varied greatly.[88] They undoubtedly made up an appreciable part of the officer's income: towards the very end of the eighteenth century, the widow of *huissier-commissaire* Blainville had claimed that commissions had indeed formed the greater part of her husband's income.[89] But, if income was one thing, wealth was something else entirely. Financial disparities undoubtedly existed between officers. Solvency was the main reason behind *huissier-commissaire* Coutans's proclivity for collecting fines,[90] though this was not a guarantee of financial stability. In 1778 and 1779, the Bureau banned the *huissier-commissaire* LeQuin twice for withholding money.[91] His colleague, Jean-François Bega, borrowed 6000 *livres* from the Bureau and mortgaged his office, worth 14,000 *livres* at the time, to settle personal debts.[92] In 1789, Hardy himself approached the Bureau to borrow the sums needed for the purchase of the office previously held by Blainville, who had died a few months earlier. Blainville's office was already heavily mortgaged; his widow estimated its worth at 9000 *livres*, but indicated that it had been repossessed.[93] Though partial, this data provides points of comparison with the offices held by Châtelet commissaires. In 1771, the asking price of such an office was 60,000 *livres*, and reached 90,000 or even 100,000 *livres* during the reign of *lieutenant de police* Lenoir.[94] Though the earnings of Châtelet commissaires are as difficult to estimate as those of the city officers, these figures allow us to appreciate the magnitude of the disparities between the two. Nevertheless, this inequality should not make us lose sight of the fact that *huissiers-commissaires*, whose responsibilities oscillated between office held and

---

88. For example, the community received 40 *livres* for meals for every firework display organised by the city. Towards the end of the eighteenth century, *huissier-commissaire* Blanchet received a bonus of 300 *livres* per year for the water rescue duties that were his responsibility. Several *huissiers-commissaires* were also sent to the rivers to monitor the supply of food to the capital, and were remunerated for these missions.

89. Paris, AN, H 1960, document 92.

90. Paris, AN, H 1957, document 68.

91. Paris, AN, H 1878, f.41 and 157-58.

92. Paris, AN, H 1878, f.244-45.

93. Paris, AN, H 1960, documents 91-92.

94. Steven Laurence Kaplan, 'Note sur les commissaires de police de Paris au XVIIIᵉ siècle', *Revue d'histoire moderne et contemporaine* 28:4 (1981), p.669-86 (670-71).

commission,[95] had in fact far more extensive powers than those we have recognised up to now.

Their careers seem to have spanned several years (sometimes thirty or forty years) and, by all accounts, some were bequeathed to other members of the family. In the eighteenth century, the *huissiers-commissaires* were no longer required to reside in the Hôtel de ville, as had been the case in the fifteenth century.[96] They were also under no obligation to live in their assigned territories, so their offices were concentrated in the streets adjacent to the Hôtel de ville, mainly on rue de la Mortellerie. In his study on the mobility of Châtelet commissaires, Vincent Milliot observed that the Grève quarter, unlike the other quarters of the Parisian police, did not have a 'rue à commissaires'.[97] Even so, such a street did indeed exist for the city commissaires. Despite the sprawl of the ports along the banks on both sides of the Seine and the relocation of many activities to the fringes of the city, in the second half of the century, the community remained grouped on the Right Bank in the centre of the capital. Other than the advantage of living in close proximity to the Hôtel de ville, the concentration of *huissiers-commissaires* is likely a consequence of their working conditions. It was not unusual for them to work jointly, and confiscations were also often on the roster.[98] The fact that the officers were clustered around the Hôtel de ville is presumably why, in the second half of the eighteenth century, many of those arrested elsewhere in the city were escorted to the Grève and port au Blé guardhouses, so the *huissier-commissaire* there could draft the arrest reports.[99]

The tasks the *huissiers-audienciers* performed were not abruptly transformed when the offices of *commissaire de police* were created in 1690. As their predecessors had in the previous period, the *huissiers-commissaires* intervened in criminal proceedings most often to serve notice of official acts. Nonetheless, there are signs that they proudly

95. Backouche, *La Trace du fleuve*, p.170-72.
96. 'Lettres de Charles VI, portant règlement pour la jurisdiction des prévôt des marchands & échevins de la ville de Paris', no.512-30, in Vilevault and Bréquigny, *Ordonnances des rois de France*, p.322-23.
97. Vincent Milliot, 'Saisir l'espace urbain: mobilité des commissaires et contrôle des quartiers de police à Paris au XVIIIe siècle', *Revue d'histoire moderne et contemporaine* 50:1 (2003), p.54-80 (72).
98. In the city of Nancy, for example, *huissiers* often seconded and acted as witnesses to each other. Claudel, 'L'intermédiaire', p.231.
99. See for example Paris, AN, Z1^h 622, 15 June, 7 July and 15 August 1765.

defended their new designation, though neither the people nor their Châtelet peers saw it as entirely legitimate. The records of Etienne Duchesne, a Châtelet commissaire active towards the end of the seventeenth century, and who resided in the place de Grève, are revealing in this regard. On 29 June 1695, Michel Lecoufle, a saddler, filed a complaint against a group of men identified as Rémy, Baillon and Pinet, as well as five other *huissiers* of the city. Lecoufle accused the men of having assaulted him in a tavern owned by a man named Brouard, a wine merchant in the port de Grève; Lecoufle had gone to Brouard's tavern to settle his debts there. Following the incident, he demanded that he be given the report of the proceedings instituted against him at the Bureau de la ville. It had been left with the *huissier-commissaire* Rémy, who was summoned. Lecoufle and Rémy quarrelled over the papers, and things turned violent when Rémy called on his colleagues for support. Both the complainant and witness testimonies registered in Duchesne's account suggest that civilians were reluctant to designate the city *huissiers* as commissaires. Brouard's wife had immediately recognised all of the accused as *huissiers*, but showed reticence towards using the term 'commissaire', adding only that 'one of them called himself commissaire, and the other a commissaire's clerk.' The *huissiers-commissaires*' defence of their new status remained stalwart: one witness had remarked that 'the plaintiff, yelling murder, called for a commissaire. One of the accused said he was a commissaire, and there was nothing to do but accept it.'[100]

By 1725, a separate incident reveals, contemporaries were coming to accept that there was parity between Châtelet commissaires and *huissiers-commissaires*. A woman who had mistakenly taken Philippe Pierre, a city *huissier-commissaire*, for a Châtelet commissaire because of his black robes asked him to intervene on her behalf with a baker, whose prices she claimed were too high. Pleased, perhaps, to have the opportunity to demonstrate his authority, the *huissier-commissaire* gladly came to her defence. A crowd began to gather and the incident attracted the attention of the guard, who then sent for a Châtelet commissaire, who in turn hastened to point out that bakers did not fall within the jurisdiction of *huissiers-commissaires*.[101] Though anecdotal, the incident nevertheless reveals that the Parisian population were growing accustomed to the change. Some years later, the *mémoires*

100. Paris, AN, H 13043, 29 and 30 June 1695.
101. Paris, AN, Y 12571, 27 October 1725, cited in Kaplan, 'The Paris Bread Riot', p.49.

submitted during the enquiry into an accident on the rue Royale give further indications of a transformation in the people's perception of *huissiers-commissaires de police*. The use of *commissaire de police* as their title and likely their assumption of the duties associated with the office were part and parcel of the power struggle between the Bureau and the Châtelet. In the *mémoire* the Châtelet commissaires submitted to the Parlement, which denounced the city officers' repeated infringements on their jurisdiction, they refused to give their city counterparts the title 'commissaire', adamantly referring to them as simple *huissiers*. Unsurprisingly, the city officers held to the opposite view, and doggedly persisted in giving the general title of *commissaire de police* to officers on both sides. This verbal back-and-forth had repercussions beyond the two rival communities jealous of their privileges. A note conserved with the papers of *procureur général* Joly de Fleury reveals that the question also presented itself whilst he was drafting his arguments before the Parlement. The note attached to the draft concerned the fifth article of his text: 'It is imperative that the article prohibit the title of *commissaire de police* from being conferred on the *huissiers* of the Bureau, and forbid *huissiers* of the Bureau from drafting commissaire reports.'[102] In 1777, the minister responsible for Paris was disturbed to learn from the *commandant de la garde* that 'the *huissiers* sought to expand their role and act in the same capacity as Châtelet commissaires.'[103] Later still, in 1780, it was the *lieutenant de police* Lenoir who warned the Châtelet commissaires against the *huissiers-commissaires*, who were carrying out tasks which jeopardised the rights and the jurisdiction of the Châtelet.[104] The continuing debate over the legitimate use of the title is evidence that the role of the *huissier-commissaire* continued to evolve over the course of the eighteenth century. The changes in the tasks and official acts they performed are further indications of this evolution.

From about 1765 onwards, the *huissiers-commissaires de police* played a greater role in how criminal cases were processed, and became essential intermediaries between adjudicators and the adjudicated. Since they were now such a crucial link in the detention procedure,

---

102. Paris, BnF, JF, 450, f.194r.
103. Paris, AN, H 1877, f.191r.
104. Paris, AN, Y 12830, letter written by Lenoir to the commissaires, 18 August 1780, cited in Alan Williams, *The Police of Paris, 1718-1789* (Baton Rouge, LA, 1979), p.172.

the Garde regularly brought detainees before them in their 'studies'[105] no matter the time of day. From that point onwards, it was they who received complaints and recorded witness testimonies, interrogated detainees and, occasionally, conducted summary investigations before drafting the criminal report used to guide sentencing. On 4 June 1765, the widow Mory, a picker who worked in the ports, was arrested by the Garde at the request of several merchants who had accused her of theft. The sergeant on duty at the port au Blé, Joseph Cantinot, first brought the detainee to his guardhouse. However, 'unwilling to assume responsibility for imprisoning the widow Mory in the Hôtel de ville', he then went to give his report to the *huissier-commissaire* Jean François Bega, who had a study on the rue de la Mortellerie. Bega then proceeded to the guardhouse to begin his investigation, questioning the defendant and the complainants in turn. The commissaire, 'attired in his robe' and in the company of the sergeant and his squad, next made his way to the widow Mory's home on the rue de la Mortellerie. There, the *huissier-commissaire* discovered a terrine full of oats under the wardrobe in her room. The oats were seized, placed in a bag secured 'with a cord, on the knots of which I [Bega] have affixed my seal with red wax', and deposited at the office of the *greffier* in the Hôtel de ville as evidence. Mory was handed over to Sergeant Cantinot, who was ordered to imprison her in the Hôtel de ville. Commissaire Bega returned home to write the criminal report, which he addressed to king and city. According to his account, he 'applied himself to drafting the report from the hours of six to nine o'clock that night'.[106]

After 1765, the *huissiers-commissaires* of the city served as the gateway in judicial procedures. The reports they drafted were precise and written immediately following the event which had prompted the intervention. The documents are nearly identical to those written by the Châtelet commissaires and record much the same information: the reports of the Garde, the declarations of complainants, witnesses and the detained, and accounts of initial searches. Once an incident report had been compiled, it was not unusual to see the *huissier-commissaire* initiate an investigation. Mory's case was not unique. On 3 September 1785, the veuve Legrand, an oat seller in the port, called for the Garde and accused Pierre Fraisier, a fugitive *gagne-denier*, of stealing a sack of oats from her. The *huissier-commissaire* Chevallier

105. Paris, AN, Z1ʰ 622, 5 October 1765.
106. Paris, AN, Z1ʰ 622, 4 June 1765.

was summoned to hear the complaint and write the report, which included the guard's statement, the veuve Legrand's complaint, and three witness accounts. Chevallier learned that the oats in question had been left with the tavernkeeper of the Vache qui corne on the rue de la Mortellerie. He proceeded to the tavern in the company of the guard, the complainant and two witnesses, and seized the sack.[107] Summary investigations such as this one often led the *huissiers-commissaires* to travel outside of the territory in which the Bureau claimed jurisdiction. While it would not have been surprising to see them search the coal barges moored in the port de Grève,[108] archival records show that they also inspected taverns and houses.[109]

In the second half of the eighteenth century, the officers' activities did not always include the transfer of their criminal report to the *procureur du roi et de la ville*. When the *procureur* did receive a report, he would occasionally request the *huissiers-commissaires* proceed with additional investigations to clarify certain points. On 6 August 1785, the Garde arrested Philippe Savard, a *gagne-denier*, on the port de Grève. They had found him in possession of 'two logs of new wood he had placed in a sack to take home with him'. The *huissier-commissaire* Doré drew up the report and ordered Savard be imprisoned in the Hôtel de ville. A few days later, Ethis de Corny, the *procureur du roi et de la ville*, sent for the *huissier-commissaire* Coutans to verify certain facts. It seems the grain merchants of the port de Grève had addressed a plea to Corny, asking for clemency in Savard's case. Coutans was tasked with authenticating the signatures on the plea. Through investigation, he managed to establish the authenticity of five signatures. Two of the merchants claimed they did not recognise their signatures, though they assured the *huissier-commissaire* 'they would have willingly signed the plea had it been presented to them, because it spoke the truth.' In the end, Coutans was unable to track down only three of the signatories. In his report, he raised the following points:

> It may so happen on occasion that two sections of wood should fall into the river while a boat is unloaded, and that Savard should have fished out the wetted wood; the commissaire who had sent him to prison would not have neglected to mention this in his criminal

107. Paris, AN, Z1ʰ 639, 3 September 1785.
108. Paris, AN, Z1ʰ 622, 27 June 1765.
109. Paris, AN, Z1ʰ 622, 4 June 1765; Z1ʰ 639, 3 September and 28 October 1785.

report. Yet the individual in question should not have removed them from public view by placing them in a sack… Such circumstances lead one to believe that his intention had been to misappropriate them, which makes him suspect.[110]

There is no way to confirm what effect these observations had on the *procureur du roi*. We know only that, in the findings he pronounced the next day, the prosecutor recommended the release of the prisoner.

The office and duties of the *commissaire de police de la ville*, created towards the end of the seventeenth century, were thus merged with those of the *huissiers de la ville*. The office encompassed more than simply a new title. It brought with it a marked change in the practices of the officeholders since, in the second half of the eighteenth century, they became unavoidable intermediaries between the accused and the Bureau's justice. The image of these officers was approximated to that of a Châtelet commissaire, as the quarrel over the legitimate use of the title *commissaire de police* brought before the Parlement in 1770 reveals. But, aside from this contention, a comparison of their practices reveals the development of common methods of policing and dispensing justice within the two institutions that shared jurisdiction over the Grève.[111]

As I have attempted to show, between 1667 and 1790, there was a marked transformation in the practices of both city and Châtelet officers who maintained order in the place de Grève. These changes were part of a more extended transformation in policing as a whole and encompassed, in particular, greater attention devoted to written procedures and their formalisation, the specialisation and professionalisation of the agents in charge of policing, and a progressive territorialisation of their activity. My analysis has also revealed a marked similarity in the strategies each institution adopted to exercise, expand and perpetuate its jurisdiction over the territory. Their strategic choices were not simply the result of the progressive centralisation of power in the hands of a dictatorial, 'power-hungry' lieutenant general of police, who imposed standard procedures on all other officers present in the capital. These choices also resulted

---

110. Paris, AN, Z1[h] 639, 12 August 1785.
111. This conclusion is in keeping with the observations made by Laurence Croq, in 'La municipalité parisienne à l'épreuve des absolutismes', p.193, that after 1740 the Hôtel de ville came to be an administration more complementary than antagonistic to the Châtelet. As she has underlined, complementarity does not mean that balance was achieved nor that the transition was smooth.

from confrontations between the stakeholders of shared and contested territories where, as was the case in the Grève, both city and Châtelet magistrates and auxiliaries walked the same space and, day by day, forged strained yet enduring relationships.

Taming public space: social exchange and the Marché-Neuf in seventeenth- and eighteenth-century Paris

CHRISTINE MÉTAYER

Université de Sherbrooke

Translated by Nicole Charley

On 15 July 1693,[1] emotions were running high in the Marché-Neuf. About a dozen *revendeuses* (female market sellers) were lodging a complaint with the lieutenant general of police. The women alleged they had been assaulted by armed officers of the Bureau de la ville – a *huissier*, an *officier aide-major* and two *archers* – who had overturned their market stalls, destroyed their wares and forcibly chased them away. They claimed they and their many female co-workers suffered similar exactions, as well as threats of even more violent reprisals, on a daily basis. It was ever thus, deplored the humble supplicants, despite the fact that, from 'time immemorial' and through the grace of good King François, honest market women 'had been given leave to display their goods along the walls from the market entrance to the pont Saint-Michel'. They demanded that justice be served and justified directing their petition to the lieutenant of police in virtue of the 7 July 1688 ruling against the Bureau de la ville, which had given the lieutenant of police the responsibility of policing the Marché-Neuf.

In the days that followed, the plot would thicken. The police subpoenaed the officers involved, who appealed to the *prévôt de la ville*, who in turn pleaded ignorance of the 1688 ruling and contested the legitimacy of the subpoena and the police's authority in this dossier. The *prévôt* certified that he alone held jurisdiction over the Marché-Neuf; consequently, it was in his absolute authority to establish order

---

1. Paris, Bibliothèque nationale (BnF), Manuscrits français (MS fr.) 21633, f.112-15, letters patent and decisions of the *prévôt de la ville*, 15 and 20 July 1693; also Paris, BnF, Fonds Joly de Fleury (JF), vol.2531, f.34-37.

through his officers if and when the appointed *placier* (the official who administered and distributed market spaces) should prove unable to do so. Furthermore, he argued, the bourgeois and other inhabitants of the quarter repeatedly asked him to intervene when the *revendeuses* selling produce inevitably set up 'in the avenues of the Marché-Neuf', along the walls of their houses and on their doorsteps. It was the *prévôt's* duty to keep the streets and surroundings clear, yet the *revendeuses* persistently defied the ordinances requiring that they relocate to the areas within the market reserved for such activities.

These arguments did not prevent the police from issuing an ordinance of their own, mandating that the women withdraw to the marketplace and formally prohibiting the *placier* from allotting spaces alongside the neighbouring houses – and leaving enforcement up to city authorities. It remained a bone of contention in the following years, and, in 1698-1699, both the city and the police would publish and post ordinances at the entrance to the Marché-Neuf, each declaring the other's null and void.[2]

Let us pause here for a moment to discuss what this affair reveals. First, there was the jurisdictional squabbling between the *prévôt des marchands* and the lieutenant general of police, as well as between the various protagonists interacting within the marketplace – the resellers and the occupants of the buildings surrounding the Marché-Neuf, the *placier*, and the officers dispatched by the city. There were also important issues at stake: the occupation of the market space, and the capacity to act in relation to it. These are the elements on which this essay will focus. The Marché-Neuf is a particularly interesting case, as it reveals how the different relationships with space intersect and become superimposed on a marketplace, and will therefore be central to this discussion. It also reveals the dynamics at play as an officially designated marketplace is created, overlaying a formal commercial status onto a space that had long thrummed with the energies of the different parties striving to lay claim to the territory, giving it its distinctive character irrespective of the new requirements of authorities preoccupied with managing the food supply in Paris. The Marché-Neuf already greatly contributed to supplying food to the quarter. And, although it was a public space, users perceived it as their own space, to which, rightly or wrongly, they believed they were

---

2. See Paris, BnF, MS fr. 21633, f.112-15, 1693 (petitions, summonses, letters patent, and judgements); Paris, BnF, MS fr. 21632, 'Police ordinance of 22 May 1699, which attests to the existence of the ordinance of 7 July 1688', f.266-67.

fully entitled. They occupied the space in the manner they chose, each attempting to maintain their position in a contest where there were no rules and where no one was in control – not even, as we shall see, the public authorities.

It is on this contest of wills – so indicative of the social practices which formed the fabric of the urban environment – that we shall linger.[3] The various struggles in the Marché-Neuf will provide insight into the agency of the *revendeuses*, *placiers* and residents who choreographed this market dance, though it was the authorities who supervised and administered the space, or at least assumed they had the authority to do so. Furthermore, the way in which the actors occupied the space, and the relationships they built with each other, will shed light on how they experienced true *citadinité*.[4] Before embarking on our discussion, however, it is important to understand how the Cité structured its mercantile activities, including those of the Marché-Neuf. The primary responsibility of the Domaine de la ville de Paris, which governed the Marché-Neuf, was to ensure that the stands would be well stocked for Parisians come market day.

Supplying food to the heart of the city

If the central Halles were the 'stomach of Paris', Paris was uncontestedly the belly of the kingdom itself. Feeding the population was a colossal challenge for the *Ancien Régime* administration. 'In an age where a large part of consumer income was expended on food, and where regular food supply largely depended on political, climatic and commercial vicissitudes, markets and food distribution were, in general, a daily preoccupation for city dwellers.'[5] This was especially true for Paris, where the supply chain was contingent on the entire country: grain was brought in from the Paris Basin, cattle from the western provinces; fruit, vegetables, cheeses and other dairy products were imported from the faubourgs and the Ile-de-France region; wines

3. The history of food supply in Paris will not be discussed in this essay. For more on the subject, see Reynald Abad's seminal study, *Le Grand Marché: l'approvisionnement alimentaire de Paris sous l'Ancien Régime* (Paris, 2002).
4. For a more in-depth discussion on the notion of *citadinité*, see Eleonora Canepari, 'Civic identity, "juvenile status" and gender in sixteenth- and seventeeth-century Italian towns', in *The Routledge history handbook of gender and the urban experience*, ed. Deborah Simonton (London, 2020), p.182-94 (185-86).
5. Jean-Michel Roy, 'Les marchés alimentaires parisiens et l'espace urbain du XVIIᵉ au XIXᵉ siècle', *Histoire, économie et société* 17:4 (1998), p.693-710 (695).

came from Burgundy, fresh fish from the North Atlantic. All flowed in a steady stream towards Paris, where it was then redistributed to the Halles, the butchers' shops, the neighbourhood markets,[6] the boutiques and the street vendors.[7] There were plenty of vending spaces of all varieties, shapes and sizes. These shaped the commercial landscape, which was increasingly densifying as demand and the urban environment developed.

The île de la Cité, a metropolis of flowing commerce

The île de la Cité was not to be found wanting (see Figure 7). Like a rolling wave, commerce flowed through the city and out onto the parapets and walkways which provided access to the Seine.[8] The archives of the police and of the *commissaires du Châtelet* show intense mercantile activity on the *quais*, in the squares and on the bridges – particularly the Pont-Neuf, which saw the most traffic, but also on the ponts Saint-Michel and Notre-Dame, which were inhabited,[9] and the Petit-Pont, populated by merchant wholesalers. Some marketplaces focused on particular products or types of clientele: the quai de la Mégisserie specialised in scrap metal; the parvis Notre-Dame was the site of an annual fair for the sale of ham; and, in the Palais de justice,

6. Some markets were in the king's domain, while others belonged to the city or were privately owned by local nobility. Still others sprang up makeshift; whether they thrived or perished depended more often on the support of the locals than on police intervention.

7. Until the 1960s, research on Paris was centred foremost on the production and the supply of grain. The focus then broadened to include the general history of food supply and, after 1975, urban consumption and regional dietary cultures, still fertile topics today. Nevertheless, with the exception of Jean-Michel Roy's study, there has been no significant research into the socio-political give and take which animated early modern marketplaces. I did broach the subject in my own work on the Saints-Innocents Cemetery market in *Au tombeau des secrets: les écrivains publics du Paris populaire – cimetière des Saints-Innocents, XVIe-XVIIIe siècle* (Paris, 2000), which can be considered a historical counterpart to the work of anthropologist Michèle de La Pradelle, *Les Vendredis de Carpentras: faire son marché en Provence ou ailleurs* (Paris, 1996).

8. Isabelle Backouche, *La Trace du fleuve: la Seine et Paris (1750-1850)* (Paris, 2000).

9. Youri Carbonnier, 'Les maisons des ponts parisiens à la fin du XVIIIe siècle: étude d'un phénomène architectural et urbain particulier', *Histoire, économie et société* 17:4 (1998), p.711-23. Nicolas Jean-Baptiste Raguenet's 1756 painting, *La Joute des mariniers entre le pont Notre-Dame et le pont au Change* (Paris, Musée Carnavalet), is one of the most detailed depictions of the commercial and residential developments on the pont Notre-Dame.

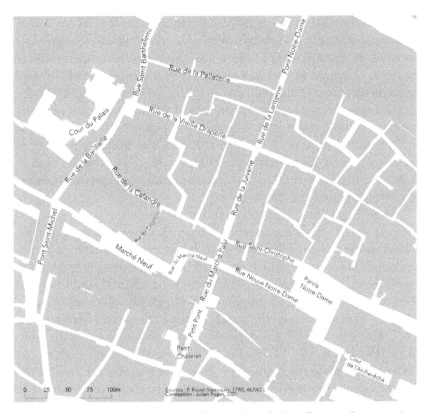

Figure 7: The Marché-Neuf. Map design: Julien Puget, Groupe de recherche en histoire des sociabilités (GRHS), Université du Québec à Montréal. Source: Paul Rouet, 'Ilots en 1791 (plan de Verniquet)', ALPAGE, Paris (2015).

one could find up to 600 shopkeepers squeezed into the arcades, hoping to satisfy the desires of their wealthy patrons.[10] To the dismay of the authorities and merchants of the capital, the Pont-Neuf also specialised in the resale of stolen merchandise[11] such as haberdashery, clothing, linens and other items of little value. Eliminating the portable stands which infested the surrounding streets would be one of the biggest challenges of the eighteenth century, both for

10. Nicolas Lyon-Caen, 'Les marchands du temple: les boutiques du Palais de justice de Paris aux XVIᵉ-XVIIIᵉ siècles', *Revue historique* 674 (2015), p.323-52.

11. See Justine Berlière, *Policer Paris au siècle des Lumières: les commissaires du quartier du Louvre dans la seconde moitié du XVIIIᵉ siècle* (Paris, 2012).

sanitary reasons and in terms of beautifying the city. These stands
that amassed during workdays 'offered a tremendously disagreeable
spectacle to the eye, depriving the many passers-by on the bridge of
the most magnificent and noteworthy view a foreigner could admire
towards the quais of the pont Royal, and of the Seine and its banks,
which extend as far as the eye can see'. In 1756, they were officially
banned.[12] Three years later, however, the police and the Bureau de
la ville would observe, with consternation, the growing number of
illegal stands in the streets and walkways neighbouring the bridge;
they were like a cancer that could not be eradicated despite all efforts
to demolish it and prevent its spread.[13]

As one might imagine, vendors and resellers of all sorts also swarmed
the busy public spaces and avenues which criss-crossed the île de la Cité,
including the rue de la Barillerie, which bordered the Palais de justice,
the rue de la Calandre, which extended from the Palais to the Marché-
Neuf, the rue de la Lanterne, which stretched north to south through
the centre of the island, the rue Neuve-Notre-Dame, which led from the
Marché-Neuf to the cathedral, and of course the rue du Marché-Neuf
itself. The sellers set up in boutiques, stalls and stands along the walls
of the Palais, the Hôtel-Dieu, the Saint-Germain-le-Vieil church, and
under the Horloge du Palais. The stall keepers ensconced outside the
houses, monuments and churches which flanked these avenues were like
living facades. Though illegal, for the most part, they were tolerated as
long as they did not encroach on the public thoroughfares, made sure
to remove their installations once night fell, and refrained from setting
up on Sundays or feast days.

Finally, roaming vendors plied every side street with the goods
they had themselves bought from the Marché-Neuf or the central
Halles. The police paid them no mind, provided they kept moving
and did not hamper the flow of traffic. On the contrary, their itinerant
trade throughout the city ensured the redistribution of produce to
areas outside of the saturated centre, reducing pressure on the Halles
and the 'licensed' markets, which barely kept up with demand. It was

12. Paris, Archives nationales (AN), H2 1866, 27 January 1756, deliberations of the
Bureau de la ville; order of the Conseil d'Etat du roi, 3 April, registered at the
Bureau de la ville on 12 April, f.285-89. Paris, AN, H2 1866, 3 April, 12 April,
28 May and 15 June 1756, f.316*v*-20 and f.335-37. A 1777 painting by Raguenet,
Le Pont-Neuf et la pompe de la Samaritaine, vus du quai de la Mégisserie, shows the
bridge stripped of its boutiques and merchants (Paris, Musée Carnavalet).
13. Paris, AN, Y 9539, police decision, 12 January 1759.

for this reason that unregulated, even illegal, points of sale – often tolerated, occasionally relocated – and sellers with multifarious, sometimes unapproved profiles dotted the territory alongside the official markets. There was one constant, however: as soon as an official marketplace was established in a quarter, generally with a roofed section, the objective of the authorities was to concentrate all transactions within that space. The Marché-Neuf is a unique example of such endeavours in many respects; through its many mutations over time and space, it illustrates how varied and rich the market experience became during the *Ancien Régime*.

Organising trade in the Marché-Neuf

The Marché-Neuf was officially created by royal decree on 21 April 1558. Henri II ordered the new market ('new' to distinguish it from the 'old' Palu Market, now deemed insufficient)[14] to be constructed on the quai Saint-Michel. The aim was to relocate the butchers and fishmongers from the fief of La Gloriette on the Left Bank near the Petit-Pont,[15] as this site was causing too much congestion in the area surrounding it. While the king did the proclaiming, it was the city who would shoulder the costs of development, beginning with a road to provide direct access to the *quai* from the old market via the rue du Marché-Palu. In compensation, the *prévôt* gained dominion over the Marché-Neuf; as its sole legal authority, he would derive all rights and benefits from it.[16]

The rue du Marché-Neuf was opened up in 1561, but did not receive its name until 1568.[17] To make way for the new market, the

14. To the south, the rue de la Juiverie became the rue du Marché-Palu, which led to the Petit-Pont. Beyond the bridge lay the fiefdom of La Gloriette and its butchers' shops. Bread, fresh and saltwater fish, vegetables and fruit were sold at the Palu Market. Unlike the Marché-Neuf, the 'old' market was a private fiefdom. Paris, BnF, MS 26310, Blondeau, Fiefs and Domains of Paris, book 3 of vol.5, f.62-67 (24 October 1671).

15. For more on this move, see Paris, BnF, MS fr. 21633, excerpt of the records of the Parlement, 11 July 1558, f.69; Paris, BnF, Fonds Moreau, MS 1061, f.157*v*, n.d.

16. Paris, BnF, Fonds Delamare, MS fr. 21633, letters patent of the *prévôt de la ville*, 20 July 1693, f.114-15, and excerpt of the records of the Parlement, 11 July 1558, f.69.

17. Paris, BnF, Fonds Delamare, MS 21692, 19 May 1571, f.14-15. See also Jacques Hillairet, 'Marché-Neuf (quai du)', in *Dictionnaire historique des rues de Paris*, vol.2 (Paris, 1960), p.101.

houses on the quai were demolished, their owners were compensated by the city, and covered market stalls were built on the south side of the *quai* near the pont Saint-Michel. Despite this, seven years after construction had begun, the city lodged a complaint with the king that the stalls had not yet been transferred from La Gloriette,[18] depriving the *prévôt* of the revenue needed to reimburse the sums invested to establish the market. Indeed, butchers' shops were highly lucrative sources of income, in part because of the rental income they represented,[19] but equally because they attracted a multitude of other vendors willing to pay for the right to set up shop nearby to avail themselves of the butcher's clients.[20] Compensation to the stall owners of La Gloriette for the losses incurred in relocating to the quai Saint-Michel had come from the *prévôt*'s own purse, which did nothing to lessen his discontent. It is reasonable to assume that the seigneurial owner of the Palu Market and the fief of La Gloriette may have worked to obstruct the transfer for the same reasons which justified the *prévôt*'s haste – revenue losses – and which in part explained the delay. Before the end of the century, however, the *prévôt* had staged a turnaround in his affairs. He issued a storm of ordinances, first banning all established points of sale outside the Marché-Neuf, then prohibiting sellers in the market from displaying their wares 'if they had neither lease, leave nor permission from ourselves to do so, or else risk a heavy fine and confiscation of their goods'.[21]

18. Paris, BnF, Fonds Moreau, MS 1061, f.187-88.
19. The city proceedings from 1652 reveal that the main sources of revenue from the Marché-Neuf were meat sales (Paris, AN, H2 *1811). The market butcher's shop possessed a covered gallery and was leased separately from the market. Leases were awarded to the highest bidder at the Bureau de la ville auction (see Paris, AN, H2 *1834, public notice, 29 March 1694, f.493-94; for eighteenth-century notices, see Paris, AN, H2 1966, 14 and 20 March 1731, 20 March 1736. For more on Paris' butchers' shops, see Sydney Watts, 'Boucherie et hygiène à Paris au XVIIIe siècle', *Revue d'histoire moderne et contemporaine* 51:3 (2004), p.79-103; Bernard Garnier, 'Les marchés aux bestiaux: Paris et sa banlieue', *Cahiers d'histoire* 42:3/4 (1997), special issue: *L'Animal domestique, XVIe-XXe siècle*, http://ch.revues.org/310 (last accessed on 19 January 2024).
20. In 1667, when the city tried transferring the bread market from the quai des Augustins to the place Dauphine, on the Ile-de-la-Cité, it was met with considerable resistance from the bakers, which the city believed was because the butchers' shops were located in the place Saint-Michel.
21. The first ordinance on this matter dates from 15 March 1559. Paris, BnF, MS fr. 21633, f.70, and excerpt from the 'Livre du juré crieur du Chatelet', f.271.

In the second half of the seventeenth century, the market underwent considerable repair and reconstruction. In 1676, the city declared it had found the perfect spot to relocate the bread market installed at the foot of the pont Saint-Michel, spilling out onto the quai des Augustins; congestion made this area impassable during Wednesday and Saturday market days. It was why the city had first tried to relocate the market to the place Dauphine in 1667. The square had been paved for the occasion, but the bakers had refused to comply. On 20 August 1673, the police obtained from the Parlement the right to regroup the bakers exclusively on the quai des Augustins. The very next day, the *prévôt* reacted to this violation of his jurisdiction by presenting his own project for the relocation of the bakers to the covered central hall of the Marché-Neuf. It had originally been built for the fishmongers, but 'had never served its primary purpose,[22] the fish merchants having deemed it more to their advantage to sell their fish in the open air'. The city authorities apparently succeeded in persuading the king that their intentions were well founded, since the project would soon proceed with the king's blessing, beginning with the demolition of the dilapidated hall and of several houses propped up against it.[23]

In 1674, the city surveyed the layout of the quai Saint-Michel market. Excluding ground-floor boutiques and the butcher's shop itself, 165 numbered spaces were identified, allowing us to finally flesh out the profiles of individual stallholders. Only five of the occupied spaces were held by men; the Marché-Neuf, unsurprisingly, was predominantly feminine – sixty-one married women, forty widows, and forty-seven unmarried young women who mostly set up in the

22. In 1618-1619, estimates for emergency repairs in the Halles, part of which had collapsed, mention only a butcher's shop on the ground floor, with an attic above (Paris, AN, H2 *1799, f.226, 263 and 290, 28 August and 6 November 1618, 15 February 1619). The fishmongers had already vacated the covered hall. It seems the work was never completed, for, in 1628, major renovations were needed 'in the main house and the central hall'. Paris, AN, H2 1803, f.20-22 (23 and 26 September 1628). A six-year lease was finally awarded in 1636. Paris, AN, H2 1899-1 (12 November 1636).

23. For more on the bread market, see Paris, AN, H2 1824, f.259-60 (February and March 1673); Paris, AN, H2 1825, f.588-93 (21 August 1673 and 28 July 1676); Paris, AN, H2 1827, f.597-600; Paris, AN, K986, BV deliberations, 7 February 1673; Paris, BnF, MS fr. 21633, f.143-44, judgements of the Conseil du roi, letters patent of the king, ordinances of the Bureau des finances (1 and 20 September 1667); Paris, BnF, Fonds Moreau, MS 1061, f.103-105*v* (7 February, 8 July and 21 August 1673).

vicinity of the buildings. During the *Ancien Régime*, second-hand and grocery professions were not generally controlled by corporations, and, as we gather from the *Cris de Paris* and the well-known case of the *Dames de la Halle* in Paris, such trades were mainly occupied by women.[24] Where the 1674 survey specifies what merchandise was sold, we find women dealing in fresh- and saltwater fish and shellfish (fifty-six), fruit and vegetables (thirty-four), dairy products (twenty-one), and fresh herbs and other leaf vegetables (ten). Only two women offered services rather than products (one garment mender and a maker of linens). The market was principally one which dealt in the essentials.

The new survey allowed the city, in 1687, to begin demarcating the lots in the Marché-Neuf; it was the first attempt to modernise the market since its creation.[25] In 1734, the city's ultimate campaign to redesign the space saw the twelve houses it had built in 1626-1627 along the quai Saint-Michel demolished. At the behest of the *prévôt* and 'for the greater enjoyment of the public street in the aforementioned market', the houses were not rebuilt. The newly disencumbered space was bordered by a riverside parapet, with stone markers defining the limits of the vending area, creating safe, spacious grounds on which to hold markets.[26] The fishmongers were to relocate their business there; only the bakers were authorised to sell their goods outside of the boundaries, if their numbers were too great. The Marché-Neuf would retain this mid-eighteenth-century layout and continue to supply the Cité until its demise in 1854.

24. James B. Collins, 'Women and the birth of modern consumer capitalism', in *Women and work in eighteenth-century France*, ed. Daryl M. Hafter and Nina Kushner (Baton Rouge, LA, 2015), p.152-76; Dominique Godineau, *Les Femmes dans la société française, XVIe-XVIIIe siècle* (Paris, 2003); Sabine Juratic and Nicole Pellegrin, 'Femmes, villes et travail en France dans la deuxième moitié du XVIIIe siècle', *Histoire, économie et société* 3 (1994), p.477-500; Katie Jarvis, *Politics in the marketplace: work, gender, and citizenship in revolutionary France* (Oxford, 2019).

25. Paris, BnF, MS fr. 21633, letters patent of the *prévôt de la ville*, f.114-15 (20 July 1693).

26. See Paris, BnF, MS fr. 21633, f.71-72 (8, 12 and 13 November 1627); Paris, BnF, JF, vol.1421, f.118-19 and 122-26 (9 September 1734); Paris, BnF, MS fr. 21692, f.199-200 (16 and 20 June 1736). 'It is decreed that a space of 5 *toises* shall be left parallel to the river, between the alignment of houses situated in the market, for the passage of vehicles and to ease the disencumbering of the market. To this effect, boundary markers of sufficient height shall be placed, 6 feet distant each from the other, inside which the activities and operations of said market shall be undertaken, and beyond which they shall not be allowed to extend.'

By the end of the sixteenth century, the Marché-Neuf had become a noisy, bustling, 'organised' space. It was tucked between the pont Saint-Michel and the Petit-Pont, and wedged in between the buildings abutting the Seine and the rows of houses, so typical of contemporary urban developments, that crowded against the rue de la Calandre.[27] The area had already long been peopled by resellers of all sorts, but the creation of a formalised market breathed new life into the space, which authorities sought to forcibly contain within the newly defined boundaries. The vitality the vendors brought to the Marché-Neuf was itself an integral component of the close sense of community woven into everyday life.

An environment full of life

The Marché-Neuf was a living entity at the heart of the city, pulsing with the energy of more than commercial transactions. Several families lived in the buildings that bordered it; a simple flight of stairs separated the stall keepers who dwelled there from their merchandise. Though the market was a stone's throw from Notre-Dame Cathedral, readily attended during grander ceremonies, the locals preferred the church of Saint-Germain-le-Vieil on the north side of the market for everyday services.[28] The children in the neighbourhood squabbled over who would get to ring the church bells while parents gathered at the tavern near the stalls in the market square to drink and eat – at the Petite Hotte in the 1680s, or in later years at the Bouteille. They were equally amenable to meeting in the establishments located in neighbouring avenues, such as the tavern on the rue de la Calandre, which the *revendeuses* particularly favoured at the beginning of the eighteenth century.

The market also housed wine merchants (the Sacrifice d'Abraham around 1687; the Cage in 1766),[29] a Guet guard post from at least 1680,[30] and the office of a few *commissaires de police du quartier de la*

---

27. Two passageways directly linked the rue de la Calandre with the Marché-Neuf: the 'Marché-Neuf passageway, also called du Boisselier, since a man by the name of Boisselier had lived there, and the rue des Cargaisons [...] through which the goods of this market were transported'. See Figure 7.
28. The portal and the bell tower were rebuilt in 1560, no doubt at the same time as the Marché-Neuf was created. The church closed its doors in 1790, was sold in 1796 and was subsequently demolished.
29. Paris, AN, Y 10724 (30 June 1687); Y 12667 (May 1766).
30. Paris, AN, H2 1827, f.597-99. It was still present in 1767. Paris, AN, Y 12668

Cité.[31] It was said that a *cour des miracles* could also be found there.[32] The young used the market square as a playground. The adults would unwind after a long day's work on the steps of their boutiques, where they had front-row seats for the processions of the shrine of Sainte-Geneviève that wound through the Marché-Neuf on the way to the cathedral. The entire neighbourhood would convene there at the slightest excuse for celebrations, crowding onto makeshift platforms, taking delight in the occasional bonfire display, or celebrating a royal victory or the birth of an heir. On occasions when the king or queen passed through on their way to Notre-Dame, the commissaire would make certain to clear the avenues, move the stall keepers aside, remove rotted awnings, have the bourgeois hang up tapestries, and even put away the stalls which leaned against the buildings.[33]

Because of its central location in Paris, the Marché-Neuf was also a convenient space for the multitudes of Parisians who crossed through on a daily basis, heading towards the cathedral or the rue Saint-Jacques, or perhaps making their way back from the Hôtel-Dieu or the Palais de justice. It was the backdrop for acts of violence and solidarity, friendly and hostile relationships, and criminality, all typical of a public space defined by its multiple uses. Inhabitants hurled insults back and forth, and ruthlessly trampled their rivals' goods to decry unfair competition, demand payment of a debt or hound a stall keeper they wished to see depart. Family conflicts played out between the stalls in front of captive audiences, and the acrimony between vendors was often echoed in the lodging houses or taverns. Opposing vendors clashed in untold numbers of skirmishes, united only according to the various goods they sold, or against bullying butchers, who were said to set their dogs on delinquent customers

---

(30 January, 9 February, 18 October, 25 October and 4 November 1767). There was another guard post at the Pont-Neuf.

31. Some of the Châtelet commissaires assigned to the municipality in the eighteenth century preferred to set up shop on the île Notre-Dame (île Saint-Louis), but most settled in the main streets of the Cité as well as in the place du Marché-Neuf: in the years following the creation of the police force, their residences could be found on the rue Carmin, rue Charles Bourdon (until 1714) and rue Claude-Louis Boulanger (from 1764 to 1780).

32. See Paris, AN, Y 10724 (30 June 1687); Y 12667 (May 1766).

33. Paris, BnF, MS 21692, f.258 (5 March 1722); Paris, AN, H2 1831, f.254-55 (5 February 1687); Paris, AN, Y 10737 (18 May 1709); Paris, AN, H2 1814, f.33-35 (6-7 September 1656). See Marie-Carmen Gras, 'Les processions en l'honneur de sainte Geneviève à Paris: miroir d'une société (XVe-XVIIIe siècles)', *Histoire urbaine* 3:32 (2011), p.5-30.

and female resellers' cats.[34] Tradeswomen and residents alike readily flocked to witness the events which transpired in the market. From sunup to sunset, they observed, commented on and participated in the hustle and bustle of the market square.

Maintaining order despite the multitude of different temperaments that coloured the Marché-Neuf environment was a daunting challenge for the authorities who had a share in resolving the conflicts that arose. The lines of jurisdiction were easily blurred with respect to the quai Saint-Michel. Quarrels in the market could quickly escalate into territorial squabbles – and which authorities would be involved in these cases was also a matter of dispute.

Endless bureaucratic bickering

From the day the Marché-Neuf was created, the city was at pains to retain exclusive jurisdiction over – and in – the market space. The king himself, in gratitude for services rendered, might take it upon himself to appoint someone of his own choosing to the position of market *éboueur* (street cleaner). He had done so in 1621, with a man named Mirande, and again in 1626, with Guillemain Guichard, while another named Dorival claimed the city had already granted him the office.[35] On occasion, the king had also magnanimously offered 'occupation without title of boutiques and stall spaces in the markets, streets, *quais*, bridges and other public places, belonging to the city and *faubourgs* of Paris'.[36] The city countered that, since the revenues generated by the Marché-Neuf were its exclusive preserve, it should be so for all associated commissions and appointments. In matters of acquired rights, it was often necessary to remind the king of agreements regarding the divisions of the territory *of* and *in* his city. In the 1670s and 1680s, for example, the crown unleashed a grand campaign to annex the territories of public markets which were not yet a part of its lands to the royal domains. Though it had previously conceded the Marché-Neuf to the city, it initiated

---

34. For more on this anecdote, see Paris, AN, Y 14371 (4 May 1684); Y 10736 (4 June and 21 December 1707); Y 10737 (4 May 1709); Y 14446 (18-23 July 1748).
35. Paris, AN, *H2 1800, f.148*v*, petition to the *lieutenant civil* to advise His Majesty, n.d., 1621; Paris, AN, *H2 1804, f.20 (10 September 1633); Paris, BnF, MS fr. 21633, f.135-36, letter to the *prévôt des marchands* to reinstate the office of *boueur*, n.d. (after 1719 and before 1721); Paris, AN, H2 1900 (4 June 1641).
36. Paris, AN, H2 1900 (3 April 1642).

administrative procedures, through the intercession of its *fermiers* (tax collectors), to regain possession of the property.[37] To forward the king's claim, *lieutenant de police* La Reynie dispatched *commissaire de police* Carmin to meet with the market resellers and 'oblige the women who had set up their stands near or in front of the houses in the aforementioned market and public places to withdraw from said places and clear the public streets, [...] [naturally,] not a single one complied'.[38] The city argued, with all the respect due to the monarch, that the Marché-Neuf should be exempt from annexation as the commercial privileges it enjoyed had been granted in compensation for its investments. In any case, contended the *prévôt*, La Reynie had not had the authority to act as he had done; the market was not within the commissaire's jurisdiction. The issue was eventually resolved in the city's favour, but a new legal dispute would soon pit the prévôt against the *fermier du roi*. The *fermier* demanded that each *revendeuse* in the Marché-Neuf present her leasing agreement and all receipts certifying her right to occupy a space in the market, and gave them three days to comply. The initiative was poorly received. The *revendeuses* flatly refused to comply; the *prévôt* condemned the measure outright and ordered his *placier* to create obstructions.[39]

This was not the only challenge to the *prévôt*'s authority, however. The *bailli du Palais* (formerly the *concierge du Palais*) was another contender. Created in 1359, the office had retained jurisdiction over civil and criminal matters within the walls of the Palais – a property of the king – and thus over the royal officers and market trades-people who lived and worked within its halls or in the neighbouring streets. At least, it had retained jurisdiction until 1674, when the old *baillage* situated outside of the enclosure was transferred to the royal jurisdiction of the Châtelet. The *bailli* was charged with implementing rules concerning market displays and the secure layout of boutiques in the Palais. Under the *Ancien Régime*, the limits of various jurisdictional territories were characteristically... fuzzy. This may explain why, in 1624-1629, the bailli deemed it was within its competence to

---

37. Paris, BnF, MS fr. 21633, f.100 (25 August 1674) and f.104-105 (1 December 1674); MS fr. 21633, f.92-95 (19 March 1674).

38. Paris, BnF, MS fr. 21633, f.100-103 (25 August, 5 September and 26 October 1674).

39. Pursuant to the lease agreement renewed in August 1676. Paris, BnF, MS fr. 21633, f.104-105 (1 December 1674); Paris, AN, H2 1828, f.638-39 (17 March 1682); Paris, AN, H2 1829, f.166-67 (19 December 1682).

adjudicate on the collective complaints of some proprietors situated in the Marché-Neuf, who were accusing *revendeuses* of obstructing the facades of their homes.[40] In 1656, it was also with the bailli that the female resellers, who had organised themselves into a confraternity, initiated proceedings to prevent the city from opening a new entrance to the covered hall of the Marché-Neuf, which they claimed would jeopardise their commerce outside of the hall.[41] It seems that the *revendeuses* cherry-picked which judicial authority they approached when they wished to express their dissent.

The city's greatest adversary arrived on the scene in 1667 with the creation of the office of the lieutenant of police. The *police générale des vivres* fell under the jurisdiction of this new entity, though the Bureau de la ville continued to govern river trade and commercial activities along the banks of the Seine. Since the Marché-Neuf was located on the quai Saint-Michel, the potential for conflict from overlapping jurisdictions was considerable.[42] In 1668, it was no longer the *bailli du Palais*, but the Châtelet police, to whom the *revendeuses* turned when the market cleaners began charging them well above the posted rate. It was a recurring grievance. This time, however, the municipality reacted by submitting a brief in support of settling, once and for all, whether judging the misconduct of the *éboueur* was within the city's jurisdiction.[43] It presented a lengthy, three-point argument demonstrating that it was indeed the city's responsibility. First, it contended, 'as regards the locality', the Marché-Neuf was situated on a *quai* (formerly called the quai Saint-Michel), ergo, it was the city's responsibility to ensure the cleaning and policing of the premises, as it did for all the *quais* in the city. Secondly, 'as regards the person', the *éboueur* was an oath-sworn officer of the city. It was the city that provisioned him, and it was to the city that the *éboueur* appealed in the event of non-payment of rent; logically, therefore, it should be to the city that the *éboueur* be accountable. Finally, 'as

---

40. In September 1629, the Parlement overturned the *bailli*'s 17 October 1624 ruling – five years after the beginning of proceedings. See Paris, AN, *H2 1803, f.20-22 and f.178-79 (1 September 1629); Paris, BnF, MS fr. 21633, f.73-74 (12 February 1630).

41. Paris, AN, H2 1814, deliberations of the Bureau de la ville, which did not halt construction, f.6-8 (18 and 19 August 1656).

42. See the essay by Julie Allard in this volume, 'A space shared, a space contested: policing the place de Grève'.

43. Paris, BnF, Factums, MS F°FM 12864 (25 June 1688); MS 21688, excerpts of the records of the Parlement, f.49 (7 July 1688).

regards the act', or justification for the liberties taken in collecting cleaning fees, the *éboueur* was again beholden to the city since it was the latter's responsibility to set tariffs in the Marché-Neuf.[44] In July 1668, the Parlement nevertheless decided in favour of the Châtelet police, alleging they were responsible for all policing duties, which included street cleaning throughout the city and, more precisely, in the Marché-Neuf. This was not the last of the disputes between the Châtelet and the city over jurisdiction of the Marché-Neuf, however. On the contrary, the Châtelet's power only continued to grow, to the detriment of seigneurial and domanial rights, including those of the city. The *revendeuses*, though under obligation to the owner of the market in which they held their stand, contributed actively to the expansion of the Châtelet's power.

In sum, the *bailli*, the *procureur du roi*, the Châtelet police, the *prévôt de la ville* each in turn tried to intervene in the territory. It was a complex struggle for power which only added to the confusion: who held jurisdiction over what and in which space within the municipality and in the Marché-Neuf was an eternal enigma. Only an analysis of the situation over a lengthier timeline can yield a more accurate measure of the situation. Even so, how did those who regularly navigated the market space perceive this conflict? One may well ask, given that they themselves seemed to contribute to the chaos. Perhaps they simply wished to take advantage of the situation in order to make their own laws, or, more precisely, exploit all available options until the jurisdictional spats were resolved.

The municipality managed to retain control of the market in the long run. Maintaining discipline over the *revendeuses* was yet another thorny problem, however, which can only be understood through the different viewpoints of those who manoeuvred in and around the Marché-Neuf. Their interactions with and through this space nourished the construction of a social and political identity. It was a space that had little to do with the legal territory the authorities administered for the benefit of the public.

---

44. Though each market set its own tariffs, the Halles were a sort of benchmark for the others. In 1695, the police began enforcing a fixed tariff in all markets. Nonetheless, in 1660, and therefore before the creation of the Lieutenance générale de police, the tariff was set by the Baillage du Palais and was still in effect in 1674. Paris, BnF, MS fr. 21633, f.88, and MS 21688, f.50-51 (5 January 1695).

Occupying the Marché-Neuf: an experiment in *citadinité*

From the moment it was created, the Marché-Neuf was meant to impose structure on the already existent commercial fabric of the quai Saint-Michel and its surroundings. Scholars are provided with a unique opportunity here, to understand the true territorial implications of such an entity at its inception from the perspective of the population. In the market environment, where there was both a desire and the capacity to act, individual power was brokered through negotiations with the collective. Through their practices and behaviours, each actor not only occupied the space but also invested it with meaning, which in return influenced their own motivations, initiatives, alliances and divisions. We gain insight into how individuals constructed their identity as *citadines*, how they shaped and were shaped by their environment and through their interactions with one another, with market authorities and with urban police.[45] Two often brutal figures of authority lorded over the daily chaos of the marketplace: the *placier* and the *éboueur*. As representatives of the city and the *prévôt*, they were responsible for maintaining order in the Marché-Neuf, and their power was manifest in their control over the territory.

The despots of the Marché-Neuf

The 1674 layout of the market proper sheds light on its physicality and the methods of localising stalls within that labyrinthian space. Of the 165 spaces plotted out, 105 were identified in relation to the market itself. Directions to stands located in the main market space might read: 'upon entering the Notre-Dame entrance to the Marché-Neuf and adjacent to the residence of so-and-so', 'around the corner behind the residence of so-and-so', 'in the first row between the two townhouses', 'the second row from the central townhouse of the Marché-Neuf', and so on.[46] Each stall occupant paid the rental rate established in 1649, 3 *livres* per year, to the *fermier du Marché-Neuf*. The survey also specifies the location and width of its fifteen inner aisles:

---

45. Isabelle Backouche and Nathalie Montel, 'La fabrique ordinaire de la ville', *Histoire urbaine* 9:2 (2007), p.5-9.
46. The largest stalls in the main section belonged to the fishmongers and measured roughly 6 feet by 6 feet; the smallest, allotted to the fruit sellers, measured 3 feet by 3 feet.

they measured anywhere from 3 to 8 feet, and were laid out 'across from the main entrance to the Maison de la ville', 'across from the stall of Michelle Lemaistre, fruit seller' or 'between the stalls of this stall keeper and that'. The remaining sixty stands were identified by the building or monument against which they leaned.[47] Only eight of these *revendeuses* declared they paid no rent; others parted with 10 or 20 *sous* per market day or per week, and some paid out as much as 10 to 15 *livres* per year to the inhabitants who gave them leave to set up shop on their doorstep.[48] There were thirteen aisles in this outer section of the central market space, measuring 3 to 6 feet wide, and five 'free spaces' of 7 to 8 *toises*. At least until the 1680 demarcation of the spaces, it appears that more than half of the stalls in the Marché-Neuf were theoretically located outside of the *placier*'s zone of authority. Yet the market was not an enclosed space. It spilled out from the main square into every available nook and cranny, clinging to the surrounding buildings, which only served to complicate the task of the *placier*.

In the seventeenth century, the auction for the *ferme du Marché-Neuf* was announced in advance by way of bills posted in the usual places – in the Marché-Neuf of course, but also on the great main door of the Hôtel de ville, and on the principal entrances of butchers' shops, the Palais de justice and the Châtelet. Adjudication took place by candlelight at the Bureau de l'Hôtel de ville, over several days or even weeks if needed; the six-year lease went to the highest bidder. In 1666, and effective the following year, Lemaire thus obtained the *ferme*, or leasehold rights, of the boutiques and butchers' shops, as well as of the less lucrative stalls, spaces and halls of the Marché-Neuf. In exchange, he undertook to keep the buildings and spaces in good repair and to return everything in good order upon expiry of the lease, which was rendered null 'in the event of war or whatever public necessity was decided upon by the municipality', or in case of non-payment of rent over three consecutive terms.[49] Either the *fermier* himself, or a

47. These stalls generally measured 4 feet by 3 or 4 feet but could be as wide as 8 feet.
48. Inequity amongst sellers was a source of violence in the marketplace, though not the principal reason for their grievances.
49. The *ferme du Marché-Neuf* conferments are found in series *H2 of the deliberations of the Bureau de la ville. In the second half of the seventeenth century, the *bail* was awarded for an annual value of between 6100 and 8200 *livres*: in 1644, 1648 and 1654, to Le Juge, merchant butcher; in 1660, to Le Caron, bourgeois and merchant from the Temple quarter; in 1666, to Lemaire, a

designated employee, served as *placier*, the inevitable go-between for all who wished to trade in the Marché-Neuf, as it was he who leased the spaces.

The municipality also counted on the services of an accredited *balayeur des boues*, who cleaned the market space of rubbish each day, carting it off beyond the city limits. The king had created the office, which could be inherited, in 1641, the Bureau de l'Hôtel de ville approving all subsequent appointments.[50] The position was unpaid; any revenues were earned from the fees the stall keepers paid at the rates advertised in the market. Several criteria seemingly went into determining the rates: the type of stall, the nature and quantity of products offered, the seller's status (master or journeyman; keeper of a permanent, stationary stall or not; retailer or wholesaler), the location (in the covered hall or outside), the type of stand (table, stall or standing with baskets; ambulatory sellers paid no fee) and, of course, especially the quantity of rubbish generated. It was therefore not surprising that a frog skinner, or her pea sheller workmate, paid 6 to 12 *deniers* a day – three to six times more than might a butter merchant.[51] This was not to say that the women willingly accepted the additional levy. Garbage collectors Leloup and Andry were known to comment that 'they would drown in expenses if they filed as many legal proceedings as they had women [pea shellers] refusing to pay' the sum owed. The women's unwillingness peaked in August as the season came into full swing and the *placier* felt entitled to increase his levies on the grounds that his workload increased with the extra heaps of shells he had to remove.[52]

---

merchant. In addition to the spaces allocated to the *revendeuses*, the *fermier* rented the very lucrative butcher's shop and Halles allotments, as well as the 'unofficial' spaces, which cost far above the mandated 3 *livres*. See Paris, AN, *H2, 1813 (12 August 1654); *H2 1815 (7-18 August 1660); *H2 1819 (23 July 1666); *H2 1820, f.510-19; *H2 1902 (July 1648).

50. Paris, BnF, Factums, MS F°FM 12864 (25 June 1688); MS fr. 21633, letter to the *prévôt des marchands* to reinstitute the *office de boueur*, f.135-36 (most likely after 1719 and before 1721).

51. The tariff in 1660, which was still in effect in 1674. Paris, BnF, MS fr. 21633, f.68. Many of the files concerning seventeenth- and eighteenth-century tariffs in the central Halles, the Marché-Neuf and other markets in the royal domain are conserved at the BnF, MS fr. 21632-33, 21635 and 21688.

52. Paris, BnF, Fonds Delamare, MS 21688, f.61-62 (3 June 1701); Paris, BnF, MS fr. 21633, f.106-109 (19 June 1701). Fishmongers and sellers of greens saw their tariffs triple during Lent (same references; see also Paris, AN, Y 9410, 26 February 1700).

Tariffs were a source of incomprehension likely to generate sentiments of injustice amongst the market occupants. The Bureau de la ville repeatedly insisted that the fees be – and remain – 'sufficiently modest as to avoid scarcity, as they are all poor folk who pay them'.[53] It kept a careful watch over the demands of the street cleaners who complained they could not cover their own costs with the meagre remittances they went to great pains to obtain from their clients.

There were separate street cleaners for the Marché-Neuf and the municipality proper. The *éboueur* for the municipality was responsible for cleaning the streets and in front of houses in the rest of the quarter.[54] Yet the buildings located within the designated selling space of the Marché-Neuf turned what at first glance was a clear division of territory and responsibilities into a muddy scramble. Tenants and homeowners who displayed goods on their doorsteps or who authorised sellers to set up there were rarely inclined to pay the double tax that was often required of them. Occasionally, both municipality and market *éboueur* positions were held by the same person, but this far from resolved the issue. In the 1680s and 1690s, a man named Beaudry, who lived at the Marché-Neuf, did in fact hold both offices, but complained that it severely handicapped him.[55] In 1701, he resigned his charge in the Marché-Neuf, keeping only his office of

53. Paris, BnF, MS fr. 21632, f.275-76, Fonds Delamare (between 1700 and 1706); Andry and Leloup were responsible for cleaning the market at the time. In 1695, police regulations stipulated that the *placier/balayeur* could tax each *revendeuse* installed in the market only once. If a fruit seller displayed multiple goods, the fee was to be established according to the merchandise which required the highest applicable tariff. See Paris, AN, Y 9410, decision of Lieutenant d'Argenson (26 February 1700).

54. See Pierre-Denis Baudriot, 'Essai sur l'ordure en milieu urbain à l'époque pré-industrielle: boues, immondices et gadoue à Paris au XVIIIᵉ siècle', *Histoire, économie et société* 5:4 (1986), p.515-28. A list of the 'cleaning contractors of the Paris quarters' was established every Friday at the Grande Police du Châtelet. See for example Paris, AN, Y 9537 (26 June 1705, 25 February 1706 and 22 October 1706). Markets did not always have an officially appointed sweeper: the post in the place Maubert market was left vacant in the middle of the seventeenth century in favour of the local *éboueur* of the quarter. Paris, BnF, MS fr. 21632, f.275-76 (between 1700 and 1706). From 1719 to 1721, it was the 'cleaning contractor of the quarter' (*entrepreneur des boues du quartier*), along with the *balayeur du Palais*, who had charge of cleaning the Marché-Neuf, which lacked its own cleaner at the time.

55. See Paris, BnF, MS fr. 21633, judgement pronounced against the inhabitants residing in the houses of the Marché-Neuf, f.116-18 (20 November and 12 December 1696).

city éboueur. Marché-Neuf duties went to a man named Andry, who would keep the position, in association with the *placier* Leloup, until his death in 1706. The imbroglio morphed from one of lost revenue into one of professional sabotage; the two associates were constantly at war with Beaudry. The latter was not above bringing the carts and wagons he also rented through the market space, filled with refuse, and stationing them near the boundary markers, where he would proceed to muck them out to 'the great chagrin of the placier [...] who was obliged to begin the job of cleaning anew'.[56]

In sum, the Bureau de la ville enjoined the *placiers* and cleaners of the Marché-Neuf to keep the *quai* well supplied and orderly. The functions were theoretically distinct, though more often informal arrangements between the parties blurred the lines between the two, resulting in multiple players intervening concurrently within the market space.[57] Andry, upon acquiring the office of *éboueur*, began closely collaborating with Leloup, who was still active in 1719 despite having reached an advanced age. In 1708, we know that Andry's widow had inherited the office, and still held it in 1721, though Leloup took over the duties of *éboueur* as early as 1711. At least, it was she who had the post reinstated – it had been abolished in 1719[58] – for herself and her young daughter. Clearly, she had remained in the Marché-Neuf after her husband had passed and continued to work in collaboration with Leloup and his wife. The Leloup and

---

56. Paris, BnF, MS fr. 21688, Fonds Delamare, letters of the *placier* and of Beaudry to the lieutenant of police, f.56-57 (14 April 1701) and ruling dismissing Beaudry, f.60 (6 May 1701).

57. This was especially so when *fermiers* who had acquired the office decided to ensure their income by contracting out part of their charge (either lot placements or merchandise) to private individuals without declaring it with the city. See Paris, AN, *H2 1820, 23 July 1666, leasing agreement to Lemaire, 'Requeste de Nicolas Lemaire à Messieurs de la Ville pour obtenir la resolution du bail des places et estaux a boucher estans au marché neuf' (16 July 1668), and the accompanying 'Accomodement de messieurs de la Ville' (23 July 1668), f.510-19.

58. The office was abolished by royal decree along with all official appointments to the ports, *quais* and *halles*, then reinstated in 1721. See Paris, BnF, orders of the Conseil d'Etat du roi, MS fr. 21632, f.305-306 (10 December 1719), and MS fr. 21688, f.64 (5 August 1721). Between 1719 and 1721, the *entrepreneur des boues du quartier* and the *balayeur du Palais* shared in the cleaning of the Marché-Neuf; an additional wagon was assigned to them and their wages increased accordingly; the police coffers covered the additional costs. Paris, BnF, MS fr. 21688, letter to Commissaire Delamare, f.74-75 (23 December 1719).

Andry families formed such a formidable partnership, spanning over twenty-five years in the Marché-Neuf, that their respective functions were sometimes mixed up.[59] In February 1701, it was thus Leloup's wife who collected payment for cleaning and waste removal, only to find that a fishmonger outraged at having to pay more than the posted tariff had been plotting against her.[60]

The city was not always informed of such associations. Indeed, the municipality's ignorance often served the illicit interests of the two market bigwigs. That the *placier* was indeed a key player, who believed he lorded it over the partitioning of a territory in which he pulled all the strings, is borne out by his attitude and behaviour. Leloup is a fascinating man in this respect: a cheat and a hypocrite, he skilfully circumvented the rules, shamelessly charged above the prerequisite rental rates, often with the help of accomplices, and rained threats and beatings on recalcitrant clients.[61] This essay opened with a description of an emotionally charged incident: it was Leloup who had moved the market women's stalls outside of the market zone and set *huissiers* and city *archers* to expel them. In a report written ten years after the incident, Commissaire Delamare condemned Leloup's persistent arrogance. Not one iota had Leloup altered his practice of placing foodstuff vendors not only outside of the boundaries, but also 'in front of houses in the streets adjacent to the market'.[62]

Another incident in 1711:[63] this time, the bakers are the victims of shady machinations that had likely been going on for some time. It seems that the new *fermier du Marché-Neuf,* named Lalonde, felt entitled to require that the market bakers lease their baskets, racks and bread paddles exclusively from him, or face a stiff increase in their tariff – from 3 to 15 *livres* – if they wished to enjoy continued access to a space in the Marché-Neuf. On 7 October, he requested the presence of Commissaire Bourdon, who resided in the marketplace,

---

59. At the start of the eighteenth century, complaints filed against abuses carried out by Leloup reveal that his extended family (sons, daughters, sons-in-law and grandsons) all participated in the business, and suggest that Andry may have been his son-in-law. See Paris, AN, Y 10735 (24 July 1706) and 10740 (25 November 1713).
60. Paris, AN, Y 10732, complaint filed by Anne Clopin (19 February 1701).
61. Again, in 1714, we read that Leloup, along with his wife, Elisabeth, and his family, 'were greatly feared in the Marché because of their verbal and physical abuses'. Paris, AN, Y 10741 (26 January 1714).
62. Paris, BnF, MS fr. 21633, f.127-28 (19 October 1703).
63. Paris, AN, Y 10739, 10741 (7 and 12 October 1711 respectively).

at six o'clock in the morning. At that early hour, the bakers had not yet arrived, but their spaces were already cluttered with baskets. Lalonde had ordered the basket merchant Gosse, who also resided in the market with his wife and his children, to distribute the woven containers. An *aide-major* and two city *archers* assisted him. Lalonde was outwardly confident he was in the right, but he must have feared some sort of resistance. The commissaire had in fact made it clear that, by order of the *lieutenant de police* d'Argenson, the bakers were free to equip themselves however they wished. This did nothing to deter Lalonde from uttering threats to the poor bakers as they arrived. Thirty-four of them capitulated to his demands they use his baskets, though Leloup, the former *placier* and current *éboueur*, had already been supplying them. This still 'left [Leloup] with twenty-one of the spaces reserved for bakers', meaning that, during his own time as *placier*, he had supplied equipment to upwards of fifty bakers! Given Leloup's track record, it is doubtful indeed that the bakers had had much choice in the matter.[64] Adding insult to injury, the city itself saw fit to send guards to support Lalonde, in line with the provision of the leasing agreement – proof, if it were needed, of the city's desire to confront the police on matters involving its *fermier*.

As *placier*, Lalonde was able to slide through the cracks breached by the quarrels over jurisdiction, testing the limits of his capacity to act in his own self-interest – as would any worthy successor of Leloup, whose career reveals the many means by which he negotiated his own independence and potential power. We had already discerned Leloup's character from his unscrupulous behaviour, certainly towards the bakers, but more particularly towards the *revendeuses*. For Leloup, the equation was simple: once the costs of his *ferme* agreement were covered, a *placier* – or his assistant – sought to increase his profit margin, accordingly adjusting his tactics, irrespective of the formal spatial or legal limits of his office. Leloup and Andry thus allowed themselves the luxury of leasing spots outside of the marked boundaries along the house fronts in the streets leading or adjacent to the market, under the pretext that the sellers were still 'in an assigned place'. Needless to say, it was all done without the consent of the *prévôt des marchands*, or that of the homeowners, who gained nothing in exchange. Agreements were often reached through intimidation, and the women looking for a strategic spot to sell their goods paid for

---

64. On Leloup's own fraudulent schemes to lease baskets to the bakers, see Paris, BnF, MS fr. 21633, f.120 and 134 (9 April, 22 May 1699 and n.d.).

them dearly. And, if one did not submit to Leloup's demands, beatings would follow, stalls would be overturned and the merchandise ruined. Yet, even inside the market perimeter, those who conformed to the regulations did not escape exaction, not when confronted with a *placier* who was completely indifferent to official market rules and did not hesitate to place them, against their will, in an unsuitable space. They might find themselves behind other vendors positioned across lot divisions, which effectively prevented customers from reaching them. It was a situation, Commissaire Bourdon had noted, which did nothing to motivate the women to abide by the rules.[65]

The archives tell of many women who, for the most part, preferred setting up their stands beyond the limits of the Marché-Neuf, though they would come to regret it, for the *placier* nonetheless came to claim his 'due'. The women lodged complaints against the *placier*'s abuses, or were themselves the object of the *placier*'s complaints. Leloup would broadcast his 'distress' at seeing his market so poorly supplied because sellers refused to set up there, hostile to the idea of having to defray the cost of a space. But, in this first scenario, the *placier* was an aggressor who bypassed regulations to his own advantage, forced to defend his case to the police, in whose authority the market women had sought protection. Unless, of course, the women approached one of the occupants of the buildings surrounding the market to escape the *placier*'s clutches. In this second situation, the *placier* became the hapless victim who, in the interest of the public, had merely wished to provide for his market. It was then his turn to make remonstrances, in which case he sought the ear of the *commissaire de police* more often than that of the *prévôt des marchands*. Perhaps he turned to the lieutenant as part of an attempt to polish his image, but it was more likely because his subterfuge did not fool city authorities. It is clear he was exploiting the territorial squabbles – but no less than his adversaries, the *revendeuses*, who were anything but victims!

The protégées of Saint Louis

By the sixteenth century, it had long been common practice for the women who sold fruit and herbs to set up their stands in the rue du Marché-Neuf along the church front and outer perimeter of Saint-Germain-le-Vieil. Religious services were often hampered by 'the

---

65. Paris, AN, Y 10730 (10 March 1698).

noise, quarrels, dissension, comments, insults and exchanges [those women] continuously produced, to the great dishonour of the glory of God and in complete disregard for his service'. Repeated judgements compelling them to relocate to the riverside reveal that this practice did not change when the new market space opened.[66] During the Fronde, however, the fish merchants decided to form an association to represent their rights. On 22 June 1649, they obtained a ruling from the Parlement to fix the annual leasing fee in the Marché-Neuf at 3 *livres*; in return, and 'to give glory to God', they established a confraternity in honour of Saint Louis and Saint Anne. In virtue of an agreement with the parish priest and churchwardens, they sponsored daily and annual services at Saint-Germain-le-Vieil. The women had reasons enough to celebrate, as they owed their victory to the queen's intervention.

The story unfolds[67] with Claude Le Juge, a merchant butcher who had been the Marché-Neuf *placier* since 1644. He was a much despised man without scruples, abusive and violent. In December 1648, and again in March 1649, the city was disturbed to learn of his troubled dealings with the various fishmongers, who claimed they were paying more in the open air, exposed to bad weather, than they had within the covered halls – and much more than the tariffs charged in other markets. The women demanded their rent be reduced to 3 *livres*. Though cases with both the city and the Parlement were pending on this matter, Le Juge managed to renew his six-year lease in 1649. This only fuelled the women's anger, prompting retaliation. Taking advantage of the queen's passage through the Marché-Neuf on her way to Notre-Dame, they held an

> assembly of all the Marché-Neuf fishmongeresses [in excess of seventy] and so pestered the queen as she was passing through that she felt obliged to help. Her support rendered the women so insolent

66. Paris, BnF, MS fr. 21693, ruling of the Prévôté concerning the confiscation of goods for the benefit of the poor of the Hôtel-Dieu, f.41 (5 August 1585); MS fr. 21692, decision of the *lieutenant civil* regarding the petition of the 'Curés, Marguilliers, et paroissiens de l'Eglise Saint-Germain-le-Vieil', f.142-43 (28 March 1591).
67. Paris, AN, H2 1809, f.105-106 (5 December 1648) and 703-705 (20 June 1650); Paris, AN, H2 1903 (17 and 26 March 1649); Paris, AN, H2 1903-2 (19 April and 30 June 1650); Paris, AN, *H2 1811 (30 August 1650 and 17 March 1652); Paris, BnF, MS fr. 21633, excerpts of the records of the Parlement, f.75-82 (22 June 1649), and edict of the king, f.87-89 (August 1651).

that they entered houses en masse, intruding with great clamour, to press for the success of their demands. We all saw them storm the great hall of the Palais in great number, crying out with importunity to obtain [satisfaction].[68]

On 22 June 1649, the Parlement ruled in favour of the women, requiring the *placier* to reimburse the amounts paid in excess since 1648. This was as much as 80 *livres* per year for the fish retailers, though the *placier* maintained he had never required more than was the custom when he had taken over the lease of the *ferme*. The saga dragged on. In April 1650, the first year of the renewed lease was nearly at an end. It became known that Le Juge, shortly after having signed the lease, had subcontracted all of the Marché-Neuf lots to the market cooper, with the exception of the butchers' shops which he kept for himself. He was undoubtedly relieved to be so easily rid of the market women. The annual cost of the *sous-fermage* was 3400 *livres*, nearly half of his own lease of 7400 *livres*, and at first it seemed a good deal. However, the rules of the game changed for the *sous-fermier*, to the benefit of the stall keepers whose yearly fees would no longer exceed 3 *livres*. Feeling cheated, the cooper had the Parlement annul his agreement, leaving Le Juge in no position to pay his debts to the city. To ease Le Juge's situation, the *prévôt* agreed to reduce the lease fees by one quarter of the initial value, no doubt aware that the butcher would find it difficult to cover his costs without taking certain liberties with the tariffs. The city itself was in an awkward position – it was precisely because the *placier* liked to line his own pockets that it could expect a good price for the Marché-Neuf lease. In point of fact, the *prévôt* would turn a blind eye on the new rental fees for the fish tubs Le Juge introduced scarcely three months later. In its defence, the city maintained that the enclosed and lidded tubs the fishmongers used had not been mentioned in the June 1649 agreement. Since those spaces were therefore worth more, it behoved the accredited *placier* to charge fittingly.[69]

68. Paris, AN, MS *H2 1811, 'Cause des lettres patentes obtenues par les maitresses de la confrairie Ste-Anne et de St-Louis en l'église de Saint-Germain-le-Vieil pour la jouissance des places du marché Neuf' (17 March 1652). The descendants of the worthy *revendeuses* who challenged the queen are indeed *Dames de la Halle* who, after storming the Bastille, marched to Versailles to lay their grievances before the king.

69. Claude Le Juge renewed his lease of the *ferme du Marché-Neuf* one last time

In response, the market women launched their own rebellion with the king in the hope that he would freeze tariffs for good at the preferential rate they had obtained in 1649. The king acceded to their demands in August 1651, 'following in this matter the example set by Saint Louis and the kings who had succeeded him, as endorsed by the queen mother and regent'.[70] In reply, the city filed an objection, the proceedings of which would last over ten years.[71] In the midst of this tug of war, the market women, in a symbolic act of resistance, transferred their confraternity from Saint-Germain-le-Vieil to the Sainte-Chapelle in the Palais de justice – and, in essence, to the king and the *bailli*.[72]

Several elements of the city's offensive are worthy of mention here. First, the *prévôt* rejected the legitimacy of the women's 'so-called confraternity'. He accused the *revendeuses* of abusing privileges they had so graciously been granted in the past. They thought to rise above their station, colouring what was a purely mercantile enterprise with religiosity. But he was no fool: it was the women's craftiness, not their devotion, which motivated their actions. Furthermore, the *prévôt* claimed, their society violated the laws and decrees of François Ier, Charles IX and Henri III in the Estates General of Blois. All three kings had forbidden artisans and craftsmen from 'colluding with each other' on pain of corporal punishment, precisely to prevent the creation of monopolies. 'This union', the *prévôt* wrote,

> sets a dangerous precedent and no good will come of it. The fishmongeresses of the Hall have repeatedly taken justice into their own hands and will do as much again [...] no sooner had the women of the Marché-Neuf won their suit against the city, usurping the city's assets and property, than they claimed that their confraternity dedicated to God was in truth a triumph against the magistrates, inciting the people to oppose those who have authority over them. Their institution is against all laws both human and divine.[73]

---

in 1654. Paris, AN, H2 1813, f.1-2 (12 August 1654); a man named Caron, a bourgeois from Paris, succeeded him in 1660.

70. Paris, BnF, MS fr. 21633, edict of the king, f.87-89 (August 1651). For more on the proceedings, see Paris, AN, H2 1905-1 (20 December 1651), and *H2 1812, f.28 (27 January 1653).

71. Paris, AN, H2 1819, petition by the city to the king against the *revendeuses*, f.24-28 (9 September 1664); H2 1905-1 (3 March 1665); BV, *H2 1819, f.199 (23 July 1665).

72. Paris, AN, H2 1819, f.24-28 (9 September 1664).

73. Paris, AN, *H2 1811, f.663-64 (17 March 1652).

The *prévôt* maintained such a confraternity should never have been registered without first consulting the city magistrates on the advisability of its creation. Furthermore, he insisted, the low rental fee set in 1649 had been a largely symbolic gesture meant to curb the women's violent behaviour. It was to have remained in effect only for the duration of the agreement with Le Juge. Once the tumult of the Fronde had subsided, it was not to have been extended. The city's rights, assets and even its property had been usurped, the *prévôt* claimed. Nevertheless, in 1666, the Parlement issued the letters patent to cap market fees, effectively undermining the *prévôt*'s authority over the women who, from then on, would turn for support to the king, their new protector, or to his servant, the lieutenant of police.

The saga does not end here: the 1649 and 1651 decisions had made the fishmongeresses 'insolent' and 'overconfident'. The bakers had struck a deal with the city, also reducing their rent to 3 *livres* if they moved from the building fronts to within the market limits. But the fishmongeresses were jealous of the rights they had fought so hard to acquire. Referencing the two rulings in their favour, they asked the police to overturn the bakers' agreement, demanding they be charged a higher fee under the pretext that they did not contribute to the fish sellers' confraternity. The original 1649 and 1651 rulings, the fish sellers argued, had never provided for the preferential treatment of the bakers.[74]

By and large, the *revendeuses* were constantly at loggerheads with the bakers who, twice a week, obstructed both market and passageways with their carts, their goods and their horses that overturned stalls. This was two days too many for the other market sellers. It is likely why, in 1719, during reconstruction work on the arches of the Petit-Pont, the *revendeuses* stubbornly refused to relocate from the Marché-Neuf to the quai des Orfèvres with the bakers. Yet the Marché-Neuf was the only space in close proximity to the Petit-Pont where the rubble from the construction could be unloaded. The city had no desire to tolerate holding a market there while the work was ongoing: 'The bakers have complied to our request and resettled in the space we had indicated [...] but the women who sell other types of goods have not yet deigned to comply, continuing to occupy many of the stalls in the Marché-Neuf and the surrounding avenues, which hinders both

74. Paris, BnF, MS fr. 21633, 'Mémoire concernant le Marché Neuf', f.65-66, n.d. (after 1651).

the delivery of stones and the work of the stonemasons.'[75] The market women clearly refused to have their movements dictated to them; on the contrary, they intended to occupy the quai Saint-Michel as they saw fit – especially while the bakers were away.

The archives abound with similar examples of the independent inclinations with which authorities were forced to contend. In March 1677, the Marché-Neuf saw a significant increase in the flow of people making their way to Notre-Dame to celebrate the Stations of the Cross, in honour of the jubilee. Given the recent demolition of the main building in the market centre, 'there was sufficient place in the Marché' to take in the women who normally set up shop in front of the houses lining the way.[76] On 6 March, the city again reiterated its prohibition against setting up there, as it only added to the obstructions and inconvenience. On 23 March, however, the bottleneck had still not eased. City officers making their rounds could do nothing more than relocate some of the women displaying their goods in the market entrance near Notre-Dame to other house fronts where they would be less of a nuisance.[77] Authorities were powerless against these women, who ruled the market, and had no other choice but to negotiate with them.

Yet, as previously noted, many were the women who agreed to rent their space from the *placier*. As he would soon find out, however, they would subsequently do as they pleased. In 1701, the *placier* filed a *mémoire* with the lieutenant general detailing the daily ploys to disrupt 'the order the women who occupy market spaces were duty-bound to uphold'.[78] Once the women had entered the market and the *placier* had allotted their space, the women formed such a tightknit community that he was left once again without authority. Some women would move on the sly to an empty space they judged more convenient. Others exchanged spaces or took over an absent friend's nearby lot so it would not be reassigned, 'on their personal authority' and unbeknownst to the *placier*.[79] Some paid for two

---

75. This had become necessary as the bridge was in a state of ruin, especially following the fire that had occurred on 26 April 1718. Paris, BnF, MS fr. 21633, police ordinance, f.138-39 (3 June 1719). The *placier* would also relocate to the quai des Orfèvres and continue charging for cleaning services.
76. See note 22.
77. Paris, AN, H2 1826, f.228 (6 and 23 March 1677).
78. Paris, BnF, MS 21688, f.56-57 (14 April 1701).
79. In the markets falling within the jurisdiction of the Domaine de la ville, permission to hold a stand was rescinded if the market seller was absent for

or three adjacent spaces in addition to their own, leaving them unoccupied to prevent women selling similar wares – or perhaps to stop some spiteful busybody from setting up in their proximity. Still others sublet the extra stalls, claiming that they wished to keep them for extended family members. Once the *revendeuses* were ensconced in the marketplace, it seems the *placier* no longer had any control over them.

For all intents and purposes, the women set their own terms when they agreed to respect the line the city had drawn around the Marché-Neuf. Their goal was to maintain some sort of autonomy – and the city had every interest in tolerating their independence if it wished to see vendors in the market. Otherwise, the women might well prefer to set up as they had always done, in front of houses. More often than not, this was done with the consent of homeowners and tenants – the women enjoyed considerable leeway with the principal occupants of the residential buildings in the Marché-Neuf, who were themselves not above turning a profit from their living storefronts. The orders to relocate to within the market – and they were legion – also instructed the residents not to sanction the sellers' presence. The August 1674 ordinance was crystal clear and unequivocal, but, to the *placier*'s consternation, and that of the city, 'not a single person would obey it'.

***

Marketplaces offer unique opportunities to observe the mise en scène of social life, rich with drama and amplified through the multiple gestures and behaviours these spaces licensed or proscribed in turn. Markets were so much more than mere settings for commercial exchange – they were an integral part of the urban dynamic. All over Paris, vendors thronged the streets for lack of sufficient spaces in official markets. These women contributed to supplying goods to the capital and, as such, their extraordinarily diversified realities required careful, constant consideration from both the city and the police. There was much at stake – order, hygiene, subsistence, finances, urban planning – but it all entailed occupying the space, navigating the social and professional negotiations which made occupation possible,

---

three or more consecutive days, which might complicate matters or result in arrangements with friends to create the appearance that the space was occupied.

and coming to terms with the various manners in which power was exercised.

The Marché-Neuf, on a much smaller scale, helps us decipher the interplay between the various actors who infused life into the urban environment. It shows us how, in the gaps between imposed rules, the actors – women – occupied their territory, and in so doing demonstrated a self-determined capacity to take action as a king's subjects, as *citadines*; and how they fashioned their own agency to gain leverage with the authorities. Competing – even opposing – interests were at play in the Marché-Neuf: the fishmonger's marketplace was certainly not the marketplace of the *placier*, nor that of the authorities. But this plurality resulted in ongoing collective and social negotiations which, in the end, kept the market open each day and allowed each social actor to exist as they would.

Throughout the early modern period, and certainly since Saint Louis had bestowed upon their destitute ancestors the right to set up stalls along the quai Saint-Michel, market women had mobilised, clamoured for their due and struggled to preserve their privileges. Many joined their kinswomen to work the market – sisters, mothers and daughters sometimes toiled together over ten, fifteen or even twenty years. Their constant presence bears witness to their desire to ply their trade in the heart of Paris, the highly sought-after location which was the Marché-Neuf market, which linked the Palais de justice to the cathedral, and where, as an added bonus, they could find a home. They had begun to congregate there well before the city had formalised the Marché-Neuf, and had never displayed the slightest proclivity towards abandoning the premises despite the hardships they suffered. It was 'their' market. In many ways, it gave them a means to exist, more especially through their words and through the seemingly unrelenting battles waged. Time and again, in this arena, they would expend their energy to be seen, heard and acknowledged. Let the *prévôt*, the police, the *bailli* – even the king – beware!

II

The police and their officers: imposing and negotiating authority

'A breeding ground for spies and informers': the Châtelet police and the surveillance of Parisian sociabilities

VINCENT MILLIOT

Université Paris 8, IDHE.S

Translated by Nicole Charley

'Espionage', L.-S. Mercier lamented in *Tableau de Paris*, 'has destroyed the bonds of trust and friendship.' Who better than he could express the radical conflict between Châtelet police practices and sociability, that 'art of pleasantly socialising with one's fellow men', which men of the Enlightenment exalted to the rank of social virtue? For Mercier, the 'odious investigations which poisoned social life' did not merely transform 'citizens into enemies, hesitant to open up to one another'. They perverted, corrupted and debased public opinion because only the most frivolous of subjects might be publicly debated. This muzzling caused the people to lose 'all concept of civic and political responsibility', to bow and scrape at the altar of official interpretation. Surveillance led to ignorance and fostered bitter prejudices. When the police constricted free social intercourse, and the circulation of texts and ideas, they interfered with both the advent of an enlightened society and the progress of 'human understanding'.[1]

Lenoir, a former lieutenant general of police, held quite the opposite opinion. In a chapter on 'Security' in his *Mémoires*, he describes the development of police surveillance as a response to the accelerated transformation of the practices of sociability in the 1780s. For the chief of police under Louis XVI, it was the changes that occurred 'in the principles, in the morals, and in society' that incited the police – protectors of public order – to 'engage in surveillance

---

1. Louis-Sébastien Mercier, *Tableau de Paris* (1781-1788), ed. Jean-Claude Bonnet, 2 vols (Paris, 1994), ch.59, 'Espions', and ch.61, 'Hommes de la police', vol.1, p.156-58 and 161-64.

measures'.[2] Lenoir makes a distinction between the 'maisons de bonne compagnie', from the Académie to the salons, and the more worrisome and increasingly numerous circles, public houses, clubs and other gatherings of 'illicit reputation' which he 'had orders to tolerate'.[3] This tolerance required certain 'precautionary measures' such as espionage, in keeping with habitual Châtelet police practices, which almost systematically favoured prevention over repression.[4]

Notwithstanding his criticisms, Mercier did concede that 'there was good alongside the bad.' The police protected honest men by eliminating the 'très mauvais sujets' (the 'bad apples') through their system of informants.[5] However, pamphlets published on the eve and at the start of the Revolution were no longer burdened by such nuances. The denunciation of 'widespread surveillance' was one of the major criticisms formulated against the office of the *lieutenant général de police*. Surveillance was one of the characteristic traits of the police's 'despotism', and was closely associated with their desire to systematically record and collect information. It was a driving force behind the construct of the *légende noire*. The institution was thought to be gangrened from its highest echelons to its lowest ranks, corrupted through and through by uncontrolled arbitrariness.

This 'legend' does not, however, account for the problematic relationship between the transformations affecting the social lives of city dwellers during the Enlightenment, and the evolution of police practices in the years following the wave of reforms fostered under Colbert in 1667. In a sense, police actors were the cause as well as the object of this evolving relationship.[6] Far from being a foreign

2.   Vincent Milliot, *Un Policier des Lumières, suivi de Mémoires de J. C. P. Lenoir, ancien lieutenant général de police de Paris, écrits en pays étrangers dans les années 1790 et suivantes* (Seyssel, 2011).

3.   Jean-Charles-Pierre Lenoir, *Mémoires*, ch.6, 'Sûreté', Bibliothèque municipale d'Orléans (BmO), Fonds ancien, MS 1422, in Milliot, *Un Policier des Lumières*, p.624-25. On the increasing surveillance of meetings of journeyman societies, see Steven Laurence Kaplan, 'Réflexions sur la police du monde du travail, 1700-1815', *Revue historique* 529 (1979), p.17-77; Michael Sonenscher, *Work and wages: natural law, politics and the eighteenth-century French trades* (New York, 1989).

4.   For a good example of policing in the book trade, see Jean-Dominique Mellot *et al.*, *La Police des métiers du livre à Paris au siècle des Lumières* (Paris, 2017); Francis Freundlich, *Le Monde du jeu à Paris, 1715-1800* (Paris, 1995).

5.   Vincent Milliot, *'L'Admirable Police': tenir Paris au siècle des Lumières* (Ceyzérieu, 2016), introduction (p.16-18) and ch.10 (p.331-59).

6.   See the essay by Laurence Croq in the present volume.

or unfamiliar 'body', the officers of the Châtelet were participants in the networks and practices of clientage, influence peddling and sociability in the neighbourhoods and parishes.[7] But the evolution of their duties and of their professional practices in the eighteenth century contributed towards reinforcing their control, if not their dominance, of all forms of social regulation.[8] Lenoir recalls in his memoirs that the officers of the Châtelet relied on various *auxiliaires naturels* to supply their information network, ease tensions and keep watch on illegal goings-on in the twenty police districts. These *auxiliaires* were the principal merchants, the master craftsmen and those in manufacturing trades, as well as tavern keepers, landlords and innkeepers, householders and principal tenants. Add to this list the parish priests, who knew the 'soul' of every citizen.[9] Each of these played a particular part in their immediate community and in the everyday sociability that punctuated work, family and domestic life, leisure activities, and the principal rites of social and religious integration. The moments and spaces of sociability were fast becoming circumscribed by a tangle of administrative obligations dictated by the Châtelet police.[10]

The police were nevertheless confounded by the underworld and its criminal organisations. They were equally so when confronted with the 'liberal' sociability which was developing in cities during

---

7.   Justine Berlière, *Policer Paris au siècle des Lumières: les commissaires du quartier du Louvre dans la seconde moitié du XVIIIe siècle* (Paris, 2012); Rachel Couture, '"Inspirer la crainte, le respect et l'amour du public": les inspecteurs de police parisiens, 1740-1789', doctoral dissertation, Université du Québec à Montréal and Université de Caen Basse-Normandie, 2013. See also the works of Robert Descimon, Laurence Croq, Nicolas Lyon-Caen, David Garrioch and Mathieu Maraud, which all deal with the Parisian bourgeoisie. For example, Laurence Croq and Nicolas Lyon-Caen, 'La notabilité parisienne entre la police et la ville: des définitions aux usages sociaux et politiques au XVIIIe siècle', in *La Notabilité urbaine, Xe-XVIIIe siècles*, ed. Laurence Jean-Marie (Caen, 2007), p.125-57; David Garrioch, *The Formation of the Parisian bourgeoisie, 1690-1830* (Cambridge, MA, and London, 1996).

8.   David Garrioch, 'The people of Paris and their police in the eighteenth century: reflections on the introduction of a "modern" police force', *European history quarterly* 24 (1994), p.511-35, and 'The police of Paris as enlightened social reformers', *Eighteenth century life* 16:1 (1992), p.43-59.

9.   Lenoir, *Mémoires*, BmO, Fonds ancien, MS 1421-23.

10. Vincent Milliot, 'La surveillance des migrants et des lieux d'accueil à Paris du XVIe siècle aux années 1830', in *La Ville promise: mobilités et accueil à Paris (fin XVIIe-début XIXe siècle)*, ed. Daniel Roche (Paris, 2000), p.21-76.

the Enlightenment. Officially sanctioned by neither Church nor state, such sociability was based on individual membership instead of the obligation to adhere to a group in the well-defined 'social chain' prescribed by the doctrine of organicism.[11] Which police assets could be trusted in these cases? How should the police adapt or reclassify their comprehension of the social world, gain better control, shape sociability? Where could they draw the line between legitimate, acceptable sociability, and that which menaced social order and was thus to be prohibited or monitored? Answering these questions means confronting the thorny subject of surveillance head on.[12]

The abundant literature on the Parisian police provides us with a number of observations on the surveillance of individuals and places of sociability, from cabarets to salons, brothels and Masonic lodges. Even so, in-depth studies of 'espionage' in eighteenth-century Paris are few and far between.[13] The difficulties in researching this subject reside in the state of extant sources, which are scattered and often incomplete. Where they do exist, they cast only partial light on the subject. Police reports, journal entries (*mémoires*) and witness accounts are a primary resource, but whose exact intent must always

11. This concept is present in Lenoir's memoirs as well as in a speech given by the *avocat général* of the Parlement, Séguier; 'Discours du 12 mars 1776', in Jules Flammermont, *Remontrances du parlement de Paris*, vol.3, p.345, quoted in Steven Laurence Kaplan, *La Fin des corporations* (Paris, 2001), p.94-95.

12. A subject which has nourished the meanderings of traditional French historiography. See Jean-Marc Berlière, 'Histoire de la police, quelques réflexions sur l'historiographie française: présentation du dossier', *Criminocorpus* (2008), special issue: *Histoire de la police*, http://journals.openedition.org/crimino-corpus/73 (last accessed on 22 January 2024). Gérard Noiriel offers another perspective in 'Les pratiques policières d'identification des migrants et leurs enjeux pour l'histoire des relations de pouvoir: contribution à une réflexion en "longue durée"', in *Police et migrants en France, 1667-1939*, ed. Marie-Claude Blanc-Chaléard (Rennes, 2001), p.115-32.

13. Some light has nonetheless been shed on the subject. See Erica-Marie Benabou, *La Prostitution et la police des mœurs au XVIIIᵉ siècle* (Paris, 1987), and Nina Kushner, *Erotic exchanges: the world of elite prostitution in eighteenth-century Paris* (Ithaca, NY, 2013). More generally, and in the context of diplomatic, military and economic activities, Alain Dewerpe, *Espion: une anthropologie historique du secret d'Etat contemporain* (Paris, 1994); Lucien Bely, *Espions et ambassadeurs au temps de Louis XIV* (Paris, 1990); Paolo Preto, *I servizi segreti di venezia: spionaggio e controspionaggio ai tempi della Serenissima* (Milan, 2010); Stéphane Genet, *Les Espions des Lumières: actions secrètes et espionnage militaire sous Louis XV* (Paris, 2013).

be questioned and interpreted by the historian.[14] For information on those who *travaillent à la police*, the informants, there is what we can glean from the archives of the *commissaires enquêteurs-examinateurs* who worked at the Châtelet and what subsists of the archives of the office of the lieutenant general deposited at the Bastille.[15] Reports and registers produced by the *inspecteurs de la Sûreté*, documents written by the morals inspectors or the inspectors of the book trade, personal files of prisoners, royal decrees, police *gazetins* (internal compilations of informant reports) also provide a mass of information, albeit with many chronological gaps. Finally, there are the entry records of Bicêtre, where the *mauvais sujets* who 'betrayed' the police were imprisoned, as well as the archives of the Ministère des Affaires étrangères.[16] They all touch on the broad spectrum of surveillance practices. Even so, whole facets of the system, such as how surveillance was financed, are missing. Only a rough sketch of the problem can be drawn.

However, before delving into what it meant to work à la police or drawing conclusions on the relationships between the police and sociability in eighteenth-century Paris, this essay will begin by exploring how shifts in urban society were linked to transformations in police practices.

14. Jean-Baptiste-Charles Lemaire, 'La police de Paris en 1770: mémoire inédit composé par ordre de G. de Sartine, sur la demande de Marie-Thérèse', ed. André Gazier, *Mémoires de la Société de l'histoire de Paris* 5 (1879), p.1-131; Lenoir, *Mémoires*; Nicolas Toussaint Le Moyne, dit Des Essarts, *Dictionnaire universel de police contenant l'origine et les progrès de cette partie importante de l'administration civile en France*, 8 vols (Paris, Moutard, 1786-1790).

15. Vincent Denis, 'Quand la police a le goût de l'archive: réflexions sur les archives de la police de Paris au XVIIIe siècle', in *Pratiques d'archives à l'époque moderne:. Europe, mondes coloniaux*, ed. Maria-Pia Donato et Anne Saada (Paris, 2019), p.183-203.

16. Paris, Bibliothèque de l'Arsenal (Ars.), Archives de la Bastille (MS Bastille), 10028, papers of Inspector Buhot, responsible for policing foreigner activities (1758); Ars., MS Bastille, 10249, surveillance of foreign residents in Paris (1749-1752); Ars., MS Bastille, 10283-93, officer reports presented to the *lieutenant général de police* (1725, 1729-1748, 1750, 1753-1754, 1761, 1767); La Courneuve, Archives du ministère des Affaires étrangères (AAE), immigration control (CE, 1-82; 1771-1791). Concerning the *gazetins de police*, see Paris, Ars., MS Bastille, 10155-70 (1726-1741). I am grateful to Laurence Croq for sharing these discoveries in the Bicêtre registries, Paris, Archives publiques des Hôpitaux de Paris (APHP), 1Q2/1-164, Bicêtre, 1725-1950.

Shifts in urban society and in police practices

Historiography generally characterises eighteenth-century cities, especially the larger ones, as 'sociable'.[17] Cities were a testing ground for the accelerated transformations in the foundations and practices of sociability. These changes were characterised by the development of an 'elective' sociability free of the officially sanctioned forms endorsed by religious and civic authorities such as academies, brotherhoods of faith and *sociétés de reconnaissance*.[18] Elective sociability was based on voluntary membership, while traditional sociability meant allegiance to an official body, and adherence to the hierarchical system of privileges and offices of the *Ancien Régime*. The one did not necessarily undermine or exclude the other. New circles of sociability willingly preserved the distinctions of rank of *Ancien Régime* society.[19] There was a hybridisation of practices and morals, rather than a clearly defined rupture. Nonetheless, this new sociability marked the expansion of the private sphere and its developing autonomy in the face of traditional powers. It favoured the establishment of a public sphere capable of criticism, where individuals saw themselves as peers and made collective use of their reasoning.[20]

For the *Ancien Régime* police, the particularly subversive potential of the principle of elective membership, at a time when the freedom to associate was not recognised, must be underlined. Belonging to an official body was a crucial element of social order, of the instruction of discipline, and of deference due to superiors. The intense conflicts which resulted from the attempt to abolish corporations in 1776 clearly underscore the obsessive fear the police had of the anarchy that a society of deregulated, de-incorporated 'individuals' would

---

17. Dominique Poulot, *Les Lumières* (Paris, 2000); *Le Temps des capitales culturelles, XVIIIe-XXe siècles*, ed. Christophe Charle (Seyssel, 2009).
18. Maurice Agulhon, *Pénitents et francs-maçons de l'ancienne Provence: essai sur la sociabilité méridionale* (Paris, 1968); Daniel Roche, *Le Siècle des Lumières en province: académies et académiciens provinciaux, 1680-1789*, 2 vols (Paris, 1989); Pierre-Yves Beaurepaire, 'La "fabrique" de la sociabilité', *Dix-huitième siècle* 46 (2014), p.85-105.
19. Pierre-Yves Beaurepaire, *L'Espace des francs-maçons: une sociabilité européenne au XVIIIe siècle* (Rennes, 2003); Antoine Lilti, *The World of the salons: sociability and worldliness in eighteenth-century Paris* (2005; Oxford, 2015).
20. Stéphane Van Damme, 'Farewell Habermas? Deux décennies d'études sur l'espace public', in *L'Espace public au Moyen Age: débat autour de Jürgen Habermas*, ed. Patrick Boucheron and Nicolas Offenstadt (Paris, 2015), p.43-61.

create.[21] The constant efforts of the Parisian police, which increased after 1750, to organise, register and make an inventory of the world of 'liberal' trades, to identify how they fit within the urban environment, demonstrates the extent to which the police were eager to codify social interactions and control social taxonomy.[22]

To complete the panorama of challenges faced by the police, we must include yet other dynamics which affected Parisian society and whose effects multiplied over the course of the eighteenth century. For one, the general population enjoyed high literacy rates, and all manner of printed material circulated widely, on top of the forms of oral communication still very much alive.[23] This only heightened the police's desire to monitor and control rumours and public discourse, and not only when key subjects of censure – the king, the Church, morality – were concerned. Public speech and opinions were enough to influence current events or even incriminate a fellow citizen.[24]

A general growth in consumption is another factor which brought change to this highly populated city. Both wealth and inequality were on the rise, and status distinctions were starting to blur.[25] *Hôtels particuliers* and *garnis*, cafés and reading rooms were added to the more traditional spheres of sociability such as cabarets, the streets and other public spaces.[26] Changes in urban planning were also very influential. The rapid expansion of street lighting allowed for an extended use of public spaces and promoted night life, as evidenced in the multiplication of performance halls, theatres and concerts.

21. Kaplan, *La Fin des corporations*.
22. Jeffry Kaplow, *The Names of kings: the Parisian laboring poor in the eighteenth century* (New York, 1972); Milliot, *'L'Admirable Police'*, p.199-232 and 281-96.
23. Robert Darnton, *Poetry and the police: communication networks in eighteenth-century Paris* (Cambridge, 2010); Lisa Jane Graham, *If the king only knew: seditious speech in the reign of Louis XV* (Charlottesville, VA, 2000); Daniel Roche, *France in the Enlightenment* (1993; Cambridge, MA, 2000); Arlette Farge, *Dire et mal dire: l'opinion publique au XVIIIᵉ siècle* (Paris, 1992).
24. A thought that obsessed the magistrate Lenoir; see Milliot, *Un Policier des Lumières*; Robert Darnton, *The Devil in the holy water, or the Art of slander from Louis XIV to Napoleon* (Philadelphia, PA, 2010); Antoine Lilti, *The Invention of celebrity* (2014; New York, 2017).
25. Daniel Roche, *The Culture of clothing: dress and fashion in the Ancien Régime* (1989; Cambridge, 1997); Michael Kwass, *Contraband: Louis Mandrin and the making of a global underground* (Cambridge, 2014).
26. Thomas Brennan, *Public drinking and popular culture in eighteenth-century Paris* (Princeton, NJ, 1988); *Sociétés et cabinets de lecture entre Lumières et romantisme*, ed. Christiane Genequand (Geneva, 1995).

Paris was a city in which the spiritual, administrative, financial and cultural elite were concentrated.[27] In the eighteenth century – and thus well before the railway revolution and the widespread exodus of the rural populations – Paris was also a city that welcomed a sizeable though often impermanent flow of migrants.[28] They were organised by industrial sector, around workshops, building projects or centres of refuge, all of which offered various means of integration into urban society and the labour market.[29] Far from being the only factor, increasing migration was not without effect on new bonds of solidarity and configurations of sociability. The seeds of a separation between work and living environments were sown during this period. The expansion of the private sphere beyond the local police station and neighbourhood likewise took root.[30] This evolution made the regulation of social relationships more complex because they were no longer dependent on local notables or religious and fraternal ties. We are still far from absolute and individualistic anonymity, but the functionalist reactions of the police to the emergence of more impersonal social ties continued to be a central concern.

The Châtelet police did not remain passive when confronted with social evolution and the new social expectations that arose from it. The density of urban society and the fear of seeing acts of unlawfulness proliferate in the vastly expanding city provoked d'Argenson, at the end of Louis XIV's reign, to overhaul the practices and protocols of the police,[31] enabling them to become more proactive, responsive and autonomous. Undercover surveillance and secret operations were favoured over the transparency of public interventions. A new body of police inspectors was also created, which answered directly to the lieutenant general and enjoyed considerable autonomy from the

27. Simone Delattre, *Les Douze heures noires: la nuit à Paris au XIXᵉ siècle* (Paris, 2000); Alain Cabantous, *Histoire de la nuit, XVIIᵉ-XVIIIᵉ siècle* (Paris, 2009).

28. Daniel Roche, *The People of Paris: an essay in popular culture in the 18th century* (1981; Berkeley, CA, 1987); Roche, *La Ville promise*.

29. Annie Moulin, *Les Maçons de la Creuse: les origines du mouvement* (Clermont-Ferrand, 1994); Laurence Fontaine, *Histoire du colportage en Europe* (Paris, 1993).

30. David Garrioch, *The Making of revolutionary Paris* (Berkeley, CA, 2002).

31. Paolo Piasenza, *Polizia e città: strategie d'ordine, conflitti e rivolte a Parigi tra sei e settecento* (Bologna, 1990); Patrice Peveri, 'Clandestinité et nouvel ordre policier dans le Paris de la Régence: l'arrestation de Louis-Dominique Cartouche', in *Clandestinités urbaines: les citadins et les territoires du secret (XVIᵉ-XXᵉ siècle)*, ed. Sylvie Aprile and Emmanuelle Retaillaud-Bajac (Rennes, 2008), p.151-70.

Chatelet commissaires.[32] These new practices are clearly at odds with the more consultative approach the police had previously been taking.[33]

The history of this department, in its infancy, is chaotic. By mid-century it had finally achieved stability, and had acquired a certain legitimacy with the population thanks to improvements in recruitment practices, efficiency of service, and compromises it had made in order to better integrate into local neighbourhood life and Parisian society.[34] The main duties of the police inspectors, as stated by Commissaire Lemaire towards the end of the 1760s, 'amounted to observation and enquiry'.[35] They rarely personally conducted either, and after 1740 were seen as 'supervisors', though it was unclear how many were under their supervision, and who were their staff, informants, spies or *mouches*. In addition to their role as supervisors and representatives of the court when in the field, inspectors largely spent their time writing summary reports, creating files and keeping records, which facilitated the cross-checking of information and fed the never-ending exchange of information between a segment of the commissaires, the lieutenant of police and his offices. The development of the Châtelet police network indeed resulted in an elaborate bureaucratic information structure which – over and above its visible components, the forty-eight commissaires and their clerks, the twenty-odd inspectors, armed law-enforcement forces such as the Paris Guard (Garde de Paris) and the French Guards (Régiment des gardes françaises) of the Maison militaire du roi – depended on a more-or-less underground infrastructure.

Nonetheless, the 'widespread' and 'omnipresent' espionage which was denounced by pamphlet authors in 1789 did not precisely reflect reality. Surveillance was in fact tailored to each specific context.[36] The monitoring of public spaces, city and market squares,

---

32. In 1708, there were forty. After 1740, there were officially twenty. See Milliot, *'L'Admirable Police'*, ch.2, p.73-137.

33. Paolo Piasenza, 'Opinion publique, identité des institutions, "absolutisme": le problème de la légalité à Paris entre le XVIIe et le XVIIIe siècle', *Revue historique* 587 (1993), p.97-142.

34. Mathieu Marraud, 'Le cérémonial urbain à Paris au XVIIIe siècle: représentation et négociation politique', in *Les Histoires de Paris (XVIe-XVIIIe siècle)*, ed. Thierry Belleguic and Laurent Turcot, 2 vols (Paris, 2012), vol.1, p.245-67.

35. Lemaire, 'La police de Paris en 1770', p.64-65.

36. Pierre Manuel, *La Police de Paris dévoilée, par Pierre Manuel, l'un des administrateurs de 1789*, 2 vols (Paris, n.n., 1790).

streets, and crowd densities during holidays and festivals stemmed from a set of defined objectives: crowd control, the suppression of pickpocketing, the prevention of dangerous outbursts of emotion particularly during periods of soaring inflation. Surveillance only coincidentally overlapped with the pressing obligation to censor speech or control the rumours which shaped public opinion. Some of the locations under watch in these cases were both 'private' (circles, clubs, salons) and public (cafés, performance halls). Some were the habitual meeting places of working-class sociability or cabals (such as cabarets), while others were new, trendier, more socially diverse settings.[37] A completely separate social sphere included the activities and places which bordered on the forbidden or the clandestine, such as gaming circles, prostitution houses or even Masonic lodges. The techniques of surveillance and information gathering were very similar in all of these situations, but the principal players in the information game were not necessarily the same.

But who exactly were the informants and observers collaborating with the police, and what was the rationale behind their cooperation?

Travailler à la police: spying for the *Ancien Régime* police

Lenoir downplays the use of surveillance in Paris at the time of the French Revolution, but he does admit to its indispensable role in ensuring security in big cities. Lemaire and Sartine had written much the same twenty years earlier.[38] The police's exploitation of *mauvais sujets* was done in the name of public interest, to neutralise even more *mauvais sujets*. Though it may seem that the general population – including the police – shared a deep contempt for *mouches*, this viewpoint should be taken with a grain of salt.

When Lenoir evokes the transformations in Parisian sociability towards the end of the *Ancien Régime*, he also calls to mind the effort expended in 'recruiting people from the *parlements*, the clergy, amongst lawyers, doctors, Freemasons and members of those societies

37. Jeffrey S. Ravel, *The Contested parterre: public theater and French political culture, 1680-1791* (Ithaca, NY, 1999).

38. Steven Laurence Kaplan and Vincent Milliot, 'La police de Paris, une "révolution permanente"? Du commissaire Lemaire au lieutenant de police Lenoir, les tribulations du *Mémoire sur l'administration de la police* (1770-1792)', in *Réformer la police: les mémoires policiers en Europe au XVIIIᵉ siècle*, ed. Catherine Denys *et al.* (Rennes, 2009), p.69-115.

which tolerance has only encouraged to grow in number'. To dispel all doubt about the population's natural inclination to collaborate with the police, he goes on to clarify, 'I had no difficulty finding those who would provide me with reports, and at little cost.'[39] Such an account points to police information being gathered with the full consent of people of very diverse ranks and social positions, though the lack of reliable archival documentation makes it impossible to come up with a decisive number. From a few rare accounting records, we can cautiously propose a workforce of around 300 spies during the 1730s. This number peaked at 3000 under Berryer (1747-1757) and was downsized to a reasonable 1000 under Lenoir (1774-1775 and 1776-1785). But who exactly was counted in these documents? Whom did the police deem to be a spy or *observateur* (the official term used)?

In the manuscript treatise written for the court of Vienna, Lemaire presents the three categories of *observateurs* mobilised within Paris. N. Des Essarts's 1786-1789 publication, the *Dictionnaire universel de police*, also makes mention of this.[40] Lemaire's treatise gives a glimpse of the diversity in terms of types of spies, their appearances, skills and where they worked. First, there were *observateurs*, who were paid to 'inform on conversations taking place in a number of public places, where *nouvellistes* [writers of underground manuscript gazettes] assembled, and where one could sometimes find citizens in a fiery lather taking shots at the government over their conduct'. Lemaire goes on to state that 'one must choose wisely when it comes to spies. Above all, they must look presentable, that is to say well turned out, and must not be suspected of engaging in this trade.' The quality of the reports presupposed their relatively seamless integration within the group or place under surveillance, whether cafés and drinking establishments, reading rooms or circles with more selective memberships.

The second category of informants could be qualified as 'unwitting' spies (*espions 'sans le savoir'*). One 'did not pay them'; they were 'people of idle occupation and without great means, big talkers, naturally curious and with their fingers in every pie, who could with ease strike up acquaintances'. He might be describing a character straight out of *Rameau's nephew*, invited to this or that salon or to share a meal at a good table.[41]

39. Lenoir, *Mémoires*, p.624-25.
40. Lemaire, 'La police de Paris en 1770', p.65-66; Des Essarts, 'Observateurs', in *Dictionnaire universel de police*, vol.7, p.340-42.
41. Denis Diderot, *Le Neveu de Rameau*, ed. Roland Desné (Paris, 1972), p.87-192.

The third group, openly despised though cynically exploited by Lemaire and Lenoir, were the *basses mouches*. They were stationed in the 'disreputable' neighbourhoods and helped to mousetrap their unlawful peers. Paid a daily wage of 3 *livres* (plus the occasional perquisite), these informers were double agents recruited from amongst *mauvais sujets*: petty thieves, compromised *libertins*, prostitutes, the unemployed and beggars. The police expected good infiltration skills from these 'penitent collaborators' whose lifestyles placed them in contact with other delinquents. In 1747, the inspector of the Halles district, Jean Poussot, enlisted two such recruits, a beggar couple at the Dammartin fair, in today's Seine-et-Marne region. He promised them 10 *sols* per day, or half the salary of a manual labourer, plus bonuses, 'for uncovering the underground lairs of robbers'.[42] 'They don't generally last long in this profession', Lemaire explained, because they quickly outlive their usefulness once they've become 'regular employees of the police'. The police kept this category of informants under constant surveillance and did not hesitate to punish 'infidelities'. The Bastille archives overflow with profiles such as these.

In reality, the informants were recruited from all walks of life, from the wretched poor paid to watch a door or a street, to dismissed servants or those still in service, ex-convicts, or nobles owing the police a favour because of some past misdemeanour or current impecuniousness. Who was recruited was a matter of opportunity and who was targeted. What preoccupied the police the most was obtaining reliable reports. They diligently cross-referenced and verified their sources. Lenoir stated it was better to rely on informants who were indebted to the police for some reason because it meant he would be 'accurately informed'. A certain number of *auxiliaires naturels* were thus in this category. Some were under regulatory obligation to collaborate with the authorities, such as surgeons, innkeepers and landlords, whose records were regularly targeted by inspectors and commissaires.[43] So, too, were those in retail professions who were regularly required to check in with the authorities and to collaborate in the fight against theft and the trafficking or sale of stolen goods. In 1763 alone, twenty-two female retailers, five second-hand-clothes sellers (or their

---

42. Paris, Ars., MS Bastille, 10136, '6 décembre 1747'.
43. Milliot, 'La surveillance des migrants'; Christelle Rabier, 'Le "service public" de la chirurgie: administration des premiers secours et pratiques professionnelles à Paris au XVIIIᵉ siècle', *Revue d'histoire moderne et contemporaine* 58:1 (2011), p.101-27.

wives) and three dealers in second-hand goods were registered as regular collaborators with Inspector Sarraire, which demonstrates the near institutionalisation of such contributions to the police-information network.[44] In addition to fines in the case of betrayal, sanctions could include expulsion from the trade or a ban on exercising their profession, even imprisonment. In the Louvre district and in proximity of the Pont-Neuf, the collaboration of 'official', duly registered female retailers with the officers of the Châtelet is well substantiated.[45]

This category of *auxiliaires naturels* was fluid, however. It regrouped individuals who collaborated very nearly statutorily with others who were forced to do so under duress or in exchange for tolerance if their activity, while not wholly illegal, was not quite legitimate either. This grey area gave the police a significant degree of latitude with respect to its regulatory power and especially in regard to the new spaces and practices of sociability. The designation of *auxiliaires naturels*, reported Lemaire in 1779,[46] thus extended to those who ran circles of 'free' sociability such as salons, gaming circles and clubs. These gatherings were overlooked if public tranquillity was not disturbed – or at least stayed within very limited confines, such as the 'materialist and atheist' salon of the baron d'Holbach – and affront to Church, king or moral values was not perceived.[47] According to Bachaumont, any transgression of these limits gave the Palais-Royal sufficient grounds to close certain clubs or circles.[48] The police lieutenant required landlords and managers of various establishments to keep him informed of whom they received and what subjects were discussed. Permission for their businesses to remain open was contingent upon respecting these obligations.[49] For example, on 17 September 1777, the sieur Robert was authorised to reopen his club, which had been closed one month earlier, on condition that he 'give a full account of the goings-on within and that he swear no gaming would take place'. These arrangements towards the end of the *Ancien Régime* call to mind

44. Paris, Ars., MS Bastille, 10144, and Paris, Archives nationales (AN), Y 18797.
45. Berlière, *Policer Paris*, p.227-30.
46. Paris, AN, K 1021, file 3, document 89, p.3-7.
47. Daniel Roche, *Les Républicains des Lettres: gens de culture et Lumières au XVIIIᵉ siècle* (Paris, 1988), p.242-53.
48. Louis Petit de Bachaumont, in *Mémoires secrets pour servir à l'histoire de la République des Lettres en France depuis 1762 jusqu'à nos jours, ou Journal d'un observateur*, 36 vols (London, John Adamson, 1771-1789), vol.28, p.198, '10 mars 1785'.
49. Paris, AN, O¹ 488, f.568.

the system of tacit permission that existed for booksellers. Authorisation was merely given verbally but, if the police harboured any suspicions, they might follow up with an investigation – which meant surveillance – that could lead to closure.[50]

Amongst the spies favoured by the police were servants and former domestic servants, note Lemaire and Lenoir. The daily task of surveilling foreigners in the capital depended on spies the police were able to recruit from the houses of diplomats.[51] In the files on 'surveillance des étrangers' conserved at the Bastille, we see domestic servants regularly remunerated by the police, such as 'a certain Duplessis, serving in the households of MM. Gundel, Faische, Mylord Thompson, and whom M. de Marville has kept on retainer for a monthly fee of 40 *livres*; he is a *fort bon sujet* who has ferreted out particularly useful items of information'.[52] When Berryer became lieutenant general, the chief secretary Duval presented him with a list of trustworthy spies: 'Bompard is in charge of taking reports from the person who keeps watch in the household of M. le comte de Los… He is a discreet and very loyal man.'[53] The role of a servant differed from that of the keeper of a *lieu de sociabilité* who was called upon to inform the police in exchange for tolerance. The near invisibility of servants conferred on them the ability to gather more finely sifted information, capture the most intimate conversations and take note of the most furtive comings and goings. Their situation was also similar to what was expected of professional gamers who were recruited for their very ability to insinuate themselves into a particular milieu. Thus, in January of 1751, when Inspector Poussot received an order of exile from the king for Simon Pierre La Bate, *dit* le chevalier de Montblanc, he did not execute it. He explained to the lieutenant of police that 'he thought the man could be of some use in gaming parties, as he was extremely *faufilé* [well insinuated in the milieu]'. As La Bate 'seemed quite sharp and well connected', Poussot referred him to Chassaigne, the inspector in charge of gambling, 'who has since employed him' with satisfaction.[54]

50. Paris, AN, O¹ 490, Secretary of State to Lenoir, 5 October 1779, f.395.
51. La Courneuve, AAE, *Contrôle des étrangers*, vol.61, Lenoir to Vergennes, 23 July 1785; see also vol.37, 1781, and vol.53, 'Lettre du 6 août 1784 de l'inspecteur Longpré, chargé des étrangers'.
52. Paris, Ars., MS Bastille, 10283-93.
53. Paris, Ars., MS Bastille, 10293, 1747, f.5-6.
54. Paris, Ars., MS Bastille, 10136, '6 janvier 1751'.

This variation in observational vantage points – the bird's-eye view of a keeper of a hospitality business versus the perspective an 'insider' could provide – also exists when we enter the world of the illicit, such as brothels, where *auxiliaires de police* were also recruited. Eighteenth-century police officers tolerated the existence of over a dozen houses of pleasure frequented by members of 'high society' such as nobles, high-ranking magistrates, financiers and visiting foreigners in exchange for daily or weekly reports from the brothel mistresses who ran the establishments.[55] One of the most famous of these, La Dhosmont, kept up a regular correspondence with Berryer. Another couple, named Brissault, reported directly to Marais, inspector of morals.[56] The women who worked in the brothels faced an even greater pressure to collaborate with the police than their well-established brothel madams. They either cooperated or faced possible internment in a workhouse. All it took was a mention in a report by an inspector attending a police hearing.

Such observations can be found in abundance. Is it possible, however, to see beyond the stereotypical image of the turncoat delinquent, the servant, the prostitute or the swindling crook and truly identify the *observateurs*? The reports drawn up by inspectors were essentially compilations of notes communicated by their sources, most of whom were not cited. Anonymity was often a shield for those who informed for the police. Sometimes, the relationships were simply too ephemeral to merit further detail.

An inventory of the different informers who worked with the officers of the Châtelet in the second half of the eighteenth century was attempted for the Louvre district.[57] The term *mouche* is rarely found in the papers of the commissaires from this sector. There is also a distinction made between paid 'undercover' spies and the *observateurs* who were more openly employed, including those who already held administrative or desk jobs, such as clerks, subinspectors and other administrative officers. Though their social status is not always apparent in the accounts, the phrase *travailler à la police* seems at times to confer a certain dignity as well as to offer protection for those who claimed the title.

55. 'Rapports venus des maîtresses des maisons de débauche', *Papiers des inspecteurs Meusnier et Marais*, Paris, Ars., MS Bastille, 10252-53.
56. Benabou, *La Prostitution et la police des mœurs*, p.238-46.
57. Berlière, *Policer Paris*, p.358-62.

Of the fifty-two individuals catalogued, an overwhelming majority were men, both young and of a more advanced age. Of the four women who appear in the registers, two had spouses who also worked à la police, and one was the widow of a military officer. Amongst those who declared their age, the largest contingent is comprised of people aged twenty to thirty-nine; the average age was twenty-nine. Those listed in the Louvre district after 1750 could, for the most part, sign their names well enough to infer a certain level of literacy, which might well be a reflection of the literacy rate of the general population, even when including the capital's lowliest citizens.

If these observateurs engaged in a professional activity outside of their work for the police, it was rarely mentioned. Sixteen of them make no mention of any occupation; fourteen declare themselves to be 'travaillant à la police', 'avec un inspecteur', 'dans la sûreté'; ten declare they are 'attaché à un inspecteur', 'employé chez' or 'par un inspecteur'; nine claim to be clerks; only one is declared 'observateur pour la sûreté'.

When a place of residence is noted, it is more often situated in the Louvre district. Some *auxiliaires* were also settled in other neighbourhoods such as the Saint-Eustache parish, or even on the Left Bank as far as the faubourg Saint-Marcel. Still others were listed as lodging with the police inspectors for whom they worked. This was the case for a man named Lacombe, who was residing with Inspector Dumont, rue Mauconseil, in August 1769; for Jean Paulmier, who was residing with Inspector Poussot, rue Sainte-Avoye, in May of 1752; and for Romain Verdun, 'one of the clerks working under sieur Lehoux, inspector, at whose home he resided, rue Bertin Poiré'. With those who were lodged, we rise above the bracket of underground *informateurs* and collaborators to the visible portion of the police structure. This seems to support the hypothesis formulated by Alan Williams, that these clerks, or *commis*, were former *observateurs* who had been promoted.[58] The social stability as well as the revenue associated with a subaltern position within the police might therefore justify the absence of some other mentioned professional occupation. Those in the lower strata of this machine, however, operated largely under the radar.

The entry records of Bicêtre are a slightly more diversified resource, though they offer information on male auxiliaires only.[59] Bicêtre was

---

58. Alan Williams, *The Police of Paris, 1718-1789* (Bâton-Rouge, LA, 1979), p.104-11.
59. Paris, APHP, 1Q2/1-164, Bicêtre, 1725-1950; women were interned in La Pitié.

where the *mouchards de la police* who had 'failed in their duty'[60] were jailed. They were held in the narrow cells of the dungeons or in *cabanons* (small, padded cells), 'segregated from the other prisoners, as they would have been torn to pieces by those they had helped to imprison and who would recognise them'.[61] An inventory of nearly two dozen records dated between 1748 and 1786 yields seventy-one entries showing individuals who were or had formerly been working for the police. Not counting repeat offenders, this represents a force of fifty-nine *observateurs*.[62] At first glance, it seems that disloyal spies were more frequently punished during Lenoir's tenure. This apparent increase may, as Mercier has noted, be due to the favouring of Bicêtre as a choice for incarceration from 1775 to 1789.[63] Other prisons may also have welcomed unfaithful *auxiliaires*, such as For-l'Evêque until mid-century, or the Bastille.

As for geographical origins, Bicêtre records show an overwhelming majority of *informateurs* hailing from Paris and nearby suburbs such as Auteuil and Montmartre; together, they make up two thirds of these *observateurs*.[64] The remaining third came from the provinces, which corresponds exactly to the demographic trend of the city; the great mass of migrants sustaining the growth of the urban population originated from within a radius of roughly 300 kilometres around Paris. This rough sketch lends credence to the idea that long-standing membership in Parisian society and neighbourhood life was an important criterion when selecting the undercover *auxiliaires* who

60. Mercier, 'Bicêtre', in *Tableau de Paris*, vol.2, ch.604, p.250.
61. Mercier, 'Bicêtre', p.250.
62. Twenty-two registers were analysed in all: Paris, APHP, 1Q2/18-20, '1er avril 1748 au 29 sept. 1750' (Berryer magistrature, three registers): 2.5 years; 1Q2/44-48, '1er août 1765 au 30 oct. 1768' (Sartine magistrature, five registers): 3 years, 3 months; 1Q2/59-72, '1er mai 1775 au 14 mars 1786' (Albert, Lenoir and Thiroux magistratures, fourteen registers): 10 years, 10 months. There are ten repeat offenders, two of whom are three-time reoffenders. This compilation covers Lenoir's second tenure as *lieutenant général*, from 1776 to 1785, and proposes similar results, after sampling, for the periods when Berryer (1747-1757), Sartine (1759-1774), d'Albert (1775-1776) and Thiroux de Crosne (1785-1789) were in office.
63. Bicêtre entries during the tenures of Berryer, Sartine and Lenoir number one, five and seventeen interned *observateurs* respectively.
64. Out of fifty-nine incarcerated *observateurs*, thirty-six are 'Parisians' and two are from surrounding parishes (Auteuil and Montmartre), for a total of thirty-eight (or 64.4 per cent). The other nineteen (32.2 per cent) are from the provinces.

worked for the police, though it is important to nuance this criterion.[65] Parish districts declared as the original place of residence highlight the geography of the old artisanal and commercial urban centre, marked by high population densities as well as heavy circulation and industry (see Figure 8). We find the districts neighbouring Les Halles: Saint-Eustache, Saint-Germain-l'Auxerrois, Saint-Jacques-de-la-Boucherie, and the working-class, artisanal neighbourhoods with their many shelters, such as Saint-Paul. Unsurprisingly, this geographical area, marked by its westward push (towards La Madeleine and Saint-Roch) and the importance of its riverbanks, corresponds to the territory occupied by the 'theatres of violence', which we can easily imagine being infiltrated by police *observateurs*.[66] Once again, we see a highly disproportionate number of Parisian police spies (thirty out of thirty-six) residing on the Right Bank. This same disproportion of inspectors' homes in relation to their most frequent hotbeds of intervention was also the norm for quite some time.[67]

In the Bicêtre records, those of 'the calling' were comparatively youthful: the average age was just over twenty-seven, whereas it was twenty-nine in the papers of the commissaires in the Louvre district. The oldest spy in the prison records was a butcher's assistant-turned-soldier of the Garde de Paris who was fifty years old at the time of his incarceration. The youngest, a servant of Inspector Le Houx, was merely eighteen.[68] The 'youngsters' who were not yet of marriageable age, which was twenty-seven or twenty-eight in Paris at the close of the century, made up roughly half of the incarcerated spies. This image is not consistent with the one Mercier proposes. He wrote descriptions of 'de petits drôles', 'adolescent spies and sycophantic informers' plying their vile trade, soon to be corrupted by the role

65. In the early 1790s, 60 to 70 per cent of the population of the Saint-Marcel and Saint-Antoine suburbs hailed from the provinces. In 1750, at least half of all married individuals in Paris were originally from those regions. Provincial migrants are consistently over-represented in the *archives de la misère*, as well as hospital and judicial archives. See Roche, *The People of Paris*; Arlette Farge, *Le Vol d'aliments à Paris au XVIIIᵉ siècle* (Paris, 1974), p.111-28.

66. Arlette Farge and André Zysberg, 'Les théâtres de la violence à Paris au XVIIIᵉ siècle', *Annales. Economie, sociétés, civilisations* 34:5 (1979), p.984-1015; Gilles Chabaud *et al.*, 'La géographie parisienne de l'accueil', in *La Ville promise*, ed. D. Roche, p.109-71.

67. Milliot, *'L'Admirable Police'*, p.212-17.

68. Paris, APHP, 1Q2/67, '8 mars 1782, Minguet', and 1Q2/70, '15 février 1784, Marin Vassot'.

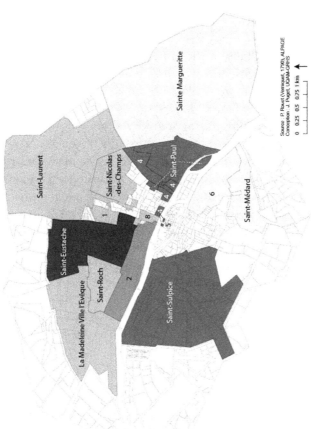

Figure 8: Geographical origins of police spies and informers. Map design: Julien Puget, Groupe de recherche en histoire des sociabilités (GRHS), Université du Québec à Montréal. Source: Paul Rouet, 'Îlots en 1791 (plan de Verniquet)', ALPAGE, Paris (2015).

1. Saint-Sauveur
2. Saint-Germain l'Auxerrois
3. Saint-Jacques de la Boucherie
4. Paroisse Saint-Gervais
5. Saint-Pierre des Arcis
6. Saint-Nicolas du Chardonnet

the police had them play.[69] However, single life did indeed reign supreme: of seventy-one declarations in the records, there are only fifteen married individuals, one widower and three with no mention of marital status. Not surprisingly, married police *observateurs* were older, on average thirty years of age and over.

In terms of professional backgrounds, we are far from the 'dregs of society' out of which 'springs public order', to quote L.-S. Mercier. Of the fifty-nine individuals imprisoned between 1748 and 1786 (some repeat offenders), twelve declared no activity other than 'travailler pour la police' and must have earned their living as professional *observateurs* alone. The rest are mostly skilled craftsmen, sometimes in luxury trades, though many were likely on the fringes of employment and frequently in bottom-level positions. There are journeymen locksmiths, glaziers, house gilders, goldsmiths, fan makers, tilers, joiners and carpenters, and apprentice tailors, wig makers, bakers, butchers, cobblers and *limonadiers* (refreshment sellers). Though the status of others is not specified, there are also cutlers, pastry cooks, stone setters – those specialised in setting gemstones into jewellery – gold and silver polishers, roofers, launderers and intaglio printmakers. The battalions of police *observateurs* jailed in Bicêtre are therefore mainly mid-level, fairly well-established representatives of urban wage earners. Still other occupations include retail or resale trades: three market vendors, two 'traders', one horse dealer. There is one barometer maker, a repeat offender, who had been a journeyman glazier four years earlier; this is a sign of how precarious these attributions were.[70] Those in unqualified service trades are rarely found: only three *observateurs* declare as their occupation *gagne-denier, commissionnaire* and *frotteur*. In addition to four traditional domestic servants and three soldiers, there are, once again, low-ranking administrative positions (two clerks, one of whom employed by an inspector), members of the urban mobility trades (three coachmen, one postilion), one apprentice surgeon and, lastly, a 'writer'. There is nothing in this assortment of trades to suggest a universe peopled exclusively by lawless, disreputable bums and brigands.

If the circumstances leading to hiring an *observateur* cannot be traced back due to the scarcity of records in the prison registers,

---

69. Mercier, 'Bicêtre', p.250.

70. Armand Crampon, a repeat offender from Picardy, states 'journeyman glazier' as his occupation on 16 March 1779 (Paris, APHP, 1Q2/63), and then 'barometer seller' on 18 May 1785 (Paris, APHP, 1Q2/71).

perhaps we can suggest a rationale behind the recruitment decisions. Beyond the 'classical' figure of the servant-spy, there are three motives which stand out. Many hired were those who were engaged in activities often associated with the fencing, transformation or dealing of stolen goods or who dealt with sensitive products such as books or images: intaglio printmakers, launderers and tailors, stone setters, precious metal polishers, goldsmiths, even various shopkeepers. Others were in trades having some connection with techniques of breaking and entering or with weapons, such as locksmiths, who could provide false keys, and cutlers. Finally, the largest group were those in trades dependent upon contact with or observation of others, from street to boutique: coachmen, odd jobbers, and those in the food, clothing and construction trades.

According to the register entries, all who were imprisoned in Bicêtre 'travaillent' or 'ont travaillé' (worked or had worked) 'pour un inspecteur', 'pour la police', 'pour la robe courte' or 'pour la sûreté'. The two phrases most frequently employed were 'pour la police' and 'pour la sûreté', the second becoming the most widely used from the 1780s onwards. The few inspectors mentioned by name were *inspecteurs de la Sûreté* Damote (1767-1770), Dutronchet (1770-1779) and Receveur (1764-1778). Bicêtre registers reveal foremost the *observateurs* who were employed by the Département de la Sûreté, which dealt with the repression of theft, an increasingly growing preoccupation for the office of the lieutenant general.

The talents required if one were to *travailler à la police* were not the qualities looked for in a *mouche* working the streets, an embassy spy, a prostitute, a professional gambler or a salon regular. The expected qualifications can be inferred from a letter written by Inspector Meusnier, head of the morals' division under Berryer's magistrature, in which he questions the reliability of an informer by the name of Girard, who worked for Inspector Framboisier. Framboisier had attributed 'superior talents' to Girard which, according to Meusnier, were subsequently offset by his 'lack of loyalty and discretion'. Girard's talents included 'always being well groomed', 'speaking decisively' and 'skill in gaining the company of servants of the highest quality'. To this list, we can add 'the art of being quick and nimble with a knife'.[71] Notwithstanding such skills, he was reproached for his secretive ways, which raised suspicion in the police: Meusnier stated that, 'throughout his employ under Framboisier's tenure, the inspector had never been

71. Paris, Ars., MS Bastille, 10248, f.298, '3 octobre 1751'.

able to ascertain his place of residence', and also added 'that it was in their interest to pierce through the mystery surrounding this man's life' since he was also employed by the magistrate. Furthermore, Girard undermined the image of the police by publicly declaring his earned wages (2000 to 3000 *livres* per annum, a relatively important sum) and boasting of his autonomy from the magistrate. His swaggering earned him a room with a view at the Bastille for the next eleven years.

Interesting disclosures and reliable reports made to one's superior officers were not enough on their own. Discretion and loyalty in all respects were the key qualities required, though what was meant by 'discretion' was open to interpretation. Inspector Sarraire firmly condemned the use of informers having stood trial in criminal proceedings that had been too widely publicised, believing that their notoriety would subsequently be a barrier to infiltrating high-risk environments. Not all his fellow officers shared this view but, as a rule, anything which could be seen to undermine the institution, its reputation or its proper functioning was actively rooted out. This is evidenced in some of the files conserved at the Bastille and the king's registers where, in addition to the *très petites gens*, *mauvais sujets*, vagabonds, crooks and gamblers, we find a great number of underlings who had behaved indiscreetly towards their inspectors.[72] Extortion, abuse of power and, especially, double-dealing and falsifying reports were severely punished.

The loyalty of an *auxiliaire naturel* towards the police was proven by faithfully executing one's duties. For resale professionals or proprietors of lodging houses, this meant keeping scrupulous records or denouncing suspicious individuals. Resellers and landlords were not of the *basse police* – on the contrary, some belonged to the class of 'established' citizens and hard-working, prosperous 'tradesmen' who contributed to ensuring the order from which all 'good citizens' benefited. Their relationships with the police were public, institutionalised. Violations of loyalty and discretion were thus met with commensurate sanctions.

Of a different nature, the loyalty expected of a *mouche* depended on the quality of the covert surveillance they provided and consisted in strictly respecting their subordination to their Châtelet officers. Should this not be the case, sanctions could be exemplary. A bootblack double agent (*contre-mouche*) who worked for smugglers and swindlers earned a one-year sentence in Bicêtre 'to serve as an example and to

72. Le Pré-Saint-Gervais, Archives de la Préfecture de police (APP), AB 362, 'Registres d'ordres du roi'.

prevent other *mouches* from falling into the same trap'.[73] It seems that such punishments were negotiable, in some sectors perhaps more than others (gaming? morals?). If the police thought they could still profit from a collaboration, and as long as the risk of scandal was not too great, they either closed their eyes on certain indiscretions or affected memory loss. If not, those they decided needed reforming could easily be replaced. Cost–benefit analyses such as these only contributed to the discourse against police corruption.

Police and sociability

The surveillance of spaces and moments of urban sociability was part of a general movement within the police organisation, which strongly encouraged the development of specialised expertise as well as the construction of a veritable information machine. The Parisian police machinery was not frozen, however. Above all, it wished to remain adaptable. But its development as well as the evolution of its methods fostered ambivalent reactions and, on the eve of the Revolution, it resisted poorly against the politicisation of sociability.

In practice, a distinction must be made between surveillance motivated by security reasons and the espionage of public or private spaces. The aim of the former was the repression of criminal activity such as theft, while the latter derived from an as yet ill-defined political and moral police engine whose purpose was the control of public opinion and the relentless pursuit of perceived affronts to public morals, the state, religion or public order.

Some inspectors focused for many years on a particular area of expertise: Meusnier and Marais concentrated on public morals, d'Hémery on the book trade, Poussot on the Halles district. The targets chosen for surveillance shaped their recruitment efforts, and the *observateurs* they deployed did not necessarily have the same skills, status or level of remuneration. Nevertheless, from one sector to the next, surveillance techniques were quite similar: eavesdrop, observe, record, 'tail' a subject, avoid detection. Regardless of the sphere of activity or the target of surveillance, what stands out is the relative commonality of practices and instruments with regard to processing, compiling, archiving and cross-checking information. The inspectors also followed similar procedures: they collected written or verbal statements, made summaries of the information which they then

73. Paris, Ars., MS Bastille, 10985, f.152-65.

transmitted to their superiors, then kept 'journals', compiled registers or perhaps created files on individual subjects. Any observation, direct or indirect, could potentially be documented. This data was completed by the written correspondences they received and was easily cross-checked, as interrogations such as those Chenon conducted in the Bastille demonstrate. The police organisation was desirous to conserve an inspector's 'papers', and, more and more frequently, the office of the lieutenant general acquired them upon his death.

The common denominator of these surveillance practices is therefore the production of written documents which became more and more standardised and uniform, whose authentication was ensured by the police and over which the police held monopoly. For example, the reports denouncing gamblers, made by a man by the name of Pons, a 'vétéran du guet' granted immunity, enumerated the names and social ranks of the players, their losses and gains, the identities of their 'bankers' and their gaming schedules.[74] In her correspondence with Berryer, La Dhosmont gave identical enumerations. The same logic held for eighteenth-century lodging registries, maintained in duplicate, in which the information itemised became more universal. This systematisation aimed to better identify travellers and migrants as well as to keep track of their movements. It was in fact a way for the royal government to institute a new system of recognition, founded on written documents, and which progressively superseded forms such as personal association or private letters, even if these methods did not disappear overnight. The administrative document insinuated itself into traditional forms of social life as well as into the surveillance of risky environments.

In addition to the widespread insistence upon the written document, the remaining distinction lies in the interlocutors with whom the police interacted. On the one hand, the Châtelet relied upon the traditional societal frameworks of the *Ancien Régime,* or at least on individuals whom it could affiliate with an orderable hierarchy and who had a vested interest in keeping their position within it: master tradesmen, shopkeepers, those in the service trades, and other *auxiliaires naturels.* In these instances, and in addition to the obligation to declare all suspect behaviour, the police looked to impose the use of forms of written registration they had themselves authorised. Properly speaking, it was not quite espionage, but a form of regulation founded on the surveillance of each by all, which relied on denunciations and regular collaboration

74. Paris, Ars., MS Bastille, 10268, 1741-1745.

with the police in the name of public interest and the fight against undesirables. This collaboration was based on a system of mutually beneficial back scratching, such as in the case of the *revendeuses* of the Louvre district who, in exchange for aiding the police to fight against theft and the trade of stolen goods, obtained the regulation of the resale market and protection from competition from unregistered (and thus without legal or social standing) 'rogue' resellers.

On the other hand, the police were confronted with activities and social practices which disrupted the world of traditional trade corporations and their habitual regulations. There was no legal or regulatory framework for such instances, no professional organisation with which to collaborate, and, when these activities were new, illicit or hidden, no legal precedent either. Since they were outside of the boundaries of 'customary' limits dictated by ordinary or licensed sociability, the police found themselves needing to invent ways of surveilling the grey areas and the criminal underworld, such as creating intermediaries who could help them pursue their objectives. It is in this grey zone that espionage in the literal sense developed. During the 1770s and 1780s, the lieutenant general's office fused surveillance activities entailing collaboration with certain leaders who viewed society in traditional and holistic terms with activities founded on the investigations and administrative work of 'specialists' or trusted affiliates. The two facets of surveillance were opposite sides of the same coin rather than distinctly articulated entities; the two went hand in hand. The boundaries between spaces of sociability and 'suspect activities' were becoming porous. The police intended to keep a firm hold on the city through any means necessary.

For Lenoir, the act of 'espionage' had two objectives: first, destroy or neutralise 'undesirables' before they could commit a crime. The lowest of the low deserved no latitude. The protection of society and of good citizens came at such a cost. Lenoir attributed a decline in the number of gangs of thieves and the exile of organised crime to the outskirts of the capital to the efficacy of a police machine drawing on years of accumulated expertise.

Second, the flow of information up the chain of command to the office of the lieutenant general was a further preventive measure Lenoir insisted upon. Through prevention of this kind, he sought to forestall scandal and protect the honour, reputations and even fortunes of families menaced by the transgressions of their libertine offspring. His intimate knowledge of certain affairs gave him the means, through negotiation or coercion, to quietly and pre-emptively defuse delicate situations which might be overwhelming to public sensibilities.[75] Inspector d'Hémery viewed his surveillance of members of the book and literary trades in the same spirit. Before deciding whether to impose censorship, a harsh and relentless punishment, he had on more than one occasion probed into the most intimate details of his suspects. Prevention was also the foundation of Lenoir's written defence of the system of *lettres de cachet* which, he further explained, were never executed without thorough investigation.

The Châtelet police fully endorsed the concept of a global, paternalist monarchy. The institution defended its right to extend its range of intervention and tutelary authority when necessary but also as a matter of principle since, as the embodiment of the king's sovereign protection, it was well within its capacity to do so. But, because the police could not prohibit all – they did not have the resources to do so – they had to content themselves with investigation and moral guidance while working to expand their field of expertise. In 1789, this led both detractors and supporters to describe the institution as an omniscient, tentacled beast. Strategies to control the public became quite ambiguous. Some were limited to the simple exploitation and manipulation of opinion, but all demonstrate the full extent and legitimacy of police power over public space. Mastery over various information networks, such as that of the *nouvellistes* who kept them abreast of the texts as they were written, allowed the police to control the information they wished to have published.[76]

This role of preventive surveillance assumed by the police, coupled with the authority to repress – quite evident with regard to 'dangerous' elements such as prostitutes or vagabonds – was concurrent with the expectations of security expressed by certain representatives of the Parisian upper classes. According to the accounts of the bookseller Hardy, the legitimacy of the system and its agents (in particular, the inspectors) had grown since the new, more repressive and administrative style of policing that began under d'Argenson had been instigated. The efforts to bolster that legitimacy were considerable, especially concerning police informers, who were subject to strict vetting and sanctions for any infidelities or abuses of power.

75. Goulven Kerien, *Pour l'honneur des familles: les enfermements par lettres de cachet à Paris au XVIIIe siècle* (Ceyzérieu, 2023).
76. Gilles Malandain, 'Les mouches de la police et le vol des mots: les gazetins de la police secrète et la surveillance de l'expression à Paris au deuxième quart du XVIIIe siècle', *Revue d'histoire moderne et contemporaine* 42:3 (1995), p.376-404.

Other segments of the population were nonetheless still hostile towards surveillance, *mouches* and some of those who *travaillent à la police*. Proof of increasing conflict between the police and civilians is not lacking in the archives. Tensions leading up to the riots of May 1750 were already palpable by the summer of 1749, when repression against vagabonds was also on the increase. *Mouches* became the perfect target for this hostility.[77] Those who were uncovered were frequently threatened and attacked. In his May 1772 bulletin, Inspector Receveur of the division of Sûreté reported the unfortunate incident of an individual beaten because he was suspected of being one of Receveur's informers.[78] In 1754, in yet another riot against a *mouche* working for the police in charge of coachmen, there were cries of 'let him hang!'[79] Death was indeed sometimes the outcome: in 1756, Pilon, a *mouche* who worked a stall on the quai de la Mégisserie, was found drowned in the Seine. Inspector Rouiller noted in his report that 'for some time there have been a number of people prowling the quai de la Ferraille and other docks, who have it in for our *mouches*.'[80] Resorting to such extreme measures was perhaps not the norm, but verbal violence and physical aggression were likely frequently observed.[81]

If, however, we choose to posit that the relationship between the police and the people of Paris was not intrinsically conflictual, then we need to puzzle out the underlying logic of such conflicts. Occasionally, undercurrents of opposition seem to derive from conflicts arising out of economic rivalry (women in the second-hand trade, the stallholders of the quai de la Ferraille) or the control of certain professional trade workers liable to take liberties with police regulations, such as coachmen and stallholders. In the turmoil leading up to the spring riots of 1750, hostility towards police discretionary power and

---

77. Paris, Ars., MS Bastille, 10138, 'Rapport de l'inspecteur Davenel, 17 juillet 1749'; Christian Romon, 'L'affaire des "enlèvements d'enfants" dans les archives du Châtelet (1749-1750)', *Revue historique* 547 (1983), p.55-95; Paolo Piasenza, 'Rapimenti, polizia e rivolta: un conflitto sull'ordine pubblico a Parigi nel 1750', *Quaderni storici* 22:64 (1987), p.129-51; Arlette Farge and Jacques Revel, *The Vanishing children of Paris: rumors and politics before the French Revolution* (1988; Cambridge, MA, 1993).
78. Paris, Ars., MS Bastille, 10127, 11 and 19 May 1772.
79. Paris, Ars., MS Bastille, 11867, f.116-29.
80. Paris, Ars., MS Bastille, 11942, f.62-75.
81. Le Pré-Saint-Gervais, APP, AB 365, 'Registre d'ordres du roi, mai 1762', and Paris, Ars., MS Bastille, 12166; see Thomas M. Luckett, 'Hunting for spies and whores: a Parisian riot on the eve of the French Revolution', *Past and present* 156 (1997), p.116-43.

arbitrary abductions was compounded by the people's opposition to the criminalisation of a specific form of sociability, the occupation of public space by youth. But the issue was not necessarily – or not uniquely – the presence of informers in the streets, cafés or circles of sociability, nor the fact that certain individuals might collaborate with the police. Other ingredients had to be present for conflict to erupt. Not all were directly linked to the police, even if the activities of those who collaborated with them might provide a pretext.

In circles of sociability more policed by practices of mundane society than were the streets and public places, the presence of police informers was expected, and one accordingly adopted a more reserved attitude. In his journal, the marquis de Bombelles relates that 'prudent individuals did not engage openly in conversation in front of others; in Paris, there was almost certainly a police spy in their midst.'[82] In a way, a police informant spying on a salon was a betrayal of the laws of hospitality. If caught, the spy was shown the door. If none was detected, one assumed a spy was present nonetheless.

However, being treated with forbearance by the police while under their surveillance was not the same as freedom. The office of the lieutenant general did make efforts to limit the discretionary power of its agents and demonstrate that the protection it provided justified their activities. Despite this, Parisian police officers struggled to contain the growing tide of criticisms formulated against them by followers of the philosophy of natural law, who sought to undermine police legitimacy towards the end of the *Ancien Régime*.[83] During the 1780s, the proliferation of clubs and the explosion of pamphletary writings exceeded the limits of what the monarchy was willing to accept without jeopardising its own authority. The Châtelet police, who had long kept a tolerant, watchful eye over what it could not repress, were progressively overwhelmed by the exponential growth and politicisation of the public sphere. The proliferation of different forms of voluntary association had long been suspected of sowing conflict with the political foundations of the monarchy. These new forms dissolved the principles of order, authority and subordination that the police had a duty to uphold.[84] Lenoir viewed the frequenting of the several dozen Masonic lodges in Paris as a harmless leisurely

82. Marc-Marie Bombelles, *Journal du marquis de Bombelles*, ed. Frans Durif and Jean Grassion, 2 vols (Geneva, 1978), vol.1: *1780-1784*, '17 juillet 1782', p.134.
83. Milliot, *'L'Admirable Police'*, p.351-53.
84. In 1731, Cardinal de Fleury justified closing the Club de l'Entresol because it

pursuit, despite being prohibited; there was a flood of other groupings, however, that aroused hostility from the government.[85]

The government's unease became palpable, the climate volatile. Increasingly, the motives for the closure of a club or an assembly would have little to do with the safeguarding of morals. In January 1788, the Secretary of State of the Maison du roi denied permission to create an English class on suspicion it was a front for a political club.[86] Before this, two associations in particular had come under investigation: the Club des propriétaires d'Amérique and that of the Amis des Noirs.[87] The baron de Breteuil's failure to implement regulations which would provide a framework for these creations was as great as his attempt to reform the use of *lettres de cachet* in order to mitigate the criticisms of partisans of judicial reform. In August 1787, turmoil followed the dismissal of the Assembly of Notables and the eleventh-hour attempts at reform. The monarchy recoiled. It tried to make clubs, salon societies and assemblies with 'subscribed' memberships cease all activity. Unrest reached the streets of Paris. Sociability by voluntary membership was under fire.[88]

By October, Lenoir's successor, Thiroux de Crosne, would oversee the enforcement of the measure but with no real success. Arthur Young, L.-S. Mercier and the bookseller Hardy all remark on the increased surveillance of cafés during the Estates General. Bachaumont came to the rapid conclusion that these societies were 'incompatible with ministerial despotism'.[89] Twenty years after Chancellor Maupeou's strike against the *parlements*, the office of the lieutenant general of police was once again the harbinger of this despotism so contrary to freedom of association and the free commerce of ideas. The bill would come due for the institution; the summer of 1789 spelled the beginning of its downfall.

The rejection of the practice of 'generalised espionage' in 1789 and afterwards can be attributed to inevitable political and ideological reasons: the implication of the police in reoccurring episodes of

was a 'veritable political academy'. René-Louis de Voyer d'Argenson, *Journal et mémoires du marquis d'Argenson*, 9 vols (Paris, 1849), vol.1, p.247-69.

85. Ran Halévi, *Les Loges maçonniques dans la France d'Ancien Régime, aux origines de la sociabilité démocratique* (Paris, 1984); Alain Le Bihan, *Francs-maçons et ateliers parisiens de la Grande Loge de France au XVIIIᵉ siècle (1760-1795)* (Paris, 1973).

86. Paris, AN, O¹ 499, f.48, 28 January 1788.

87. Paris, AN, O¹ 494, 1 October 1784 (Propriétaires d'Amérique), O¹ 499,647, 26 October 1788 (Amis des Noirs).

88. Paris, AN, O¹ 498, f.567, 27 August 1787.

89. Bachaumont, *Mémoires secrets*, vol.35, p.412, '28 août 1787'.

repression against Parliament magistrates; demands for the rule of law against absolutism and its arbitrary nature; the affirmation of the values of individual freedom against the logic of corporations. This rejection might also be due to the desire to put a stop to collaboration with the police, which had affected all levels of society and not only delinquents or 'marginals'. It is important to avoid an anachronistic interpretation of this collaboration. It was not compromise with a liberticidal government, but a form of social regulation, though one incompatible with the rapid transformations that rocked Parisian society as a whole. In this respect, the 'police system' of Paris had been, since the end of the seventeenth century, caught up in the process which led both to the reconfiguration of the relationships between the powers that be (municipality, Parliament, Châtelet, Maison du roi...) and to the evolution of relations between the police and the population. 'General espionage' was one aspect of the effort to adapt in order to administer such a major city.[90] It was made possible through the construction of a veritable information-gathering apparatus created by an agency whose workings were progressively fine-tuned. And, in so doing, it defined the limits of tolerance, the potential for negotiation, and even efforts to exploit public debate and the new forms of community life, which received their de facto validation. The Enlightenment police searched hard for the means to shape Enlightenment sociability. But it was unwilling – and unable – to smother this new sociability despite its steadily increasing potential to subvert a society framed in traditional and holistic terms.

90. Because we know little or nothing on this topic, it is hard to say that the kingdom's largest cities did not dream of setting up an observation system inspired by the one in Paris. In Toulouse, the *capitouls'* police force probably resorted to espionage methods in the field of games policing. The projects came to nothing because of a lack of resources, but the intention was there, as it was in Strasbourg at the end of the eighteenth century. See Jean-Luc Laffont, 'Policer la ville: Toulouse, capitale provinciale au siècle des Lumières', doctoral dissertation, Université Toulouse II Le Mirail, 1997, 3 vols; Vincent Denis, 'Peut-on réformer un "monument de la police"? La réforme de la police de Strasbourg en débat à la fin de l'Ancien Régime, 1782-1788', in *Réformer la police: les mémoires policiers en Europe au XVIIIᵉ siècle*, ed. Catherine Denys *et al.* (Rennes, 2009), p.131-50.

Policing religious sociability

DAVID GARRIOCH

Monash University

It may seem strange, in a book about policing, to devote an entire essay to religious sociability. Historians of the police in this period, if they mention religion at all, perceive it to be of secondary importance, well behind issues of food supply, public health and the maintenance of order. Similarly, most work on urban sociability in eighteenth-century France has little to say about religious associations, although Maurice Agulhon's pioneering book on *La Sociabilité méridionale* revealed the importance of lay religious confraternities in the south of France.[1] While there has been some recent interest in these associations, in urban contexts, it has been mainly among religious historians who are primarily concerned with their devotional dimension.[2] Most work on urban sociability has been more interested in new forms that are perceived to have played a key role in disseminating secular ways of thinking and behaving and hence in undermining the religious and social underpinnings of absolutism. Although recent work on Jansenism has questioned the assumption that piety is inconsistent with questioning authority, religious sociability, especially confraternities or charity companies, is generally seen as reinforcing monarchical principles and religious orthodoxy.[3]

---

1. *La Sociabilité méridionale: confréries et associations dans la vie collective en Provence orientale à la fin du 18ᵉ siècle*, 2 vols (Aix-en-Provence, 1966).
2. Partial exceptions are Stefano Simiz, *Confréries urbaines et dévotion en Champagne (1450-1830)* (Paris, 2002), and Philippe Desmette, *Dans le sillage de la Réforme catholique: les confréries religieuses dans le nord du diocèse de Cambrai (1559-1786)* (Brussels, 2010).
3. Catherine Maire, *Les Convulsionnaires de Saint-Médard: miracles, convulsions et prophéties à Paris au XVIIIᵉ siècle* (Paris, 1985); B. Robert Kreiser, *Miracles, convulsions, and ecclesiastical politics in early eighteenth-century Paris* (Princeton, NJ, 1978); Jeffrey Merrick, *The Desacralization of the French monarchy in the eighteenth*

It is therefore perhaps surprising that descriptions of the Paris police, throughout the eighteenth century, should begin not with food supply or public order, but with 'religion'. In the account written during the Revolution by the former police chief Jean-Charles-Pierre Lenoir, he recalled that on taking office in 1774 he was told by the comte de Maurepas, Louis XVI's key minister, that religion was 'le premier objet de la police'. Admittedly, Lenoir saw 'irreligion' as the key factor undermining the Old Regime, and was keen to explain why the police were helpless to prevent the collapse.[4] Yet his list of priorities, in religious matters, included not only enforcing respect due holy places, observance of feast days and Sundays, and preventing the distribution of antireligious writing, but also 'to pursue abuses under the titles of pilgrimage and confraternity'.[5] It is revealing, too, that he begins not with the *Encyclopédie* or with Voltaire, but with the Catholic reform movement known as Jansenism. He is at pains to point out that this movement included 'true' Jansenists whose morality was irreproachable, but also a number of religious fanatics, together with a third, more dangerous group of individuals who wanted to change the French Church and government. It was their power, he maintains, that hamstrung the police and allowed free rein first to the defenders of religious toleration, then to the *philosophes*, whose pernicious works completed the damage.

It is also revealing that the first concrete example that Lenoir gives to illustrate the spread of irreligion in Paris is not, as one might expect, of a decline in religious observance, but rather of a form of religious sociability. The police discovered, in the late 1770s, a large group of fan makers living and working together in the rue Quincampoix. They included couples who were cohabiting without being married, did not go to church and were not having their children baptised. They were taught, the police discovered, 'by an intellectual who came from time to time to lecture and encourage them'. The police chief had them all

---

century (Baton Rouge, LA, and London, 1990); Dale K. Van Kley, *The Religious origins of the French Revolution: from Calvin to the Civil Constitution, 1560-1791* (New Haven, CT, 1996), esp. ch.2 on Jansenist sociability. Monique Cottret, *Jansénismes et Lumières: pour un autre XVIIIᵉ siècle* (Paris, 1998), p.241-63, and Nicolas Lyon-Caen, *La Boîte à Perrette: le jansénisme parisien au XVIIIᵉ siècle* (Paris, 2010), p.110-20, 142-52.

4.   Vincent Milliot, *Un Policier des Lumières, suivi de Mémoires de J. C. P. Lenoir, ancien lieutenant général de police de Paris, écrits en pays étrangers dans les années 1790 et suivantes* (Seyssel, 2011), p.22-25, 28-32.

5.   Milliot, *Un Policier des Lumières*, p.473.

locked up, concluding that 'I thought I had dissipated the beginnings of a gathering of so-called illuminated people.'[6] Religious sociability, for the police, was an indicator of social health, and needed to be monitored closely.

While Lenoir's account is shaped by his desire to respond to his critics and to account for what he saw as the disaster of the Revolution, as Vincent Milliot has pointed out it is in many ways characteristic of police reform *mémoires* of the second half of the eighteenth century. In fact, Lenoir took the structure of his description directly from earlier works about the Paris police, particularly from an equally self-justificatory document written by the *commissaire* Lemaire in 1770.[7] Lemaire too began with 'Religion', offering precisely the same list of police activities that Maurepas later supposedly gave to Lenoir.[8] Once again, overseeing various forms of conventional religious activity and sociability – religious services, processions, pilgrimages and confraternities – was given pride of place. But Lemaire's account was not entirely original, either. It in turn adopted elements of the structure used by his predecessor Nicolas Delamare in the *Traité de la police* of 1705-1719 that had become a standard guide to policing across Europe. Delamare's work commenced with a long historical framing, but, when he described the police of Paris, like Lenoir nearly a century later he asserted that 'religion is the first and foremost concern of the police'. He then listed six of the seven areas of policing mentioned by Lemaire and Lenoir, omitting the surveillance of irreligious writing.[9]

6. Milliot, *Un Policier des Lumières*, p.481-82.
7. Jean-Baptiste-Charles Lemaire, 'La police de Paris en 1770: mémoire inédit composé par ordre de G. de Sartine, sur la demande de Marie-Thérèse', ed. André Gazier, *Mémoires de la Société de l'histoire de Paris* 5 (1879), p.1-131. Milliot, *Un Policier des Lumières*, p.88. Vincent Milliot, 'Ecrire pour policer: les "mémoires" policiers, 1750-1850', in *Les Mémoires policiers, 1750-1850: écritures et pratiques policières du siècle des Lumières au Second Empire*, ed. Vincent Milliot (Rennes, 2006), p.15-41. Steven Laurence Kaplan and Vincent Milliot, 'La police de Paris, une "révolution permanente"? Du commissaire Lemaire au lieutenant de police Lenoir, les tribulations du *Mémoire sur l'administration de la police* (1770-1792)', in *Réformer la police: les mémoires policiers en Europe au XVIII*ᵉ *siècle*, ed. Catherine Denys *et al.* (Rennes, 2009), p.69-115.
8. Lemaire, 'La police de Paris en 1770', p.13-14.
9. Nicolas Delamare, *Traité de la police*, 2nd edn, 4 vols (Paris, n.n., 1729), vol.1, p.249, 305-354. On Delamare's *Traité*, see Nicole Dyonet, 'L'ordre public est-il l'objet de la police dans le *Traité* de Delamare?', in *Ordonner et partager la ville, XVII*ᵉ*-XIX*ᵉ *siècle*, ed. Gaël Rideau and Pierre Serna (Rennes, 2011), p.47-74. All translations are my own unless otherwise indicated.

Right across the eighteenth century, then, the police gave a high priority, at least in theory, to overseeing religious sociability.

That term, of course, is a modern one that they did not use. Yet Delamare began his chapter on the policing of religious confraternities by asserting that 'Man was so born for society that in this world he makes it his favourite object and his principal satisfaction. Hence it is that [...] not content with this first bond, which made of the whole human race only one great society, he has eagerly sought closer unions, [...] even more intimate societies, through jobs and particular professions.'[10] In this essay, I use the term 'religious sociability' to refer to organised groups of lay people that had a specific membership, and for which religious practice was one of the major goals. I first describe the various forms of religious sociability in eighteenth-century Paris. I then examine the attitudes of the religious and secular authorities towards them, the legislative framework and, most crucially, the actual process of policing, since in practice the laws were often not applied.

In this area, policing was undertaken not only by the personnel of the Châtelet – who included both the police and the lower courts – but by a variety of Old Regime institutions. As in other domains, both the Parlement and the King's Council issued decrees that had direct application to Paris. In religious affairs, of course, the archbishop also had a key role, sometimes issuing formal instructions of his own but delegating most matters to his subordinates, notably his deputy the *grand vicaire*. Many matters were also handled by the diocesan court, the Officialité, which dealt mainly with requests for permission to marry within the prohibited degrees and with misbehaviour by members of the clergy, but also with religious disputes of different kinds, including those involving confraternities.[11] At the very local level, the parish clergy and religious orders also played a key regulatory role. While a key aim of all these policing agents was the maintenance and strengthening of an ideal moral, social and political order, their understanding of what this meant and the ways they went about it often differed.

---

10. Delamare, *Traité*, vol.1, p.347.
11. John McManners, *Church and society in eighteenth century France*, 2 vols (Oxford, 1998), vol.1, p.191-92. Bernard d'Alteroche, *L'Officialité de Paris à la fin de l'Ancien Régime (1780-1790)* (Paris, 1994).

Forms of religious sociability

Paris contained a wide variety of religious associations. Most numerous were confraternities, groups of lay people that organised religious services for their members, mainly regular masses, funerals, processions and occasionally other ceremonies. Most also offered prayers, particularly after the death of a member, and obtained indulgences to reduce time spent in purgatory. Some also had charitable goals: poor relief, the release of people imprisoned for debt or, in a couple of cases, the redemption of Christians sold into slavery. A couple ran hospices, and some paid for religious services or processions that non-members could also attend. In the course of the eighteenth century, a number also branched out into mutual aid, allowing members to contribute to a fund that could be drawn on in case of sickness or unemployment.[12]

Each confraternity had one or more patron saints, or was dedicated to a divine manifestation like the Trinity, an event such as the Annunciation, or else directly to Jesus Christ, most often in the form of the Blessed Sacrament. Most confraternities rented a chapel in a parish or monastic church, where they held services, and they took pride in its decoration. In Paris, unlike in some other places, the members were almost exclusively lay people, who met for services but also, in some cases, to elect their administrators and make financial and other decisions. While a few are well documented, often we know only that they existed at a particular moment, which is perhaps one reason they have been largely overlooked. Their level of activity also varied greatly. Some held services only on the feast days of their patron saints, perhaps half a dozen times a year, but many had a mass every month or even each week, in addition to funeral services for members who died. Like modern clubs, some associations declined and disappeared, but might be revived a few years later by a committed group with new energy.

Confraternities came in all sizes. The prestigious Archiconfrérie du Saint-Sépulcre had around 400 members in 1765. In the early 1780s

---

12. For useful overviews on French confraternities, see Marie-Hélène Froeschlé-Chopard, *Dieu pour tous et Dieu pour soi: histoire des confréries et de leurs images à l'époque moderne* (Paris, 2006), and McManners, *Church and society*, vol.2, p.156-88. On Paris, see David Garrioch, 'Mutual aid societies in eighteenth-century Paris', *French history and civilization* 4 (2011), p.22-33, and David Garrioch, 'Les confréries religieuses, espace d'autonomie laïque à Paris au XVIIIᵉ siècle', in *La Religion vécue: les laïcs dans l'Europe moderne*, ed. Laurence Croq and David Garrioch (Rennes, 2013), p.143-63.

the Blessed Sacrament confraternity at Saint-Roch had some 260 paying members, whereas the same confraternity at Saint-Jacques-de-la-Boucherie had only 69. The Grande Confrérie de Notre-Dame had some 600 members in the early years of the century.[13] The occupational confraternities, which in principle included all members of the trade, also varied enormously in size: the dyers had only a dozen or so members, while the mercers numbered in the thousands. Yet, although all those belonging to the trade were automatically members of the confraternity, not all of them participated. There were probably a couple of thousand journeymen shoemakers in Paris, but between 1759 and 1774 anywhere from 70 to 360 voted in the elections of administrators of the confraternity.[14]

Both the number and the longevity of the Paris confraternities are astounding. In the early years of the eighteenth century there were around 460, just over half of which (about 240) were for specific occupational groups. In the 1760s, the overall number seems to have peaked at about 530, roughly one for every 1100 or so inhabitants.[15] If we assume (conservatively) that each confraternity had fifty to one hundred members, then between 5 and 10 per cent of the Paris population – and a higher proportion of the adult population – belonged to one in the middle years of the century. In 1776, however, the government abolished over 200 guild associations, and others disappeared for a variety of reasons, so that by the 1780s there were probably only around 120 confraternities left. Even this much smaller number, however, indicates that we should not imagine pre-revolutionary Paris as a modern secular city.

Confraternities took a variety of forms. It is conventional to make a broad distinction between occupational and 'devotional' confraternities, the latter seen as more purely religious, the former as less pious and more occupied with trade matters.[16] This was sometimes true, but not always. In practice, both types were very

---

13. Paris, Archives nationales (AN), T1489 (1-2), pièce 3, 29 December 1765. AN, LL790. Jean Gaston, *Les Images des confréries parisiennes avant la Révolution* (Paris, 1910), plate 25, 1782, p.25-26. Laurence Croq, 'Le déclin de la confrérie Notre-Dame aux prêtres et aux bourgeois de Paris sous l'Ancien Régime', *Paris et Ile-de-France: mémoires* 50 (1999), p.243-89.

14. Paris, AN, S118, 'Register of deliberations'.

15. Daniel Roche estimates the city's population at *c.*500,000 in 1700 and *c.*600,000-700,000 by 1789. Daniel Roche, *The People of Paris: an essay in popular culture in the 18th century* (1981; Berkeley, CA, 1987), p.20.

16. Marc Venard, 'Si on parlait des confréries de métiers...', in *Sacralités, culture*

diverse. Occupational confraternities were in principle limited to a single trade, and many were closely associated with one of the guilds. The goldsmiths, a particularly wealthy group, even had their own free-standing chapel, dedicated to Saint Eloi. The far more numerous bakers had confraternities, all devoted to Saint Honoré, in several different Paris churches. Yet many occupational groups that had no official guild nevertheless had their own confraternities: the postmen, the fishwives of the central market, and the workers at the glass factory in the faubourg Saint-Antoine, for example. So too did most of the small groups whom the monarchy – for financial reasons – had transformed into officeholders, such as the men who measured firewood on the river ports and those who monitored the sale of pork.[17] Some occupational confraternities, though, were open to more than one trade: the carters and the horse merchants apparently shared one, as did workers in the hatting and dyeing trades. Some guild confraternities included journeymen artisans as well as masters, while in other trades they assembled separately: across the eighteenth century over fifty associations, in some thirty-seven different male trades, were solely for journeymen.[18] Their confraternities functioned in much the same way as the official guild ones, organising regular religious services and celebrating the feast day of their patron saint. Some of them played a role in assisting men to find work, although most guilds tried to stop journeymen gaining control over labour supply. These were not *compagnonnages* – the semi-secret associations that existed in many other parts of France and that catered to young, mobile journeymen. The evidence suggests that the confraternities were primarily for men who were permanently established in Paris, often married.[19]

---

et dévotion: bouquet offert à Marie-Hélène Froeschlé-Chopard, ed. Marc Venard and Dominique Julia (Marseille, 2005), p.221-38.

17. Paris, Bibliothèque nationale de France (BnF), Fonds Joly de Fleury (JF) 1590, f.28, 34, 195-97. Paris, AN, S7492B.

18. *Almanach spirituel de Paris pour l'année 1737* (Paris, n.n., 1737), December. Paris, BnF, JF 1590, f.32. David Garrioch and Michael Sonenscher, 'Compagnonnages, confraternities and associations of journeymen in eighteenth-century Paris', *European history quarterly* 16 (1986), p.25-45. I have found some twenty more journeymen's confraternities since this article was written.

19. Michael Sonenscher, *Work and wages: natural law, politics and the eighteenth-century French trades* (New York, 1989), p.89. David Garrioch, *The Making of revolutionary Paris* (Berkeley, CA, 2002), p.76. Garrioch and Sonenscher, 'Compagnonnages', p.38-40.

Certain 'devotional' confraternities were also restricted to particular groups of people. Some were for pilgrims: those of Saint Jacques de Compostelle and of Saint Michel (the latter for people who had been to the mont Saint-Michel). I have found only one confraternity that was for a particular ethnic or provincial group, that of the Saint-Ange-Gardien which was exclusively for 'Savoyards de nation'. A few were only for women, while the Passion of the Saviour at Saint-Paul was primarily for young people. Some associations were by invitation only, such as the Grande Confrérie de Notre-Dame at the church of Sainte-Madeleine or that of the porters of the reliquary of Saint Geneviève, the latter restricted to forty members at any one time.[20] These last two were prestigious and attracted wealthy people, as did the confraternity of the Passion at the Jacobins, which in 1782 included most of the royal family and many high-ranking nobles. In the 1780s the Archiconfrérie de Jérusalem similarly recruited members of the military and judicial nobility.[21] By contrast, the Blessed Sacrament confraternities, present in most of the Paris parishes, had a very low annual fee and encouraged poorer people to join. Except in the small number of female-only occupations, the Paris confraternities were run by lay men, but many admitted both sexes as ordinary members, and even in male trades the wives and widows of masters often partic-ipated in religious ceremonies.

Alongside their spiritual sociability, most religious associations engaged in forms of closely related festive activity. Although the statutes of eighteenth-century confraternities usually forbade feasting and drinking, there is evidence that some of them celebrated the day of their patron saint in some style. The mercers' employees reportedly feasted on Saint Louis' Day. The eighteen 'associates of the Blessed Virgin' in the rue aux Ours – not, perhaps, a standard confraternity – celebrated both the day and the octave of Corpus Christi in 1776 with a copious meal. The thirty-five-member governing body of the

20. Marcel Fosseyeux, 'La dévolution des biens de l'hôpital Saint-Jacques-aux-Pèlerins aux XVIIe et XVIIIe siècles', *Bulletin de la Société de l'histoire de Paris et de l'Ile-de-France* 41 (1914), p.117-34. Paris, BnF, JF 1590, f.29, 263. Croq, 'Le déclin de la confrérie Notre-Dame'. Edouard Pinet, *La Compagnie des porteurs de la châsse de sainte Geneviève, 1525-1902* (Paris, 1903).

21. Paris, BnF, D-52463; *La Solide Dévotion à la passion de Notre Seigneur Jésus-Christ, à l'usage des confrères et sœurs de la confrérie royale de la Passion du Sauveur et de Notre-Dame de Pitié* (Paris, n.n., 1782), p.15, 52. Paris, Bibliothèque historique de la ville de Paris (BHVP), 130963, *Tableau de l'Archiconfrairie royale du Saint-Sépulcre de Jérusalem* [Paris, n.n., 1790].

Blessed Sacrament confraternity in the parish of Saint-Jacques-de-la-Boucherie held dinners on the same two feast days, at the expense of their two leaders – who knew that they would attend for free in future years. They noted dutifully that, as Corpus Christi was a day when meat was not allowed, they served only fish and vegetables, and, since they took the precaution of inviting the parish priest to both meals, the clergy could hardly object. Other confraternities were reported to enjoy similar celebrations. That of the notaries held a lavish annual dinner, although after 1672 each member was required to pay for his own meal.[22]

Eating and drinking reinforced the spiritual bonds between the members. The clearest example of this is the sharing of *pain bénit*, bread taken to the church, usually following a roster, to be blessed during the mass. The blessing was often done with some pomp, the bread decorated with candles, and, in the case of the saltpetre makers, with small flags.[23] Presenting the bread was both a duty and an honour, especially on a major feast day. This was sometimes done by women – the wife or daughter of a member – even in male-only associations, illustrating the unofficial way in which families were part of the spiritual community of the confraternity.[24] The blessed bread was then divided among those present at the service and taken to be shared with family members, with the sick or with others who could not attend. According to a *Traité du pain bénit* of 1777, this was a 'signe d'union fraternelle et de communion ecclésiastique, afin qu'encore qu'ils soient plusieurs, ils ne forment qu'un tout, comme plusieurs grains ne font qu'un seul pain'.[25] That some members of confraternities shared this belief is suggested by examples where journeymen

22. Paris, BnF, JF 1590, f.167. Paris, Archives de Paris (AP), D5 B6 472. Paris, AN, LL791, f.6, 8, 9. Pierre Robin, *La Compagnie des secrétaires du roi (1351-1791)* (Paris, 1933), p.57. For further examples, see Paris, AN, S118, *Recueil des titres de la confrérie de Saint-Crespin et Saint-Crespinien* (Paris, n.n., 1754), p.6. Paris, BnF, JF 1801, f.70. Paris, BnF, Manuscrits français (MS fr.) 21663, 'jardiniers', and MS fr. 21793, f.177.

23. Paris, BHVP, CP 3548, 'Mémoires pour servir à l'histoire de l'église Notre-Dame des Victoires (c. 1740)'.

24. Paris, BnF, MS fr. 21872, 'booksellers'. Paris, AN, H4648, 'Conception à Saint-Séverin'. Paris, BnF, JF 232, 'Mémoire pour les sieurs curé et marguilliers de St Jean en Grève, contre la confrairie de St François de Sales établie en l'église St Jean [1746]', f.331-34.

25. Nicolas Collin, *Traité du pain béni [sic], ou l'Eglise catholique justifiée sur l'usage du pain-béni* (Paris, n.n., 1777). See Thierry Wanegffelen, 'D'une dévotion à l'autre? L'évolution de la pratique du pain bénit mise en rapport avec le processus de

artisans gathered in a café after the service of their confraternity to share the blessed bread and some bottles of wine in what was very explicitly a continuation of the communion of the mass. We know they did this because the guild leaders attempted to present it as evidence of 'plots' and illegal meetings. In 1740, roofers were engaged in legal action against employers who were taking on apprentices to replace journeymen, and the members of the confraternity refused to share the bread with other men who were present, explicitly excluding one man who was a master and not an employee. The sharing of the bread reinforced solidarity by symbolically enacting both inclusion and exclusion. A second example, in 1741, also occurred in the context of a dispute, this time among the dyers, who also met near the chapel of their confraternity. Here, however, both masters and journeymen were sharing the bread, to the chagrin of the guild leaders who invited the police to document their 'plotting' and to take the names of the masters who were present.[26] A very similar use of the blessed bread can be seen in the context of another, very bitter dispute in 1698, among the carpenters. A journeyman who was 'master' of the confraternity went to offer blessed bread to an employee of one of the guild leaders, clearly attempting to get the man to support the journeymen's grievance, the bread symbolising solidarity.[27] These examples point clearly to the symbolic significance of the *pain bénit*: ordinary bread would not have had the same value as a marker and driver of collective identity and action. Complementing attendance at confraternal masses, at funerals and processions, the sociability of eating and drinking created a very particular bond between the members – what the statutes of one confraternity termed 'a holy union that the *confrères* form among themselves'.[28]

"sortie de la religion"', *Histoire des dévotions* (2000), https://hal.archives-ouvertes. fr/hal-00285123 (last accessed on 23 January 2024).

26. Paris, AN, Y11159, 28 April 1740; Y15364, 17 September 1741; Y11159, 28 April 1740. On the roofers' dispute, see Sonenscher, *Work and wages*, p.88-89.

27. Sonenscher, *Work and wages*, p.256-66. For another example, see p.89.

28. *Instructions et prières tirées de l'Ecriture sainte et des Saints Pères, pour la confrérie de Saint Jean Baptiste, érigée en l'église royale de Saint-Victor-lez-Paris* (Paris, n.n., 1684), p.22. On the inseparability of sacred and profane in this period, see Alain Cabantous, *Entre fêtes et clochers: profane et sacré dans l'Europe moderne, XVIIe-XVIIIe siècle* (Paris, 2002).

A spectrum of associations

Confraternities were the principal form of religious sociability, but other bodies had some of the same features. The Frères tailleurs and the Frères cordonniers, for example, were groups of tailors and shoemakers who lived and worked together in small Christian communities. Founded in the mid-seventeenth century and continuing right through the eighteenth, they were generally described as confraternities, and like them rented a chapel in a church for regular services. They had a highly democratic internal structure, but had both an ecclesiastical and a secular patron. They took the title of 'brother', imposed a one-year noviciate on new members, wore a distinctive costume and took an oath of celibacy.[29] In these ways, they were closer to the model of religious orders. So were most of the 'third order' associations supported by the Carmelites, the Franciscans, the Dominicans, the Mathurins and the Augustinians. The Franciscan Third Order members had a spiritual director, took a habit and swore a formal vow to observe the rule of the order, undertook a noviciate and chose a religious name. Men and women met separately. Yet most were lay people who continued their ordinary professions, and like confraternities they maintained a chapel where their services took place.[30]

As these examples show, confraternities were part of a spectrum of religious associations that had common features but that might vary in significant respects. Another variant was the mutual aid societies that proliferated during the century. In this period, Paris confraternities rarely provided material assistance, focusing instead on spiritual support and on the salvation of the soul. Mutual aid societies, by contrast, had the secular aim of assistance in the here and now. That, however, is a modern distinction, and at the time they did not always distinguish between their religious and secular functions: in 1770 the employees of the *fripiers*, who sold second-hand clothes, sought permission to create 'a confraternity whose purpose is to help both those of them who are out of work and those who are ill, and even in the event of death to give them a Christian burial'.[31] The earliest

---

29. Paris, AN, H4060. Archives de l'Archevêché de Paris, 4o r P 12; *Règlement des Frères tailleurs établi à Paris en 1647 suivant le texte ancien et nouveau, avec des éclaircissements et des additions faites en l'an 1725* (Delatour, n.n., 1727).
30. Paris, BnF, JF 1590, f.31-33. Paris, AP, 3AZ 4, no.126, 'registre de professions'.
31. Paris, BnF, JF 1590, f.92. See Garrioch, 'Mutual aid societies'.

mutual aid societies in Paris appear to have developed within the confraternities run by the grave diggers and by journeymen joiners and hatters. Another grew out of the late medieval confraternity of Saint-Prix, which in 1763 adopted new statutes providing for any member who fell sick to receive monetary assistance, and which for the first time limited the age at which new members were admitted – clearly so that the association would not be swamped by the old and infirm.[32] The only mutual aid societies we know of that were entirely separate from confraternities, in eighteenth-century Paris, existed among journeymen printers in the 1760s.[33] Yet mutual aid associations were not always coterminous with a confraternity, and nor were they solely for journeymen. Those created in the parishes of Saint-Nicolas-du-Chardonnet in 1768, Saint-Laurent in 1780, Saint-Eustache in 1782 and Saint-Médard in 1783 were linked to a confraternity, but their finances and organisation were separate, and at Saint-Médard the mutual aid society had a different name. The link remained, since only members of the confraternity were admitted, but at Saint-Médard they had to be under forty years of age, while at Saint-Nicolas only one hundred individuals were allowed to join the mutual aid group at any one time.[34]

Where mutual aid was undertaken within a guild confraternity, any direct link was broken by the edict of 1776 that banned all such confraternities. Nevertheless, Lenoir refers in his memoirs to 'a charitable institution to which a group of bourgeois of little means joined by a simple verbal agreement'. They gathered for mass on Sundays and major feast days, each man donating 12 *sous* to assist members who fell sick. As Lenoir recognised, this was a continuation of the musicians' guild confraternity of Saint-Julien, although it is not clear whether other occupations were now admitted.[35]

32. Paris, BnF, JF 1590, f.119-26.
33. Philippe Minard, *Typographes des Lumières* (Paris, 1989), p.156-57. Nicolas Contat, *Anecdotes typographiques* (Oxford, 1980), p.78-79.
34. Paris, Bibliothèque Mazarine, 42891, pièce 3, *Statuts, règlemens et bulle de Notre S. P. le Pape Alexandre VII, concernant l'association d'assistance mutuelle des cent associés de la confrairie de Saint Jean-Baptiste et de Saint Jean l'Evangéliste, érigée en l'église paroissiale de Saint Nicolas du Chardonnet* (1769); *Règlemens en forme de statuts, pour la confrérie du Très-Saint-Sacrement, érigée en l'église paroissiale de S. Médard de Paris, pour la société des boursiers-confrères de ladite confrérie, sous l'invocation de S. Pierre* (Paris, n.n., 1783). Jean Bennet, *La Mutualité française des origines à la Révolution de 1789* (Paris, 1981), p.759-60.
35. Orléans, Bibliothèque municipale (BmO), Fonds ancien, MS 1422, f.454.

Other organised groups with a specific membership and often a very local focus were clearly not confraternities but also resembled them in certain ways. On the pont au Change, a group of the inhabitants created a 'Christian society' whose primary purpose was to construct a station (*reposoir*) where the procession of the Blessed Sacrament could stop during the Corpus Christi celebrations each year. Although apparently originally founded in 1693, the society had fallen into abeyance and was renewed in 1717 when a meeting agreed on a 'concordat and statute' that they entered into their register of deliberations. Those present agreed to each donate 25 *livres* per year – a quite substantial sum – and obtained further support from 'a select number of the town's leading citizens of piety and probity'. They affirmed their belief in the Bible, and promised to obey God's commandments and those of the Church. The following year they signed the agreement before a notary, 'as we have planned to forge a stronger bond of friendship than ever before'.[36] It is possible that similar societies existed elsewhere, since *reposoirs* were constructed in different parts of the city, some funded by local residents.[37] One on the corner of the rue aux Ours, in the mid-1770s, was built by the 'associés de la sainte Vierge', already mentioned, led by their 'roy' (king). Their name and location suggest that they also looked after the chapel at the corner of the street that housed a statue of the Virgin, famous for having bled when stabbed by a Swiss Protestant. Each year, on 3 July, the Swiss was burned in effigy, a celebration once seen as an appropriate rejection of Protestant heresy but that by the late eighteenth century was criticised as superstitious and puerile. It is not clear whether the 'associés' also organised this bonfire: someone must have provided the firewood and built the giant straw figure that a crowd paraded around the neighbourhood before setting it alight.[38]

36. Paris, AN, MC, CVIII 332, 10 April 1718. Thanks to Nicolas Lyon-Caen for this document.
37. Christine Gouzi, 'Tapisseries nomades et déplacements de sacralité dans l'espace paroissial parisien au XVIIIe siècle', *Europa moderna: revue d'histoire et d'iconologie* 4 (2014), p.40-57. McManners, *Church and society*, vol.2, p.122. An agreement of 1685 indicates that the cost of another station in the faubourg Saint-Germain was borne by the local bourgeois: Paris, AN, MC, XCI 454, 17 July 1685.
38. Paris, AP, D5 B6 472. Louis-Sébastien Mercier, *Tableau de Paris*, ed. Jean-Claude Bonnet, 2 vols (Paris, 1994), vol.1, p.837-38. Pierre Thomas Hurtaut and Claude Drigon de Magny, *Dictionnaire historique de Paris*, 4 vols (Paris, n.n., 1779), vol.4, p.417-18.

Unorthodox sociabilities

All these forms of religious sociability were broadly consistent with mainstream Catholicism, but alongside them were quite a number of less orthodox groups. The most significant, numerically, was Freemasonry. While generally thought of as secular or deist, in Paris it often took an explicitly religious form. The Bible, particularly the New Testament, played a prominent role in Masonic ceremony in the 1740s, and men like Andrew Ramsay, who had a big influence on French Freemasonry well after his death in 1743, conceived of the order as a way of reuniting the different Christian churches.[39] Some strands within French Freemasonry were more exclusively Catholic. Over half of the 183 lodges that affiliated with the Grande Loge de France had a religious name, either that of a saint or that of the Trinity or the Holy Cross.[40] The 1755 statutes of the Grande Loge not only recognised God as their leader but required all members to attend mass on the feast day of Saint John and to hold a second Catholic service to commemorate Freemasons who had died. Most lodges provided funerals for their members, which all the brothers were supposed to attend.[41] Catholicism, then, was one of the central elements of Paris Freemasonry during the middle decades of the century. It was only after 1773, with the creation of the Grand Orient, that explicitly confessional elements largely disappeared from the general statutes, although some lodges not affiliated with the Grand Orient retained them.[42]

Jansenism also gave rise to unorthodox forms of religious sociability, initially built on connections between merchant families active in parishes where Jansenism was strong. But in the late 1720s, much wider groups of people gathered regularly at the tomb of François de

---

39. Kenneth Loiselle, *Brotherly love: Freemasonry and male friendship in Enlightenment France* (Ithaca, NY, and London, 2014), p.27-28, 67-68. Joseph de Maistre, in 1781, agreed: Georges Goyau, *La Pensée religieuse de Joseph de Maistre* (Paris, 1921), p.39.
40. Based on the list in Alain Le Bihan, *Francs-maçons et ateliers parisiens de la Grande Loge de France au XVIIIᵉ siècle (1760-1795)* (Paris, 1973), p.313-24.
41. Le Bihan, *Francs-maçons et ateliers*, p.393-439. Pierre Chevallier, *Histoire de la franc-maçonnerie française*, 3 vols (Paris, 1974-1975), vol.1, p.120-21. See the dossiers in Paris, BnF, FM 2; Paris, Bibliothèque de l'Arsenal (Ars.), MS 11556; and Pierre-Yves Beaurepaire, *L'Autre et le frère: l'étranger et la franc-maçonnerie en France au XVIIIᵉ siècle* (Paris, 1998), ch.10.
42. Le Bihan, *Francs-maçons et ateliers*, p.134, 153. On the centrality of Christian belief, see Loiselle, *Brotherly love*, p.60-69.

Pâris, a priest whom many Parisians regarded as a Jansenist saint. As Nicolas Lyon-Caen has shown, a veritable 'community of belief' developed as miracles were reported taking place on Pâris's tomb at Saint-Médard. Complex parish and city-wide networks developed around the defence of the Jansenist cause.[43]

The most intense unorthodox form of sociability associated with Jansenism was that of the so-called 'convulsionaries'. In 1731 a number of people who came seeking cures and who lay on the tomb of François de Pâris experienced extraordinary convulsions. After the authorities closed the cemetery, groups began meeting in private houses, where the contortions continued, increasingly inspired by a belief that the last days were at hand and that only a few would be saved. They said prayers, read from Scripture and sang psalms, exchanged stories and in due course some of them would enter a state of exaltation and experienced convulsions. Like many mystics, they believed that God was speaking through them. This movement – thousands of people, according to Robert Kreiser – has been variously interpreted, but it was certainly a form of religious sociability, albeit an extraordinary one. The convulsionaries' gatherings involved small numbers of people, rarely more than twenty or thirty, recruited from a wide social range, yet they were apparently highly egalitarian, both in their theology and in their interaction. Since each group met regularly, they must have come to know each other reasonably well, even if, for fear of persecution, individuals often remained anonymous. It was clearly a highly charged emotional environment.[44]

The convulsionaries, along with other Jansenist sympathisers, engaged in other forms of religious activity that also had a sociable dimension. One group organised processions through the streets at night. There were pilgrimages, first to Saint-Médard and later to the site of the monastery of Port-Royal, a symbol of Jansenist resistance, destroyed by order of Louis XIV in 1710-1711. These events continued as late as the 1760s, as did the convulsionaries' regular meetings. More spontaneous, it seems, were excursions such as the one undertaken by a group of female lace workers who, one summer's day, assembled in a garden in the faubourg Saint-Marcel – not far from Saint-Médard – with some religious books, no doubt to read and say prayers.[45]

43. Lyon-Caen, *La Boîte à Perrette*, p.85-152. Maire, *Les Convulsionnaires*.
44. Kreiser, *Miracles*, p.245-75. Lyon-Caen, *La Boîte à Perrette*, p.148-50.
45. Kreiser, *Miracles*, p.313, 338, 393. Lyon-Caen, *La Boîte à Perrette*, p.114-21.

Other strange assemblies, apparently unconnected with the convulsionaries, appeared from time to time. One, in the 1770s, was the
group of fan makers I mentioned at the start of this essay, described
by Lenoir as 'illuminated'. They were living and working together in
a small community, engaging in free love and rejecting conventional
religious practice. The bookseller Hardy describes them as a 'sect'
led by 'dame sainte Catherine' – Catherine Théot, whose praise for
Robespierre was to be used against him in 1794. Since she claimed
to be pregnant with the future Messiah, this was apparently another
millenarian group.[46]

Another religious minority in Paris was Protestants. Despite
Louis XIV's persecutions, Huguenots in Paris probably numbered
4000 to 7000 at any one time. Early in the eighteenth century,
there is evidence of clandestine meetings for prayers, sermons and
psalm singing, which helped to maintain connections within an
otherwise fragmented community. Later in the century, a core of
regulars worshipped in the chapels of the English, Dutch and Swedish
ambassadors: in 1766, around ninety families regularly attended
services at the Dutch chapel. Intermarriage and other connections
show the continued existence, partly thanks to shared worship, of
real communities of the faithful. In addition to Reformed Protestants,
small communities of Lutherans lived in Paris, mainly Danes, Swedes
and German-speakers, who also frequented the ambassadors' chapels.
They were at times quite separate but at other moments cooperated,
for instance to open a fourteen-bed hospital in 1743. The Germans
also ran their own library. There is some evidence that all these
groups socialised both at religious services and in other contexts.[47]

Religious sociability thus took many different forms. At its heart
were always meetings for worship, which created and consolidated
emotional and spiritual ties between individuals that were invariably
extended into other forms of interaction. This was usually a deliberate
goal. Confraternities and Freemasonry, with their language of
brotherhood, set out to create ritual connections that were similar

46. Siméon-Prosper Hardy, *Mes loisirs, ou Journal d'événemens tels qu'ils parviennent à
    ma connoissance (1753-1789)*, ed. Pascal Bastien *et al.*, 11 vols (Paris, 2012-2024),
    vol.6: *1779-1780* (2017), p.139-40 (22 April 1779).
47. David Garrioch, *The Huguenots of Paris and the coming of religious freedom,
    1685-1789* (Cambridge, 2014), p.126-54. Janine Driancourt-Girod, *L'Insolite
    Histoire des luthériens de Paris: de Louis XIII à Napoléon* (Paris, 1992), p.136-40
    and *passim.* Janine Driancourt-Girod, *Ainsi priaient les luthériens: la vie religieuse,
    la pratique et la foi des luthériens de Paris au XVIII* siècle* (Paris, 1992).

to those of kinship.[48] So too did the Jansenists, and also smaller groupings like the association on the pont au Change that aimed to build a *reposoir* but explicitly sought to create bonds of friendship among its members.

Policing

The police took a keen interest in religious sociability. They were always suspicious of meetings that were not held in public, since, as Fréminville's *Dictionnaire, ou Traité de la police* put it in 1771, 'these kinds of assemblies always smack of libertinism, and have nothing but evil ends in view.'[49] Both the Parlement and the police repeatedly banned 'private meetings' unless formally authorised by royal letters patent. In practice, though, the legislation was very selectively enforced, depending on police priorities of the moment and on their evaluation of the threat that particular forms of sociability represented. Usually they supported the ecclesiastical authorities in suppressing unorthodox practices, but the collaboration between religious and secular agencies varied significantly across the century.

It is perhaps surprising to find that the authorities regarded confraternities with some ambivalence. On the one hand, they wished to encourage pious associations that might provide a buffer against Protestantism, a major concern both of the Catholic Church and of successive French monarchs. In 1699 the *commissaire* Delamare argued that it was important to maintain the Blessed Sacrament confraternity at Saint-Barthélemy because the parish was full of 'new Catholics' (the official euphemism for Protestants).[50] Yet not all confraternities, he later pointed out in his *Traité de la police*, were good: alongside purely devotional bodies that were entirely legitimate, there were pernicious confraternities 'who cover themselves with the specious veil of religion to disturb the state'.[51] Such suspicions went back a long way. In 1560 the monarchy had banned confraternities altogether, although the edict was not enforced.[52] A later one, in 1666, required all new

---

48. *The Politics of ritual kinship: confraternities and social order in early modern Italy*, ed. Nicholas Terpstra (Cambridge, 2000). Loiselle, *Brotherly love*, p.47-80.
49. Edme de La Poix de Fréminville, *Dictionnaire, ou Traité de la police générale des villes, bourgs, paroisses et seigneuries de la campagne* (Paris, n.n., 1771), p.13.
50. Paris, BnF, MS fr. 21609, 24 April 1699, f.368.
51. Delamare, *Traité*, vol.1, p.372-73.
52. Froeschlé-Chopard, *Dieu pour tous*, p.19.

confraternities to have their statutes approved by royal letters patent, which needed to be registered with the secular courts. Ordinances intended to control the guilds also targeted the trade confraternities. An edict of 1539 had abolished all the guild confraternities – although it too was not enforced – while in 1670, guild officials were forbidden to organise meetings without police officials being present, whether 'on the pretext of levying funds, confraternities and any other business whatsoever'.[53]

The requirement for all confraternities to have letters patent was renewed in 1749, when another edict formally abolished all those created since 1636 that did not have any. It added a test of public utility for any new ones.[54] This made the suppression of confraternities easier if they attracted unfavourable attention, yet, once again, there is little evidence that the rules were enforced. Whether or not confraternities had letters patent, the secular courts routinely recognised them as 'moral persons', allowing them to take legal action and to own, buy and sell property. In other words, confraternities were 'corporations', like the guilds and many other bodies in Old Regime France. Sometimes, too, technically illegal confraternities won support from the ecclesiastical authorities. Confraternities were both a form of piety and a source of income for monasteries and parishes, and for both reasons they were welcomed and defended. The Brothers of Saint-Jean-de-Latran even intervened in a legal case to support the journeymen printers' confraternity in their church in 1700.[55]

In the second half of the eighteenth century, however, tolerance of confraternities began to dissolve. Surveillance increased, initially as a by-product of the religious disputes between partisans of the papal bull *Unigenitus* and their Jansenist-leaning opponents, who were able to mobilise Gallican feeling in support of their cause. Both the crown and the courts had long been concerned about papal influence, which they saw as a threat to the 'liberties' of the French Church and, as a result, to the close alliance between Church and state on

53. Delamare, *Traité*, vol.1, p.375. Steven Laurence Kaplan, 'Réflexions sur la police du monde de travail, 1700-1815', *Revue historique* 529 (1979), p.17-77.
54. Pierre-Toussaint Durand de Maillane, *Dictionnaire de droit canonique et de pratique bénéficiale*, 2 vols (Paris, n.n., 1761), vol.1, p.637-40. Joseph-Nicolas Guyot, *Répertoire universel et raisonné de jurisprudence civile, criminelle, canonique et bénéficiale*, 64 vols (Paris, n.n., 1775-1783), vol.14, p.335-38.
55. Sonenscher, *Work and wages*, p.81.

which the monarchy was based. As Jansenist influence in the Paris Parlement increased, it clamped down on Jesuit activity, and, given that the Jesuits had been leaders in the creation of confraternities, these too came under suspicion. In 1757, an anonymous denunciation provided a pretext for new legislation. It informed the magistrates of the Parlement of a large association at the Collège de Tours, part of the University, where some 150 workers and servants were attending a sermon and church service on Sundays and holy days. It further claimed that this association was sponsored by an ally of the archbishop of Paris, a major target of the pro-Jansenist forces. Such mobilisation of working people rang alarm bells, and the Parlement decided to reinforce the requirement for confraternities to obtain royal letters patent, but to apply it to existing bodies as well as new ones. In May 1760 it required all confraternities to present their letters patent to the Parlement, which would decide which ones would be authorised to continue. This time the measure was initially enforced: the Parlement gathered information on several hundred confraternities and suppressed a certain number.[56] After 1764, however, once the Jesuits had been exiled from France and disbanded, the heat went out of the issue and the laws on confraternities were once more widely disregarded. Nevertheless, there remained a general suspicion of associations established in monastic churches. Hence, Joseph-Nicolas Guyot declared in 1777, in his comprehensive compilation of French jurisprudence, that confraternities housed by religious orders were potentially dangerous, because, unlike parish ones, they were 'secret'.[57]

These political considerations were reinforced by a long-standing religious critique. Since the Catholic Reformation of the sixteenth and seventeenth centuries, practices that had previously been accepted and even encouraged, such as pageantry, feasting and drinking, had come to be condemned as 'abuses', wasteful and even sinful. A religious work of 1714 accused many confraternities of 'dissolution, vanity, indecency, superstition and sacrilege'.[58] Reforming theologians, particularly Jansenist ones, worried about excessive devotion to the

56. Paris, BnF, JF 1590, f.320, and JF 573, f.401. Kaplan, 'Réflexions', p.61-62. Gustave Dupont-Ferrier, *Du Collège de Clermont au Lycée Louis-le-Grand, 1563-1920*, 3 vols (Paris, 1921-1925), vol.1, p.406.
57. Guyot, *Répertoire*, vol.14, p.344.
58. *Des confréries érigées en l'honneur des saints: traité moral et historique, dans lequel on s'attache particulièrement à combattre les abus qui y règnent* (Avignon, n.n., 1714), p.5, 16, 58, 113. Froeschlé-Chopard, *Dieu pour tous*, p.30-35.

saints, which they saw as potentially superstitious.[59] Such critiques led to bans, by both religious and secular authorities, on confraternal feasting, drinking and gift giving, and even to attempts to limit the pomp with which religious services were celebrated. Guild confraternities were particularly singled out, since they were often more independent of the clergy than the parish ones and therefore able to continue the older forms of sociability. The major royal edict of 1691 that reorganised the Paris guilds explicitly forbade confraternal feasting.[60]

Accusations of 'abuses' in confraternities were further fuelled by rivalry and suspicion between the secular clergy of the parishes and the monastic orders whose churches sheltered many lay associations. Parish churches were directly subject to the bishops, who were key agents of the Catholic Reformation, whereas religious orders had their own, separate lines of authority and were often perceived to be sustaining practices that had been eradicated elsewhere. Furthermore, adding financial injury to pious indignation, many services funded by confraternities channelled income away from the parishes and into convents and monasteries.[61]

In the later eighteenth century, accusations that confraternities encouraged 'superstition' and that those in monastic churches diverted both the faithful and key resources away from the parishes, on which Christian piety and charity should centre, became a key refrain of enlightened anticlericalism, primarily directed against the religious orders. In 1756, Voltaire had condemned confraternities for their 'extravagant ceremonies'. Louis Philipon de La Madelaine's *Vues patriotiques sur l'éducation du peuple*, of 1783, urged the complete abolition of 'these associations which, by persuading people that their confraternity is the centre of salvation, also distract them from the essential duties of religion and the work of their condition, make them intolerant or superstitious, and even mould them into a factional spirit'.[62] These views were already influencing jurists. Fréminville,

---

59. Simiz, *Confréries urbaines*, p.249-52. Dominique Julia, 'Jansénisme et "déchristianisation"', in *Histoire de la France religieuse*, vol.3: *Du roi très chrétien à la laïcité républicaine*, ed. Philippe Joutard (Paris, 1991), p.249-57.

60. Etienne-Olivier Pary, *Guide des corps des marchands et des communautés des arts et métiers tant de la ville et fauxbourgs de Paris, que du royaume* (Paris, n.n., 1766), p.19. See also Alfred Franklin, *Dictionnaire historique des arts, métiers et professions exercés dans Paris depuis le treizième siècle* (Paris, 1906), p.291.

61. Froeschlé-Chopard, *Dieu pour tous*, p.273-75.

62. Voltaire, *Essai sur les mœurs* (1756), 2 vols (Paris, 1829), vol.2, p.319. Louis

in his *Dictionnaire, ou Traité de la police* of 1771, was less worried about sedition than by the threat to religion and morality. While undoubtedly founded with pious intentions, he asserted, confraternities 'have finally degenerated, often into disputes, factions and disorder [...] into superstition and libertinism'. Because of this, they needed to be policed.[63]

In practice, policing was done in the first instance by the clergy rather than by the state. A surge of new statutes in the late seventeenth and early eighteenth centuries reflects the desire of successive archbishops to 'rechristianise' their flock. Hence the rules of the confraternity of Saint-Jean-Baptiste, at Saint-Victor, approved by the archbishop in 1684, stressed spiritual union between the members, emphasised the need for them to take the sacraments regularly, to examine their individual conscience and live a holy life, then die a Christian death. Each administrator, in addition to having a particular devotion to Saint Jean, was expected to be 'selfless, hard-working, clean and modest'. The chaplain who conducted services for the confraternity was to be named by the prior of the monastery, and both priests were to participate in the elections of new administrators.[64] This was a new confraternity, but during this same period many older ones were refounded and granted revised statutes that met the more stringent expectations of the reforming clergy. In 1688, for instance, two confraternities in the parish of Saint-Sulpice – the late medieval one dedicated to Saint Christophe and Saint Geneviève and that of the Ascension that dated at least to the early seventeenth century – were provided with new statutes. A few years earlier, when the confraternity of Notre-Dame de Liesse moved from the Benedictine monastery to Saint-Sulpice, it too was obliged to revise its statutes. The new rules explicitly banned feasts and banquets, strengthened the authority of the parish clergy over the confraternity, and placed severe restrictions on what administrators could spend without explicit permission from the meeting of the governing body, of which the parish priest was a leading member. The insistence of parish priests on naming chaplains to provide religious services to confraternities, providing a greater

Philipon de La Madelaine, *Vues patriotiques sur l'éducation du peuple, tant des villes que des campagnes* (Lyon, n.n., 1783), p.239.

63. Fréminville, *Dictionnaire*, p.244-45, art. 'Confrairies'. See also N. Collin, *Traité des confrairies en général et de quelques-unes en particulier* (Paris, n.n., 1784), p.123-33.

64. *Instructions et prières*.

degree of control, led to many disputes with lay administrators who claimed this right for themselves.[65]

The almost identical wording and provisions of many of the new statutes also reveal the desire of the archdiocese not only to reform but also to standardise the practices of confraternities, even when individual associations drafted their own rules. The election process specified in the statutes became broadly the same, as did the number of administrators and the supervisory role of the governing body, composed of former administrators.[66] At the same time, the Blessed Sacrament confraternities, which the clergy particularly wished to encourage, were given special honours, such as a leading place in processions, use of the main altar and priority in receiving communion.[67]

After about 1720, the archdiocese also seized the opportunity to reform confraternities when they came before its court, the Officialité. The court ruled on disputes over elections, precedence in processions and similar matters, and routinely began to demand to see the statutes of confraternities based in monastic churches. In 1721, the administrators of the confraternity of Notre-Dame et de la Reine Marguerite, at the monastery of the Petits-Augustins, failed to produce the relevant documents, so the court suspended its religious services. Two years later, it did the same when asked to rule on an internal dispute concerning the Archiconfrérie du Saint-Sépulcre de Jérusalem. The confraternity of Notre-Dame de Grâce at the Cordeliers convent was referred to the archbishop, presumably because it had no statutes or letters patent, since the court subsequently approved detailed new statutes.[68]

65. For example, Paris, BnF, 4-Z Le Senne 1395, *Factum pour les maîtres, gouverneurs et administrateurs, tant anciens qu'en charge, de la confrérie du S. Sacrement de l'Autel, première érigée en l'église paroissiale S. Nicolas-des-Champs [...] contre maître François Mommignon, [...] curé de ladite paroisse* (Paris, n.n., 1682).

66. Paris, AN, L569, no.36, 'Statuts de la confrérie de l'Immaculée Conception, Saint-Germain-l'Auxerrois', 18 July 1676. Paris, AN, Z1O 77, f.23*v*-25, 8 August 1722, 'Règlement de la confrérie de Notre-Dame de Grâce'.

67. Paris, Bibliothèque de Port-Royal, Fonds patrimoniaux, LGd 4281, *Recueil d'instructions et de prières à l'usage de la confrairie du Saint Sacrement, érigée le 9 août 1690, en la paroisse de Sainte Marguerite, fauxbourg S. Antoine, à Paris* (Paris, n.n., 1780), p.129-35. Paris, Bibliothèque Mazarine, 42684, *Reglemens de la confrérie du S. Sacrement de l'église paroissiale de S. Barthelemy, donnez par son éminence Monseigneur le cardinal de Noailles* (Paris, n.n., 1708).

68. Paris, AN, Z1O 76, f.97 (3 September 1721), 99 (27 September 1721), 101 (18 October 1721). Z1O 77, f.44*v* (14 April 1723). Z1O 77, f.2*v* (22 November 1721); f.23*v*-25 (8 August 1722).

The secular authorities rarely intervened in this process. In fact, despite the battery of restrictive legislation and their mistrust of civil society, except in the early 1760s they largely ignored confraternities as long as there were no complaints. But they were quick to intervene when journeymen's associations became involved in industrial campaigns. This was a natural outcome of the sociability that accompanied religious celebrations. After the mass, journeymen would repair to nearby wineshops, where they naturally discussed their work, particularly when there were disputes over wages and conditions. In the absence of any other form of organisation, it was often the leaders of the confraternity who took the initiative. In 1746, the journeymen locksmiths' confraternity organised meetings to raise funds to bring a court case against their guild. The guild officials were quick to accuse them of insubordination, and the police, always hostile to worker organisation, agreed. While it was permissible for the journeymen to take legal action, unauthorised meetings were forbidden. As soon as stop-work action began, the authorities arrested the leaders of the confraternity and the strike quickly collapsed. In this case, the Parlement also issued a specific ban on meetings of journeymen, even for the affairs of their confraternity.[69] There are similar examples in other trades. Even then, however, the police sometimes displayed a certain reticence about the legal limits of intervention, as in 1769 when a police inspector requested a formal order from the king in order to arrest the leaders of a journeymen's confraternity who, he pointed out, 'are resident, have wives and children, [...] even have a certain status'.[70] In practice, too, police action and even bans were short-lived. The journeymen roofers' confraternity was abolished no fewer than five times across the seventeenth and eighteenth centuries, but after each ban was again active within a few years.[71]

These actions, like much of what the police did, were an immediate response to a particular situation. So was the very unusual intervention by the police in an internal dispute in the Archiconfrérie du Saint-Sépulcre, which had the privilege of making an annual address to the king. The association had long been run by

69. On this and for other examples, see Garrioch and Sonenscher, 'Compagnonnages', p.33-37. Paris, AN, AD XI 26, pièce 7: *Arrest de la cour de Parlement du 23 juillet 1746*.

70. Paris, Ars., MS 12369, f.12.

71. Garrioch and Sonenscher, 'Compagnonnages', p.31.

shopkeepers and artisans, but in the mid-1770s was taken over by a group of lawyers and wealthy merchants. A bitter struggle ensued, which ended when the merchants got police chief Lenoir to obtain a royal order giving them control.[72] It was normally the law courts that decided these kinds of disputes, but in this case the courts had ruled against the merchants. Lenoir clearly felt that this prestigious association should be in the hands of more illustrious men.

On the whole, though, the police left the confraternities alone. Until the 1770s, the main way in which action by the secular authorities affected the trade confraternities was indirect. It arose from the government's own attempts to extract more money from the Paris trades, which led it to limit confraternal access to guild funds. After 1716, special commissioners began retrospective audits of guild expenditure, and, for the first time, they rigorously separated guild finances from those of the confraternities, declaring that anything spent on religious services had to have been explicitly raised for that purpose. This considerably reduced the amounts available, and combined with other changes in the trades prepared the way for the decline of the confraternities, although that was not the intention. It was nevertheless linked to a new perception, on the part of the royal authorities, that commerce and religion were entirely separate spheres.[73]

The eventual abolition of the trade confraternities in 1776 was connected to the long-standing perception that they fostered cabals. It was part of the assault by *contrôleur général* Turgot on trade organisations in general, and was intended to prevent their members from fixing prices or controlling labour. The fact that trade confraternities continued to be banned when the guilds were re-established at the end of 1776, however, reflects the criticisms of both religious reformers and enlightened thinkers. This is clear in Lenoir's language and actions. Hostile to what he termed 'confréries de cabarets' and their 'pratiques superstitieuses', he nevertheless continued to tolerate a small number of bodies '[which] had as their object the communal exercise in work and in good practices of charity and devotion'.[74] He allowed the Frères tailleurs to continue, although insisted that they could not recruit new members, and he approved of the musicians' mutual aid society. As

---

72. Paris, AN, T1489; Paris, AN, Y13620.

73. David Garrioch, 'Confréries de métier et corporations à Paris (XVIIᵉ-XVIIIᵉ siècle)', *Revue d'histoire moderne et contemporaine* 65 (2018), p.95-117.

74. Milliot, *Un Policier des Lumières*, p.763-64, 777-78. Garrioch, 'Confréries de métier'.

the jurist Joseph-Nicolas Guyot noted in 1777, many confraternities that did not have royal letters patent were tolerated because they were contrary neither to morality nor to religion and 'by the spiritual benefits that could be derived from it'.[75]

Official attitudes towards other sorts of religious sociability were pragmatic, although any association clearly at odds with orthodox Catholicism received short shrift. The fan makers of the rue Quincampoix, with their rejection of church attendance, were promptly locked up, without any judicial process or chance of appeal. The case of the convulsionaries was more complicated, because they were closely linked to Jansenist circles that included many judicial and merchant families. The religious politics of the period were acrimonious, pitting the archbishop against the Parlement, with the royal government backing first one side and then the other.[76] While the police chiefs René Hérault and Claude Feydeau de Marville, between 1725 and 1747, took vigorous action against Jansenism, their efforts were stymied by the fact that, as the diarist Barbier pointed out in 1731, 'three quarters of [their] clerks, commissioners and exempts are for this cause'.[77] The parish clergy, by contrast, had by the 1730s been largely purged of Jansenist priests, and many of them actively pursued lay Jansenists. This made them deeply unpopular and earned many of them retribution from the Parlement.[78] It is not surprising, then, that repression of the convulsionaries and other Jansenist groups was highly selective: most of those arrested, between the 1730s and the 1760s, were plebeian women and a few flamboyant aristocrats. As Nicolas Lyon-Caen points out, after first trying (but not always too hard) to suppress the movement, the police strategy was to contain the phenomenon by keeping it quiet.[79]

They took broadly the same approach with the Protestants, after the failure of rigorous repression in the late seventeenth century. Although

---

75. Guyot, *Répertoire*, vol.14, p.345.
76. Kreiser, *Miracles*. Dale K. Van Kley, *The Jansenists and the expulsion of the Jesuits from France, 1757-1765* (New Haven, CT, 1975).
77. Edmond-Jean-François Barbier, *Chronique de la Régence et du règne de Louis XV, 1718-1763*, 8 vols (Paris, 1857-1866), vol.2, p.211.
78. David Garrioch, *The Formation of the Parisian bourgeoisie, 1690-1830* (Cambridge, MA, and London, 1996), p.17-40, 86-102. Dale K. Van Kley, *The Damiens affair and the unraveling of the Ancien Régime, 1750-1770* (Princeton, NJ, 1984), p.104-63.
79. Kreiser, *Miracles*, p.393. Lyon-Caen, *La Boîte à Perrette*, p.143-52. Catherine Maire, *De la cause de Dieu à la cause de la nation: le jansénisme au XVIIIᵉ siècle* (Paris, 1998), p.143-47.

some of the clergy felt that the best way to convert the Huguenots was to gain their trust, others felt that the secular authorities were not doing enough, and it was most often priests who denounced Protestants. The police and the Parlement, however, were worried that persecution would renew the exodus of artisans and merchants, and they had no wish to provoke religious violence by advertising the Protestant presence. They kept an eye on meetings of Protestants until the 1760s, and any who gathered too openly or who were suspected of trying to convert Catholics were very quickly arrested. But they were usually released quite quickly, and the intention was clearly to persuade them to keep a low profile. Provided they did so, after the 1720s they were rarely much bothered.[80]

Freemasonry posed more of a problem for both the police and the Church, because it came to include many of the social elites. In 1737 the general assembly of the police, composed of the leaders of the Parlement, the police and the municipality, was informed of the existence of this new organisation and decided to ban it. They particularly disliked its closed character, its mixing of different religious groups and its links to England. Through the 1740s the police conducted arrests, although, as they increasingly found themselves dealing with men of the social elites, they targeted the innkeepers who hosted the meetings and provided the dinners afterwards. In 1743 a member of the royal family became the new grand master, and by the 1760s the Paris authorities were only interested in preventing public scandals. In the 1780s, Lenoir was informed of meetings in advance, but he seemed by then to regard the lodges as harmless philanthropic entertainment.[81]

Dilemmas and outcomes

Policing religious sociability was no easy task. Disputes over religion divided Parisians more than any other issue in the eighteenth century, government policy shifted repeatedly, and the different authorities themselves did not always agree. On the one hand, many of the clergy had reservations about confraternities but continued to see them as encouraging piety, and therefore preferred reform to abolition. They were also well aware of the revenue that confraternities brought

80. Garrioch, *Huguenots of Paris*, p.45-74, 182-85.
81. Paris, BnF, MS fr. 11356, f.333*v*-34*v*. Chevallier, *Histoire*, vol.1, p.14-15, 24-124. Orléans, BmO, MS 1422, f.103.

to monasteries and churches. The secular authorities, on the other hand, were mistrustful of 'cabals' and 'secret' meetings, especially in guild confraternities and those in monastic churches. They therefore imposed additional requirements, eventually abolishing the guild confraternities outright and suppressing others.

Where Protestant gatherings were concerned, it was the Catholic clergy who took a hard line, whereas the police feared the economic and social consequences of persecution. They, on the whole, were less swayed by theological factors than by political and practical ones, and most saw God-fearing Protestants as little threat to the state. Over Jansenism, too, both the secular courts and many police officials were often at odds with the clergy. Yet neither the secular nor the ecclesiastical authorities were always unanimous among themselves. Some of the regular clergy, male and female, tolerated practices among the confraternities that the parish clergy did not, while divisions over Jansenism were less predictable and ran much deeper. On the secular side, in mid-century the Parlement took issue with royal policy over Jansenism, leaving the police, servants of the king but subordinate to the Parlement, unhappily in the middle.

On many issues, the police were pragmatists. They had limited resources and much to do. In dealing with religious associations, they preferred them to be in the open, even if they were suspicious, rather than underground. They were also highly sensitive to 'public' opinion, that of the social elites and of the educated, propertied Parisians to whose ranks they themselves mostly belonged. They could clamp down on plebeian organisations, but could not easily arrest noblemen who participated in lodges or gatherings of convulsionaries, or even parish notables who supported Jansenist dissidents. Confraternities, in particular, were part of the social structure that the police were there to defend, legally constituted bodies that conferred rights on their officeholders, even if these were men of modest status, such as journeymen.

Yet both the nature of policing and that of religious belief were changing. The late seventeenth-century police chiefs had to deal with unruly noblemen and their servants, the violence of soldiers and unsafe streets. They feared revolt and interconfessional conflict. In religious matters they suppressed anything they felt was contrary to Catholic doctrine or to the interests of the state, but broadly left oversight of confraternities to the Church. By the later eighteenth century, like the monarchy itself, the police had become more interventionist and more responsive to 'enlightened opinion', suppressing practices that critics both within and outside the Catholic Church condemned as 'abuses'. This included even forms of celebration that had once been seen as pious, such as confraternal feasts and pageants. Police chief Lenoir wished to end the annual burning of the mannequin at the rue aux Ours, finding it disorderly and superstitious, although he reversed this decision when warned of growing irreligion in the quarter and tried simply to ensure that the celebrations were not too rowdy. But this was a temporary reprieve, as the early revolutionary municipality was to suppress the custom on exactly the same grounds![82]

Ironically, while defence of the Catholic Church and of the existing social hierarchy was always a key aim, the policing of religious sociability inadvertently accelerated a variety of changes that helped to undermine both. Many priests and nuns were keen reformers, seeking to encourage a deeply felt personal faith, and their efforts helped to produce a critique of orthodox Catholic practice. They attempted to root out practices they saw as incompatible with true Christianity, such as excessive devotion to the saints. Seconded in the later eighteenth century by enlightened thinkers and by the secular police, their attacks on the rowdy sociability of the older confraternities made religious associations less attractive and helped hasten their demise. The disappearance of confraternities greatly reduced the numbers of religious services and processions.[83] By the 1780s, religious sociability in Paris was far less inclusive and lively than it had been at the start of the century. There were many reasons for this, but among them the policing undertaken by both secular and religious authorities was an important factor, and it accelerated the secularisation of the city.

---

82. Milliot, *Un Policier des Lumières*, p.482-83.
83. David Garrioch, 'La sécularisation précoce de Paris au dix-huitième siècle', *SVEC* 2005:12, p.35-75.

Accommodation: the policing of used playing cards in late eighteenth-century Paris

JEFFREY S. RAVEL

Massachusetts Institute of Technology

One Tuesday morning in June 1786, a confrontation broke out on the rue Saint-Denis, a busy thoroughfare on Paris' Right Bank.[1] Around mid-morning, a group of men who worked for the Régie générale, a recently restructured royal tax-collection bureau, and a *commissaire*, approached a man named Pierre François Houdin. They had received information that Houdin, an out-of-work fishmonger, was selling decks of used playing cards composed of discards he had purchased from some of the city's gambling parlours and from servants working in the houses of elites. Questioning him, the tax collectors and the judge discovered that he possessed a sack containing forty-eight decks of used cards for sale. At first Houdin refused to reveal his identity; once he began to do so, a crowd gathered around him and his interlocutors and threatened to intervene, perhaps violently, in the investigation. The tax collectors and the judge were forced to call the Paris Guard to curtail the disturbance. Once order was restored, the inspectors, the judge and the police had Houdin lead them to a room he rented on the fourth floor of a building on the same street. There they found dozens of pounds of used playing cards that Houdin had stored in boxes, wardrobes, baskets and an empty *chaise percée*, or toilet.[2] The inspectors inventoried Houdin's cards and other materials,

The author wishes to thank Cristelle Baskins, Thierry Depaulis, David Garrioch and an anonymous reviewer for Oxford University Studies in the Enlightenment for their invaluable comments on earlier drafts of this essay.

1.   Details of this encounter can be found at Paris, Archives nationales (AN), G² 192, entry no.3, dated 20 June 1786; and Paris, AN, Y 15999 B, 'Procès-verbal d'emprisonnement de Pierre François Houdin', dated 20 June 1786.

2.   I have translated *une livre* in French as 'a pound' throughout this article. The term *livre* as used by the *régisseurs* in the eighteenth century was an imprecise measurement of weight; it varied from region to region across the kingdom.

wrapped them up in packages, and deposited them in the commode, which they then paraded back to their headquarters. Houdin was led off to prison by the Guard, and later fined the exorbitant sum of 1000 *livres*, which was thousands of times the going rate in Paris for a used deck of playing cards.

The incident, comical in one respect and harrowing in others, raises questions. The image of the tax agents and the police emerging from Houdin's building with a *chaise percée* full of 'evidence' resembles a slapstick parody of overly officious, bumbling bureaucrats. At the same time, the determination to ferret out used playing card purveyors is striking. Why were the tax collectors and the Paris police so interested in a poor, unemployed fisherman who was trying to eke out a living by selling repackaged, resorted cards on the streets of the city? Surely the royal government had better ways to balance its budget. Was not the crushing fine imposed on Houdin out of proportion to the nature of his infraction? Confiscation of his cards and other supplies would put him out of business; payment of the fine was beyond his means, and would leave him destitute. Beyond the individual consequences for Houdin, the reaction of the crowd to this policing initiative suggests that more was at stake in this encounter than the suppression of contraband commerce that infringed on the crown's tax revenues. The state was implicitly reinforcing its authority by its determined pursuit of supposed playing card offenders like Houdin, and the king's subjects were responding, quite explicitly, with a threatened riot that the Guard had to suppress.

This investigation was one of many undertaken by excise tax collectors and policing agents into the commerce in used cards across the Paris Basin in the 1780s.[3] Throughout the decade, agents

---

Furthermore, the *régisseurs* did not carry a scale with them during inspections; sometimes they used the term *poignée*, or 'fistful', to quantify the loose cards they seized.

3. The core of this essay is an analysis of 107 inspections of individuals suspected of buying, selling or otherwise possessing 'illegally' constructed decks of used playing cards. These inspections were carried out in the Paris Basin by agents of the Régie générale between 1779 and 1789; two thirds of them occurred in 1780. Paris, AN, call numbers G^2 190-92 consist of three registers which summarise the results of ninety-nine of these inspections, including the fines paid and their distribution among the collectors and the Régie. Details on the other eight cases not recorded in the Paris, AN, G^2 190-92 registers can be found in the papers of the *commissaire* Mathieu Vanglenne, Paris, AN, Y 15990-16009. Supplementary material on a few of these cases is also available in Paris, AN, Y 9516, the deliberations of the Paris Police Chamber. In several cases, the three registers

of the Régie générale, accompanied by representatives of the Paris police, staked out public spaces and barged into small merchant shops and private apartments across Paris and its suburbs in search of trimmed, resorted decks of used cards. They claimed that these cards were 'fraudulent', by which they meant that the recycled packets contravened royal regulations governing the manufacture and taxation of playing cards. We might be tempted to question the nature of the 'fraud', and to side with Houdin and the crowd that gathered on the rue Saint-Denis to defend him. But we should also think more critically about the motivations of the tax-collecting and policing arms of the kingdom. By the late eighteenth century, the Bourbon government increasingly acknowledged a responsibility not only to the reigning monarch but to his subjects. Corruption, inefficiency and appalling abuses existed, but serious plans were also put forth to reform the workings of the state, and to collect taxes that would finance an enlightened government designed to protect the lives, livelihoods and property of French men and women.[4] The other essays in this volume demonstrate various levels of compatibility between policing policy and practices of sociability in seventeenth- and eighteenth-century Paris. While Parisians who played cards enjoyed their games and the thrill of gambling, the tax-collection initiatives and policing support upon which they relied were not designed to foster these forms of social interaction. The primary goal of these officials was to increase excise tax revenues for the state. The

---

in the G² series also contain loose-leaf documents recording more detailed legal accounts of the inspections, known as *procès-verbaux*. Elisabeth Belmas, *Jouer autrefois: essai sur le jeu dans la France moderne, XVIᵉ-XVIIIᵉ siècle* (Seyssel, 2006), p.343-53, offers an extended, insightful study of the data found in the Paris, AN, G² 190-92 registers and some of the Paris, AN, Y 9516 cases; she focuses primarily on the consumers of these cards. The interpretation below makes use of additional sources in Paris and the French provinces to contextualise the data in these registers, and considers more fully the interest of the monarchy in taxing and policing the commerce in used playing cards.

4. Vincent Milliot, 'Aimer et détester la police? Le peuple et les polices au siècle des Lumières', in *Paris et ses peuples au XVIIIᵉ siècle*, ed. Pascal Bastien and Simon Macdonald (Paris, 2020), p.49-64. See also Vincent Milliot, *'L'Admirable Police': tenir Paris au siècle des Lumières* (Ceyzérieu, 2016); Vincent Denis, 'L'histoire de la police après Foucault: un parcours historien', *Revue d'histoire moderne et contemporaine* 60:4 (2013), p.139-55; and David Garrioch, 'The paternal government of men: the self-image and action of the Paris police in the eighteenth century', in *A History of police and masculinities, 1700-2010*, ed. David G. Barrie and Susan Broomhall (London and New York, 2012), p.35-54.

tax collectors and policing agents charged with maximising this royal revenue stream, however, understood that they could not impose the harsh penalties against the resale of used playing cards called for by the crown. While high-level royal officials argued about enforcing these policies in the last decades of the Old Regime, the royal agents charged with their implementation often found ways to bend the rules in a humane fashion. In the realm of used playing cards, one cannot argue that policing and sociability were compatible, but one can assert that the agents of the crown were able to accommodate the sociable gaming practices of the capital's commoners.

The regulation of used playing cards in France, 1751-1789

The state's efforts to tax playing cards manufactured in the French kingdom dated to 1583, but royal ordinances did not explicitly turn to the question of used playing cards until the mid-eighteenth century.[5] In 1751, the crown established a Royal Military Academy to train the male children of impoverished or orphaned nobles for the officer corps. The monarchy decreed that revenue from an increase in the excise tax levied on playing cards would help to finance the new institution. To guarantee income from the playing card tax, the Bourbon government shifted the responsibility for collection from the tax farm, a semi-feudal practice under which the government sold the right to collect taxes to private individuals, to the Régie, a state-financed bureaucracy whose employees also had permission to pocket some of the taxes they collected on behalf of the crown. On 9 November 1751, the King's Council issued new orders that more strictly regulated the commerce in playing cards.[6] These rules included explicit prohibitions on the resale of used cards; all subjects of the king were prohibited from cutting, trimming and resorting used cards and packaging them to look like new decks. Article 17 of the statute explicitly forbade café and cabaret owners, tennis court proprietors, *épiciers*, *merciers* and many other categories of merchants

---

5. On the taxation of playing cards in France from 1583 to 1790, see Henry-René d'Allemagne, *Les Cartes à jouer du XIVe au XXe siècle*, 2 vols (Paris, 1906), vol.1, p.314-30; Thierry Depaulis, 'Between Germany and France: cardmakers in Landau and Kehl', *The Playing-card* 49:2 (2020), p.50-61; and Belmas, *Jouer autrefois*, p.287-306.

6. *Arrest du Conseil d'Etat du roi, portant règlement pour la perception du droit sur les cartes, 9 novembre 1751.* Paris, Bibliothèque nationale de France (BnF), F-23662 (317).

and small businessmen and women from buying, selling or otherwise possessing playing cards not manufactured under the auspices of the Régie, under threat of a fine of 1000 *livres*. Nor could they refuse the agents of the Régie entry to their homes or places of business for the purpose of searching for fraudulent playing cards, on pain of a 500-*livre* fine. Article 20 authorised visits by the agents of the Régie to *châteaux*, townhouses, convents and other habitations for the purpose of searching for illegal playing cards. It also, however, required the agents to obtain authorisation from a royal judge, or to have a judge accompany the agents on their inspections. The statutes therefore confirmed the state's rights to tax playing cards while also requiring the legal system and the police to protect the king's subjects from capricious behaviour on the part of the agents of the Régie.

Not surprisingly, the Régie did not always adhere to the constraints placed upon it in the 1751 statutes, leading individuals subject to excessive scrutiny to call upon the law and the police for redress. In Rouen in the late 1760s, for example, the local *intendant* began to receive letters complaining about alleged abuses by the agents of the Régie, including forced entry without the presence of a judge, falsification of reports and exorbitant fines for infractions that seemed trivial. In one instance, in December 1769, an *écuyer* named Du Verdray who had a townhouse in Rouen and a residence in a village north of the city reported that the *régisseurs* had shown up at his country home at nine o'clock on a Sunday morning as he was preparing to attend church.[7] They had no magistrate with them, but insisted on inspecting the residence, in spite of the owner's claim that he rarely played cards and had only a few legitimately purchased decks in the house. When his servant Simon told the agents that he kept a handful of used cards, whose backs were blank, for IOUs and sending notes to others in the neighbourhood, the *régisseurs* spent three hours turning the house upside down in search of playing cards. Du Verdray protested against the invasion of his home, saying the law did not authorise the agents to 'conduct searches contrary to the security and liberty of citizens', nor did it allow them to pry into 'the secrets and the most hidden affairs of families'.

---

7.   This incident is recounted in two *supplications* to the *intendant* of Rouen in Rouen, Archives départementales de Seine-Maritime (ADSM), C 605, dated 3 February 1770 and 28 February 1770. Several other *supplications* from the late 1760s recounting similar incidents can be found in this dossier. All translations are my own unless otherwise indicated.

Inspired most likely by this event and other alleged abuses, the Parlement of Rouen, the region's highest law court, issued an order on 19 March 1770 in which it forebade the Régie agents under any pretext to enter the assembly halls, *châteaux* and houses of the king's subjects unless accompanied by a *commissaire*.[8] Noting that playing cards, initially an amusement for high society, had become 'an almost necessary pastime' at all social levels, the judges upheld the legitimacy of the excise tax on their manufacture, especially since it now directly benefited the Royal Military Academy. Nevertheless, they wrote, the *régisseurs* in Normandy were entering homes armed, without police accompaniment, and subjecting citizens to harsh enquiries, after which they would seize playing cards and destroy them without following the proper procedure. Given these repeated abuses, the judges of the Parlement argued, they had no choice but to issue a call to respect the safeguards set up to protect the king's subjects in his several ordinances dating back to the start of the century.

This decision drew a swift rebuke from the King's Council sitting in Versailles. In an opinion a month later, the Council nullified the order of the Rouen Parlement, arguing that the experiences of the 1750s and 1760s showed that the work of the Régie was not comparable to other forms of justice.[9] It was sufficient for the agents to take an oath in front of a royal judge before they undertook inspections of private residences and other venues. The king's statute of 9 November 1751 provided sufficient protection for his subjects against abuses, the Council asserted; any further constraints placed on the work of the *régisseurs* would result in unacceptably reduced revenues for the Royal Military Academy. At the kingdom-wide level, this clash of wills in Normandy should be understood as one episode in the gathering political storm that led to the crown disbanding all twelve *parlements* at the end of 1770, an event subsequently labelled the 'Maupeou coup' after the royal chancellor who oversaw it.[10] But at the local level it reflected the tensions in the system set up by the monarchy to profit

8. See the printed *Arrest de la cour de Parlement de Rouen* [...] *du 19 mars 1770*, in Rouen, ADSM, C 604.
9. *Arrest du Conseil d'Etat du roi* [...] *du 21 avril 1770*. See the copy in Paris, BnF, Cabinet des estampes, Kh 380 (7), item 40.
10. Durand Echeverria, *The Maupeou revolution: a study in the history of libertarianism, France, 1770-1774* (Baton Rouge, LA, 1985); Shanti Marie Singham, '"A conspiracy of twenty million Frenchmen": public opinion, patriotism, and the assault on absolutism during the Maupeou years, 1770-1775', doctoral dissertation, Princeton University, 1991.

from the steadily growing popularity of card games among the king's subjects. The conflict the year before at the country home of Du Verdray had revealed that the motivations of the tax agents and the desire of the king's subjects for protection from arbitrary abuses of power were not easily balanced.

A royal reform of the Régie towards the end of the 1770s brought these issues into even greater relief. From 1777 to 1780, the director general of finances, Jacques Necker, transferred most of the responsibility for collecting indirect taxes under the auspices of the Régie.[11] As part of this reorganisation, the state decided to divert the flow of playing card revenues from the Military Academy to the coffers of the Royal Treasury. Henceforth, taxes on playing cards would finance a variety of government policies, rather than the professional training of the hereditary elite, thereby linking this income to the general welfare of the king and his subjects. At the same time, the Régie tried to address a decline in revenue collection from playing cards that had arisen since 1751. A nine-page circular dated May 1779, and a second printed letter from the same source at about the same time, set the tone of these discussions.[12] Both documents identified manufacturing fraud as a major threat to revenue collection under the new administration of the playing card tax. The practices of some card makers, who counterfeited official face card designs and wrappers intended to be printed only under the direct supervision of the *régisseurs*, were one aspect of the problem. Equally present in the 1779 administrative decrees issued by the Régie, however, was a determination to root out 'fraud' committed by the king's subjects who reconstituted decks from used playing cards. From a consumer perspective, these repurposed decks served the needs of consumers who could not afford decks with higher taxes; reports from at least two provinces noted that the rise in prices during wartime had made essential goods so costly that less wealthy consumers could no longer afford official decks.[13] From the

---

11. Although there is no study on the Régie in the eighteenth century comparable to the major work by Yves Durand on their counterparts, *Les Fermiers généraux au XVIIIᵉ siècle* (Paris, 1971), one may consult Aline Logette, 'La Régie générale au temps de Necker et de ses successeurs (1777-1786)', *Revue historique de droit français et étranger* 60:3 (1982), p.415-45.

12. Paris, AN, G² 185, dossier 12, 'Circulaire sur la répression de la fraude', and undated, printed three-page letter that begins: 'De tous les abus qui portent atteint au produit des droit sur les cartes'.

13. Paris, AN, G² 25, dossier 1, 'Etat de localité des villes et banlieues de Strasbourg'.

perspective of the Régie and at least some *cartiers*, however, these fraudulent decks hurt both the Royal Treasury and the bottom line of the guildsmen who manufactured cards.

Accordingly, the new directives issued in 1779 renewed authorisation for employees of the Régie to go into private homes and businesses such as cabarets and cafés in search of fraudulent cards. The circular distinguished between the homes of nobles, upper-level clerics and *bourgeois notables* on the one hand, and the small businesses and domiciles of less wealthy and prestigious subjects of the king. The households of the kingdom's elites presented substantial problems for the Régie because domestics had access to decks of cards deemed too worn to be usable at the card tables of their masters. The circular and letter issued by the Régie in 1779 encouraged its employees to remind the heads of wealthy households to remove official envelopes and wrappers of new decks immediately upon purchase and destroy them, so that their domestics would not package reconstituted decks of used cards with them. At the same time, however, the circular cautioned Régie employees against overly aggressive intrusions into the households of the wealthy and important. Only the most senior Régie officials should conduct *visites de politesse* to these households, and then only when accompanied by local judges or other legal officials. If they discovered fraudulent activity, an oral *avertissement instructif* was preferable to an official written report and the levying of a fine. No such precautions were advised, however, when visiting the homes and businesses of *personnes d'un état médiocre*. This category included people who ran gambling parlours, cafés, cabarets, tennis courts and billiard parlours. The social distinctions made explicit in this circular informed the actions of the *régisseurs* in Paris and the provinces throughout the 1780s as they pursued their mission of suppressing the commerce in fraudulent playing cards.

The circulation of used playing cards in the Ile-de-France *c.*1780

It was perhaps inevitable that, by the 1780s, the Paris Basin would be the focus of the tax agency's renewed efforts to curtail the trade in used playing cards among the popular classes. Boasting perhaps as many as 600,000 residents, the capital was by far the largest city in the realm, with more potential gamblers and casual card players and a greater need for cheaply available decks of cards than any

Figure 9: Authorised band for a deck of cards. At the top of the
document, an authorised band for a deck of cards manufactured
in France, and on the bottom an authorised band for a *sixain*,
or six-pack, of cards. Rouen, Archives départementales de la
Seine-Maritime, dossier C 604.

other urban area. The size of the capital and its surrounding towns
encouraged the organic development of a more complex, diversified
distribution network for used playing cards than that found in any
other urban area in the kingdom. The Régie, in response to the
challenges posed by the commerce in used cards in the Ile-de-France,
relied on physical identifiers established earlier in the century to
indicate that manufacturers had paid the proper tax before bringing

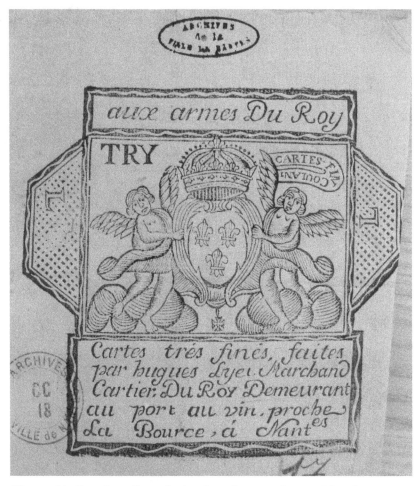

Figure 10: Envelope for a deck of cards manufactured by the master card maker Hugues Lyet in Nantes, second half of the eighteenth century. Nantes, Archives municipales de la ville de Nantes, CC 18, pièce 17.

their product to market. For example, for most of the century, the state required that official decks of cards be wrapped in printed bands designed and distributed by the Régie and then sealed in an approved envelope (see Figures 9 and 10).

In 1701, following a royal decree, the tax agents collected the woodblocks previously used by the card makers to produce face cards and destroyed them. The revenue collectors then substituted newly cut woodblocks for printing face cards. The card makers were required to bring their paper to the tax agent's office in order to print the outline of the face cards. Taxing agents were provided with copies of this official imprint, which they could compare with cards in circulation to make sure no one was producing illegal, or 'false', playing cards. Examples of these official imprints can be found in Parisian and provincial archives (see Figure 11).[14]

Another technique, first implemented in 1751, required card makers to print their cards on paper supplied by the crown, with a special watermark. Complaints from card makers about the poor quality of this paper, or the insufficient amount of official paper supplied by the state, are common in the archives. For its part, the state was constantly arresting paper makers who surreptitiously supplied unauthorised paper to card makers who wanted to manufacture playing cards illicitly.[15] Taken together, these four elements (bands, envelopes, face card design and paper watermarks) allowed the inspectors of the Régie to quickly ascertain whether a deck of cards was 'fraudulent' (i.e. not in compliance with manufacturing techniques that assured the excise tax had been paid).

Earlier in the century, these indicators had been used to crack down on card makers who attempted to produce new decks of cards outside the royal inspection systems. Often these artisans would stock a duplicate shop hidden from the inspectors that would allow them to produce cards clandestinely.[16] While these secret workshops persisted until the Revolution, after 1751 the *régisseurs* also used the identifying bands, envelopes, face card designs and watermarks to ferret out repackaged decks of used cards that turned up during inspections. The inspection registers that the Paris *régisseurs* maintained in the 1780s allow us to evoke in some detail the circulation of these used playing cards from the time they left the homes of the capital's elites

14. For more on these procedures, see Thierry Depaulis, 'Le portrait des cartes à Lyon: la Révolution et après', *Le Vieux Papier* 408 (2013), p.49-56 and plates 8 and 9.
15. For a 1780 case involving paper smuggling from Rouen into Paris in 1780, see Paris, AN, G² 190, entry no.29; and Paris, AN, Y 10800 A, papers of *commissaire* Graville, 7 July 1780; and a 1782 case at Paris, AN, Y 15991, papers of *commissaire* Vanglenne, *Procès-verbal du 31 juillet 1782*.
16. A particularly well-documented example of such a clandestine workshop can be found at Paris, AN, Y 9516, dossier 'Nicholas Isaac Delaistre, 1747'. As the century wore on, some card counterfeiters located their workshops in particularly audacious spots, including the basement of the Tuileries Palace in Paris and the Bordeaux mint.

Figure 11: Face cards printed from a woodblock held by the Régie office in Bordeaux, *c.*1773. Note the wax seal on the lower left and the handwritten notation at the bottom certifying that this is an imprint from an official woodblock in the possession of the Régie. Bordeaux, Archives départementales de la Gironde, C 1204.

or the city's *académies de jeu* (authorised gambling parlours), discarded because they were too worn, until they made their way to more modest shops selling alcohol, tobacco and other minor consumer goods in Paris and the towns outside the city walls.[17]

The records indicate that the Régie uncovered more than half a dozen individuals in Paris in the 1780s whom we might label as 'wholesalers' of used playing cards. These people obtained large lots of used playing cards from gambling parlours or the houses of elites who could afford to buy dozens of new decks of playing cards at a time, then discard the decks when they became worn. Most of the wholesalers were workers who supported themselves or supplemented their incomes as used card dealers. The *régisseurs* in the 1780s, in addition to writing up a fishmonger like Houdin, also cracked down on a salt seller, a former member of the Régie, and even a member of the card makers' guild itself for wholesale trafficking in reconstituted decks of playing cards. Some of them were men working on their own, while others were married couples; a few were women supervising male domestics. There is no typical profile for these wholesalers, but a detailed look at a few of their operations illustrates the movement of used cards from the tables of the wealthy to the drinking and eating establishments of the working classes in Paris and its suburbs.

Pierre-Joseph Thuillon had formerly been a footman in the service of the princesse d'Enghien.[18] In 1771, in return for his loyalty, the princess had bestowed a 300-*livre* annuity on him, which he was still receiving in 1785 when the Régie had him thrown in prison and ultimately fined for dealing in used playing cards. Thuillon was forty-two years old at the time of his arrest, living in the Saint-Germain neighbourhood on the Left Bank. He identified himself to the *régisseurs* who showed up at his door on 18 July that year as a *bourgeois de Paris*, or a resident of the city existing by his own means, no longer in the service of another. In his fourth-floor room, the inspectors found signs that he lived comfortably, including a large bed luxuriously furnished with sheets and blankets, fashionable clothes, six framed engravings and a portrait of himself in a gilded oval frame, a flute, a barometer, a timepiece, a coffee service, a snuffbox and eight bound volumes, including a *Vocabulaire français*. They also found 'a large

---

17. On the *académies de jeu*, see Francis Freundlich, *Le Monde du jeu à Paris, 1715-1800* (Paris, 1995).

18. Paris, AN, Y 15997, 'Procès-verbal d'emprisonnement de Pierre-Joseph Thuillon', 18 July 1785.

quantity' of used playing cards originally manufactured by official guild card makers that had been trimmed and resorted, and the tools necessary to forge counterfeit bands and envelopes in which to wrap them. Later that day, Thuillon led the inspectors and a police escort guarding him to a sixth-floor room he rented under a false name in a building near the Saint-Germain abbey, where they seized 148 six-packs of playing cards, 460 counterfeit bands for wrapping single decks of playing cards, 900 bands for wrapping six-packs, 83 pounds of unsorted used playing cards, and various implements necessary to repackage and resell used playing cards. Under interrogation, he claimed that another man named La France, 'now living in Italy', had forged the wrapping bands, while he wrapped the cards and resold them to 'different persons'. The price for a six-pack of his repurposed cards was 20-24 *sous*. After Thuillon had languished in prison for two months, the lieutenant general of police ordered that he be fined 5000 *livres*, far above the standard sum authorised by statute, and forfeit all the possessions found in his primary residence.

Other used card wholesalers investigated by the agency did not live quite as ostentatiously as Thuillon, but operated on a similar scale. A year earlier, in August 1784, in the course of their ordinary rounds, the *régisseurs* noticed a *colporteur*, or street vendor, who was hawking playing cards in the square in front of the Saint-Sulpice church on the Left Bank.[19] They detained him, discovering that he had eighty-one decks of used, resorted cards in his possession. During the course of questioning he explained that he had obtained the cards he was selling from an individual he described as a *garçon papetier*. Two days later the *régisseurs* and an accompanying police officer staked out a meeting that the vendor had arranged in the Luxembourg Gardens with his supplier. When the latter appeared, the agents arrested him and seized three six-packs of used cards on his person that he had assembled from a variety of different decks. Under interrogation the man, a forty-six-year-old unemployed domestic in ill health named Michel Jovenne, first tried to argue that he was also only a retailer. Since his last master's death, he had been unable to find another service position; he had been trying to make ends meet by running errands and doing other small tasks, including selling the occasional deck of used cards. Under examination, however, Jovenne admitted that he had a more extensive card repackaging operation, and led

19. Paris, AN, Y 15995 A, 'Procès-verbal d'emprisonnement de Michel Jovenne', 18 and 20 August 1784, and Paris, AN, Y 9516, dossier 'Jovenne'.

the agents to his residence on the fifth floor of a building on the rue Condé, not far from the Luxembourg Gardens. There they found hundreds of used cards sorted by face value, some of which had been regrouped into decks, and more than a thousand counterfeit wrapper bands and the instruments to produce them. The inspectors also found a letter from a customer dated June 1780 in which Jovenne was asked to supply dozens of fifty-two-card decks. After two months in the Grand Châtelet prison, Jovenne was sentenced to pay a 1000-*livre* fine, and his cards and tools were confiscated by the Régie. In February of the following year, though, unable to pay the fine and languishing in the prison's hospital in poor health, he was released pending the discovery of further information in the case.

The case of a third wholesaler named Guillaume Lurier, investigated by the Régie in June 1786, provides an even clearer picture of the circulation of used cards in Paris at the end of the Old Regime.[20] Lurier, a carpenter no longer able to exercise his trade, was arrested at a northern city gate while attempting to sell used decks of cards. The *régisseurs* found 136 piquet decks in a sack he was carrying. Lurier explained that he bought some of the used cards by the pound from the *académie de jeu* in the Hôtel d'Angleterre, paying 15 *sous* per pound, and the rest from a domestic serving in the residence of the marquis de Chabonnet. He made his living by repackaging these cards and selling them to cabaret owners in La Courtille, a working-class neighbourhood just outside the city walls north of Paris, allegedly for 2 *sous* per deck. Three days after his arrest and confinement in the Hôtel de la Force, a royal prison where many of those who ran afoul of the Régie were sent, Lurier admitted that he had given them a false residential address. The agents then briefly pulled him from the prison and took him to his true residence in a third-floor room in a building in the Courtille neighbourhood, where they found many more packaged decks of used cards and several pounds of unsorted used cards. Lurier confessed that he actually sold his reconstituted decks of used cards to cabaret owners for 1 *livre* for a piquet deck of thirty-two cards, and 2 *livres* for a full deck of fifty-two cards. Two months later, Lurier was condemned to pay a 1000-*livre* fine, and reimburse the Régie and the police 62 *livres* for their expenses.

The registers detailing the inspections undertaken by the Régie in the 1780s also provide insight into the customers of the

---

20. Paris, AN, G^2 192, f.1; Paris, AN, Y 1599 B, 'Procès-verbal d'emprisonnement du nommé Guillaume Lurier', 5 June 1786.

wholesalers, the 'people of mediocre condition' who sold wine
and spirits out of their homes and who kept a few decks of used
cards for the pleasure of their customers. In the five months from
June to October 1780, the *régisseurs* conducted fifty-six inspections
of small-scale purveyors of alcohol and other goods suspected of
making used playing cards available to their clients.[21] This concentrated period of activity preceded the three operations detailed
above, which all took place in the mid-1780s. None of the fifty-six
shops inspected in the summer and autumn of 1780 was found to
have more than twenty decks of used cards in its possession, and
most had fewer than ten. None had loose counterfeit bands or
envelopes, or the tools needed to fabricate them, further distin-
guishing them from the wholesalers who supplied them. Of the
fifty-six shops inspected, forty-one were run by husband-and-wife
couples. Table 13 tallies the occupations of these fifty-six merchants
as identified to the Régie agents.

Table 13: Stated occupations of individuals found with
twenty decks of used cards or fewer in their possession,
June-October 1780[22]

Stated occupation	Number of cases
Marchand de vins	20
Marchand limonadier	17
Marchand ou débitant de tabac	10
Cabaretier	5
Marchand épicier	4
Marchand de bière	2
Aubergiste	2
Traitteur	2
Marchand Saulnier ou regrattier de sel	2

21. Summaries for all fifty-six cases can be found in Paris, AN, G^2 190-91.
22. Occupations mentioned only once, not listed above: *marchand pâtissier,
    marchand mercier, compagnon cartier, ancien débitant de cartes, marchand vinaigrier,
    marchand boursier, billardier tenant académie.* Some individuals gave more than
    one occupation for themselves, hence the table displays a total number of
    occupations greater than fifty-six. Source: Paris, AN, G^2 190-91.

The table makes clear that, during this five-month period in 1780, the Régie agents targeted shops that provided stimulants such as wine, *limonade* (an inexpensive liqueur in the eighteenth century), tobacco and other consumables to their customers.[23] A few offered both alcohol and tobacco. These purveyors, no doubt operating on small margins, could not afford new decks of playing cards, so they sought used cards through various networks to enhance the experience of their patrons. Unlike the wholesalers discussed above, all of whom had set up shop within the city walls of Paris, twenty-one of these fifty-six establishments were located outside the city, including venues in Chaillot, Nanterre, Saint-Denis, Suresnes and Vincennes. The agents visited these extramural locations because they had received word that they were supplied by Paris wholesalers, or by domestics serving in wealthy households within the city who had access to their masters' used cards.

An inspection conducted during these months at the home of a *marchand de vins* named Claude Jacob and his wife is typical of these encounters between the Régie and small shopkeepers.[24] On the morning of 31 July 1780, three employees of the Régie knocked on the door of their home in the Saint-Marcel parish in Paris in search of fraudulent playing cards. When Jacob and his unnamed wife opened the door, the agents, who did not have a police judge accompanying them, presented their credentials. They requested entry onto the premises, and asked the couple to show them all the decks of playing cards they had in their possession. The Jacobs told the agents that they had none, and that no one ever played cards in their residence. Undeterred, the agents informed them that they would need to inspect every room in the house. In the kitchen, they asked Jacob's wife to open the *buffet*, a wooden chest used to store tableware and linen. At the bottom of the chest, the inspectors found six piquet decks of playing cards, as well as half a pound of unsorted, used playing cards. Three of the decks had been wrapped together in a piece of paper, while the other three were unwrapped. All six were composed

23. On distinctions between taverns, cabarets and other drinking establishments in eighteenth-century Paris, see Thomas Brennan, 'Taverns and the public sphere in the French Revolution', in *Alcohol: a social and cultural history*, ed. Mack Holt (Oxford and New York, 2006), p.107-20.
24. The summary of the Jacob inspection detailed here is register entry no.44 in Paris, AN, G^2 190; I have supplemented this account with the *procès-verbal* based on the inspection, which is an unattached three-page document tucked into the register and dated 31 July 1780.

of used cards, presumably selected from the other cards found at the bottom of the chest.

During the inspection, Jacob fled the house, leaving his wife to explain the situation. Her default role as the face of this husband-and-wife enterprise emphasises the importance of women in these small, family-run businesses, and in the trade in used playing cards. The couple may also have thought she would be punished less severely. Upon discovery of the cards, the agents asked Mme Jacob why, in spite of rules forbidding reconstituted decks of used playing cards, they had found the six suspect decks in her kitchen. They wanted to know where she had obtained the cards, how much she had paid for them and how they were being used in her home. Dropping the couple's initial claim that they had no used cards on hand, she explained that she had received the cards in the chest in an unsorted pile from a female domestic of the chevalier de Carle, a lieutenant-colonel in the king's infantry. She herself had assembled the six piquet decks from the cards the servant of the *chevalier* had given her; the intention, she said, was to provide them to customers who came to drink wine in their home, not to resell them. Upon hearing this explanation, the inspectors wrote a detailed report of their investigation and findings, which they then read to her. She refused to sign the report, or perhaps did not know how to write her name. The agents then confiscated the cards, wrapped them in a white piece of paper, closed it with the agency's red Spanish wax seal and left the premises. Eleven days later, Jacob and his wife paid a fine of 24 *livres* and agreed to allow the collectors to keep the cards they had confiscated. The case was then closed.

While the Jacobs, a married couple who formulated piquet decks from a stash of cards they kept hidden in their kitchen, are in many ways typical of those targeted by the agents, the Régie came across others who were not wine sellers or had different connections to the used card trade during this period of intense investigations in 1780. Alexandre Billod, for example, whom the Régie agents encountered a month earlier than the Jacobs, identified himself as a *marchand limonadier*, a tobacco vendor (*débitant de tabac*) and a journeyman card maker.[25] Operating alone out of a shop on the rue Saint-André-des-Arts on the Left Bank, he was found to have seven trimmed and resorted piquet decks in his possession, one of which had been placed in an envelope with his own logo on it, as well as half a pound

25. Paris, AN, G² 190, entry no.16, 20 June 1780.

of unsorted cards. He agreed to pay a fine of 48 *livres*. Three weeks later, Bernard Thellement and his wife, also *marchands limonadiers* and tobacco sellers who ran a small watering hole on the rue Mazarin near the Saint-Sulpice church, forfeited eleven piquet decks to the agents.[26] They claimed that the decks had been left in their shop by men exiting the nearby gambling parlour who came to their bar to drink. They also settled for a 48-*livre* fine. In both cases, these Parisian purveyors of alcohol and tobacco had found a way to acquire modest amounts of used cards for the amusement of their customers.

The Parisian traffic in used cards in the 1780s extended beyond the town walls. On 1 July the *régisseurs* accosted a couple in the public square of Courbevoie, a village just to the west of Paris, who claimed to be pastry makers, *traiteurs* and wine sellers.[27] They were carrying sixteen piquet decks, composed of used cards that had been resorted and placed in blank envelopes. They told the agents they had bought them from a domestic for 3 *sous* apiece to give to the customers who came to their establishment to drink. The agency negotiated a settlement of 48 *livres* with the pair. Almost three weeks later in Nanterre, also west of the city, the agents raided the shop of a *marchand épicier* named Delaunay and his wife, in which they found seven decks of trimmed and resorted cards, including six wrapped in envelopes sporting the mark of the 'Roy de Siam', a well-known brand of the Mandrou firm, one of the best-known Paris playing card manufacturers.[28] Delaunay told the inspectors that his sister, who was a servant in a house in Paris, had passed him the cards. For their transgressions, the Delaunays were forced to pay 60 *livres*. And five days after that, in the village of Suresnes just south of Courbevoie and Nanterre, the agents confiscated four trimmed and repackaged piquet decks from another spice merchant and tobacco seller named Nicolas Billard and his wife, who recounted that they had bought the decks from a domestic in the 'streets of Paris' who had been selling them for 3 *sous* per deck.[29] This time the agents extracted 36 *livres* from the unfortunate couple.

---

26. Paris, AN, G^2 190, entry no.32, 11 July 1780.
27. Paris, AN, G^2 190, entry no.25, 1 July 1780.
28. Paris, AN, G^2 190, entry no.35, 19 July 1780. On the Mandrou card manufacturing family, see Thierry Depaulis, 'Des "figures maussades & révoltantes": Diderot et les cartes à jouer', *Le Vieux Papier* 412 (2014), p.256-64; 413 (2014), p.289-98; 414 (2014), p.342-53; and 415 (2015), p.409-21.
29. Paris, AN, G^2 190, entry no.37, 24 July 1780.

This survey of the flow of used cards from the tables of the elites and the city's gambling parlours to neighbourhood bars and watering holes in Paris and its outskirts suggests the structure of this commerce. Some middlemen gathered large lots of used cards which they fashioned into facsimiles of officially packaged decks that emulated playing cards manufactured by official members of the card makers' guild. Other intermediary agents sold or gave away lesser lots of cards to smaller retailers or merchants, who in turn resold them or provided them to customers who sought amusement in neighbourhood spaces. Many of those encountered by the *régisseurs* claimed that they had no idea that the trade in repurposed playing cards was illegal; some of course were pursuing a strategy to avoid prosecution, but others, it would seem, may have believed there was no harm in circulating used cards on which an excise tax had already been paid. Major wholesalers such as Thuillon, Jovenne and Lurier who manufactured fake bands and envelopes in their crowded apartments had little room to contest the technical charges of fraud brought against them by the Régie, although the larger question of the merits of serving customers who could not afford a pack of new cards remained open. But what damage was being done by a couple like the Jacobs, who acquired a small cache of used cards from time to time to enhance their business and serve customers who did not have the means to buy newly manufactured decks for their enjoyment?

'Accommodating' the used card network in the Ile-de-France in the 1780s

We know of the elaborate Paris Basin network of used card wholesalers, retailers and consumers outlined above thanks to the meticulous records kept by the employees of the Régie and the Paris policing agents with whom they collaborated. The goal of the Régie was to expand royal tax revenues, especially after the 1778 reform that redirected the taxes they collected from the Royal Military Academy to the Treasury for unrestricted use. But did the compensation structure for the director of the bureau and for its staff on the ground also provide an incentive to identify and fine as many participants in this network as possible? What motivated the agents of the Régie, and in the final analysis how successful were they at increasing the agency's revenues and controlling the trade in used playing cards? Were their actions moderated by the theoretical imperative, espoused by eighteenth-century enlightened police reformers, that the state should ensure the security and material well-being of the people as well as buttress the authority of the monarch?[30]

The records of Régie inspections from the years 1780 and 1781 allow more insight into the potential conflicts of interest at play when the *régisseurs* knocked on the doors of small-time merchants in Paris and its suburbs. For these two years as a whole, we have records of eighty-nine inspections conducted by the agents of the Régie. The 9 November 1751 royal statute permitted the Régie to levy a fine of 1000 *livres* for possession of fraudulent cards, and 500 *livres* for refusing the *régisseurs* entry to inspect a home or workplace. Attempts to collect fines at this level were made later in the 1780s in the case of some of the used card wholesalers we have discussed, but, in the 1780-1781 period under consideration here, the agents of the Régie negotiated 'accommodations' with those they found in possession of used playing cards, rather than insisting on the officially sanctioned amounts. As a result of these eighty-nine inspections, the agents collected fines totalling 3040 *livres*, 8 *sous*, for an average of 34 *livres*, 3 *sous* per investigation. None of the fines exceeded 200 *livres*, and seventy-five of them yielded less than 50 *livres*. A total of 775 decks of used playing cards were confiscated, or an average of 8.7 decks per event. The three highest confiscation totals were ninety-nine, sixty and forty-two decks; no other haul exceeded twenty decks, and seventy-three of the inspections yielded ten decks or fewer. At first glance, therefore, the outcome of these two years of intensive surveillance of the Paris used

---

30. Before delving more deeply into the motivations of the Régie, an archival caution is in order. It is clear that the *régisseurs*, in partnership with the Paris police, surveyed the Parisian market in used cards throughout the decade. But we only have registers detailing the full extent of their work for three years: 1780, 1781 and 1786. The registers for the other years have gone missing, or perhaps never existed. Police reports on major contraventions in the other years, from different archival deposits, confirm that tax oversight of the market for used cards was continuous up to the outbreak of the Revolution. But we must extrapolate the full nature of this activity across the decade from these three more fully documented years and the surviving individual cases from other years, and especially from the 1780-1781 period when the eighty-nine relevant investigations occurred. The total number of investigations in registers in Paris, AN, G[2] 190-92 breaks down as follows: 1780 (G[2] 190): 58 / 1781 (G2 191): 33 / 1786 (G[2] 192): 10. For purposes of the analysis that follows of 1780 and 1781, two of the investigations have been excluded; one took place in October 1779, and one in 1780 involved the seizure of a shipment of paper for making illicit playing cards rather than the trade in the cards themselves.

card market hardly seems worth the trouble, given that the efforts
of the Régie resulted in gross revenues to the Royal Treasury of 1.3
million *livres* per year by the eve of the Revolution.[31]

In the vast majority of the eighty-nine cases recorded in 1780
and 1781, the *régisseurs* negotiated the amount of the accommodation
based in part on the quantity of material confiscated, and in part on
the agents' assessment of the individual's ability to pay. There was no
clear correlation between the number of decks seized and the amount
of the accommodation; the fine was set each time via negotiation
between the agents and those they had found with used cards. The
régisseurs may have informed individuals like the Jacobs that they were
technically subject to a fine of 1000 *livres*, which the working-class
couple was in no position to pay. The agreed-upon accommodation
was usually one twentieth or less of the fine authorised by royal
statute. The agents then recorded the distribution of the negotiated
accommodation, noting in the register that the Régie had consented
to the accommodation in lieu of the far greater, but most likely
unobtainable, judgement permitted in the 1751 guidelines.[32] The
agents recorded that each settlement was split equally three ways:
between the director of the Régie charged with oversight for the tax
on playing cards, the two to four agents who undertook the operation,
and the Régie itself. Over the course of 1780-1781, the director of the
Régie, Ferdinand Charles Cambon, collected almost 500 *livres* each
year, a sum that effectively gave him up to a 10 per cent bonus on
top of his annual salary and other benefits.[33] The agents under him

31. Belmas, *Jouer autrefois*, p.305. Belmas argues further that the agency's
    investment in labor and equipment necessary to produce this revenue signifi-
    cantly diminished the net proceeds.
32. See, for example, the third entry in the 1780 register, Paris, AN, G² 190,
    which reads as follows: 'Accommodation made with sieur Oudaille on 24 May
    1780 with the consent of the Régie générale for the sum of 12 *livres* to avoid
    judgement, confiscation of the cards agreed to'. Almost all of the eighty-nine
    register entries for these two years record the same formula, with only minor
    variations in wording.
33. Paris, BnF, Cabinet des estampes, Kh 380 4°, document entitled 'Bureau
    particulier des exercices' is a detailed list of the salaries of Régie agents in
    1779 that shows Cambon, the director, receiving a total of 5160 *livres* per
    annum in salary, bonuses and other supplements. Most of the agents, whom
    we will discuss in more detail below, received 900 *livres* that year in salary and
    supplements, exclusive of their share of the accommodations they collected. Of
    course, they may have received income from other Régie operations that were
    not recorded, or have not survived in the archives.

collectively acquired a slightly lesser sum, 960 *livres*, over these two years, and the remaining amount of 960 *livres* appears to have gone to the operating budget of the bureau. The fiscal rewards for the bureau, then, were not massive, but they did add income on the margins for both the employees and the operation as a whole.

The registers also list the teams of inspectors, known as *commis* or *employés*, that staffed each of the eighty-nine inspections. A total of twenty-three agents worked in teams of two, three or four on each inspection. In 1779, the year before the period in question, these employees were each paid a salary of 900 *livres*.[34] We do not know how the twenty-three employees divided the 960 *livres* they collected as their share of the proceeds over the 1780-1781 period, but two variants appear plausible. If we assume that they split their take evenly, each man would have received a little less than 42 *livres* over the course of these two years, or about 4 per cent of their 1779 wages. The work, however, was not distributed evenly among the agents. Two of the more senior *commis*, Christophe Millot and Daniel Louis Ballet, respectively staffed forty-two and thirty-eight of the eighty-nine cases.[35] Five other agents participated in ten to twenty of the inspections, and the remaining sixteen agents worked on seven cases or fewer. If we divide the accommodation from each inspection evenly among the participating agents, Millot and Ballet would have each received a little over 180 *livres* across the two years for their efforts, or about 10 per cent of their annual income from the Régie, a rate equal to that taken home by Director Cambon. Under this scheme, the other five most active agents would have each received between 15 and 30 *livres* per year in supplemental pay, or the equivalent of 1.5-3 per cent of their annual wages. Either way, divided evenly or pro-rated according to the number of cases each agent worked, the results would have been insubstantial for almost all of the *commis*. The policy of negotiated 'accommodations' meant that monetary rewards for the *régisseurs* were minimal. The evidence does not lead one to conclude that the agents

34. Paris, BnF, Cabinet des estampes, Kh 380 4°. Two of the twenty-three, Jacquetot and Deloffre, were *contrôleurs* rather than *commis*, and therefore received 1200 *livres* that year. But these two men only worked two of the eighty-nine cases recorded in the registers for 1780-1781.
35. Paris, BnF, Cabinet des estampes, Kh 380 4°. Millot, who was a widower without children, had been with the Régie bureau devoted to playing cards since 1760. Ballet, with a wife and a child, had joined the agency in 1769.

were cracking down on the circulation of used playing cards among the Parisian popular classes to line their own pockets.

Nor did their work make the *régisseurs* popular with Parisians and those living in the city's near suburbs. We have already seen that the questioning of the fishmonger Houdin in 1786 nearly caused a riot on the rue Saint-Denis. Earlier, in the 1780-1781 period, the *régisseurs* also occasionally encountered resistance as they went about their inspections. In four of the eighty-nine cases in these years, the individuals suspected of possessing fraudulent cards refused the *régisseurs* entry to their domiciles, noting that they were not accompanied by a local judge. In only two of these instances were the agents able to negotiate an accommodation by arguing that the 1751 statute gave them the right to levy a 500-*livre* fine for refusal to allow an inspection; in one case, they collected 48 *livres* and in the other only 6 *livres*.[36] In four other cases, the inspection degenerated into a violent confrontation between the *régisseurs* and the alleged *fraudeurs*. On 27 June 1780, for example, during an inspection being carried out by Millot, Ballet and a third agent named Bourgogne, the aggrieved wife of a *marchand limonadier* and two of her servants 'violently' ripped four or five pounds of unsorted used cards out of the hands of the *régisseurs* as they were taking inventory of the items they had seized. Order was eventually restored; interestingly, the accommodation negotiated by the agents, 120 *livres*, was the second highest sum collected in these two years, presumably as compensation for the physical resistance they encountered.[37] Finally, three accommodations negotiated in this period were subsequently vacated in 1783, due to the extreme poverty of the accused or for technical reasons. In one of these cases in the suburb of Bagnolet, the widow Querelle, a formerly legitimate seller of new playing cards, was found in September 1781 with eleven decks of used, resorted and fraudulently wrapped playing cards. In June 1783, Lieutenant General of Police Jean Charles Pierre Lenoir sentenced her to pay the full 1000-*livre* fine mandated by the 1751 statute, presumably because she should have known better as a

---

36. The 48-*livre* fine for refusal to permit inspection is recorded at Paris, AN, G² 191, entry no.3; the 6-*livre* fine is at Paris, AN, G² 191, entry no.24. The two refusals that yielded no accommodation are at Paris, AN, G² 190, entry no.50; and Paris, AN, G² 191, entry no.19.

37. The case of Fleury – the *marchand*'s wife – is recounted at Paris, AN, G² 190, entry no.22. The other three instances of violence can be found at Paris, AN, G² 190, entry no.39; Paris, AN, G2 190, entry no.58; and Paris, AN, G² 191, entry no.5.

former playing card merchant. But she was excused from this onerous penalty later that year after a Bagnolet priest wrote a letter testifying that she was utterly destitute.[38]

The picture that emerges of the agents of the Régie, therefore, is not one of a group of Old Regime officials easily able to exploit an inequitable situation for their own profit. They had to accept settlements at a rate far below that authorised by the royal ordinances. Their willingness to do so may indicate the Régie's realistic assessment of those whom it caught with used playing cards; the agency had to follow the instructions of the royal government, but its agents tacitly acknowledged the inappropriately high fiscal penalty specified in the 1751 statute. When the agents happened upon individuals whom they thought might be violating the regulations, they were sometimes unable to conduct inspections, or encountered violent resistance; in a few instances, their work was overturned by higher-ups. It is not surprising, therefore, that after 1781 the number of cases pursued by the Régie appears to have declined, while the few cases they chose to investigate focused mostly on wholesalers like Thuillon, Jovenne and Lurier, with greater potential for seizing valuable possessions and collecting the larger fines authorised by royal statute. The agency may have determined that the best way to meet its goals was to focus on the high-volume middlemen who might generate more tax revenue.

One of the most extensively documented wholesaler cases, that of a forty-five-year-old man named André Diel arrested in November 1782, illustrates the changing objectives of the Régie after the flurry of inspections in the 1780-1781 period.[39] Diel, a native of Lausanne in Switzerland, claimed to be a men's tailor; he inhabited several rooms on the third floor of a building on the corner of the rue Beaurepaire and rue Montorgueil on the Right Bank. The Régie received a tip in mid-November 1782 via Jacques Guillaume Mandrou, from the prominent Parisian *cartier* family mentioned above, that someone living at Diel's address was counterfeiting the firm's trademarked playing cards, bands and envelopes. When a team of three agents

38. The Querelle case is at Paris, AN, G^2 191, entry no.23, 6 September 1781. The other two abandoned cases are at Paris, AN, G^2 190, entry no.17, 21 June 1780; and Paris, AN, G^2 190, entry no.55, 14 September 1780. In January 1783 the Régie decided not to pursue these cases because the judge who had initially authorised them was no longer available; the agency noted that it would have been too difficult to reconstruct the cases.
39. The Diel case is amply documented at Paris, AN, Y 9516, 'Dossier André Diel'; and Paris, AN, Y 15991, 16 November 1782 and 17 December 1782.

from the Régie and the *commissaire de police* Mathieu Vanglenne arrived at Diel's apartment on 16 November 1782, they found several rooms full of tools and materials devoted to the repackaging of used cards, and a large number of falsely packaged decks. The *commissaire* questioned Diel while the Régie agents seized the cards and tools, after which Diel was hauled off to prison.

During interrogations over the following month, it came out that Diel had previously worked for fourteen years, from 1764 to 1778, in the playing card unit in the Lille bureau of the Régie, where he carried out inspections similar to those conducted in Paris. When the Régie was consolidated nationwide in 1778 Diel lost his post. Although he claimed to have been working in Paris since then as a men's tailor 'to earn a living', he was not affiliated with the tailors' guild. When questioned about the used cards, tools, bands and other suspicious card-making implements found in his apartment, he insisted that they belonged to a man from Flanders named Pierre Gaudin, much as Pierre-Joseph Thuillon would blame a mysterious 'M. La France' for the equipment found in his apartment and separate workshop in 1785. Diel reported that this roommate had left Paris earlier in November 1782, and stated that he had been allowing Gaudin to run his operation out of the Right Bank apartment. Diel of course knew the regulations regarding the trade in used cards from his time in Lille; he assured *commissaire* Vanglenne that he had repeatedly told Gaudin he was risking serious trouble by trafficking in used cards. The police of the Châtelet, who were by now handling the case, examined the extensive inventory of items found in Diel's apartment, calling in engraving experts to verify that the bands they had seized were forgeries. Diel repeatedly denied that he had stolen material from Lille to equip his alleged used card business in Paris. Meanwhile, as early as December 1782, a month after Diel's arrest, the Paris police began to circulate notices calling for the arrest of Gaudin, the man whom Diel alleged was behind the used card operation. In January 1783, the police authorised a town crier to publicise the search for Gaudin by voice and trumpet in all the major public spaces of Paris. He never materialised, however, and in June 1783 the police court found Diel and Gaudin (in absentia) guilty of falsifying bands and otherwise manufacturing fraudulent packets of playing cards. Diel, still languishing in prison, was fined 3000 *livres* for his alleged transgressions.

In its vagaries, the Diel case typifies the questions raised by the efforts of the Régie and the police to suppress the trade in used playing cards in Paris during the 1780s. It was a tip from Mandrou, a prominent member of the card makers' guild, that originally led the Régie and the police to Diel. In this sense, the tax collectors and the policing agents were fulfilling their duty to protect the livelihoods of the king's subjects, and to preserve revenue-generating tax streams that supported the crown. But the extensive efforts to prove Diel's guilt and locate his alleged accomplice Gaudin were only partially successful, and the surviving documents do not confirm that the Régie was able to collect the substantial fine from Diel. The evidence preserved leaves some doubt about Diel's guilt. It was true that his fourteen years in the Lille office of the Régie had provided him with the technical expertise necessary to forge the bands and envelopes wrapped around new decks, and letters the agents found in his rooms from his son and another acquaintance in Lille might plausibly be interpreted as support for his allegedly fraudulent practices in Paris. But another letter in the same folder to Gaudin in Flemish supported the idea that he, not Diel, was the true forger. The extensive but ultimately unproductive effort to bring Gaudin into custody suggests that the police found Diel's claims against his Flemish roommate plausible. During one interrogation, when *commissaire* Vanglenne insisted repeatedly that Diel admit his guilt, the former *régisseur* finally replied in frustration that 'he was incapable of a commerce in playing cards wrapped in false bands, that he had always conducted himself with honour and integrity throughout his entire life, and that he begged [the *commissaire*] to be persuaded of this truth'.[40] Diel's exasperated, pleading tone, quite different from the curt, confident responses he usually made to assert his innocence during these interrogations in late 1782 and early 1783, reads as much like a legitimate cry for justice as a cynical effort to escape ruin. *Commissaire* Vanglenne and the *régisseurs* did not act arbitrarily to increase personal or public profits. Rather, they made an effort within the bounds imposed by procedure, custom and the limited profits generated by the used card trade to fulfil the goals of generating indirect tax revenue for the crown without abusing its subjects. The hardships that their inspections visited on so many in the Paris Basin in the 1780s reveal the struggle involved between 'good policing' and the material difficulties faced by the poor and middling classes at the end of the Old Regime.

40. Paris, AN, Y 9516, 19 December 1782, p.4.

'Une tyrannie horrible'?

Commentary surrounding a case that arose four years later in Bordeaux provides an ideological conclusion of sorts to the Diel affair, and to many of the other cases in Paris in the 1780s that we have been examining. In late September 1786, a team of *régisseurs* based in that city entered a wine shop located in the home of one of the town's noblewomen, Mme Le Blanc de Mauvesin.[41] The shop, kept by a married couple named Arnaud Marès and Pétronille Boucand who also worked in her home as domestics, sold wine made in her Bordelais vineyards. Marès had been a porter, transporting Le Blanc de Mauvesin around town in her chair, until he became too old. Now sixty-four, he and Boucand served other porters and *gens de la lie du peuple* in their shop. The couple also provided their customers with worn playing cards that had been discarded by their mistress. During their inspection of the shop, the Régie agents seized eight six-packs and three other unique decks of playing cards, all of which bore clear signs of use and were packed in unmarked, dirty wrappers. Ten days later, the Bordeaux Régie imposed a 1000-*livre* fine and a requirement that the elderly couple also pay for printing and posting of posters publicising their fine and transgression. As in Rouen in 1770, the affair was brought to the attention of the *intendant*, in this case by Mme Le Blanc de Mauvesin herself, who argued that the exorbitant fine was incommensurate with the infraction, and would ruin her long-time servants. In a pleading on behalf of Marès and Boucand submitted to the *intendant*, their representative seconded that argument, adding that they were not aware of the regulations and could not have imagined they were doing anything wrong by recycling cards given to them by their mistress. Furthermore, echoing points made in Rouen and Paris, the Régie had already extracted its cut when Mme Le Blanc de Mauvesin first purchased the cards from local Bordeaux card makers who worked with the tax collectors. Thus, the unfortunate couple were in no way depriving the Royal Treasury of its legitimate revenue.

By the following March, the case had made its way to the Bordeaux high court. The Régie at this point had already reduced the fine to 500 *livres*, perhaps in the hope of salvaging some of the

---

41. For details regarding this case, see Bordeaux, Archives départementales de la Gironde (ADG), C 1204, documents dated 7 and 29 October 1786 and 10 March 1787.

monies they felt they were owed. In a summary commenting on the case, the magistrates observed that it was true, under the terms of the 1751 royal statute, that the defendants were guilty. 'But with what type of contravention are we dealing?' they asked.[42] This was not a case of false commerce in cards made outside the kingdom, nor a case of cards made with illegal woodblocks, both of which clearly violated the king's right of taxation. This infraction, they opined, did not seem serious enough to merit the ruin of an elderly couple. And in the final verdict, copied in the margin of the case summary found in the Bordeaux archive, an anonymous observer noted that 'the proposal of the Régie agents in this matter constitutes a horrible tyranny [*une tyrannie horrible*], and that there is cause to reduce the amount to 10 *livres*, since the law makes it clear that a fine must be paid'.[43]

While one might be tempted to understand the language of tyranny invoked in this dossier as a common rhetorical flourish of the age or a foreshadowing of the coming revolution, we need to look past the semantics. The Bordelais high court, like the agents of the Régie and the police and magistrates with whom they worked, understood that the statutes on playing card taxation were a starting point for negotiations. The King's Council might debate the merits of the excise tax with his *parlements*, and the directors of the Régie might write circulars outlining procedure. On the ground, however, the *régisseurs* and the police, and the subjects with whom they interacted, often found a way around the letter of the law that did not curtail the pleasures enjoyed by commoners when playing a game of cards. The government's agents did not arrive at justice for all, but they did find an accommodation for most.

42. Bordeaux, ADG, C 1204, 10 March 1787.
43. Bordeaux, ADG, C 1204, 10 March 1787.

III

The people of Paris: negotiating and resisting authority

Sex in the city: policing debauchery in eighteenth-century Paris

Lisa Jane Graham

Haverford College

> In a city whose population is composed of men from all over, where events unfold in rapid succession, where the passions are never still, and where differences of habit and lifestyle inevitably exist among the inhabitants, it is impossible to maintain at all times a consistent, equal and rigorous moral discipline.[1]

Contrary to popular images of the period, eighteenth-century Paris was not a libertine's paradise. Lenoir was one of the last police chiefs of Paris of the Old Regime. His remark foregrounds the place of moral discipline in the crown's efforts to pacify urban space. This agenda targeted public venues like theatres, gardens and cafés and the activities associated with them such as prostitution, drinking and gambling. As the 1713 royal edict concerning 'debauched women' proclaimed, 'The task of repressing moral licence and corruption, which seem to spread every day, [is] one of the main objects of vigilance for the police officers of our good city of Paris.'[2] This refrain about the rising tides of debauchery and the need for policing was amplified over the century and persisted into the Revolution. Moreover, it bridged the ideological divisions of the late eighteenth century, joining the voices of *philosophes* and physicians to those of magistrates and ministers.

Although we expect to find these concerns guiding royal edicts, it is surprising to hear them echoed by *philosophes* like Rousseau who

---

1. J. C. P. Lenoir, cited in Vincent Milliot, *Un Policier des Lumières, suivi de Mémoires de J. C. P. Lenoir, ancien lieutenant général de police, écrits en pays étrangers dans les années 1790 et suivantes* (Seyssel, 2011), p.495. All translations are my own unless otherwise indicated.
2. François-André Isambert *et al.*, *Recueil général des anciennes lois françaises, depuis 420 jusqu'à la Révolution de 1789*, 29 vols (Paris, 1821-1833), vol.20, p.603.

deplored cities as 'the abyss of the human species' and chroniclers like Louis-Sébastien Mercier who exclaimed in his *Tableau de Paris*, 'If the last act of debauchery is hidden, why shouldn't the first step be equally so? It is not libertinage that stifles all virtue, but its deadly publicity.'[3] Both men agreed that cities bred vice by publicising it. Like the police, they identified debauchery as a threat to civic morality and collective existence. Yet, while *philosophes* debated the limits of liberty in salons and on the page, police officers confronted disruptive desires on the ground in their daily patrols. They alert us to the central role of sexual relations, the licit and the illicit, in maintaining social harmony.

Debauchery illuminates the connections between sex, sociability and policing in the eighteenth-century city. As Michel Foucault observed, 'sex became a police matter in the eighteenth century'.[4] More than repression, policing entailed the regulation of sexual behaviour in the name of public utility. The city, however, expanded opportunities for meeting and mingling at all hours of the day and night. Paris quickly emerged as an 'erotic capital' with a reputation as a 'den of vice', both in France and beyond its borders. Over the century, moralists, novelists and urban chroniclers amplified this image of a city that offered visitors delights and dangers.[5] The worlds of pleasure and crime overlapped in terms of people, places and practices.

When did an individual's pursuit of pleasure constitute a problem of public order, and what criteria determined the need for intervention? These questions acquired urgency in the context of the enlightened promotion of happiness and individual liberty. By rejecting a providential narrative, the *philosophes* made society the product of human design and endeavour.[6] Influenced by Locke's

---

3. Louis-Sébastien Mercier, *Tableau de Paris*, ed. Jean-Claude Bonnet, 2 vols (Paris, 1994), vol.2, p.21.

4. Michel Foucault, *History of sexuality: an introduction* (1978; New York, 1990), p.24.

5. See the introduction by Sylvie Chaperon *et al.* to the special issue of *Genre, sexualité & société* 10 (2013), *Eros parisien*, ed. Sylvie Chaperon *et al.*, https://journals.openedition.org/gss/3039, and the article by Clyde Plumauzille, 'Le "marché aux putains": économies sexuelles et dynamiques spatiales du Palais-Royal dans le Paris révolutionnaire', https://journals.openedition.org/gss/2943 (last accessed on 25 January 2024).

6. Carl Becker, *The Heavenly city of the eighteenth-century philosophes* (1932; New Haven, CT, and London, 1966), p.97. Also see Keith Michael Baker, 'Enlightenment and the institution of society: notes for a conceptual history', in *Main*

epistemology, they insisted on the malleability of human nature and the formative role of one's environment. God's distance, however, shifted the responsibility for government to human ingenuity and error.[7] Even materialists like Diderot worried that, without Christian morality, unfettered desire might lead to ruin. The weakness of man, therefore, required policing to provide the restraints necessary for collective life. Thus, the emergence of liberal society did not eliminate the problem posed by debauchery but reconfigured the criteria and procedures for intervention.

Unlike magistrates who punished violations of the law, the police had broad regulatory powers over different aspects of urban life. Their policies towards vice mirrored those they applied in other areas like censorship and the grain trade.[8] In all three instances, they gathered information to identify threats and prevent crime. This prophylactic ethos, to borrow Vincent Milliot's phrase, reflected their mission to ensure the 'well-being of the king's subjects'.[9] Although they were agents of a paternalistic state, they were also products of the communities they policed. In the course of the eighteenth century, they adapted their practices to meet changing expectations about professional conduct and personal liberty.[10]

In this essay, I will trace evolving views of social morality and tolerance through discussions of debauchery that appeared in police reports and requests for sealed arrest warrants known as *lettres de*

trends in cultural history, ed. W. F. B. Melching and W. R. E. Velema (Amsterdam and Atlanta, GA, 1994), p.187-205; Charly Coleman, 'Resacralizing the world: the fate of secularism in Enlightenment historiography', *The Journal of modern history* 82 (2010), p.368-95 (373); Damien Tricoire, *Die Aufklärung* (Cologne, 2023).

7. Charly Coleman, 'Religion', in *The Cambridge companion to the French Enlightenment*, ed. Daniel Brewer (Cambridge, 2014), p.105-21 (106), and David A. Bell, *The Cult of the nation in France: inventing nationalism, 1680-1800* (Cambridge, MA, 2001), p.25-30.

8. On censorship, see Raymond Birn, *Royal censorship of books in eighteenth-century France* (Stanford, CA, 2012); Simon Burrows, *Blackmail, scandal, and revolution: London's French libellists, 1758-1792* (Manchester, 2006); Robert Darnton, *Censors at work: how states shaped literature* (New York, 2014), p.21-86. For markets, see Steven Laurence Kaplan, *La Fin des corporations* (Paris, 2001) and *Raisonner sur les blés: essais sur les Lumières économiques* (Paris, 2017).

9. Vincent Milliot, *'L'Admirable police': tenir Paris au siècle des Lumières* (Ceyzérieu, 2016), p.184.

10. David Garrioch, *Neighbourhood and community in Paris, 1740-1790* (Cambridge, 1986), p.31.

cachet. What did debauchery signify, when was it invoked, by whom and to what ends? Although we associate debauchery with sexual indulgence, it captured concerns about excess triggered by the rise of a commercial society. Under the Old Regime, debauchery acquired coherence through its weight in the crown's policy of administrative confinement implemented through *lettres de cachet*. The police were responsible for investigating these requests for detention that peaked in the first half of the century. Starting in the 1760s, the campaign for criminal law reform attacked both the *lettres de cachet* and the role of the police in implementing them. Although the revolutionaries abolished the *lettres de cachet* in 1790 and temporarily dismantled the police, the problem of sexual discipline persisted under the First Republic and Empire.

Policing morality: protection and correction

In the wake of the Reformation, princes across Western Europe sought to pacify and unite territories that had fractured along confessional lines. In France, the violence unleashed during the Wars of Religion threatened to tear the country apart. In response, jurists and ministers promoted the principle of divine right that fused the king's spiritual and political duties.[11] The crown pursued this agenda through censorship and edicts against gambling, clandestine marriages, soliciting sex and brothels, vagrancy and begging, rape and seduction. The decrees emphasised their prophylactic goals such as 'preventing women from falling into prostitution' or 'reducing the number of places for debauchery'.[12] Louis XIV made Paris a centrepiece of his efforts to build a moral polity that would reinforce and radiate royal authority.

Early in the reign, he established the General Hospital to coordinate the operations of existing facilities including the Salpêtrière (for women) and Bicêtre (for men) under a single director

11. Dale K. Van Kley, *The Religious origins of the French Revolution: from Calvin to the Civil Constitution, 1560-1791* (New Haven, CT, 1996), and Paul Monod, *The Power of kings: monarchy and religion in Europe, 1589-1715* (New Haven, CT, 1999).
12. 'Prévenir la débauche des femmes' and 'diminuer les lieux de débauche'. The Fonds Joly de Fleury (JF) in the Manuscripts room at the Bibliothèque nationale de France (BnF) in Paris, site Richelieu, contains volumes of these edicts arranged chronologically and topically. For example, the volume dealing with *Religion, mœurs, santé* includes edicts against brothels, luxury, dirty books and air pollution. See Paris, BnF, JF 9059, f.172-78.

appointed by the king. The General Hospital was not a medical facility but an apparatus for detention and correction.[13] The 1656 edict targeted vagrants, beggars and delinquents who 'cluttered' the capital and threatened the safety of its residents. The Parisian model was exported two decades later, in 1662, when the crown founded analogous facilities in major cities throughout the realm. In these same decades, the Counter-Reformation Church converted existing hospitals and religious houses into detention centres and workhouses.[14] To implement this vision of urban space, Louis XIV created a new charge in 1667, the lieutenant general of police, a magistrate who oversaw policing activities in the capital. The lieutenant general commanded a force of commissioners, inspectors, guards and informants, and he met with the king on a weekly basis. The police became key players in the theatre of urban life, gathering information, surveilling markets and repressing crime.

The creation of a police force reinforced the disciplinary role of work and family as seen in the criteria for detention in the 1684 edicts: 'Children [...] who mistreat their fathers or mothers, or those who refuse to work either from libertinage or laziness, and girls who have been debauched, and those at risk of being debauched, all will be detained in the designated sites, meaning: Bicêtre for boys and the Salpêtrière for girls.'[15] The preamble described the mission as 'reforming bad habits' through a combination of religious instruction and hard labour. Internment satisfied three goals and reflected assumptions about crime and character. First, by removing the debauched, it contained risk since vice was contagious. Second, it offered the possibility of correction and re-entry into society. Finally, by putting the detainees to work, the crown transformed idle hands into productive labour.

13. Michel Foucault refers to this policy as 'le grand renfermement', and describes the General Hospital as 'a strange power that the king establishes between the police and the judiciary, at the limits of the law: the third order of repression'. See Michel Foucault, *Histoire de la folie à l'âge classique* (Paris, 1972), p.61. Also see Erica-Marie Benabou, *La Prostitution et la police des mœurs au XVIIIe siècle* (Paris, 1987), p.79-85; Tim McHugh, *Hospital politics in seventeenth-century France: the crown, urban elites and the poor* (Ashgate, 2007), p.84-101; Clyde Plumauzille, *Prostitution et révolution: des femmes publiques dans la cité républicaine, 1789-1804* (Ceyzérieu, 2016), p.175-78, and Alan Williams, *The Police of Paris, 1718-1789* (Baton Rouge, LA, 1979), p.233-36.
14. Foucault, *Histoire de la folie*, p.61, and McHugh, *Hospital politics*, p.83.
15. Isambert *et al.*, *Recueil général*, vol.19, p.442-43.

The edict's language alerts us to the importance of the family as an institution of order and the belief in the therapeutic powers of work to correct character, since 'the children will be treated with gentleness to the extent that they offer proof of their reform'.[16] The crown boasted of these institutions as showcases of rational government. By clearing the streets of marginal and mobile populations, the police improved urban life and reduced crime. These repressive measures were complemented by the introduction of street lighting in Paris and other large cities.[17] The capital was cleaner, brighter and more salubrious.

The preceding edicts identified debauchery, idleness and insubordination as threats to public order. They constituted a grey zone of delinquent activities handled by the police at the crown's behest. In addition, the police had recourse to extraordinary justice to address individual cases of what might be called problematic sociability. In this system, a family asked the crown to confine an individual whose behaviour, often labelled debauchery, resisted correction. After receiving a request, the police investigated the allegations to determine whether detention was merited and, if so, the lieutenant general of police dispatched a sealed arrest warrant known as a *lettre de cachet*. Circumventing the law courts, the *lettres de cachet* guaranteed speed and secrecy for the families involved. Rather than fines or corporal punishment, they used detention to curtail bad behaviour since the accused had no legal recourse for recovering their liberty.[18]

The process forged an alliance between the king and his subjects to defend family honour and avoid scandal. In his memoirs, one of the last lieutenants of the Old Regime, J. C. P. Lenoir, recalled:

> In those days, we followed the principle that the dishonour of an individual rebounded on his family; in that case the government and the police came to the aid of parents who had a legitimate reason

16. Isambert *et al.*, *Recueil général*, vol.19, p.444.
17. For street lighting, see Craig Koslofsky, *Evening's empire: a history of the night in early modern Europe* (Cambridge, 2011), p.128-56; Darrin M. McMahon, 'Writing the history of illumination in the *siècle des Lumières*: Enlightenment narratives of light', in *Let there be Enlightenment: the religious and mystical sources of rationality*, ed. Anton M. Matytsin and Dan Edelstein (Baltimore, MD, 2018), p.103-28, and Sophie Reculin, 'Le règne de la nuit désormais va finir: l'invention et la diffusion de l'éclairage public dans le royaume de France, 1697-1789', doctoral dissertation, Université Charles de Gaulle – Lille III, 2017.
18. Claude Quétel, *De par le roy: essai sur les lettres de cachet* (Toulouse, 1981) and *Une Légende noire: les lettres de cachet* (Paris, 2011); Brian E. Strayer, *Lettres de cachet and social control in the Ancien Régime, 1659-1789* (New York, 1992).

to fear dishonour. This procedure definitely improved security. It prevented crimes, and was necessary in a large city like Paris where the youth is exposed to all of the dangers of corruption: despite all that has been said and written against these *lettres de cachet*, they were never as abusive as has been claimed.[19]

Lenoir's assessment captured the paternalist assumptions that guided the police in their approach to sexual improprieties. For Lenoir, the *lettres de cachet* offered an effective response to debauchery as long as the police applied consistent criteria in their investigations. He was unequivocal that the benefits outweighed the abuses.

Modern scholars who study the *lettre de cachet* system concur with Lenoir, even if they are less sanguine about their abuse. Arlette Farge and Michel Foucault identified debauchery as a dominant motive in family requests for administrative confinement.[20] Foucault insists that the *lettres de cachet* expressed a 'moral consensus' located in the family and the community, *not* the arbitrary power of an absolute monarch.[21] The majority of the requests were initiated by families, not ministers.[22] We must keep this in mind when considering both the meaning of debauchery and the role of the police. As a category of delinquency, debauchery shaped and was shaped by the *lettres de cachet*. In investigating the requests, commissioners navigated between popular and royal expectations regarding tolerance and punishment for sexual deviance.

According to Alain Rey, the modern meanings of debauchery appeared in the fifteenth century, when it signified 'to lead someone astray or indulge in vice'.[23] When applied to work, *débaucher* was the opposite of *embaucher* (to hire) and meant to fire an employee or

---

19. Milliot, *Un Policier des Lumières*, p.609-10.
20. Arlette Farge and Michel Foucault, *Disorderly families: infamous letters from the Bastille Archives* (1982), translated by Thomas Scott-Railton (Minneapolis, MN, 2016), p.35. See also Goulven Kerien, *Pour l'honneur des familles: les enfermements par lettres de cachet à Paris au XVIIIᵉ siècle* (Ceyzérieu, 2023). Unfortunately, Kerien's book appeared after my essay was submitted and I was unable to incorporate it into my analysis. This research provides a new synthesis and chronology for studying the *lettres de cachet* in eighteenth-century Paris that will guide future work.
21. Michel Foucault, *The Punitive society: lectures at the Collège de France, 1972-1973*, ed. Bernard Harcourt (New York, 2015), p.130.
22. For the generality of Caen, Quétel estimates that 97 per cent of the *lettres de cachet* were issued in response to family requests; see *De par le roy*, p.123-35.
23. 'Débauche', in *Dictionnaire historique de la langue française*, ed. Alain Rey (Paris, 1995), p.557.

poach them from an employer.[24] The two meanings overlapped, since work prevented dissipation. Finally, the verb 'to debauch' designated an individual such as a tutor or a priest who abused the confidence of those he was entrusted to guide.[25] It was frequently used to warn parents and their children about the dangers of sexual corruption, especially in the urban environment. In all instances, debauchery designated risk, vulnerability, scandal and disorder.

In order to monitor debauchery, the police needed information and assistance. They employed informants who reported on individuals, conversations and activities. They compiled these reports in internal newspapers, the *gazetins*, which located the accounts spatially in the gardens, theatres, cafés and *petites maisons* where Parisians gathered for news and diversion. The reports covered every imaginable topic, from weather and grain prices to political rumours and sexual scandals. By tracking gossip and reactions to events, the *gazetins* distilled fleeting conversations into a compendium of public opinion for the crown. In the process, they alerted the king to grievances and potential sources of unrest. The reports, however, must be treated with caution: they were neither neutral nor transparent. They filtered observations through police assumptions about human nature, social hierarchy and paternalistic government.[26] Moreover, officers used the reports to promote their role as guardians of the capital and its denizens.

The *gazetins* mapped a city of vice and pleasure through meticulous notes on brothels and their clients, gambling dens and licentious parties. For example, in late November 1725, an inspector on patrol near the Palais-Royal discovered the house of the sieur Marais which contained two brothels and another on the rue de Richelieu: 'Between a saddler and a laundress, there is a school of Cythera [brothel] where people indulge in all sorts of vices, and they bring in very young people to school them in libertinage and discharge the fruits

24. 'Débauche', in *Dictionnaire de l'Académie française*, 4th edn (Paris, La Veuve de Bernard Brunet, 1762).
25. Pierre-François Muyart de Vouglans, *Institutes au droit criminel* (Paris, n.n., 1757), p.19. Vouglans cited the example of a doctor who poisoned his patients as an instance of criminal intent and abuse of trust.
26. On how the police understood their role, see Lisa Jane Graham, *If the king only knew: seditious speech in the reign of Louis XV* (Charlottesville, VA, 2000), p.25-55; David Garrioch, 'The paternal government of men: the self-image and action of the Paris police in the eighteenth century', in *A History of police and masculinities, 1700-2010*, ed. David G. Barrie and Susan Broomhall (London and New York, 2012), p.35-54; Milliot, *'L'Admirable Police'*.

of incontinence.'[27] The report juxtaposes the respectable commerce of the saddle maker and the laundress to the illicit business of the brothel on the same street. This moral topography revealed how the police *read* the city and its population for the crown.

The police prided themselves on safeguarding urban spaces for licit activities of leisure and labour. They identified children, women, apprentices and provincials as vulnerable prey for swindlers and crooks. In particular, they targeted the aggressive efforts to seduce young girls and recruit them into prostitution.[28] Moreover, such activities often compounded physical violence with sexual exploitation. In late December 1747, Sergeant Malivoir reported on a brothel run by Mme Sanson,

> Last night around five o'clock, MM. de Primond and Mottel, both musketeers, took me to a prostitute named Sanson in the rue des Mauvais Garçons, Saint-Germain, the first alley on the left [...] third apartment, where I found about twenty young men playing cards, they invited me to return and encouraged me to bring my friends, saying that they played every day most often until the crack of dawn, nothing but games of chance, and that when one wanted to dine with pretty girls, Mme Sanson made sure to procure some.
>
> This brothel is composed of nothing but gentlemen from the king's household, officers and some students of law and medicine. Almost every day a fight breaks out, most often these disputes end in duels; on the 29th of this month, two men took up swords at nine o'clock in the evening in the courtyard of the Saint-Germain fairground, one of the musketeers involved was injured.[29]

Malivoir's self-image of stewardship reflected the official understanding of the policing mission in the metropolis. The latent violence justified surveillance.

Thus, in 1725, a report noted acclaim for Lieutenant General of Police Hérault's crackdown on brothels: 'He is being praised by many who think this renewed attention will eliminate many evils from the capital of the kingdom, by continuing this exemplary severity.'[30] Echoes

27. Paris, Bibliothèque de l'Arsenal (Ars.), Archives de la Bastille (MS Bastille), 10155, 27 November 1725, f.145*v*.
28. Nina Kushner, *Erotic exchanges: the world of elite prostitution in eighteenth-century Paris* (Ithaca, NY, 2013), p.46-71, and Plumauzille, *Prostitution et révolution*, p.59-69.
29. Paris, Ars., MS Bastille, 10029, 31 December 1747, f.8.
30. Paris, Ars., MS Bastille, 10155, f.145*v*.

of this sentiment recurred, for example, in April 1741: 'the public was apparently delighted with the suppression of gambling at the *hôtels* of Soissons and Gêvres. We saw some men, whose livelihood depended on gambling, reduced to tears. [...] Nobody talked about anything else but gambling today.'[31] The *gazetins* foregrounded public opinion as a badge of approval for police intervention to quell disturbances.[32]

Was this a police fantasy of popular support, or did it reflect an underlying consensus? It is hard to tell but likely a bit of both. For example, prostitution was a perennial issue in the capital, one that forced the police to navigate between repressive laws and tacit tolerance. Although neighbours and respectable residents denounced brothels, the *gazetins* echoed debates about the best policy: regulation versus repression. One officer noted that several people worried about the unintended consequences of repression:

> At the Regency café, people were saying that the Inquisition has arrived in Paris because all one hears about is nightly round-ups by the police. It seems that M. Hérault wants to make the sin of sodomy fashionable, given all of the women being arrested. There is no doubt that there will be more disorder than already exists in the city, and that respectable women will not be safe in the streets, because, in a city like this, one needs prostitutes in order to prevent worse crimes.[33]

This excerpt illuminates how the police and the populace understood the city's sexual economy. A shortage of outlets would not suppress male libido but divert it to other men or married women. Both fostered deviance and threatened respectable families.

The *gazetins* compiled evidence for the crown that debauchery was spreading in the eighteenth century with the construction of new neighbourhoods and the influx of people searching for work. This perception reinforced the fears of municipal officials, political economists and royal ministers. Both David Garrioch and Erica Marie Benabou note the rising tide of ordinances that targeted vagrants, beggars and prostitutes in an effort to 'civilise and improve'

---

31. Paris, Ars., MS Bastille, 10168, 7 April 1741, f.106*v*.
32. Jeffrey Ravel notes a similar self-perception of protecting an orderly from a disorderly public; see the example of Exempt Duveau in Jeffrey S. Ravel, *The Contested parterre: public theater and French political culture, 1680-1791* (Ithaca, NY, 1999), p.158-59.
33. Paris, Ars., MS Bastille, 10170, f.167*v*. Papers in this file are undated, although they span the years 1742-1748. Hérault was lieutenant general of police from 1725 to 1739.

the city. Transient populations, including soldiers, escaped community surveillance and were associated with crime. The task of enforcing these various edicts fell to the police as part of their efforts to make the city safe for residents and visitors, traders and travellers. The law courts rarely intervened to punish vice unless it reached the level of a *cause célèbre* or political scandal.[34]

Surveillance and prevention reinforced by internment or banishment allowed the police to bypass the cumbersome and costly procedure of the courts. They intervened strategically to avoid escalation. As Lenoir recalled, the police prioritised discretion: 'To tolerate errors and, above all, keep them hidden when they do not disturb public order was an obligation prescribed to the police in enforcing moral discipline.'[35] This shared investment in secrecy justified the recourse to extraordinary justice when other preventive measures failed. Publicity advertised vice and encouraged bad behaviour. It was undesirable for the police but also the people who feared shame and dishonour.

Pleasures and vices

While the crown developed an apparatus for repressing debauchery, the Enlightenment expanded opportunities for indulgence and the arguments for tolerance. It should not surprise us that the policing of morality grew more specialised and urgent in a society transformed by urbanisation, commerce and literacy.[36] These material changes converged with philosophical and scientific ideas that rejected the negative view of human desire as sin. This liberation of the passions was exemplified by the meteoric career of the Scottish financier John Law and the crash of his System in 1720. The rue Quincampoix quickly became a symbol for the dizzying luxury and devastating loss that accompanied unbridled speculation.[37] The rue Quincampoix stood in the heart of the city, adjacent to the central marketplace, Les Halles,

---

34. Garrioch, 'The paternal government of men', p.38; Benabou, *La Prostitution et la police des mœurs*, p.28.
35. Milliot, *Un Policier des Lumières*, p.503.
36. Daniel Roche, *France in the Enlightenment* (1993; Cambridge, MA, 2000) and *A History of everyday things: the birth of consumption in France, 1600-1800* (1997; Cambridge, 2000).
37. Charly Coleman, 'The spirit of speculation: John Law and economic theology in the age of lights', *French historical studies* 42:2 (2019), p.203-37 (216-27), and Arnaud Orain, *La Politique du merveilleux: une autre histoire du Système de Law (1695-1795)* (Paris, 2018).

and not far from the Palais de justice and the Palais-Royal. The urban landscape reflected the proximity of provisioning, policing, prostitution and pleasure. The introduction of street lighting in Paris in the early eighteenth century encouraged informal sociability outside of the traditional venues and hours. Although lighting improved safety, it also increased crime with more people out and about at night.[38] The police struggled to adapt to the shifting rhythms of city life and its population.

We see these challenges in a memoir addressed to Cardinal Fleury, chief minister of Louis XV, from bourgeois Parisians who complained of insecurity in the capital. In addition to beggars and thieves, they cited 'the large number of libertines and drunkards who roam the streets day and night, provoking disputes with bystanders and insulting women and girls'.[39] These rowdy bands scared respectable folk and hindered commerce. The authors insisted that the primary victims were coachmen and market women heading to Les Halles, the central marketplace, between three and four o'clock in the morning. Both risked being insulted and attacked on their way to work. The authors criticised the police for 'retiring at the time when they are most needed, something which runs counter to good sense and good government'.[40] They demanded that more officers be assigned to the Night Watch and forced to patrol in the wee hours to protect these vendors. This document reveals expectations about the responsibility of the police to protect labourers from libertines.

As seen in the *gazetins*, the police presented themselves as partners with the populace in enforcing the moral norms that secured public order. At the same time, they recognised that material and cultural developments had shifted the threshold for tolerance and repression. The *philosophes*, for instance, extolled happiness as a worthy goal of human endeavour and reclaimed it from the spiritual afterlife to the material present.[41] This rejection of a worldview framed by sin,

---

38. On nocturnal sociability, see Koslofsky, *Evening's empire*, p.157-97. On leisure, see Garrioch, *Neighbourhood and community in Paris*, p.169-203, and for theatres, see Ravel, *The Contested parterre*.

39. Paris, Bibliothèque historique de la ville de Paris (BHVP), MS 713, 'Mémoire adressé par les habitants de Paris au Cardinal Fleury contre les voleurs, libertins, etc. qui infestent la capitale et contre certains officiers de police', f.54r.

40. Paris, BHVP, MS 713, 'Mémoire adressé [...] au Cardinal Fleury', f.55.

41. Robert Mauzi, *L'Idée du bonheur dans la littérature et la pensée françaises au XVIIIᵉ siècle* (Paris, 1969), p.514; Darrin M. McMahon, *Happiness: a history* (New York, 2006), p.197-252, and Ritchie Robertson, *The Enlightenment: the pursuit of happiness, 1680-1790* (New York, 2021).

however, required qualifications about the conditions for happiness. Authors like Diderot worried that a society predicated on individualism might implode, since 'every man's desire is despotic'.[42] Proponents of enlightened freedom preached moderation and self-control in order to direct the passions towards beneficial ends.[43] This calculated view of managing the passions dominated the emerging fields of demography and political economy in the second half of the century. As the Italian jurist Cesare Beccaria observed in his treatise *On crimes and punishments*, 'Just as the constant and very simple laws of nature fail to prevent perturbations in the movements of the planets, so human laws cannot prevent disturbances and disorders amid the infinite and utterly conflicting attractions of pleasure and pain.'[44] Reformers were forced to acknowledge the limitations of the law in the face of emancipated desire.

Paris was simultaneously the capital of pleasure and vice engendered by commerce and individualism. The tireless chronicler Louis-Sébastien Mercier decried 'the contagion of debauchery' to reinforce the perception that the city fostered promiscuous intimacy.[45] He contrasted the 'coarse pleasures of the capital' to the 'pure morals' of an idealised countryside where 'debauchery is a word without meaning'.[46] For Mercier, carceral institutions like the Salpêtrière spread debauchery by lumping together professional prostitutes with unwed mothers and destitute women: 'The hospital where they are locked up does nothing to improve their morals; they leave even more dissolute than when they arrive because there is nothing more fatal for women than example, and nothing more contagious than libertinage.'[47] Note Mercier's use of contagion to conflate the medical and moral risks of sexual promiscuity.

42. Michel Delon, 'Morale', in *Le Monde des Lumières*, ed. Vincenzo Ferrone and Daniel Roche (Paris, 1993), p.41-48 (46). Becker makes a similar argument in *The Heavenly city*. Also see Thomas Laqueur, *Solitary sex: a cultural history of masturbation* (New York, 2004).

43. Thomas Kavanagh calls this effort 'epicurean stoicism'; see Thomas Kavanagh, *Enlightened pleasures: eighteenth-century France and the new Epicureanism* (New Haven, CT, 2010), p.3.

44. Cesare Beccaria, *On crimes and punishments, and other writings*, ed. Richard Bellamy (Cambridge, 1995), p.103.

45. Mercier, *Tableau de Paris*, vol.2, p.20.

46. Jean-Jacques Rousseau, *Emile, or On education*, ed. Allan Bloom (Chicago, IL, 1979), p.59, and Mercier, *Tableau de Paris*, vol.1, p.599.

47. Mercier, *Tableau de Paris*, vol.2, p.1092.

Mercier condemned the monarchy for failing to adapt its repressive tactics to the problems of a modern metropolis. Early demographers like Jean-Baptiste Moheau concurred in railing against cities where promiscuity threatened fertility because 'the inhabitants are less robust' and 'the taste for luxury and moral perversity makes them fear a large family'.[48] Moheau summoned the crown to limit urban growth through fiscal incentives designed to lure people back to the countryside.[49] As the previous examples suggest, the link between cities and sterility loomed over debates about sexuality and policing in the second half of the century.

When Lieutenant General of Police Nicolas René Berryer overhauled the police force in 1747, he appointed an inspector to lead the Morals Brigade. This bureau monitored brothels, prostitutes and kept women, as well as gambling dens, lodging houses and public theatres. The first man assigned to the job, Inspector Meusnier, kept meticulous notes on the demimonde of eighteenth-century Paris. In addition to his own observations, Meusnier employed informants to alert him to suspicious activities and individuals. His files captured his liminal position as an agent of the crown and a resource for the local population in enforcing moral discipline.[50]

Meusnier received denunciations on a weekly basis from priests, parents and neighbours. Clearly, the police relied on Parisians for assistance as much as they surveilled them. Their files overflowed with complaints from residents disturbed by indecent behaviour and threats of scandal. For example, a parish priest wrote to Inspector Meusnier in the winter of 1750 about a woman who had moved into an apartment on the rue Cristine eight months earlier: 'In the beginning, her house did not draw visitors; nonetheless, everybody knew that she was no prude, and for the past few months, there has been a constant flow of all sorts of people at all hours of the day and night, including priests and clergymen seen going to her house.'[51]

The priest confronted the woman and threatened to denounce her unless she moved out of the neighbourhood. Immediately after

---

48. Jean-Baptiste Moheau, *Recherches et considérations sur la population de la France, 1778*, ed. Eric Vilquin (Paris, 1994), p.134.

49. Moheau, *Recherches et considérations*, p.304.

50. Benabou, *La Prostitution et la police des mœurs*, p.96-104; Kushner, *Erotic exchanges*; and Plumauzille, *Prostitution et révolution*. See also the essay by Vincent Milliot in this volume.

51. Paris, Ars., MS Bastille, 10248, 'Lettre de Leger, curé de St André, le 6 février 1750'.

agreeing, she changed her mind and resumed her licentious behaviour. Her defiance prompted the priest to alert Meusnier on behalf of his parishioners: 'all of the neighbours are scandalised by her libertinage and have complained to me about it, they are all respectable folk; there are few lowlifes residing in this street.'[52] The priest emphasised the propriety of the neighbours to bolster his request for intervention. He asked Meusnier for a *lettre de cachet* to send the woman to a workhouse or evict her from the parish.

In another instance, Meusnier learned of the dangers posed by a woman named Linière who had recently been released from a nine-month stint at the Salpêtrière. A neighbour accused Linière of 'debauching' the thirteen-year-old son of a stocking merchant named M. Le Lièvre. The boy's mother threatened to denounce Linière if she did not stop seeing her son, but Linière ignored the warning. The next time that the boy delivered a pair of stockings to Linière, the two spent four hours one afternoon in a rented coach. In addition to their role as transportation, coaches offered accommodation for trysts. Unlike lodging houses that required landlords to register clients and verify marital status, coaches kept no records of their passengers. The informant concluded, 'it is shocking that an unmarried woman of twenty-seven or thirty years old is debauching a young man or boy of twelve or thirteen. I am convinced that the mother of the young man knows nothing of their recent meeting last Wednesday. You must warn the father or mother of the young man.'[53]

The denunciation insisted on two points. First, the age difference between the seducer and her victim violated the hierarchies of gender and age that defined licit relationships. Moreover, the public nature of the behaviour caused scandal. Second, the ignorance of the boy's parents and the danger that threatened their son. The witness turned to Meusnier to protect the boy and his family from Linière's corrosive influence. It is unclear whether Meusnier followed up on this report or if Linière was sent back to the Salpêtrière. Nonetheless, it demonstrates the complicity between the police and the people in enforcing the rules of rank, gender and age that structured community life.

As the city grew and attitudes evolved, the police worked with Parisians to uphold the norms for social relations. The breakdown of traditional constraints, whether spiritual, material or familial,

---

52. Paris, Ars., MS Bastille, 10248, 'Lettre de Leger, curé de St André, le 6 février 1750'.
53. Paris, Ars., MS Bastille, 10251, f.54.

augmented the perceptions of vulnerability and risk in the urban environment. When laws failed to check bad behaviour, the police and the populace turned to the *lettres de cachet* to restore order. The *lettres de cachet* were makeshift tools for addressing conflicts between individuals and their families that avoided the expenses and publicity of ordinary justice. The police were instrumental, since they investigated the requests and advised the crown on how to proceed. Their files registered the shifting threshold of tolerance for moral infractions and repression over the course of the century.

Stop the scandal

The *lettres de cachet* developed in tandem with the carceral institutions of the Old Regime to clear the streets of disruptive individuals whose behaviour did not qualify as crimes in a technical sense. As a rule, the magistrates were reluctant to prosecute moral infractions and turned them over to the police.[54] The police acted as liaison between the king and the community in administering the *lettres de cachet*. Given their intimate knowledge of the city and its denizens, they were well placed to determine the need for correction.[55] Their internal reports revealed an equal concern for public order and public opinion when deciding whether to intervene.

This policy of administrative confinement reinforced the paternalist ideology that guided policing and structured corporate society under the Old Regime. As former Lieutenant General of Police Lenoir observed, 'the *lettres de cachet* should be viewed as an extension of paternal authority' and 'the king's order was in effect a sanction for parental concern'.[56] When the family initiated the request, generally the father or other male relatives, it paid the fees for detention. Otherwise, the crown footed the bill. The logic that guided *lettres de cachet* prioritised the avoidance of scandal and the dishonour that flowed in its wake.

The requests rehearsed assumptions about bad behaviour and its impact on family and community. In each document, the supplicant identified the villain and their victims to substantiate the allegations of danger and the need for intervention. For example, in 1716, Secretary of State d'Aguesseau received several letters denouncing Lucas de Bellebat, a middle-aged man accused of sodomy: 'We have established

---

54. Benabou, *La Prostitution et la police des mœurs*, p.29.
55. Milliot, *Un Policier des Lumières*, p.274.
56. J. C. P. Lenoir, 'Mémoires', in Milliot, *Un Policier des Lumières*, p.746.

that he has a habit of luring young boys to his apartment, fifteen- to eighteen-year-olds including students, the children of picklocks and unemployed lackeys, on the pretext of finding them a position in a good household, he buggers them and abuses them with violence.'[57] Bellebat was arrested and taken to Bicêtre on 4 January 1716. He was released a year later and exiled to his house in Marcoussis, just outside of Paris, to remove him from his potential victims.

Apparently, Bellebat ignored the decree and, five years later, we find the following report from Inspector Simmonet:

> The Sire Bellebat was detained for correction at the end of Louis XIV's reign for seducing and corrupting young men; since he persists in this behaviour and is incorrigible, he deserves no grace (to be convinced, you simply need to observe him). He lives in the street that ends on the place de la Sorbonne and the rue des Cordiers, and he will do a great deal of harm because there are lots of young men in this area who lack careful supervision.[58]

Simmonet had watched Bellebat for some time, and insisted on his 'incorrigibility' to justify the *lettre de cachet*. His report demonstrates how the police considered factors like location, age and opportunity in calculating the risk posed by a delinquent individual. They acted, as Jeffrey Merrick argues, to prevent men like Bellebat from corrupting these 'unsupervised' young men.[59] The inspector saw himself as a substitute for absent kin or other guardians. Simmonet insisted, 'public welfare and good order require that he [Bellebat] be placed in a correctional facility and forced to repent'.[60] After nine months in Bicêtre, Bellebat was released for the second time in November of 1723 on the condition that he leave Paris for Marcoussis. There were no further reports on his case.

This effort to shield young men and women from predators was a recurring motif in the files. In 1741, Commissioner Rochebrune

---

57. Paris, Ars., MS Bastille, 10619, f.83.
58. Paris, Ars., MS Bastille, 10619, f.103.
59. Jeffrey Merrick, 'Sodomitical scandals and subcultures in the 1720s', *Men and masculinities* 1:4 (1999), p.365-84 (380). See also Jeffrey Merrick, 'Sodomitical inclinations in early eighteenth-century Paris', *Eighteenth-century studies* 30:3 (1997), p.280-95, and Michel Rey, 'Police and sodomy in eighteenth-century Paris: from sin to disorder', in *The Pursuit of sodomy: male homosexuality in Renaissance and Enlightenment Europe*, ed. Kent Gerard and Gert Hekma (New York and London, 1989), p.129-46.
60. Paris, Ars., MS Bastille, 10741, f.231.

requested a *lettre de cachet* for three prostitutes who occupied the first and second floors of a house at the corner of the rue Brisemiche and Saint-Médéric 'to put a stop to their debauchery'. Both Rochebrune and the local priest certified '[t]hat they have received numerous complaints about these three women who are supported by soldiers, that they solicit clients publicly and debauch young girls of thirteen and fourteen years old, we ask that they be locked up in order to stop the scandal that they are causing in the neighbourhood'.[61]

The combination of prostitutes and soldiers raised a red flag that threatened the virtue of proper women and their families. Similar to Simmonet's response to Bellebat's case, Rochebrune underscored the need to prevent young girls from falling into the demimonde.[62] Like the *gazetins*, this file insisted on the tension between respectable and disrespectable sociability, and the extent to which one threatened to engulf the other. For Rochebrune, the case was clear-cut: 'since it is in the public interest to put a stop to this criminal and dangerous commerce, I recommend that an order be dispatched to arrest them.'[63] The plea to 'stop the scandal' by removing the offending parties reverberated in the requests for *lettres de cachet* and signalled community consensus.

By disrupting the fiscal and libidinal economies of work and family, debauchery threatened the ecology of the neighbourhood. The two economies were interconnected, since 'commerce' referred both to sexual relations and material exchange. Moreover, marriage managed human and material resources by disciplining desire. This convergence was explicit in the case of the widow Morel, who was detained first in 1715 to little effect. Eight months after her release from the Salpêtrière, she resumed 'her previous disorders, and her debauchery is scandalising her neighbours'.[64] Morel's neighbours wrote to the regent, the duc d'Orléans, in February 1717 to request a second *lettre de cachet* to send her back to the Salpêtrière. They denounced her 'scandalous relations' in seducing a married man, a cook's apprentice named Chaillon: 'she not only disturbed the tranquillity of his household but worse, she advised him to treat his wife cruelly and then obliged him to abandon her.'[65] Apparently, a second detention

61. Paris, Ars., MS Bastille, 11484, f.26.
62. Kushner, *Erotic exchanges*, p.46-96.
63. Paris, Ars., MS Bastille, 11484, f.26.
64. Paris, Ars., MS Bastille, 10621, f.160-62 for the quotations from the Morel case.
65. Paris, Ars., MS Bastille, 10621, f.163.

failed to reform Morel, who resumed her relationship with Chaillon, forcing him to abandon his wife and children and sell his clothes 'to pursue his debauchery'.

The Morel case crystallised the dangers of debauchery in one episode: sexual promiscuity, broken households, debt, violence and scandal. To make matters worse, Morel was pregnant with 'the fruit of her debauchery'. The upstanding neighbours demanded her detention to stop the disorder caused by this relationship. After investigating the allegations, Commissioner Camuset recommended that Morel return to the General Hospital. Even if she refused correction, her arrest would force Chaillon to put his household in order. The neighbourhood used the *lettre de cachet* to recall Chaillon to his paternal and conjugal obligations. If Chaillon failed to provide for his wife and children, he not only set a bad example but also imposed a financial burden on the community.

Morel's recidivism was not uncommon given the conditions at the Salpêtrière. Although some women secured their release, many resisted correction. In May of 1715, Christophe Battelier, a munitions officer, had his fifty-year-old wife, Marguerite Rochon, detained at the Salpêtrière for drunken excesses that led her to beg for money. One year later, however, she convinced her family of her repentance and promised 'not to fall back into these excesses in the future, having benefited from her detention'.[66] Perhaps Rochon succeeded in convincing the crown that she was 'corrected' and deserved her freedom. Or her husband may have tired of paying the fees and decided that the punishment had served its purpose. The motives were never clear in these requests either for detention or for release. In general, however, the decision to release was initiated by the family, not the crown.[67]

More often than not, however, the police confirmed Mercier's assessment that the Salpêtrière exacerbated rather than improved behaviour. For example, a woman named Sourdeval was detained four times for drunkenness and violence. Sourdeval's husband died during her first detention in 1715, and she moved in with relatives upon her release in 1716. The police observed 'that she is definitely more disorderly now than before her detention'.[68] After a second arrest and release,

66. Paris, Ars., MS Bastille, 10619, f.67-70.
67. Foucault, *The Punitive society*, p.128.
68. Paris, Ars., MS Bastille, 10622, f.103.

She moved in with her mother but refused to work at anything that was offered to her, on the contrary, she took up her old habits that they tried to reform and to hide as much as possible, always hoping that she would change, [...] she left her mother's house to live in greater freedom and pursue her drinking binges that provoked outbursts of violence, fits of rage towards her neighbours, currently reduced to a bed she cannot leave since she sold her clothes to pay for her debauchery [...] threatening to set the room on fire.[69]

The request emphasised the family's shame and their obligation to lock up a relative who endangered the community with drunkenness and dissipation.[70] Sourdeval returned to the Salpêtrière for the fourth time in March of 1721, at her family's expense: 'But far from correcting herself, she gave herself over to debauchery more than ever.'[71] Sourdeval's case revealed the limited resources available for managing such problems.

Non-conjugal sexual relations loomed large in accusations of debauchery and requests for intervention. Contrary to the libertine image cultivated in novels of the period, many French men and women condemned adultery and misalliances for their destructive consequences. The influx of single men and women into Paris created an environment for chance encounters and extramarital sex.[72] Declining religiosity and absent parents left the young and uprooted without guidance for sexual relations. Traditionally, marriage aimed to consolidate rank and secure the transmission of property. In the eighteenth century, however, reformers promoted a companionate model that emphasised affection between the future spouses. In both cases, parents and neighbours sought to guide young people towards the stability of marriage even after sexual relations and pregnancy.[73] Pre-marital sex was not the problem; the refusal to legitimate it through marriage was.

Such behaviour qualified as 'scandalous' when, for example, the

---

69. Paris, Ars., MS Bastille, 10622, f.97-98.
70. Garrioch, *Neighbourhood and community in Paris*, p.56-95.
71. Paris, Ars., MS Bastille, 10622, f.105.
72. Garrioch, *Neighbourhood and community in Paris*, p.84-87, 203-204. On mobility, see Vincent Denis, 'The invention of mobility and the history of the state', *French historical studies* 29:3 (2006), p.359-77.
73. Arlette Farge, *Fragile lives: violence, power, and solidarity in eighteenth-century Paris* (1986; Cambridge, 1993). Julie Hardwick offers a comparative analysis of Lyon; see *Sex in an Old Regime city: young workers and intimacy in France, 1660-1789* (Oxford, 2020).

thirty-three-year-old heiress Henriette-Emilie de Bautru, comtesse de Nogent, ignored her mother's choice of suitors in favour of an eighteen-year-old water carrier named Thomas Dufour whom she dressed up and paraded around in her carriage. Mme de Nogent requested a *lettre de cachet* to detain her daughter in a convent, alleging 'her indiscreet taste for independence'. In a twenty-page memoir, she insisted that her daughter's disregard for propriety 'drew the attention of her neighbourhood and caused a huge scandal'.[74] The family claimed that Henriette-Emilie intended to elope to Holland with Dufour and abscond with the family fortune since she was the sole heir. After being sent to a convent in 1740, Henriette-Emilie hired a lawyer whose inflammatory memoirs transformed her into a *cause célèbre*. By mobilising public opinion, Mlle de Nogent forced the crown to release her one year later.

According to her mother, Henriette-Emilie set a bad example to her domestic staff and surrounding neighbours. By dressing up Dufour and elevating him through intimacy, she displayed the arbitrary nature of social distinctions and the power of sex to subvert them. Similar efforts for sexual regulation also appeared among working Parisians whose livelihoods were endangered by troublesome behaviour. Around the time of Nogent's detention, Robert Loyer found himself under investigation. His mother requested a *lettre de cachet* for her twenty-three-year-old son who had stopped attending church and was 'living in libertinage' with a woman twice his age, Marie Bouton. Loyer's mother denounced Bouton, a fruit seller, as 'a slut who sleeps around with guys from the neighbourhood and elsewhere, gets drunk with them and is known for her bad reputation and misconduct'.[75]

Despite the family protests, Robert was determined to marry Marie Bouton, 'which causes much scandal, she is the reason that this young man refuses to listen to the reprimands of his mother, or other members of his family, and he wants to marry her in order to dishonour his family'.[76] The family cast Robert's intended marriage as a spiteful act designed to tarnish their hard-won reputation. The argument found a sympathetic ear in Commissioner Blanchard who investigated the case. After interviewing neighbours, he recommended

---

74. Paris, Ars., MS Bastille, 11504, f.5. For the Nogent affair, see Lisa Jane Graham, 'Scandal: law, literature and morality in the early Enlightenment', *SVEC* 2005:04, p.232-40.
75. Paris, Ars., MS Bastille, 11484, f.193.
76. Paris, Ars., MS Bastille, 11484, f.198.

two *lettres de cachet* in order 'to put a stop to the scandal'.[77] Marie was sent to the Salpêtrière and Robert to Saint-Lazare, where he was monitored to prevent suicide given his distress over the separation.

Individuals who abandoned work and family to pursue debauchery inspired shame. The breakdown in governance constituted a breach of trust within the community that required repair. These assumptions guided the uncles of Pierre Caze, who requested a *lettre de cachet* for their nephew who was orphaned as a child. They raised him and apprenticed him to a tailor,

> But, despite their efforts, they failed to correct his bad penchant for libertinage, he often stole bits of fabric from them to sell them to pay for his debaucheries, when their reprimands became too much of a burden, he left the house [...] the entire family requests an order to detain him in a safe place in order to shield themselves from his insults and preserve their honour and favourable reputation.[78]

The family needed the police to protect its honour, and the police needed the family to discipline its members. Together they circumscribed the delinquent and filled the void left by absent or dead parents.[79]

In a similar vein, the kin of nineteen-year-old Noël Henriette Cheris pooled resources to care for the girl who had been abandoned by her parents at birth. Trained as a button maker, Noël initially showed promise and satisfied her employers. Yet, just as she began supporting herself, she quit her job, moved out and gave herself over to the most 'appalling debauchery'.[80] Her relatives asked for a *lettre de cachet* to send her to a workhouse; 'having shaken off the yoke of their domination, she abandoned herself to a shameful libertinage that make them fear more deplorable repercussions than those which currently disgrace them.'[81] Noël's grandmother emphasised the family's sacrifices to raise the girl and her ingratitude. Moved by the family's plight, the prime minister Cardinal Fleury noted that 'the conduct of this girl is deplorable' and recommended detention.

---

77. Paris, Ars., MS Bastille, 11484, f.197.
78. Paris, Ars., MS Bastille, 11485, f.218.
79. Garrioch argues that Old Regime society was structured as a great chain of patriarchy culminating in the king. The police were expected to intervene when individual links broke down; see 'The paternal government of men', p.37.
80. Paris, Ars., MS Bastille, 11486, f.10.
81. Paris, Ars., MS Bastille, 11486, f.13.

Noël was arrested in January 1741 and sent to the Salpêtrière for six months to reform her behaviour.

This survey of petitions for detention illuminates the central place of sexual misconduct in the ecology of urban life. Debauchery designated the disruptive behaviour and its reverberations on the family and the community. The police were the middlemen between the crown and its subjects, investigating requests and evaluating motives. They were summoned to protect the innocent and the vulnerable, but they had to tread cautiously since their intervention could quickly turn repressive. Their reports displayed sympathy for families and victims of disorderly behaviour and remind us of the limited resources available for addressing these problems. As ideas about the family and sexuality evolved, however, so too did expectations about policing and punishment.

A society of individuals

The requests for *lettres de cachet* peaked in the first half of the eighteenth century. Although requests continued into the opening months of the Revolution in 1789, the archives thin out after 1760.[82] Various factors converged to change royal policy and public attitudes towards moral infractions in the later decades. The discourses of natural rights and individual liberty moved criminal law reform to the centre of the *philosophes'* agenda and public debates. This movement targeted the *lettres de cachet* as symbols of despotism. Mounting criticism, however, did not signal the dawn of sexual liberation, but rather ushered in a new approach to the problems associated with urban space and sexual discipline.

Both David Garrioch and Vincent Milliot emphasise the impact of enlightened ideas on attitudes towards the police and policing. Garrioch argues that sentimental currents in French culture reconfigured the traditional image of fathers as distant and austere figures. These biases inevitably affected the paternalistic assumptions that guided policing in Paris. Evidence confirms that the police embraced this conciliatory model in their interactions with the populace. From this perspective, the *lettres de cachet* appeared as outmoded tools of patriarchal authority. The cult of affection and the image of the 'good father' reconfigured notions of policing and public order.[83]

---

82. Farge and Foucault, *Disorderly families*, p.26-27.
83. Garrioch, 'The paternal government of men', p.45-49, and Lynn Hunt, *The Family romance of the French Revolution* (Berkeley, CA, 1992), p.17-52.

The proliferation of police memoirs in the second half of the century attested to the impact of natural rights theory and judicial reform on notions of public service.[84] To cite just one example, Lieutenant General Lenoir identified protection and pedagogy, not surveillance and repression, as the goals that guided his administration. Moreover, he insisted that his agents were a professional force of public, not royal, servants.[85] This vision of policing integrated respect for individual liberties into the traditional concerns for order and the public weal. The two visions proved incompatible but, up to 1789, the police tried to stretch moral tolerance to accommodate individual liberties.

The emergence of political economy in the second half of the eighteenth century moved criminal law to the centre of reform efforts within philosophical and ministerial circles. The French translation of Cesare Beccaria's *On crimes and punishments* in 1764 spearheaded a movement to denounce the crown's archaic judicial system. The redefinition of delinquency as a product of environment, not original sin, made the old penal methods appear barbaric and ineffective. If society made criminals, it could also reform them. In addition, Beccaria called for the calibration of penalties to reflect the severity of the crime. Detention in a workhouse or medieval fortress was both useless and irrational since it produced no benefit either for the offender or for society. For writers like Voltaire and Louis-Sébastien Mercier, the *lettres de cachet* exemplified the arbitrary nature of royal justice and policing. These arguments mobilised public opinion to clamour for reform, and inspired ministers and magistrates to join the campaign.

In 1784, Secretary of State Breteuil sent a memorandum to Lieutenant General Lenoir and provincial *intendants* of the realm that reflected new attitudes towards moral infractions. He singled out debauchery and the *lettres de cachet* in his diagnosis of the penal system. He advocated reducing the length of detention or abolishing it altogether. Although he recognised the aversion to scandal that propelled the requests, he insisted that the crown distinguish between 'inconveniences' and 'true dishonour' when evaluating them. Of course, it was annoying for an upstanding family to be humiliated by the profligacy or promiscuity of a relative,

---

84. *Les Mémoires policiers, 1750-1850: écritures et pratiques policières du siècle des Lumières au Second Empire*, ed. Vincent Milliot (Rennes, 2006).

85. Garrioch, 'The paternal government of men', p.45-49, and Milliot, *Un Policier des Lumières*, p.345-49, 273.

But nothing in all that has been mentioned seems to offer strong enough cause to justify depriving such individuals of their liberty, they are, according to the laws, *sui juris*. They do harm only to themselves; they bring disgrace only to themselves and their parents do not share it, therefore, the latter have no right to request that the crown intervene on their behalf.[86]

Breteuil's comment captures the liberal pivot in royal circles in the 1780s in regards to the administration of justice and policing. A moral misdemeanour did not constitute a social crime that merited detention: the crown could no longer justify private repression. Breteuil recognised the individual as an independent legal entity and rejected the familial model of discipline that justified the recourse to *lettres de cachet*. These same reformers also promoted scientific methods in jurisprudence, including more rigorous standards of proof for conviction.

The police applied these methods in their investigations and refused to arrest individuals on allegations of debauchery. In September of 1789, the family of twenty-two-year-old Victoire Beauregard requested a *lettre de cachet* in the same terms as those used a half-century earlier for Noël Cheris:

Starting in her youth, she began showing a taste for scandalous pursuits and despite the sacrifices her family made to stop these pursuits [...] she topped off her debauchery by moving out of the house; was brought back to Versailles on the condition that she lead a better life, but she was pregnant with the fruits of her debauchery and returned to Paris to abandon herself to a sordid life. The family, which is above reproach, fears an inevitable disgrace and hopes that you will grant the request for an order to detain her.[87]

As part of his investigation, Lieutenant Clos, the police chief for Versailles, interviewed two of Victoire's former employers, who testified that the girl had committed some minor thefts. None of the witnesses, however, substantiated the family's allegations of debauchery. Clos denied the request since, 'on this charge, I could not find anything convincing besides the minor offences already noted. These strike

---

86. A copy of Breteuil's *circulaire* is published in Frantz Funck-Brentano, *Les Lettres de cachet à Paris, étude suivie d'une liste des prisonniers de la Bastille (1659-1789)* (Paris, 1903), p.xlii-xlv.

87. Paris, Archives nationales (AN), O¹ 361, f.255.

me as too petty to justify locking up the girl called Beauregard in a *maison de force.*'[88]

Moreover, Clos had a legal argument to support his decision, since Victoire indulged in debauchery in Paris, not Versailles. Technically, therefore, her behaviour fell outside of his jurisdiction. Nonetheless, his report foregrounded judicial principles as opposed to legal technicalities to make the case, and demonstrated new attitudes towards policing debauchery. The family's fear of scandal no longer sufficed without strong proof of criminal activity to justify an individual's detention. Three months into the Revolution, Clos's report revealed the impact of natural law discussions on how the police understood the balance between individual liberty and public order in relation to sexual improprieties.

Had French society grown more tolerant, or had the police raised the threshold for intervention that recognised a right to privacy and personal autonomy? It is hard to generalise, but their reports emphasise standards of proof and conviction that guided judicial reform in these decades. For example, in June of 1789, the family of twenty-three-year-old Pierre-Nicolas Jean *dit* Rivière asked the crown for a *lettre de cachet* to detain the young man at Bicêtre because 'he has indulged in terrible libertinage since age sixteen, his conduct and his dissipations [...] have always alarmed his family'. Pierre-Nicolas was caught stealing as well, although he was acquitted. Even though the family offered to pay for his detention at Bicêtre, the minister, Villedeuil, denied the request since 'there was no proof of the alleged theft. If the family has no other accusations than those imputed, I don't think there is good reason to grant the request to deprive him of his liberty; the suspicion of a misdemeanour is insufficient for locking up someone who could not be convicted in a court of law.'[89] Villedeuil, who was controller general of finances, shared the views of ministers like Breteuil, Malesherbes and Lenoir: allegations of debauchery no longer warranted incarceration without strong proof. Family honour receded before individual liberty. Although families continued to send requests, they were less likely to find sympathetic ears in the royal administration.

The attack on the *lettres de cachet* represented the conflict between the liberal and corporate social models. Did calls for individual rights include behaviour that threatened community norms of moral

88. Paris, AN, O¹ 361, f.255.
89. Paris, AN, O¹ 361, f.235.

propriety? Secretary of State Malesherbes reflected at length on this question. In order to justify repression, he distinguished between liberty and licence, the latter being 'as dangerous to true liberty as despotism'. For Malesherbes, the prophylactic principles that guided policing remained as pertinent as ever. In fact, policing was the prerequisite for liberty:

> And for everybody to be truly and entirely free, we ask that nobody be free to trouble public order. Safeguard us, Sire, against the excess of liberty, the liberty of vice, continue to impose the barrier of *une police exacte*; but at the same time, eliminate all abuses in policing through circumspect procedures that prevent it from becoming oppressive, all the more necessary for the police to preserve their full authority.[90]

Malesherbes sought to reconcile his attachment to public order with principles of natural law and liberty. By contrast, the *lettres de cachet* represented arbitrary authority that threatened personal liberty by denying individuals access to the law courts and due process.[91]

For Malesherbes, extraordinary justice had to go for the monarchy to survive. To fill the void left by the *lettres de cachet*, he proposed creating a public tribunal to receive the complaints that motivated petitions for detention. Malesherbes recognised the necessity of policing, and expedited justice to protect society against disruptive behaviour. Yet he suggested that the police could participate in the tribunal when their expertise was pertinent to the cases under review. The police would preserve their authority by joining forces with the tribunal to maintain public order in the capital and other large cities of the realm.[92]

The problems associated with debauchery did not disappear with the abolition of the *lettres de cachet* in 1790. As Vincent Denis demonstrates in his essay in this volume, the revolutionary police continued to monitor sociability in the name of public order and social harmony. In the last decades of the Old Regime, the evidence suggests that the criteria and forms for police intervention evolved in favour of individual autonomy over repression. These attitudes converged with philosophical, medical and judicial calls for reform and the abolition of torture. New laws and institutions distinguished, for example, cases

---

90. Draft of a memoir in Malesherbes's papers. Paris, AN, 399AP 142, f.10.
91. Julian Swann, *Exile, imprisonment, or death: the politics of disgrace in Bourbon France, 1610-1789* (Oxford, 2017), p.415.
92. Draft of a memoir in Malesherbes's papers. Paris, AN, 399AP 142, f.10.

of mental infirmity from prostitution and criminality in terms of punishment and treatment.

Debauchery: past and present

Through the lens of debauchery, this essay suggests that moral discipline was integral to maintaining the social ecology of eighteenth-century Paris. Debauchery reminds us that sociability involved conflicts as well as consensus, the corporeal and the discursive. The erosion of temporal and spatial hierarchies abetted by the commercialisation of leisure augmented fears of sexual danger in both the intimate and the public spaces of the city. The crown expanded its policing powers in response to the growth of the metropolis. Policing combined information gathering and surveillance to monitor the population and defuse conflicts. The police were integral to the community's capacity to define and enforce normative sociability. As we saw in the *gazetins*, these agents represented themselves as astute observers and guardians of the communities they served. They alert us to a thriving economy of illicit activities that threatened to engulf the licit worlds of work, parish and family.

The preceding analysis suggests that debauchery bridged the passage from a traditional to a liberal society. As defined through the petitions for the *lettres de cachet*, debauchery subverted principles of hierarchy and corporate identity that structured Old Regime visions of state and society. In the context of the Enlightenment, debauchery represented the lack of self-government so critical to a society of individuals. Debates about debauchery were ultimately debates about the task of moral discipline in a free society. Was freedom compatible with free love? Who was responsible for resolving conflicts over disruptive sexual relations and behaviour? Should communities or states regulate sex and, if so, how and according to what criteria? Given their intermediary role between the crown and the populace, the police offer us some answers.

Debauchery threatened the integrity of the household in terms of sexual scandal and financial ruin, as seen in the petitions for *lettres de cachet*. It also tested the republican promotion of marriage as a site for reproductive sexuality and civic education. As philosophical and medical expectations about family and sexuality evolved to accommodate rational choice, utility and pleasure, debauchery acquired a political charge in the context of Jacobin efforts to found a republic of virtue in 1792-1794. The French Revolution and the virtuous republic it sought to establish did not put an end to debauchery, which continued to proliferate after the abolition of the *lettres de cachet*. However, the mechanisms of surveillance were quite different in the nineteenth century, as the police shared the work of moral discipline with other experts and agents of the modern state. The tensions between licit and illicit sexuality, and their relative visibility in the urban landscape, produced new forms of surveillance and regulation.

The condemnation of mesmerism:
a police affair?

BRUNO BELHOSTE

Université Paris 1, IHMC

Translated by Nicole Charley

In August 1784, two separate royal commissions formally condemned Franz Anton Mesmer's doctrine of animal magnetism, or mesmerism: a royal commission made up of scientists from the Académie des sciences and doctors from the Paris Faculté de médecine, and another commission made up of members of the Société royale de médecine. The affair enthralled public opinion; over the next few months, those for and against his doctrine would confront each other through various means such as libels, newspaper articles and theatrical plays. At issue was not only the medical aspect, but science as a whole, and truth itself; even liberty was thought to be at stake. Even so, before Robert Darnton's first book on the subject, *Mesmerism and the end of the Enlightenment*,[1] this contentious sequence of events had failed to capture the attention of most historians. Darnton was also the first to have considered the affair within its true context. He argued it was not only a medical bone of contention, but also a political one; the debate on mesmerism was part and parcel of the escalating contestations which characterised the 1780s and ultimately led to the Revolution. The quarrel was a moment of clarity for those who opposed absolutist power; it provided not only common ground, but also – and most importantly – powerful moral and analytical resources to add to the debate. Other studies have since followed Darnton's, clarifying, developing or amending his thesis, but without fundamentally challenging it.[2]

---

1. Robert Darnton, *Mesmerism and the end of the Enlightenment in France* (Cambridge, MA, 1968).
2. See David Armando and Bruno Belhoste, 'Mesmerism between the end of the Old Regime and the Revolution: social dynamics and political issues', *Annales historiques de la Révolution française* 391 (2018), p.3-26.

In this essay, I would like to examine the mesmerist debate from the point of view of the authorities instead of from that of the mesmerists. For it was as much the royal administration as it was Mesmer and his partisans who made animal magnetism a public affair. Indeed, the government had orchestrated its condemnation, transforming the matter into a medical debate and a battle for public opinion. For what reasons would they oppose a movement which was tolerated by police authorities? How did their about-turn over mesmerism occur? What was it the crown feared, and what did they hope to get out of the affair? These are the questions I will attempt to answer.

To begin, I will consider the condemnation of mesmerism as a police concern. The movement had a bearing on public order, and was therefore naturally subject to the jurisdiction of the police. The question here is on the nature of the enforcement itself. In their research, Vincent Milliot and other historians have clearly demonstrated what challenges the police faced in the eighteenth century.[3] The police apparatus evolved concomitantly with police ideology, and occurred in response to the profound social, political and environmental transformations in the fabric of urban life, which traditional policing structures were increasingly at pains to effectively address. Reducing the risk of delinquency and unrest was an important objective, true, but mitigating threats to food supply, sanitation and hygiene was equally critical. To do this, more effective measures of control, prevention, protection and, ultimately, repression were needed; achieving this goal meant developing knowledge and information networks. The police consequently became a huge governmental entity, mobilising vast amounts of moral, material and intellectual resources. The response to mesmerism involved two separate police imperatives, the policing of public health and the policing of opinion; each exploited different agents, lines of reasoning and forms of action. This greatly complexified the condemnation of mesmerism as a police affair.

Politics played a decisive role in our narrative. Robert Darnton was the first to note this, though his focus was uniquely on what he called the 'radical strain in mesmerism'. For him, the run-of-the-mill mesmerists, though well represented in court circles, were nothing more than middling illuminists, harmless and reactionary. But one cannot ignore that the affair took on a political cast as early as 1784,

---

3.   Vincent Milliot, *'L'Admirable police': tenir Paris au siècle des Lumières* (Ceyzérieu, 2016); see also Nicolas Vidoni, *La Police des Lumières, XVIIᵉ-XVIIIᵉ siècles* (Paris, 2018).

when Mesmer and his partners established the Société de l'harmonie universelle. The baron Louis Auguste de Breteuil began invoking the threat of moral and political turmoil posed by mesmerism upon his arrival at the ministry of the Maison du roi, exploiting the issue of medical policing as a means to ingratiate himself with the royal couple. From its earliest incarnation, therefore, the condemnation of mesmerism appears to have been an exercise in policing with a twofold agenda: to discredit a movement which gravely threatened the troubled medical institutions; and to initiate a political campaign with the aim of dismantling an organisation whose web of influence extended to the highest levels of the state and of the court. The struggle for dominance was an ongoing battle in the corridors of power. The government risked revealing its weakness in attacking Mesmer and his partisans. Yet the operation was a success: Breteuil won his battle of opinions, and animal magnetism rapidly lost its appeal with the enlightened public. It is this aspect of the affair I wish to examine in closing.

From medical quarrel to police affair

Animal magnetism was first and foremost a medical doctrine and a treatment method. Since its discovery in 1774, it sparked considerable controversy among doctors. The discussion centred on the medical and scientific merits of the treatment as well as on its effectiveness. The question of whether to forbid this therapy only gradually gained leverage. After that, animal magnetism was not only a hotly contested subject, but also, for the police, a sanitary matter.

A medical bone of contention

In 1774, Franz Anton Mesmer, a medical doctor in the Faculty of Vienna, announced he had discovered something he called animal magnetism. According to Mesmer, a type of magnetic fluid circulated throughout the universe, penetrating all bodies, including humans; this fluid ebbed and flowed just as gravitational tides did. When some sort of blockage obstructed its internal movements, this resulted in sickness. The medical cure consisted of re-establishing these movements by transferring the magnetic fluid accumulated in the body of the mesmerist or in some other reservoir to the sick patient, either remotely or through direct contact. The reservoir could be a natural repository, such as a magnetised tree, or artificial, such as one of Mesmer's famous tubs.[4] Mesmer's discovery of animal magnetism was promptly disputed by the leading doctors of Vienna; the inoculator Jan Ingenhousz accused Mesmer of charlatanism and was foremost amongst his critics. Nevertheless, Mesmer found partisans of his doctrine in Vienna and elsewhere in Germany. For three years, he tried without success to have his findings recognised, basing his argument on several alleged medical successes. In 1778, after failing to cure Maria Theresia von Paradis, a blind pianist and one of the empress' protégés, he left for Paris in a bid to have the Académie des sciences, the most prestigious scientific institution in Europe, validate animal magnetism. It was also likely, as rumour had it, that Mesmer's decision to leave Vienna had been motivated by an imposed ban. The interdict, if there had indeed been one, was never officially disclosed.

In Paris, the Académie des sciences – and the Société royale de médecine – refused to approve Mesmer's discovery. Yet he remained in France,[5] settling first in Créteil, then in the Marais in Paris. He tended to patients with relative discretion, and his activities were tolerated though he was neither a member of the Faculté de médecine in Paris nor a *médecin privilégié*. They alone were granted permission to practise medicine in Paris, but the prestige of Mesmer's title of medical doctor of the Faculty of Vienna gave him some protection. Charles Deslon, *docteur-régent* in the Faculté de médecine, became one of Mesmer's disciples, and colleagues readily sent patients to Mesmer. His case was clearly not unique; Colin Jones' comparison of the medical and literary markets in late eighteenth-century Paris reveals the emergence of a veritable medical black market, subject to little oversight despite official regulations on the practice of medicine and the use of remedies.[6]

Yet animal magnetism, like many other professed therapeutic discoveries, though tolerated, was unceasingly challenged. In 1780, the controversy began to intensify. At first, the debate was medical,

4. See Frank A. Pattie, *Mesmer and animal magnetism: a chapter in the history of medicine* (Hamilton, NY, 1994); and Alan Gauld, *A History of hypnotism* (Cambridge, 1995).

5. See Bruno Belhoste, 'Mesmer et la diffusion du magnétisme animal à Paris (1778-1803)', in *Mesmer et mesmérismes: le magnétisme animal en contexte*, ed. Bruno Belhoste and Nicole Edelman (Paris, 2015), p.21-61.

6. Colin Jones, 'The great chain of buying: medical advertisement, the bourgeois public sphere, and the origins of the French Revolution', *American historical review* 101:1 (1996), p.13-40.

focused on whether magnetic fluid truly existed and on its practical effectiveness. Many of Mesmer's adversaries maintained that animal magnetism was pure fraud and that the police in charge of public health should therefore look after the matter. The doctor and journalist Jacques Dehorne denounced Mesmer's trickery in a libel published in July 1780.[7] Another medical journalist, Jean-Jacques Paulet, went further still in an article he wrote for the *Gazette de santé*.[8] The attack against Mesmer and Deslon, his disciple, was in response to their attempt to secure the support of the Faculté de médecine de Paris for animal magnetism. Indeed, after having failed to convince several *docteurs-régents*, Mesmer had proposed that the Faculty conduct its own controlled trials comparing his method with traditional therapies.

To counter the opposition, Deslon wrote an account of the cures which they had obtained. This only served to provoke outrage in some doctors, who accused their fellow *docteur-régent* of having abused of his title by promoting animal magnetism.[9] On 1 September 1780, the Faculty convened to resolve the dispute between Deslon and his adversaries, and, after hearing both sides, pronounced its verdict. Deslon was given a warning 'to be more circumspect in future', and one year to publicly disavow his publication on pain of expulsion from the Faculty. Their condemnation was directed exclusively against Deslon; Mesmer's propositions were dismissed out of hand.[10] The Faculty clearly viewed the latter as no more than a foreign charlatan who was thus beneath contempt. Deslon's sin was far graver: in promoting animal magnetism, he had compromised the reputation and honour of the esteemed academic body to which he belonged.

A condemnation had to be issued twice more to become binding. The Faculty did pronounce a second condemnation on 7 October 1780, but put off making a third for fear of creating a scandal. Finally, at the express request of Deslon himself, who wished to settle matters once and for all, they met again on 20 August 1782, and condemned him a third time. This ultimate condemnation marked a crucial

7. Jacques Dehorne, *Réponse d'un médecin de Paris à un médecin de province sur le prétendu magnétisme animal de M. Mesmer* (Vienna and Paris, Delalain le jeune, 1780).

8. Jean-Jacques Paulet, 'Les miracles de M. Mesmer', *Gazette de santé* 28 (9 July 1780) and 29 (16 July 1780).

9. Charles Deslon, *Observations sur le magnétisme animal* (London and Paris, n.n., 1780).

10. See Adolphe Pinard *et al.*, *Commentaires de la Faculté de médecine: 1777 à 1786*, 2 vols (Paris, 1903), vol.1, p.545-73.

turning point for mesmerism. Before then, the conflict with partisans and opponents of animal magnetism had been entirely medical. As fierce as the attacks had been, on both sides, they had never gone beyond the limits of what was acceptable in this type of disagreement between doctors. Even the dishonourable accusation of charlatanism levelled against Mesmer was part of the rhetorical repertoire typically deployed during such professional jousting, which could often become quite vicious. However, striking Deslon from the ranks of the Faculté de médecine was to exclude animal magnetism from legitimate medical discussion entirely. It meant that, in the interest of patient protection, the threat of prohibition hung over Mesmer and his doctrine.

Nevertheless, if the professors of the Faculté de médecine adopted a radical stance against Deslon and animal magnetism, it was not only due to the dangers his doctrine posed for patients. The context in which their pronouncement was made – the gravely weakened authority of the Faculty – must also be taken into consideration. The *docteurs-régents* were increasingly confronted with the growing demands of surgeons and pharmacists who, with the complicity of the government, sought emancipation from the Faculty. The greater threat stemmed nonetheless from the state's own medical authority; the government was intent on weakening the corporations and gaining direct control over the practice and instruction of medicine. The *docteurs-régents* considered the founding of the Société royale de médecine, in the same year Mesmer arrived in Paris, as an 'usurpation' of their rights and a veritable declaration of war. The new society was under the direct authority of the royal government; it promised an enlightened approach to medical questions founded on an increase in the number of investigations and the application of the physical sciences. This broke with traditional scholastic and Galenic practices, of which the Faculté de médecine of Paris was the eminent representative.[11]

It also dealt a terrible blow to the Faculty, more so since their weakening state was already manifest in the quality of their instruction. Their narrow, run-down buildings on the rue Jean-de-Beauvais were put to shame by the brand-new quarters housing the Collège de chirurgie, the Collège royal de France and the Jardin du roi. Members of the Faculty were weighed down by limited resources and

11. Laurence Brockliss and Colin Jones, *The Medical world of early modern France* (Oxford, 1997), p.760-82.

an archaic organisational structure; incapable of keeping abreast of recent developments in medicine, their teaching remained essentially theoretical. Clinical medicine was entirely ignored, chemistry completely overlooked and practical anatomy (practised on human cadavers) marginalised. Students looked outside of the Faculty, to private classes, the Collège de chirurgie, the royal institutions and the occasional hospital to complete their education. The signs of decline were clear: in the final years of the *Ancien Régime*, a scant 100 students enrolled in the Faculté de médecine, against 800 in the Collège de chirurgie.[12]

Though discussion centred on the academic controversy, the commercial aspect was another serious bone of contention between the Faculté de médecine and the new Société royale de médecine. Most physicians in Paris, whether doctors in the Faculté de médecine or in princely houses, commercialised their practice, often partnering with those who dispensed remedies. But medicine was equally practised and monetised by many outside of the corporations. Since the Faculty had been unable to eliminate these activities, they learned to cohabit, even make affiliations, with such players, and were satisfied with simply denouncing the most scandalous cases of charlatanism. The creation of the Société royale de médecine would destroy this fragile equilibrium. The new body was not content with merely assessing medical progress: it controlled the manufacture and sale of remedies, and meant to have the final say regarding new therapeutic procedures. It was for this reason, when Mesmer arrived in Paris in 1778, that the Société wished to evaluate his discovery. The *docteurs-régents* of the Faculty perceived their rival's presumptuousness as a threat; they had become accustomed to working discreetly alongside healers and medicine makers of all sorts. But, to avoid providing their opponents with ammunition against them, the Faculty had to appear as intractable as the Société towards charlatans.[13] Mesmer might have been ignorant of these confrontations. Deslon certainly was not, but he misread the situation. He tried to capitalise on the hostility the *docteurs-régents* felt towards the Société royale de médecine, arguing that '[the Société] would find it extremely disagreeable to see this discovery succeed by virtue of [the Faculty's] ministrations'.[14] What

12. Toby Gelfand, *Professionalizing modern medicine: Paris surgeons and medical science and institutions in the 18th century* (London, 1980).

13. Gelfand, *Professionalizing modern medicine*, p.622-70.

14. Deslon's speech to the Faculté de médecine de Paris, 18 September 1780, cited

he did not anticipate was that, to reaffirm its authority, the Faculty would decide to relentlessly pursue anything which threatened to disrupt medical orthodoxy. It was therefore out of the question that they approve a doctrine as controversial as animal magnetism.

The Société de l'harmonie universelle and the royal commissions

The Faculté de médecine's condemnation of animal magnetism in 1780 led to one unintended consequence: it propelled Mesmer and his method into the spotlight. Far from being discouraged, patients began to flock to Mesmer to seek treatment. Many were powerful individuals whom Deslon, a familiar figure in court, brought to see his mentor. First Deslon, then Mesmer himself, began to entertain the idea that they could circumvent the opposition by appealing to public opinion and to the royal court. Their strategy seemed to bear fruit, since the queen herself intervened on behalf of Mesmer in March 1781. In exchange for a lifetime pension of 20,000 *livres*, he was to relinquish the secret to his supposed treatment; but Mesmer haughtily refused the government's conditions, and announced his firm intent to leave France, although, instead, he remained in Paris.[15]

Disillusioned by Mesmer's attitude, Deslon gradually grew estranged from his former master. He decided to take up mesmerising independently, without waiting for Mesmer to initiate him. As we saw earlier, in August 1782, he presented himself for a third time before the Faculté de médecine and demanded they examine thirty cures he maintained to have effected through animal magnetism. The Faculty refused, and pronounced their final condemnation. Mesmer, who felt betrayed by his former disciple, accused Deslon of having appropriated his method. With the support of new disciples (and former patients, foremost amongst them the lawyer Nicolas Bergasse and the banker Guillaume Kornmann), he conceived of a joint-stock company to promote animal magnetism; he would reap the financial rewards, and humanity would benefit from a novel universal remedy. Mesmer spent 1783 in preparations. Subscriptions to the Société de l'harmonie universelle were issued in March of that year. An ill-fated attempt at reconciliation between Mesmer and Deslon delayed the

---

by Franz Anton Mesmer in *Précis historique des faits relatifs au magnétisme animal jusqu'en avril 1781* (London, n.n., 1781), p.175.

15. Mesmer gives an account of the negotiations in his *Précis historique*. See Darnton, *Mesmerism*, p.51.

inauguration of the business venture until the end of 1783, but open it did, to tremendous success. Among the subscribers were Mesmer's patients and doctors, but also prominent personalities, courtiers, financiers and military figures. The affair of the mesmerist movement was imminent.

Three factors were instrumental in triggering the affair. The first was the rivalry between Mesmer and Deslon. The latter, preoccupied with waging his two-front war against both his colleagues in the Faculté de médecine and Mesmer, insisted that an official commission to examine animal magnetism be appointed. This was a way to not only circumvent the Faculty, which had condemned him, but also beat Mesmer to the punch. Essentially, Deslon reproached Mesmer for breaking the medical community's monopoly of animal magnetism by initiating those who were not medical practitioners to the treatment. Deslon intended to reserve such knowledge to medical graduates. To that end, he announced the opening of his own clinic, on the rue de Montmartre, where he received and instructed his colleagues.[16] The second catalyser was the appointment of the baron de Breteuil to the ministry of the Maison du roi, which had oversight of both scholarly institutions and Paris affairs. Breteuil had been witness to Mesmer's difficulties in Vienna while he had served as ambassador there, and was convinced that Mesmer was a charlatan.[17] He therefore consented to meet with Deslon and supported his demands for an official evaluation of animal magnetism.[18] No doubt there were other reasons for Breteuil to arrange for the evaluation; animal magnetism was beginning to take hold in the highest reaches of the state and in the royal court. The final inflammatory element was the remarkable success of the Société de l'harmonie universelle.

The Société opened for business at the Hôtel de Coigny, in the centre of Paris, where Mesmer resided.[19] A clinic led off from the

---

16. Letter written by Deslon and published in the *Journal de Paris* on 10 January 1784.
17. *Journal du marquis de Bombelles*, ed. Frans Durif and Jean Grassion, 2 vols (Geneva, 1978), vol.2, 16 April 1785, p.51.
18. See the letter written by Breteuil to Deslon, dated 13 January 1784, postponing their appointment, Paris, Archives nationales (AN), O*/1/495.
19. The descriptions we have of the Hôtel de Coigny are those made by two of Mesmer's adversaries, Jean Jacques Paulet and Charles-Pierre Brack. See also the testimony given by Marie Daniel Bourrée de Corberon on the meetings of the Société de l'harmonie universelle, reproduced in Darnton, *Mesmerism*, p.180-82.

meeting room, with tubs and 'crisis rooms' for patients. And however prohibitive the cost of subscription may have been – 100 louis – membership grew rapidly, from 15 at the start of 1784 to roughly 40 by February, 100 by the beginning of April and 200 by August. The Société primarily recruited from Parisian high society. Members included doctors and surgeons, some hailing from the provinces. While not officially enrolled, two princes of the blood, the prince de Conti and the duc de Bourbon, also regularly attended. The Société was kept under close watch by the police, though there was no great attempt at concealment – as early as December of 1783, they had accepted the membership of Jean Guillemain, a police inspector.[20] Mesmer gave his first class in February 1784, with four scribes recording the session; he published the lecture in booklet form, complete with engraved illustrations, which he distributed to the first hundred subscribers. A second class followed in April. Animal magnetism was on everyone's lips, at least in high society; it was discussed in the salons, in the press and in private correspondence. There were enthusiastic partisans of the doctrine, and hostile opponents, but predominantly sceptics unwilling to commit to an opinion. There was no other way to fully resolve the matter but to call for an official examination.

In response to Deslon's request, the decision to create a royal commission of enquiry was made, with the king's blessings, in March of 1784. The government first approached the Faculté de médecine de Paris with the task.[21] On 12 March, the *lieutenant de police*, on behalf of Breteuil, invited the dean, Jean Charles Henri Sallin, and two other *docteurs-régents*, Jean Darcet and Joseph Ignace Guillotin, to join the commission. Paschasius Borie would quickly be added to the panel, but he died soon after and was replaced by Michel Joseph Majault. With relations already strained, the effect on the medical community was immediate: excluded from the commission, the Société royale de médecine, also on 12 March, insisted it be associated with the enquiry; it tasked one of its members, Michel Augustin Thouret, with collecting information on animal magnetism. Sallin and his colleagues categorically refused the Société royale's participation

---

20. For more on the Société de l'harmonie universelle and its members, see the Harmonia Universalis database, https://harmoniauniversalis.univ-paris1.fr (last accessed on 26 January 2024); see also David Armando, 'Armonie discordi: una rilettura del movimento mesmerista alla fine dell'Antico regime', *Rivista storica italiana* 131:3 (2019), p.847-88.

21. Pinard *et al.*, *Commentaires de la Faculté de médecine*, p.1246-49.

and instead, since Mesmer claimed to have made a major discovery in physics with his magnetic fluid, requested the minister call on 'celebrated physicians' to aid their investigation. On 2 April, Breteuil appointed Benjamin Franklin, Jean Baptiste Leroy, Antoine Lavoisier, Gabriel de Bory and Jean Sylvain Bailly, all members of the Académie des sciences, to the Royal Commission. They now numbered nine in all. And finally, on 5 April, to pacify the Société royale de médecine, Breteuil appointed several of its members to a second commission. Pierre de Poissonnier, Claude Antoine Caille, Jean Etienne Mauduyt, Antoine Laurent Jussieu and Charles Louis François Andry would conduct an independent enquiry.

The entire process was imposing and rather complex, with three institutions – the Faculté de médecine, the Académie des sciences and the Société royale de médecine – mobilised in two commissions, and one special rapporteur, Thouret, from the Société. Despite their division, they all came to similar conclusions, with the exception of Jussieu, who would submit his own report. The enquiry commenced in May 1784, and, though its focus was on animal magnetism, it ignored Mesmer entirely. Only Deslon and an independent mesmerist, M. Jumelin, were interrogated. True, it was Deslon who had requested the enquiry, but it is surprising nonetheless that the commissioners did not seek to probe the creator of the doctrine. Perhaps they had known that Mesmer would have denied their authority in the matter. Whatever the case, he never protested his omission. He denounced Deslon's ignorance and dishonesty, and merely made to reject whatever conclusions the commissioners might draw from an enquiry carried out without his consent.[22]

On 9 May, both commissions paid a visit to Deslon's clinic on the rue Montmartre, where they listened to a preliminary presentation on the doctrine of animal magnetism given by his assistant, Lafisse. Next, they observed the treatment. The commissioners were unconvinced by the spectacular demonstrations of animal magnetism and its purported healings which, they noted, might be attributed to other causes, or simply to the imagination. They next attempted magnetic treatment on each other twice a week, to no result. They demanded that Deslon give them physical proof, but he was unable to do so.

22. See Mesmer's letter to Franklin, dated 14 May 1784, published in a pamphlet entitled *Lettres de M. Mesmer à Messieurs les auteurs du Journal de Paris et à M. Franklin* (1784), p.8-14, reproduced in the compilation Franz A. Mesmer, *Le Magnétisme animal: œuvres*, ed. Robert Amadou (Paris, 1971), p.241-43.

They also made a few observations on treatments done by Jumelin, who practised mesmerism but had received no training from Mesmer.

Finally, with Deslon's consent, they experimented on isolated patients using the principles of a single-blind study: patients were made to believe either, incorrectly, that they had undergone mesmerism, or, conversely, that they had been mesmerised without their knowing, and their reactions were observed. In one example, a child Deslon had brought to Franklin fell unconscious as he approached a tree he had been falsely told was magnetised. In Lavoisier's home, they tested magnetised cups of water: twelve cups were presented to a woman Deslon had said was sensitive to magnetism; only the last one had in fact been magnetised, yet the woman went into convulsions at the fourth cup and drank the twelfth without effect. Lavoisier, who is believed to have conceived these experiments, remarked, 'therefore, imagination alone produces the effects attributed to magnetism, and magnetism without imagination produces no effect whatsoever'.[23]

In August 1784, after three months of investigation, the commissioners published their conclusions. Thouret's report, which the Société royale de médecine approved on 9 July, appeared in book form at the beginning of the next month.[24] He concluded that the doctrine of animal magnetism was no different from that of the Paracelsians, which had already long been shown to be ineffectual. By far the most important report was the one Bailly wrote for the Royal Commission, dated 11 August,[25] in which he stressed the role of the imagination and denied all physical existence of magnetic fluid. Bailly presented a summary of his report to the Académie des sciences on 4 September: 'animal magnetism,' he concluded, 'has not proven entirely useless to the discipline which has condemned it; it is yet one more item to consign to the history of humankind's follies, and a

23. Antoine Laurent Lavoisier, 'Sur le magnétisme animal', in Œuvres de Lavoisier, vol.3 (Paris, 1865), p.499-527 (522). See also Iml Donaldson, 'Antoine de Lavoisier's role in designing a single-blind trial to assess whether "animal magnetism" exists', *Journal of the Royal Society of Medicine* 110:4 (2017), p.163-67.

24. Michel-Augustin Thouret, *Recherches et doutes sur le magnétisme animal* (Paris, Prault, 1784).

25. Michel-Joseph Majault et al., *Rapport des commissaires chargés par le roi de l'examen du magnétisme animal* (Paris, n.n., 1784); English translation: Benjamin Franklin et al., 'Report of the commissioners charged by the king with the examination of animal magnetism', *International journal of clinical and experimental hypnosis* 50:4 (2002), p.332-63.

valuable experiment on the power of the imagination.'[26] The report of
the commission of the Société royale de médecine, dated 16 August,
simply confirms the earlier report. Yet some days later, Jussieu, who
had dissociated himself from his colleagues, published his own report,
in which he maintained that animal magnetism was not a mere
product of the imagination, and demanded further investigation.[27]

A threat to the established order

And yet, if mesmerism was so vigorously condemned, it was because it
was indeed considered a threat. Why and how a mere medical debate
suddenly became an affair which inflamed public opinion is not yet
clear. There was something about animal magnetism which resonated
with contemporary concerns, but we still need to give substance to the
inflammatory context ignited by the commissioners. Robert Darnton
has been the first, perhaps the only one, to have attempted to do so
thus far. Following his approach, with perhaps some fine-tuning or
further elaboration on certain points, may be the key to answering
these questions.

Policing medicine, policing science

At the start, mesmerism was nothing more than a hotly contested
medical doctrine. But over the course of the next few years, it became
a matter many believed necessitated policing. As we have seen, from
1780 onwards, the Faculté de médecine in Paris viewed the doctrine as
a threat to their authority; this led to their threefold condemnation of
Charles Deslon, Mesmer's disciple, and to Deslon's subsequent expulsion
from their ranks. Following the official condemnations, the Faculty
zealously redoubled its efforts to repress the movement. On 28 August,
they decided that all *docteurs-régents* who had publicly defended or had
practised mesmerism would be required to sign a written retraction. A
list of the guilty was drawn up, exposing 19 of their 260-odd *docteurs-
régents*.[28] Most complied and renounced their adherence to Mesmer's
doctrine, except of course Deslon who had already been condemned,

26. Jean-Sylvain Bailly, *Exposé des expériences qui ont été faites pour l'examen du
    magnétisme animal* (Paris, n.n., 1784).
27. Antoine Laurent de Jussieu, *Rapport de l'un des commissaires chargés par le roi de
    l'examen du magnétisme animal* (Paris, veuve Hérissant, 1784).
28. Pinard *et al.*, *Commentaires de la Faculté de médecine*, p.1155.

and Charles Varnier, who appealed to the Parlement de Paris against the decision. Varnier's judicial *mémoire*, written by Jean-François Fournel, a lawyer and one of Mesmer's students, would circulate widely in Paris.[29] Though the Parlement confirmed that Varnier had been struck off the registry, the affair considerably damaged the Faculty's reputation; the public disapproved of their zeal, which it perceived as blind and excessive. That this repression was specific to one institution becomes readily apparent when one compares the Faculty's reaction to the attitude adopted by the Société royale de médecine. The Société had equally condemned Mesmer's doctrine, but in a far less virulent manner. None of its members who were partisans of animal magnetism had had reason to be fearful of censure. Some, such as Jean Noël Hallé and Henri Horace Roland Delaporte, would go on to pursue brilliant careers.

It might be said that the institutional reaction of Paris' Faculté de médecine was proportional to the spell mesmerism had cast even over medical professionals, including its own members. The list of offenders published by the Faculté de médecine in August 1784 is actually missing a few names. Quite a few *docteurs-régents* had shown an interest in animal magnetism but had not been harassed. Some, like Jussieu and Jumelin, were themselves mesmerists, but had not appeared on the list. For certain enlightened doctors, mesmerism was a means to profoundly reform the practice of medicine. Jean Goulin, the editor of the *Gazette de santé*, had frequented Deslon's clinic for two months, and appeared at first to have been convinced;[30] but, like most medical professionals, he would eventually abandon mesmerism altogether. Behind the quarrel over the therapeutic effectiveness of the treatments lay the underlying thorny issue which split partisans and adversaries of animal magnetism into two camps: who was for Enlightenment, who against? It was scholars, much more than *médecins*, who wielded the authority to decide.

It was for this reason that the five members of the Académie des sciences played such a central role in the condemnation pronounced

29. [Jean-François Fournel], *Mémoire pour Me Charles Louis Varnier, docteur régent de la Faculté de médecine de Paris et membre de la Société royale de médecine, appelant d'un décret de la faculté* (Paris, n.n., 1785). See also Pinard *et al.*, *Commentaires de la Faculté de médecine*, p.1271-88. On the political role of judicial *mémoires* published towards the eve of the Revolution, see Sarah Maza, *Private lives and public affairs: the causes célèbres of prerevolutionary France* (Berkeley, CA, 1993).
30. Jean Goulin, 'Sur le magnétisme animal', Reims, Bibliothèque Carnegie, MS 1063, f.34-39 and 45-76.

by the Royal Commission. The affair of animal magnetism was for them an opportunity to further their long-standing campaign against superstition and the false sciences. In 1775, the Académie des sciences had already decided to refuse examining further demonstrations of the quadrature of the circle, the trisection of an angle, the duplication of a cube and perpetual motion, which supposed discoverers never ceased to put forward. As noted by Condorcet, the permanent secretary of the Académie, the mission of savant societies was 'to be a barricade against charlatanism in all its forms; it is for this reason so many charlatans railed against them'.[31] It was indeed with this perspective that the scholars of the Académie investigated mesmerism in 1784. Their objective, from the start, had been to dispel an illusion: the fluid did not exist, and any curative effects were products of the imagination and pure imitation.

Bailly and Lavoisier were the most active of the commissioners. Bailly was close to the baron de Breteuil, and had authored the report, but it is Lavoisier who appears to have played the lead role. It was he who had devised the protocol for the single-blind experiments and who had guided the commission's conclusions. For Lavoisier, the enquiry into mesmerism was but one skirmish in a grander crusade against scientific quackery: Mesmer and his partisans were not the only targets; fanciful theories and 'systems' of any kind were in his line of sight, including those proposed in the Académie des sciences. Less than a year after mesmerism was condemned, Lavoisier turned his attention to supporters of the phlogiston theory, a principle of fire which most chemists believed composed all combustible substances. He denounced this theory in the same terms he had used for animal magnetism. The similarity is uncanny: phlogiston, like magnetic fluid, did not exist; it was no more than a product of the imagination.[32]

The offensive that Lavoisier and his partisans launched against the pseudosciences was a major watershed for official scientific endeavours and the public's perception of science. Within the Académie itself, the conception of science as exacting, a discipline founded on calculations, measurements and experimentation, gained a firm foothold and was fiercely defended by the Newtonists of the time. The public was

31. Paris, Bibliothèque de l'Institut, MS 876, draft of a letter on the report of the Académie des sciences and the *académies de province*, 1783, f.95-96, reproduced in *Marat avant 1789*, ed. Jacques de Cock (Lyon, 2003), p.375-76.
32. Bruno Belhoste, *Paris savant: parcours et rencontres au temps des Lumières* (Paris, 2011), p.214-17.

unfortunately much more divided: many denounced the tyranny of the academics, which they likened to ministerial despotism. The crusade against scientific imposture thus fed back into an anti-academist sentiment which would lead to the suppression of the institution during the Revolution.

Mesmer's nemesis, the baron de Breteuil

Though doctors and scholarly experts viewed animal magnetism as a false remedy, even deliberate deception, the royal powers-that-be behind the enquiry also considered it a dangerous doctrine, if not exactly for the same reasons. In fact, the government had not at first been hostile to Mesmer. It was only in 1784 that the administration's shift against mesmerism occurred. This about-turn seems to have been effected more for political reasons than on medical grounds. The baron de Breteuil, minister for the Maison du roi, most likely played a critical part in the affair.

First, let us circle back to the attitude of government authorities towards Mesmer from his arrival in France. We have seen that he had aroused the hostility of the imperial family in Vienna, and, despite the support he enjoyed in certain circles of power, this led to his disgrace. He remained isolated upon his arrival in Paris, and there is nothing to indicate in the beginning that he had been in Marie-Antoinette's good graces. Progressively, Mesmer gained the trust of prominent individuals. His disciple, Deslon, doctor to the comte d'Artois, brought him patients who had been presented at court, and some were even close to the royal family. In 1780, then-minister for the Maison du roi Antoine Jean Amelot de Chaillou had personally referred a patient to Mesmer. Finally, the queen herself developed an interest in mesmerism. She sent her former favourite, the duchesse de Chaulnes, to Mesmer for treatment, and arranged for him to obtain a grant from the government. On 28 March 1781, and on behalf of the queen, the state minister Maurepas received Mesmer in Versailles and made him a few offers, but Mesmer broke off the negotiations. The *lieutenant de police* Lenoir would later record that, though Maurepas did not believe in animal magnetism, he did not see the need to persecute Mesmer and his partisans; by his estimation, Mesmer deserved 'only ridicule and contempt'.[33] It is possible that

---

33. Bibliothèque municipale d'Orléans (BmO), Fonds ancien, MS 1421, *Mémoires de Jean-Charles Pierre Le Noir, lieutenant général de police de la ville de Paris sous le règne*

Maurepas was more interested in the doctrine than Lenoir claimed, even in regard to his own health, though we shall never know for sure. Maurepas died on 21 November 1781, a few months after his meeting with Mesmer.

Following Maurepas's demise, the role of state minister was de facto occupied by Vergennes, the minister of Foreign Affairs, who did not seem to be interested in Mesmer or in mesmerism. It was quite the opposite for the baron de Breteuil, who succeeded Amelot in the Maison du roi on 18 November 1783, a few months after his return from his ambassadorship in Vienna. Breteuil was extremely ambitious. He and Calonne, the new *contrôleur général des finances*, were Vergennes's close rivals. The two men had strong ties with the queen's entourage, but Breteuil also had his own agenda: to one day become the state minister. To achieve this end, he had begun to scheme as soon as he had arrived at the ministry. The plan was to gain the confidence of Marie-Antoinette by protecting her from anything which might be compromising, while 'sidelining the queen's society', or the group of intimates who attended her at court.[34]

Discrediting Mesmer and his many courtly partisans in the eyes of the queen might achieve the desired result, especially since Breteuil was already convinced that mesmerism was a sham. After receiving Deslon early in 1784, Breteuil therefore acquiesced to his demand to create a commission of enquiry. At the time, the nobility had not yet rallied to the Société de l'harmonie universelle. It was not until May, when the enquiry was already in full swing, that courtesans in the queen's retinue, such as the duc the Coigny, the duc de Lauzun and the chevalier de Crussol, began to follow Mesmer's teachings.[35] At first, Breteuil's quarry was therefore more likely the men who had instigated the plan for the Société, who were two of Mesmer's

de Louis XVI, écrits dans les années 1790 et suivantes, bundle 1, p.132, http://aurelia. orleans.fr (last accessed on 26 January 2024). From an excerpt not reproduced in Milliot's edition of the *Mémoires*. Vincent Milliot, *Un Policier des Lumières, suivi de Mémoires de J. C. P. Lenoir, ancien lieutenant général de police de Paris, écrits en pays étrangers dans les années 1790 et suivantes* (Seyssel, 2011).

34. See Munro Price, *Preserving the monarchy: the comte de Vergennes, 1774-1787* (Cambridge, 1995). Munro Price paints a flattering portrait of Breteuil in *The Fall of the French monarchy: Louis XVI, Marie-Antoinette and the baron de Breteuil* (London, 2002).

35. See the bibliographical entries in the Harmonia Universalis database. However, the princesse de Polignac and her lover, the comte de Vaudreuil, do not seem to have taken an interest in mesmerism.

patients, and both cut-throat businessmen: Bergasse was a lawyer who represented his self-named Lyon trading company in Paris; but Kornmann, a banker and speculator from Strasbourg, was especially in Breteuil's line of sight – Kornmann's involvement in the property dealings of the Quinze-Vingts had recently led to its insolvency. Breteuil may also have been aiming at Kornmann's protector, the cardinal de Rohan, his predecessor in Vienna, whom Marie-Antoinette detested; Breteuil's actions would precipitate Rohan's fall from grace the following year during the infamous diamond necklace affair.

Alongside the enquiry, Breteuil had almost certainly prepared a secret dossier to show to the royal couple. Its purpose was not merely to denounce false science and misrepresentation, but to uncover a veritable menace. The *lieutenant de police* Lenoir was well versed in the affair; in his *Mémoires*, though written later in life (and of dubious exactitude), he mentions 'anonymous letters' warning the police 'that seditious talk against religion and against the government circulated during the mesmerist assemblies'. He then added, no doubt with reference to Breteuil, that, 'on the heels of this police denunciation, one of the king's ministers proposed to banish the foreigner Mesmer, generally believed to have inaugurated the practice in France, and who had been expelled for the selfsame reason from Vienna, Austria.'[36]

According to Jean-Louis Soulavie, who was himself well informed, when Marie-Antoinette learned of what transpired around the tubs, she abruptly withdrew her support from Mesmer:

> the queen was shown letters wherein several women who, in the midst of their convulsions, reproached the princess with infidelities, with having stripped the royal coffers for the benefit of Joseph II, and with having incontrovertibly poisoned M. de Vergennes. The queen's strong disinclination towards the French lent credence to the letters in her eyes. De Breteuil seized the opportunity to pursue the mesmerists, and the whole of the queen's party gave him their blessing.[37]

This account may be nothing more than malicious gossip, and should therefore be taken with a grain of salt. Nevertheless, the authorities certainly were as concerned about moral conduct as they were about

36. Excerpt from an early draft of Lenoir's *Mémoires* which was not reproduced in the Milliot edition, cited in Darnton, *Mesmerism*, p.86-87.
37. See Jean-Louis Soulavie, *Mémoires politiques et historiques du règne de Louis XVI*, 6 vols (Paris, 1801), vol.1, p.261.

the effectiveness of magnetic treatment. When the enquiry concluded, Bailly, who was close friends with Breteuil, submitted a secret report to the king denouncing mesmerism as a menace to morality; the contents of the report would not be revealed until 1797.[38]

Politics and sexuality

While the medical and scientific condemnation of animal magnetism had underscored the fraudulence and the ineffectiveness of the treatment, the moral and political excoriations, though later in coming, were no less categorical: those who practised the method exposed themselves to grave disorders. The apparent threat applied more particularly to women of course, who outnumbered male patients, and concerned their relationships with the medical mesmerists. It is important to note that the medical professionals had never raised this last point; they had criticised the adverse physiological effects of the fits and convulsions. In their report, the commissioners of the Société royale de médecine had reaffirmed that convulsions 'heightened tensions in the fibres to an extraordinary degree in individuals with acutely sensitive nerves' and especially denounced 'the public dimension [of the therapy], which exposed the patient to the risk of contracting spasmodic and convulsive habits, and which may become the source of greater illnesses'. There is no mention here of morality. In truth, officials of the administration had been the ones to suggest that the magnetic cure might include an element of indecency. Lenoir was the first to mention it when he addressed Deslon in their presence on 9 May 1784: 'I ask you, as a lieutenant general of police: when a woman is mesmerised and is seized by a fit, does this not

38. Bailly's *Rapport secret sur le mesmérisme* was published in *Le Conservateur, ou Recueil de morceaux inédits d'histoire, de politique, littérature et de philosophie tirés des porte-feuilles de M. François de Neufchâteau de l'Institut national* (Paris, Year VIII), p.146-55. And yet the existence of the 'secret' report was intentionally disclosed at the close of the enquiry. The *Journal historique et littéraire* thus indicated in October 1784: 'What's more, we have been informed that the commissioners of the Academy and of the Faculty have submitted to the king a supplement to their report, just two or three pages long, which His Majesty has permitted only two people to read. We believe it is in regard to public morality which, despite all efforts to imbue the therapy with decency, magnetic treatment does not seem to sufficiently respect.' The secret report was translated into English in 2002: Jean-Sylvain Bailly, 'Secret report on mesmerism or animal magnetism', *International journal of clinical and experimental hypnosis* 50:4 (2002), p.364-68.

make her vulnerable to abuse?'[39] Deslon is said to have answered in the affirmative, which was consistent with his desire to restrict the practice of animal magnetism to medical doctors.

The accusation of immorality was first publicised in an anonymous anti-mesmerist pamphlet entitled *Mesmer justifié*, which appeared early in June 1784.[40] The author, who was in fact Jean-Jacques Paulet, was well acquainted with mesmerism; the pamphlet was rife with insinuations, the worst of which was an embarrassing scene which had transpired in Deslon's clinic:

> I am speaking of a case of satyriasis which of a sudden overtook a man at the sight of a young lady who was with her mother. It had gone so far that the mother had risen to restore order; but M. Deslon had cried out in a prophetic voice, 'Leave them, leave them be or they shall die!' And it was with such deliberate barbs that certain misguided individuals have reported the goings-on in Mesmer's office.[41]

We have a more trustworthy account of the incident written by Goulin, the sceptical journalist-doctor from the *Gazette de santé*, who had kept a journal during the weeks he had frequented Deslon's clinic. We learn from his account that the satyr in question was a patient named Charles Auguste Bourlet, principal valet to the comte d'Artois, who entered into a state of somnambulism when he was mesmerised. The scene Paulet described took place on 2 June 1784. A very agitated Bourlet had circled the tub with a lost look and, 'upon seeing a woman in convulsions, had lifted her from the armchair on which she was sitting, sat down in her stead and settled the woman on his lap, as if deeply moved. It was then that M. Deslon said, "Leave them, otherwise they shall die."' But Goulin contradicts Paulet at this point, following immediately with, 'In any case, there had been nothing indecent, no embarrassment, no fondling, no licentious behaviour, as the recently published pamphlet entitled *Mesmer justifié* would have us believe.'[42]

The secret report which Bailly compiled shortly after, signed by the other commissioners, discussed the immorality of the cures at length.

39. Bailly, *Rapport secret*, p.151.
40. Jean-Jacques Paulet, *Mesmer justifié* (Constance and Paris, Chez les libraires qui vendent les nouveautés, 1784).
41. Paulet, *Mesmer justifié*, p.32.
42. Jean Goulin, 'Sur le magnétisme animal', Reims, Bibliothèque Carnegie, MS 1063, f.37r, 1 June 1784.

First, he underscored the different organic constitutions of men and women, which caused the latter to be more prone to imitation, and which would also explain why women experienced more frequent, more prolonged and more violent convulsions. He noted that women were more frequently mesmerised, yet mesmerists were inevitably men. For Mesmer, the 'magnetic crisis', a state of disorder often marked by spectacular convulsions, even visions, was a moment of release during which the accumulated magnetic fluid began to flow freely. But, for Bailly, it was a manifestation of sexual excitement, a veritable orgasm brought on by stroking gestures and other acts of the mesmerist. He wrote, 'Undoubtedly many women have not experienced these effects, and others have not understood the cause of the effects they experienced; the more modest they are, the less they would be likely to suspect it. But it is said that several have perceived the truth, and have withdrawn from the magnetic treatment, and those who have not perceived it ought to be deterred from its pursuit.' This was why 'The magnetic treatment must necessarily be dangerous to morality.' What was more disturbing, according to Bailly, was that the effects of mesmerism were contagious. He worried the convulsions might spread like an epidemic through towns and villages and across future generations, and he therefore declared that 'morally they must be condemned'.[43] Bailly seemed to fear that animal magnetism would result in the propagation of unbridled sexuality.

The threat to morality also took on a distinctly political dimension. While medical doctors and scholars saw in mesmerism the resurgence of ancient Paracelsian medicine, government authorities saw the revival of the Jansenist convulsionary movement. 'In 1780,' wrote Lenoir in his *Mémoires*, 'the vogue of magetism began in Paris. It was necessary for the police to take cautious and deliberate measures against the abandoned practice of convulsions, which the public viewed with too much unconcern.'[44] Lenoir indicates elsewhere, though it is impossible to substantiate his claim, that the theologians of the Sorbonne had been consulted, and had concluded that mesmerism was indeed a practice which was 'incompatible with religion, and similar to that of Jansenist convulsions'.[45]

---

43. Bailly, 'Secret report', p.366.
44. BmO, Fonds ancien, MS 1421, *Mémoires de Le Noir*, bundle 1, p.132. This is an excerpt from the draft version of the *Mémoires* and is not reproduced in the Milliot edition.
45. *Mémoires de Le Noir*.

And yet the threat was of an even greater magnitude than it had first been assumed: mesmerism was uncontrollable; it tricked the mind; it troubled the body; it subverted authority and upset reality itself; it was, therefore, politically perilous. 'For,' Lenoir continued, 'mesmerism may have been one of the means used to form and maintain assemblies in which a cultish or factional mindset has been instilled.' Aside from the doctrine which, all things considered, was quite confused, and quite apart from the treatment, which was scarcely more scandalous than that of medical electricity (another contemporary 'treatment'), what worried the authorities was the passion it awakened, the behaviours it stimulated and the assemblies it provoked.

The magnetic crisis itself could manifest as convulsions, which took on strong sexual overtones, but it could also be hypnotic, presenting as a state which Mesmer would later call 'critical' sleep (*sommeil critique*), in which the patient was expected to 'predict the future and bring the deepest past to light'.[46] With the discovery of magnetic somnambulism by one of Mesmer's disciples, the marquis de Puységur, in the summer of 1784, the experience of the critical states, which had already been observed at the Hôtel de Coigny where Mesmer officiated, could be prolonged. Chassaignon writes of one such experience: the abbé Petitot, *second secrétaire* of the Société de l'harmonie universelle, thus prophesised the impending doom of the French nobility: 'Enjoy your titles while you can, for the honour of your blazons is in its final throes; in two lustra [ten years], all will be made level.'[47] There was Madeleine as well, a young seer whom Dr Aubry, a close friend of Mesmer, had mesmerised; she had warned the comte de Haga, Gustav III (the king of Sweden), who had stopped by incognito at the Hôtel de Coigny, of the risk of assassination.[48]

Repression or ridicule?

The Royal Commission's August 1784 condemnation represents the highest point in the controversy over the science and medicine

46. Franz Anton Mesmer, *Mémoire de F. A. Mesmer, docteur en médecine, sur ses découvertes* (Paris, Fuchs, 1799), p.60.
47. Jean-Marie Chassaignon, *Les Nudités, ou les Crimes du peuple* (Paris, n.n., 1792), p.121-22. See the Harmonia Universalis database for the entry on Pierre Petiot.
48. Aubin Gauthier, *Histoire du somnambulisme*, 2 vols (Paris, 1842), vol.2, p.246-49. There is an entry regarding Madeleine in the Harmonia Universalis database.

of animal magnetism. Despite this, it was but one move in the campaign to neutralise Mesmer and his partisans. The strategy which the government adopted following the publication of the reports combined both threat and persuasion. It was remarkably effective: Mesmer was compelled to leave the country and Deslon forced to withdraw; with its principal gurus dislodged, after 1785, the great mesmerist wave receded.

A measured response

As we saw earlier, following its condemnation of mesmerism, Paris' Faculté de médecine had opted to impose punitive measures, and obliged its members to retract their mesmerist allegiances. At first, the royal administration also seemed to be oriented towards prohibitive action. On 29 August 1784, the King's Council adopted a ruling forbidding any person, 'regardless of rank or station', from assembling and experimenting with respect to magnetic fluid, on pain of banishment from the kingdom in perpetuity; it also threatened internment in Charenton – 'until such time as the recovery of their reason has been properly and duly ascertained' – to persons of either sex 'who have been affected and are convinced they have personally taken part in trials or experiments relating to the dubious effects of the so-called magnetic fluid'.[49]

In order to be effective, the Council's decree still needed to be registered in the Parlement. Mesmer and his friends had evidently been informed of this and decided to forestall events. They could count on the support of certain members of the Parlement, such as the councillor Duval d'Eprémesnil, who was a member of the Société de l'harmonie universelle and one of the leaders of the anti-ministerial party in the Parlement. In a printed petition dated 30 August and addressed to the Grand' Chambre, Mesmer raised the point that Deslon had betrayed his trust and was neither his disciple nor his interpreter; furthermore, he was outraged that the commissioners the king had named had been allowed to form an opinion on his doctrine based on what Deslon may have claimed. He demanded justice from members of the Parlement, and enjoined them to nominate medical professionals who could judge for themselves the

---

49. A copy of the decree of the Conseil du roi is held in the archives of the Société royale de médecine, Paris, Bibliothèque de l'Académie nationale de médecine, SRM 126, dr 13, no.25.

veracity of the healings he had effected. In response, the Parlement ruled on 6 September that Mesmer would be allowed to present his doctrine and his methods before a panel of eight commissioners.[50]

The ruling was never followed up. Since Mesmer had restricted the circle of initiates to whom he would reveal his secrets exclusively to members of the Société de l'harmonie universelle, he was unable to accept the proposed arrangement. Fearing his arrest, he fled Paris and spent the next few weeks in England. Nevertheless, there is every reason to believe that Mesmer's true objective in initiating proceedings with the Grand' Chambre had been not to obtain the re-evaluation of animal magnetism, but to prevent the enactment of the King's Council's decision to prohibit it. If this was indeed the goal, then his scheme succeeded, since the decree was never promulgated. It also proved that the government was incapable of applying authoritative measures to repress a movement which had such strong support. The royal administration ultimately came across as weakened in the face of opposing factions so keen to publicly denounce its ministerial despotism. For, if Breteuil had initially aimed his attack at courtly rivals to gain the trust of the queen, it was indeed the Parlement which he confronted when he tried to have mesmerism blocked. In 1786, he would find himself in the same situation when the Parlement acquitted the cardinal de Rohan and Cagliostro in the affair of the diamond necklace.

If the government could not ban mesmerism altogether, it would seek to hinder its dissemination. And yet it tolerated the pro-mesmerist publications which were sold freely in bookshops.[51] In 1785, the government forbad only the *Journal de Paris*, the sole daily newspaper in Paris, from reporting further on animal magnetism (it had written abundantly on the subject in the previous year).[52] In

---

50. Mesmer's letter, the Parlement's ruling and all associated documents have been reproduced in Pinard *et al.*, *Commentaires de la Faculté de médecine*, p.1251-65.
51. As an example, the bookseller André Médard Gastelier, whose bookshop was located on the parvis Notre-Dame, published a catalogue in June 1786 listing sixty-six books and pamphlets on animal magnetism which were sold in his shop.
52. See the announcement in the *Journal de Paris*, 2 March 1785. The *Journal de Paris* accordingly refused to publish the letter Deslon addressed to them on 4 March 1785, which was published elsewhere shortly after, undated, and explicitly entitled *Lettre adressée par M. Deslon aux auteurs du 'Journal de Paris' et volontairement refusée par eux, concernant l'"Extrait de la correspondance de la Société royale relativement au magnétisme animal' rédigé par M. Thouret et imprimé au Louvre.*

his *Mémoires*, Lenoir claims to have informed the *garde des sceaux*, Armand Thomas Hue de Miromesnil, that 'impious discourse was held and grossly indecent acts had transpired' in Deslon's clinic, but the *procureur général du Parlement de Paris* had renounced prosecution following opposition from several *parlementaires*.[53] Though we can scarcely give credit to Lenoir's account, as imprecise as it is, we do know from a letter Deslon wrote on 10 November 1785 that the *garde des sceaux* had forbidden him from publishing a book on the doctrine and practice of mesmerism. Presumably, authorities had also pressured Mesmer, who was facing possible deportation as a result. This might explain why he left Paris in the summer of 1785, as well as his considerable discretion in the years leading up to the Revolution.

The triumph of propaganda

Even so, it was far more through the masterful use of propaganda than with repression and intimidation that the government opposed mesmerism. Indeed, if the administration allowed Mesmer's partisans to publish the great quantity of books and pamphlets which circulated freely in the kingdom, they also did not hesitate to use this tactic against them, secretly supporting the doctrine's detractors. From the start, Breteuil's objective was to discredit mesmerism, in the eyes of the royal couple at first but also in those of public opinion. He had entrusted the Royal Commission with this very undertaking in the spring of 1784, and the enquiry had fulfilled its mission. Though the government was unable to capitalise on this advantage or forbid mesmerism outright, it could still find benefit in the battle for public opinion. The official reports condemning mesmerism had indeed been written with this in mind, and used a language that not only doctors but also an enlightened readership could understand. It seems Breteuil had personally overseen the formulation of the findings. In an exchange of letters between the lead doctor, Joseph Marie François de Lassone, and the secretary of the Société royale de médecine, Vicq d'Azyr, we learn that the Société's report had been revised at

_____

On the *Journal de Paris* and mesmerism, see Anne-Marie Mercier-Faivre, 'La science au quotidien: l'affaire Mesmer dans le *Journal de Paris* (1783-84)', in *Metamorfosi dei Lumi*, ed. Simone Messina and Paola Trivero, vol.6 (Turin, 2017), p.148-68.

53. From the Milliot edition of the *Mémoires de Lenoir*, in Milliot, *Un Policier des Lumières*, p.49.

the minister's request: 'there is a bit of meaningless repetition before we get to the conclusion which must be removed,' wrote Lassone, 'especially in light of M. de Breteuil's repeated admonishments that the report is far too long and phrased so only medical doctors may decipher it, though it was destined to be read by the general public.'[54]

The official reports were widely covered and reproduced in the newspapers. Government authorities were nonetheless fully conscious that scientific censure alone would never suffice; Mesmer must be made odious, his doctrine absurd and his followers ridiculous. A campaign for public opinion would have to be staged, mocking animal magnetism and its founder through songs, posters and theatrical performances as much as through writing. Two authors in particular were enlisted to wage the pamphletary battle: Jean-Jacques Paulet and Charles-Pierre Brack, both brilliant polemicists who were well acquainted with all that went on in the Société de l'harmonie universelle. The weapon of choice was satire.

Paulet was an erudite medical practitioner best known for his work in mycology. He was also a *docteur-régent* at the Faculté de médecine de Paris, and had sided with his fellow members in the conflict with the Société royale de médecine, from which he had withdrawn his membership. As we also saw earlier, he was the owner and editor of the *Gazette de santé*, a medical journal in which he had branded Mesmer a charlatan in 1780. However, finding himself in financial difficulties, he was forced to sell the *Gazette* early in 1784. The exact circumstances which led him to write on mesmerism are unknown, but he was very much in need of both position and money. Though there is no formal proof, Paulet was most likely financed by the government and given strict instructions to discredit Mesmer and his partisans. The three volumes he published anonymously on the subject received quite a bit of attention. His first two titles were a biting and extremely well-documented satire on Mesmer and the Société de l'harmonie universelle entitled *Mesmer justifié*, and a much more in-depth study of the doctrine and its history, *L'Anti-magnétisme, ou Origine, progrès, décadence, renouvellement et réfutation du magnétisme animal*. Both appeared before the publication of the Royal Commission reports, and seem to anticipate the line of reasoning the

54. Paris, Bibliothèque de l'Académie nationale de médecine, SRM 126, dr 13, no.6, letter written by Poissonnier to Vicq d'Azyr, secretary of the Société royale de médecine, n.d.

commissioners would follow.[55] In 1785, Paulet delved one last time into the subject in *Réponse à l'auteur des Doutes d'un provincial*. It was addressed to the Grenoblois lawyer Joseph Michel Antoine Servan, mesmerism's most talented advocate in the wake of the controversy following the publication of the reports.[56]

The identity of the second author, Brack, is less certain. He claimed to be a surgeon, but may instead be Charles-Pierre Brack, the son of a surgeon. He was a literary scholar and tutor to Miromesnil's children.[57] In June 1784, Brack anonymously published a volume entitled *Histoire du magnétisme en France*, which he followed up in August with *Lettre de Figaro au comte Almaviva sur la crise du magnétisme animal*. Both works were well researched and adopted the same sarcastic tone Paulet had used.[58] Brack issued a third pamphlet in the following year, *Testament politique de M. Mesmer, ou la Précaution d'un sage*, a satire which recalls Paulet's *Mesmer justifié*. The police confiscated the pamphlet because it revealed the names of important members of the Société de l'harmonie universelle. It would not be allowed to circulate.[59]

The theatre was also mobilised for the cause. In November 1784, the Théâtre-Italien produced a *comédie-parade* (a type of farcical *opéra comique*) called *Les Docteurs modernes*;[60] incidentally, one of

55. Paulet, *Mesmer justifié* (1784), and, by the same author, *L'Antimagnétisme, ou Origine, progrès, décadence, renouvellement et réfutation du magnétisme animal* (London, n.n., 1784).

56. [Jean-Jacques Paulet], *Réponse à l'auteur des Doutes d'un provincial* (Paris, n.n., 1785).

57. Charles-Pierre Brack (1742-1830) was the private tutor of the son of the *garde des sceaux* Miromesnil, and a well-recognised member of Parisian scholarly circles. In 1782, Pierre Simon Laplace, a learned mathematician, referred Brack to his Berlin colleague Lagrange. In 1785, on Miromesnil's recommendation, and perhaps in recompense for his services in the Mesmer affair, he was appointed assistant to the *directeur général des traites* in the Hôtel des fermes.

58. [Charles-Pierre Brack], *Histoire du magnétisme en France, de son régime et de son influence, pour développer l'idée qu'on doit avoir de la médecine universelle* (Vienna, Chez Boyer, 1784); by the same author, *Lettre de Figaro au comte Almaviva sur la crise du magnétisme animal* (Madrid, Chez les marchands de nouveautés, 1784).

59. [Charles-Pierre Brack], *Testament politique de M. Mesmer, ou la Précaution d'un sage, avec le dénombrement des adeptes, le tout traduit de l'allemand par un Bostonien* (Leipzig and Paris, n.n., 1785). For more on the censorship imposed on Brack, see the letter in the Archives de la Société royale de médecine signed 'Brac, chirurgien', Paris, Bibliothèque de l'Académie nationale de médecine, SRM 136, dr 15, no.2.

60. Pierre-Yves Barré and Jean-Baptiste Radet, *Les Docteurs modernes: comédie-parade en un acte et en vaudevilles, suivie du baquet de santé: Divertissement analogue mêlé de*

the Théâtre's new halls, situated near the Grands Boulevards, had been inaugurated by Marie-Antoinette the previous year. The play's intrigue was minimalistic: Cassandre, seeking to make a large and timely fortune, has pinned his hopes on animal magnetism. To persuade his colleague to join his undertaking, Cassandre offers his daughter, Isabelle, in marriage. But Isabelle is in love with Léandre, the colleague's nephew; the feeling is mutual. Léandre goes to Cassandre to be cured of his love, and by chance runs into Isabelle, who mesmerises him. The doctors surprise the two lovers, but in the end consent to their union. The play is light and funny in tone, and centres on deception, the greediness of the doctors, and the gullibility of the two patients. The first scene, where Cassandre initiates his valet, Pierrot, is particularly clever. The threat to morality which the commissioners had underlined has given rise to a scene in which a mesmerised patient, Aglaé, swoons with pleasure. The vaudeville show follows with a *divertissement-parade*, where patients sing around a tub, go mad and are taken to the 'crisis chamber'. The triumphant doctors are the only two to remain on the stage. Cassandre (played by Jean René Rosière) ends by turning to the public and declaiming, 'the author is here, in the crisis room', but, after the curtain call, the actor returns to announce, to the amusement of all, that 'the author had been in the crisis room but we don't know what has become of him'.

The show premiered on 16 November 1784, and was an immediate success. In the *Correspondance littéraire, philosophique et critique*,[61] Jacques-Henri Meister commented on how

> crowds flocked to the Théâtre-Italien each time they presented *Docteurs modernes*. At each couplet, peals of laughter would burst from the stalls and the boxes; none of the solemn characters – Cassandre, the doctor, his valet, their patients – could hold to their gravitas. There is reason to believe that this little comedy will do more harm to the novel sect than the reports of all the academies and the faculties, or the rulings of the Council and of the Parlement, which had solemnly proscribed both the doctrine and the methods.

---

couplets; représentée pour la première fois à Paris par les Comédiens italiens ordinaires du roi, le mardi 16 novembre 1784 (Paris, Brunet, 1784).

61. F. M. Grimm, *Correspondance littéraire, philosophique et critique par Grimm, Diderot, Raynal, Meister, etc.*, ed. Maurice Tourneux, 16 vols (Paris, 1877-1882), vol.14, p.78.

Mesmer's supporters appeared even more foolish when they denounced the show and tried to have it banned. D'Eprémesnil accused the playwrights, Pierre-Yves Barré and Jean-Baptiste Radet, of calumny; the two denied, unconvincingly, ever having wanted to ridicule Mesmer: 'We assume that it was not forbidden to poke a little fun at an illusion, that it might be useful to attack a novelty believed to be dangerous.'[62] Radet, worried he might be dismissed as librarian to the duchesse de Villeroy, an initiate of mesmerism, later declared the true author was Barré.

Les Docteurs modernes was almost certainly financed by the government. Whether or not this is true, the play was compatible with their strategy to discredit Mesmer and, judging by the outrage in those it criticised, successfully achieved that goal. The cultured *beaux esprits* were the targeted demographic, and ridicule acted like a powerful repellent. Members of Parisian high society had been the most vocal supporters of mesmerism, but they were highly sensitive to which way the wind blew, and what they feared above all was to be seen as foolish. As Meister noted above, if mesmerism's star fell as quickly as it had risen, it was far more likely due to the influence of this play than to the reports of the experts.

To its bitter end, animal magnetism remained confined to the salons of aristocrats and bourgeois, never reaching the masses. The campaign to discredit mesmerism was consequently directed exclusively towards the elites. An anecdote describing how the project of an engineer named Nicolas Lhomont underwent transformation offers further support, *e contrario*, for our argument. In the midst of the craze for balloons, Lhomont conceived of the idea of a 'grand aerostatic grape harvester', an experiment in popular science inspired, as Lavoisier himself put it, by both 'balloons and mesmerism'.[63] He proposed to launch a balloon in the shape of a grape-picker holding a tub on his head and a banner in his right hand which read, 'Adieu

---

62. Grimm, *Correspondance littéraire*, vol.14, p.76-78. Mesmer submitted a petition to the king demanding justice (the only known copy of this petition is in the collections of the Wooden Library). See also the petition presented by Mesmer's students to Joly de Fleury, dated 3 December 1784, calling for a ban on *Les Docteurs modernes*, Paris, Bibliothèque nationale de France (BnF), Fonds Joly de Fleury (JF) 1789.

63. Letter written by Lavoisier to Bailly, 15 October 1784 (no.529) in Antoine Laurent Lavoisier, *Correspondance*, vol.4: *1784-1786*, ed. Michelle Goupil (Paris, 2012), p.43-44.

Baquet, vendanges sont faites'.[64] However, when the balloon was
finally launched at the Tuileries on 12 March 1785, the banner
was no longer to be seen; either the mesmerist devotees had paid
to have it removed or the police had not authorised it.[65] It had also
been rumoured that an Italian comedy piece staged on the rue
Saint-Honoré had been organised in the final days of the carnival:
Pierrot had supposedly held a Chinese banner on which 'Harmonica'
(in reference to the Société de l'harmonie universelle) was written in
bold letters; he had followed behind a doctor astride a donkey, led by
Folly bearing a shield which read 'Gratis aujourd'hui' (free of charge
today). The play seems to have been pure fabrication on the part of
Pierre-Jean-Baptiste Nougaret, author of the *Tableau mouvant de Paris*.[66]

***

In the end, the policing operation was a success. Admittedly, the
government had been unable to put an end to mesmerism. The
fashion persisted, particularly in the form of magnetic somnambulism, and the number of its followers did not diminish. The themes
at the core of the doctrine contributed to fashioning revolutionary
sensibilities, as Darnton and more recently Armando have shown.[67]
Even so, the government had fulfilled its overall objective: it had
lastingly discredited mesmerism in the eyes of enlightened opinion,
and strangled the immediate threat it seemed to represent.

64. A play on words alluding to mesmerist tubs. We could propose 'Your grapes are
    crushed; the game is up' (note from the translator).
65. *Journal de Paris*, 14 March 1785, p.301.
66. Pierre-Jean-Baptiste Nougaret, *Tableau mouvant de Paris, ou Variétés amusantes*,
    3 vols (London and Paris, n.n., 1787), vol.2, p.270-71.
67. Darnton, *Mesmerism*; David Armando, 'Magnetic crises, political convulsions:
    the mesmerists in the Constituent Assembly', *Annales historiques de la Révolution
    française* 391:1 (2018), p.129-52.

Negotiating fraternity: Paris police and *soupers fraternels* during the Terror

VINCENT DENIS

Université Paris 1, IHMC

Translated by Nicole Charley

'And for five or six days now, *repas fraternels* have been organised throughout the streets of Paris. They begin at nine each night and end at eleven and twelve o'clock.' It was with these words that Nicolas-Célestin Guittard described the rising trend in *soupers fraternels* or 'fraternal feasts' which filled the sweltering streets of Paris in July 1794.[1] The victory of the French armies at the Battle of Fleurus on 26 June had triggered an unprecedented wave of nightly banquets bringing together thousands of dinner companions in the streets. The feasting would continue for weeks in a veritable eruption of largely spontaneous sociability, distinct from the official celebrations of the revolutionary regime. It overwhelmed and unsettled authorities who, after several days of a wait-and-see attitude, would issue warnings and a public injunction to put an end to the banquets. The cycle of festivities ceased as rapidly as it had first sprung up. Why, then, should this fairly marginal and little-known phenomenon of the Revolution be of interest to us? The resurgence of widespread, spontaneous festive practices taking place against the backdrop of a revolutionary government in decline reveals a number of issues. First among them, a particular form of sociability: the feast. Between 1789 and 1793, the Revolution had dismantled most forms of organised sociability, such as processions and religious holidays, replacing them with more rigidly structured and ritualised incarnations such as revolutionary celebrations.[2] Plainly, fraternal feasts are a form of sociability, but they have not been widely studied from this point of view.

---

1. Raymond Aubert, *Journal d'un bourgeois de Paris sous la Révolution* (Paris, 1974), p.410, 14 July 1794.
2. Mona Ozouf, *Festivals and the French Revolution* (Cambridge, MA, 1991); Michel

After 1789, new policing and political configurations were underway, while some of the more ancient forms of Parisian sociability in which men and women met and gathered were abolished or 'reformed'. How did the Revolution reshape Parisian society? How were the various elements of sociability, so widely studied during the Enlightenment, recombined or reconstructed? What new practices were introduced over the course of the long eighteenth century? There have been sectorial studies on the topic, but a general overview for Paris is beyond the scope of this essay.[3] I will instead attempt to address some of the above questions by exploring the unique phenomenon of the fraternal feast.

Of the many spaces and practices we might observe, the wave of *soupers fraternels* that occurred in the summer of 1794 is of particular interest. The banquets were relatively unplanned events of considerable magnitude. There was an ephemeral dimension to them characteristic of other celebrations, but they were also a form of festivity situated in an 'intermedial zone' – not illicit, exactly, but not quite licit either. The National Convention, the government committees and the police heads of the capital were completely unprepared to deal with this new situation. They could not ban the feasts outright, nor could they be seen to tolerate them. This 'grey zone' – where irregular dealings, pressure tactics and diverse transactions take place – was indeed the domain of the police, charged with enforcing public order. The observations we glean from studying the frameworks that evolved out of these events may help to more broadly elucidate how the relationship between police and forms of Parisian sociability developed during the Revolution. The *Ancien Régime* police force no longer reigned over the capital. What innovations did the 'fraternal meals' represent for the new police organisation? What concrete measures did the police adopt to draw the line between what was

---

Vovelle, *Les Métamorphoses de la fête en Provence, 1750-1820* (Paris, 1976); for a more recent analysis of revolutionary celebrations, see Hervé Leuwers, 'Pratiques, réseaux et espaces de sociabilité au temps de la Révolution française', in *La Révolution à l'œuvre*, ed. Jean-Clément Martin (Rennes, 2005), p.41-55.

3.   Hervé Leuwers did attempt this. See Leuwers, 'Pratiques'. More recent studies have expanded in scope to the Directoire; see esp. *Réseaux et sociabilités littéraires en Révolution*, ed. Philippe Bourdin and Jean-Luc Chappey (Clermont-Ferrand, 2007). Less organised, more ephemeral, forms of sociability are still fairly unknown, however. On soupers fraternels, see Serge Aberdam, 'L'heure des repas de rue (juillet 1794)', in *Les Nuits de la Révolution française*, ed. Philippe Bourdin (Clermont-Ferrand, 2013), p.237-50.

lawful or illicit? How did revolutionary authorities convey their ideal of 'good' sociability? And how did Parisians compromise, collaborate or forge relationships with the police in their bilateral negotiations on fraternity?

The dynamics of *soupers fraternels*

A capital under surveillance

Soupers fraternels occurred against a well-known backdrop; the preceding months had seen all potential centres of political autonomy systematically asphyxiated. On 9 September 1793, only four days after having voted to compensate workers who attended sectional assembly meetings, the Convention put an end to 'permanent sittings' and limited the number of weekly general assemblies to two. The law of 14 frimaire Year II transferred control of institutions to the Comité de salut public and the Comité de sûreté générale, and made the Convention the gravitational centre of the government. Any coordinated action at the sectional level was considered subversive.[4] During the winter of 1793-1794, the *sociétés populaires* (plebeian societies) therefore became havens for critics. The societies were exempt from legal constraints as they were formally recognised as private meetings. The regime tried manoeuvring to reduce their influence, but ended up provoking a new crisis: in March 1794, the leaders of the Club des Cordeliers, including Hébert, who had criticised the revolutionary government, were arrested, judged and executed. A second wave of repression against the Indulgents also saw its members, including Danton, arrested. On 5 April, they were guillotined. In the weeks that followed, the Comité de salut public orchestrated the suspension or dissolution of thirty-seven *sociétés populaires*, effectively snuffing them all out.[5] Similarly, the Paris Commune and the various administrative bodies, which had until then maintained autonomy, were purged. In May, the leaders were arrested and replaced by 'reliable' members; such was the case of Mayor Jean-Nicolas Pache, who was succeeded by the more docile Fleuriot-Lescot.

A sort of dual police system maintained public order in the capital. In 1789, revolutionary authorities had substituted a new set

4.   Micah Alpaugh, *Non-violence and the French Revolution: political demonstrations in Paris, 1789-1794* (Cambridge, 2014).
5.   Aberdam, 'L'heure des repas', p.237-38.

of structures for the *Ancien Régime* police force. Appointment was by election and did not require prior professional qualification. Members were, for the most part, selected from their respective sections, and worked closely with them. The newly formed sections functioned as political and administrative cells, at the centre of which was a *commissaire de police* in charge of maintaining order and documenting crimes and misdemeanours. The police commissaires were profoundly linked to the political life of their section; they had been chosen in recompense for militant activism or for loyalty to local 'leaders', or because of a natural aptitude for representing their fellow citizens.[6] The public police force itself, the Garde nationale, included a battalion of elected officers and was also organised by section. This force was a mix of professional soldiers and citizens conscripted into their section's battalion. In theory, all male citizens were obliged to enlist. At the beginning of 1794, tens of thousands of men were marshalled under the command of Géneral Henriot, making him the most powerful head of police and public order in the capital.[7] The Garde made its presence felt through constant patrols, lining thoroughfares and strategic points of the capital with barracks and guard posts.

The local policing structures were augmented by the revolutionary committees, sometimes called *comités de surveillance*, that had been created during the political, military and social crises of March 1793. The committees, comprised of twelve elected citizens, were charged with monitoring and arresting foreigners, local officials and the citizens in their section. This body had been granted considerable authority; their effectiveness lay in citizen denunciations as much as in their own investigative powers (and, sometimes, in their henchmen). They were independent of the *commissaire de police* but could commandeer his services and were thus a formidable political police force.

All of these local structures had been founded in 1792-1793 on an exalted ideal of direct democracy, but the level of autonomy they ought to be granted had been a constant subject of debate since 1789, invariably fuelling tension with municipal authorities. The Paris Commune was the sole master of policing in the city via its police administration, to which the *commissaires de police* were equally subject. The battalions of the Garde nationale were also under the authority of

---

6. Vincent Denis, *Policiers de Paris: les commissaires de police en Révolution, 1789-1799* (Ceyzérieu, 2022).
7. For an overview on the topic, see Roger Dupuy, *La Garde nationale, 1789-1871* (Paris, 2011).

a municipal *état-major*. The autonomy of local police reached its zenith in 1793, though the revolutionary government remained tireless in its efforts to seize control. By 1794, the district police were in the iron grip of the Convention committees, which had secured control of the Commune and replaced its leaders the previous spring. In 1793-1794, the *comités de surveillance* were trimmed back and merged with the revolutionary government, becoming local auxiliaries and docile intermediaries of the Comité de sûreté générale. The revolutionary government now had control over the upper echelons of the police system without having cut the ties between the sections and their local police, whose allegiance remained ambiguous, caught as they were between obedience to an ever more centralised authority and compromise with the local population. These ambiguities became glaringly apparent when citizens began organising *repas fraternels*.

Characterising soupers fraternels

Fraternal banquets evolved against the backdrop of police surveillance of public spaces and muzzled dissidence, buoyed by news of the victory at Fleurus and the retreat of the First Coalition forces on 26 June 1794. As Serge Aberdam has shown, the *repas* were a refuge of sociability and a substitute for political expression, which for months the revolutionary government in Paris had largely stifled.[8] The banquets themselves occurred within a chronologically limited time frame. The first *repas* seems to have been held on 5 July in the île de la Cité; Henriot alludes to the celebration in his journal on 8 July.[9] The bourgeois Guittard confirms 5 July as the beginning of the movement in the capital, recording that 'the feast opened with a few individuals in the Cité, and everyone else followed suit'.[10] Though Conventionnel Bertrand Barère would denounce the movement merely days later, he declared at the time that 'the idea was contagious and had rapidly spread. Many sections spontaneously proclaimed there was to be a *fraternité* on the morrow. Little by little, our public spaces became banquet halls and the light of joy seemed to shine all at once in several Paris neighbourhoods.'[11] The movement did indeed spread to the rest

8.   Aberdam, 'L'heure des repas'.
9.   *Le Sans-culotte* (24 messidor Year II), excerpt of the orders from 20 messidor, p.2055.
10. Aubert, *Journal*, p.411.
11. Bertrand Barère, *Rapport fait au nom du Comité de salut public* [...] *sur la suppression*

of the city. The banquets reached Guittard's neighbourhood near the Saint-Sulpice church, in the Mucius Scaevola section, on 15 July, though he reckoned the initial wave to have begun five or six days earlier. On that date, he noted in his journal, 'This night we held the *souper fraternel* in all neighbouring streets as well as ours, and on the place Saint-Sulpice.'[12] The banquets reached their peak during this period, overlapping with the celebrations of 14 July. In the section of the Amis de la patrie, there was a banquet on 8 July, and again on 14 July. The sections of the Gardes françaises and the Roule both hosted one on 14 July, while the Arsenal held theirs on the night of 15 July.[13] The street celebrations, full of joyful exuberance, starkly contrasted with the sober official festivities in the Jardin national (ex-Tuileries) to which Parisians had been invited.[14]

The accounts we find scattered throughout the archives help define the unusual nature of the *soupers fraternels*, as Parisians named them. In and of itself, the practice of communal feasting had been as much a common occurrence during the *Ancien Régime* as it was under the Revolution. Such celebrations had been frequent in the trade corporations, for example, with candidates for masterhood or corporate honours regularly offering sumptuous feasts to guild masters.[15] However, *souper fraternels* were likely more akin to the relatively egalitarian feasting that punctuated life in the journeyman associations or – to the dismay of the Church – in religious confraternities.[16] In the summer of 1794, neighbourly sociability brought

---

des repas civiques et des fêtes sectionnaires: séance du 28 messidor, l'an deuxième de la République française une et indivisible, imprimé par ordre de la Convention (Paris, n.n., 1794).

12. Aubert, *Journal*, p.412.
13. Le Pré-Saint-Gervais, Archives de la Préfecture de police de Paris (APP), AA 49 (Amis de la patrie), 22 and 26 messidor Year II; APP, AA 70 (Arsenal), 27 messidor Year II; Paris, Archives nationales (AN), W/47, file 3138 (Le Gray) on the banquet in the section of the Gardes françaises on 26 messidor Year II.
14. See as an example *Le Sans-culotte* (27 messidor Year II), p.2068.
15. Steven Laurence Kaplan, 'Idéologie, conflits et pratiques politiques dans les corporations parisiennes au XVIIIᵉ siècle', *Revue d'histoire moderne et contemporaine* 49:1 (2002), p.5-55.
16. *Jacques-Louis Ménétra: Journal de ma vie, compagnon vitrier au XVIIIᵉ siècle*, ed. Daniel Roche (Paris, 1982), p.345-46; Edme Martin de Saint-Léon, *Le Compagnonnage* (Paris, 1977), p.267; David Garrioch, 'Les confréries religieuses, espaces d'autonomie laïque à Paris au XVIIIᵉ siècle', in *La Religion vécue: les laïcs dans l'Europe moderne*, ed. Laurence Croq and David Garrioch (Rennes, 2013), p.143-63 (152-53).

Parisian citizens together far more often than the solidarity of the corporations, which had been dissolved. But professional association still did provide opportunities to host banquets, as shown in the lamp lighters' intention to 'faire un repas de fraternité' on 19 July in their workplace, the general warehouse in the section of the Amis de la patrie.[17]

In the wake of the 1789 Revolution, banquets proliferated rapidly, becoming one of the preferred forms of civic celebration. The prevalent incarnation was for an individual or group of citizens to offer a banquet and invite guests to celebrate. In July 1790, during the Fête de la Fédération, sections, municipalities and individual Parisians all prepared feasts for the departmental delegates of the Garde nationale. Other banquets were organised, with each participant sharing equally in the cost of a predetermined menu.[18] The *soupers fraternels* differed from such traditional forms in that each guest was only expected to contribute what they could: 'Let each one of us bring down his table, bare of cloth,' wrote Guittard, 'and set it next to his house or straddling the gutters. We will have only forks made of iron and spoons of tin. Let neighbours from all houses mingle with each other. Let each bring what he can, and we shall sup together as a large family.'[19]

Soupers fraternels: *two case studies*

The archives tell us that the *soupers* were generally all organised in the same manner. They were open, egalitarian celebrations in which men and women, young and old, came together over a communal meal taken in the open air. Extant documents from a feast held on 8 July in the Ponceau section (renamed section of the Amis de la patrie on 10 August) reveal some of how the *soupers* fitted in with local society and the urban environment. The Ponceau district, situated in the former parish of Saint-Martin-des-Champs, between the rue Saint-Martin and the rue Saint-Denis, was one of the most densely populated in the capital. It was home to a heterogeneous population of journeymen, *gagne-deniers* and entrepreneurs representing mostly craft trades and manufactories, and energised by lively economic and neighbourly

17. Le Pré-Saint-Gervais, APP, AA 49, filed by Citoyen Damour, 28 messidor Year II.
18. See Aberdam, 'L'heure des repas'.
19. Aubert, *Journal*, p.410.

interactions. As one of the hubs of craft and industry in central Paris, it catered to a wide range of activities, from textiles and ribbonry, fashion accessories, luxury trades, construction and metalworking, to the entire leather industry which sold skins that made wallet makers flourish in the district. Like the neighbouring section of Gravilliers, it supported one of the most diverse, well developed, large-scale economic structures in Paris.[20] The section was situated next to the gates of the capital along the main thoroughfares leading to *la route du Nord*, to Lille and Flanders. Life in the section was punctuated by the constant traffic of wagons and carriages, their drivers unloading and acquiring merchandise, and of the travelling merchants who filled the inns lining the rues Saint-Martin and Saint-Denis. Industrial activity and residential housing were closely intertwined. The density of buildings and commercial holdings only increased with the renting out of the îlot de la Trinité to business developments. The section's diverse population, which lived and worked in the courtyards and along the passageways, was generally close-knit due to strong neighbourly bonds and close economic relationships within the trades.[21]

The rue du Ponceau was the geographic heart of the district. It was one of the rare roads to cut across the massive rectangular zone, though it did so with difficulty, following a tortuously winding course.[22] Our first case study unfolds along this road on the night of 22 messidor (8 July), at number 55. Here, a gate led to a courtyard hidden deep within the district.[23] At a quarter past eleven that night, the inhabitants of the building initiated a *souper fraternel* 'in the courtyard of their residence'. Several men sat around the tables they had placed there: Armand Fidèle Guillaume, a goldsmith; Jean-Baptiste Vrainot, Pierre Alard and Jacques Charles Thirard,

---

20. Maurizio Gribaudi, *Paris ville ouvrière: une histoire occultée, 1789-1848* (Paris, 2014). See p.163-80 for the impact of the Revolution ('Une industrialisation organique' and 'Un artisanat industriel renouvelé').

21. See Gribaudi, *Paris ville ouvrière*, p.224-40.

22. Bobigny, Archives départementales de Seine-Saint-Denis (ADSSD), RES/A15113/21, '6ᵉ arrondissement ancien, Porte Saint-Denis', sheet 1. Redrawn in Figure 12.

23. Le Pré-Saint-Gervais, APP, AA 49, complaint filed against Citoyen Gambette, 24 messidor Year II. Number 55, which led to the cour du Roi François, corresponds to the property identified as number 42, rue du Ponceau on the cadastral map of 1810. For more on variations in Paris street numbering at the time, see Vincent Denis, 'Les Parisiens, la police et le numérotage des maisons du XVIIIᵉ siècle à l'Empire', *French historical studies* 38:1 (2015), p.83-103.

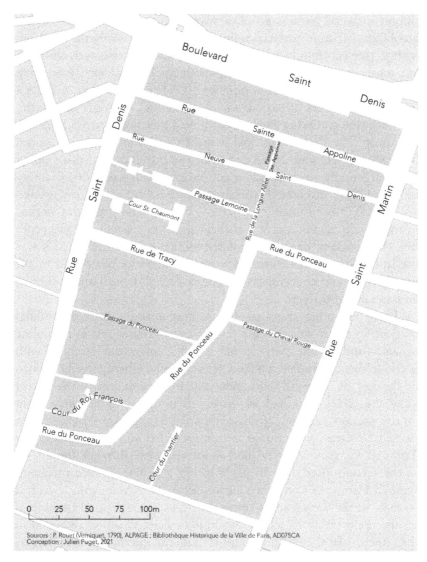

Figure 12: The Ponceau district. Map design: Julien Puget, Groupe de recherche en histoire des sociabilités (GRHS), Université du Québec à Montréal. Sources: Paul Rouet, 'Îlots en 1791 (plan de Verniquet)', ALPAGE, Paris (2015); Archives de Paris (AP), Paris, Plans parcellaires, RES/A1513/21.

ribbon weavers; Nicolas Krief, a sword cutler; and Antoine Audry, a cobbler. All were artisans representing typical economic activities within the community. With them sat their wives and children, but also acquaintances from neighbouring houses, such as a man named Giraud, who lived at number 49. There seemed to be quite a turnout of revellers of various social standings. The only peculiarity was that this gathering took place in an inner courtyard and not in the street. The decision to hold it there was undoubtedly influenced by practical necessity and a desire for the intimacy and discretion a courtyard might offer. It was a convenient, vital space of sociability around which dwellings, workshops and boutiques were clustered and food was occasionally prepared for those who lived and worked in the buildings, making it a natural spot for residents to gather. In this close-packed, densely populated section of the inner city, it was not in the streets that narrowly circumvented city blocks but in the passageways and courtyards that people ebbed, flowed and gathered, and sociability thrived.

There are other snippets of information about these communal outdoor festivities we can tease out from the archives. After partaking of food and drink, participants wound down the banquet with patriotic singing. Dancing added to the joyful exuberance. On 14 July, in the rue du Bourg-l'Abbé, men and women danced in the street amid the tables they had set up for their meal.[24] That same night in the section of the Gardes françaises, companions of a citizen named Le Gray, who would later appear before the Revolutionary Tribunal for comments he had made, roamed through the streets of the section after their meal, 'dancing a country dance in one of them'.[25] Fireworks and other festive detonations were also a central feature. In the days leading up to the feasts, peddlers had capitalised on the opportunity to sell pyrotechnic devices, which were set off in the streets.[26] In the rue du Bourg-l'Abbé, the guests had even placed little copper cannons on the tables.[27] In the Arsenal section, the night lit up with *fusées volantes* launched between the quai des Célestins and the rue Antoine. A number of firecrackers also went off, which irked

24. Le Pré-Saint-Gervais, APP, AA 49, 26 messidor Year II.
25. Paris, AN, W 47, file 3138, 1 thermidor Year II, appearance of Richard and Fabrègue before the police administration.
26. See the testimony of Victor Pelletier, arrested for having fired rockets. Le Pré-Saint-Gervais, APP, AA 49, 26 messidor Year II.
27. Le Pré-Saint-Gervais, APP, AA 49, 26 messidor Year II.

the police administration no end, leading them to dispatch an irate letter in the middle of the night to the civil committee of the section.[28]

Spontaneity, equality, commingling and exuberance: these were the features of the nocturnal *soupers*, and as many potential sources of friction with authorities.

From wait-and-see to seeing red: the official response

Police and political leaders were initially caught off guard by the new movement, their attitude quickly shifting from one of indulgence to public condemnation. *Soupers fraternels*, despite their intense, albeit brief, popularity, have not attracted much attention from the academic world and, as they do not fit the typology of revolutionary celebrations, are typically missing from reference volumes.[29] Yet they are clearly part of what Mona Ozouf has termed 'alternative' celebrations (*l'autre fête*), which revolutionary authorities widely condemned, unwittingly echoing the tone in which pastoral letters and civic corporations' decrees had denounced certain 'traditional' *Ancien Régime* celebrations.[30] The inherent spontaneity and exuberance of the feasts clashed with the desired solemnity of the Davidian ceremonies organised by local Jacobin leaders. More sober commemorations usually prevailed, such as at the 14 July celebration of 1794 in the Jardin national. However, a recent study by Serge Aberdam has revealed their subversive power. This protean movement was also in part an improvised form of criticism of the politics of the 'government committees', at a time when ways of expressing dissent were being stifled.

In the first few days, the authorities displayed an ambivalent, laissez-faire attitude towards this patriotic, grassroots movement the Parisians had robed in civic virtue: on 11 July, at the very moment the movement was gaining in momentum, the Commune decided it would no longer inspect security documents until after midnight, thus easing the police chokehold on the night.[31] Then came a complete about-turn. Général Henriot's general orders after 18 July reflect the remarkable volte-face from praise and paternalistic goodwill to censure and growing hostility. On 19 July, he wrote, 'My brothers in

---

28. Le Pré-Saint-Gervais, APP, AA 70, Night Watch report from 27-28 messidor Year II.
29. Serge Aberdam's study is an exception: Aberdam, 'L'heure des repas'.
30. Ozouf, *Festivals*, p.84-88.
31. *Le Sans-culotte* (27 messidor Year II), p.2068.

arms, I am confident that these feasts, during which true republicans were afflicted with an indecency unbecoming of free men, have come to an end. Henceforth, let only wisdom, decency and reason be our guides.'[32] The day before, the Jacobins had launched their counterstrike: the *agent national* of the Commune, Payan, had denounced the banquets. Hard on his heels, Barère gave his own condemnation in a memorable speech before the Convention assembly that was subsequently printed and circulated in the press. Next, Robespierre spoke at the Club des Jacobins, warning the people against the trickery of those who hid behind a mask of fraternity, seeking instead the downfall of the revolutionary government.[33]

Barère's long indictment is the most detailed official statement on *soupers fraternels*. It also exemplifies the Jacobin stance on 'good' sociability. Barère violently stigmatised the mixedness and exuberance of the *soupers*, which he qualified as 'saturnalia'. Morality itself was primarily at stake, for 'how on earth could morals be regenerated in such a bizarre confusion of citizens, amidst such reckless intermingling of the sexes, in the thick of the banquets, shrouded in night's shadows, and after meals where wine and the most immoderate joys have presided, sometimes coupled with perverse intentions?'[34] On this point, Barère's opinion diverged little from that of the encyclopedists, who denounced the 'abuses' of traditional celebrations as opportunities for debauchery and unrestrained passion. The feasts were the absolute antithesis of the regimented celebrations the revolutionaries dreamed of.

Barère claimed that the Convention, as the supreme authority, should exercise complete monopoly over all festivities. But their monopoly was being challenged in the sections and by the citizens who had initiated the wave of banquets. 'It is the exclusive right of the Convention', Barère wrote, 'to organise national celebrations and civic ceremonies. It is the prerogative of the Convention to invite citizens to take part, through general gatherings, in the joyous events of the Revolution.' A 'coup' was in play between the revolutionary government and, among others, the local democratic bodies, the Commune and the sections, though, in the previous months, it had

---

32. *Le Sans-culotte* (24 messidor Year II), p.2055; *Le Journal de la Montagne* (15, 17 and 19 July 1794).
33. *Le Journal de la Montagne* (17 July 1794); Convention nationale, sitting of 28 messidor, p.660.
34. Barère, *Rapport*, p.10.

been held in check. Barère was unequivocal: 'Under no circumstances shall a commune, military commander, civil or sectional committee be allowed to tear citizens from their labours, block the routes so essential to commerce, close down boutiques, or force expenses upon the citizens.'[35] The right to celebrate was at stake in this struggle which opposed, on the one hand, a highly centralised conceptualisation of government by the will of the people, represented by the National Convention, and, on the other hand, the equally justified decentralising tendencies embodied by local collective and individual initiatives. The people constructed their own patriotic legitimacy through action, though at the risk of opposing, impeding or going beyond the purview of the revolutionary government.[36] The battle the government thought it had won in the winter of 1793 seemed to have reared its head once more. The Jacobins, at the very least, interpreted the new wave of *soupers* as a possible resurgence of that menace, interpreting all gatherings and aspects of sociability as potential political risks as well as matters of public order. This, of course, meant surveillance far beyond what took place during simple public festivities: advance authorisation for all gatherings, including private ones, became a requirement. Since all private gatherings were now perceived as expressions of individual interest, and thus contrary to the will of the general population, this regime became the norm.[37] A meal served under cover of darkness could mean its participants were a coterie of some sort. Or worse: they could be fellow conspirators. The death knell began to toll on *soupers fraternels*; such mistrust regarding festive gatherings led a simple wine merchant hosting a wedding feast to prefer declaring to the police in the section of the Amis de la patrie 'that his clients might linger a little deep into the night'.[38] Suspicion ran deep for all forms of sociability which might escape the control of Jacobin leadership or, in the case of private events, the imperative of transparency.

   Barère's pronouncements, and Robespierre's address to the Jacobins the next day, cut short the momentum initiated by the first

---

35. Barère, *Rapport*, p.10.
36. Haim Burstin, *Révolutionnaires: pour une anthropologie politique de la Révolution française* (Paris, 2013), p.234.
37. Lynn Hunt, 'Révolution française et vie privée', in *Histoire de la vie privée*, ed. Georges Duby and Philippe Ariès, vol.4: *De la Révolution à la Grande Guerre*, ed. Michelle Perrot (Paris, 1985), p.21-52 (21).
38. Le Pré-Saint-Gervais, APP, AA 49, 30 messidor Year II (Mathey).

souper. And yet, it had been the initial silence of authority figures –
their tacit, benevolent sanctioning of this unprecedented movement
– which had allowed it to develop so freely. The thankless task of
contending with the *soupers fraternels* fell on the police. It was they who
were forced to draw the line between what was licit and what was not.
Caught between the citizens of their own district and their loyalty to
the directives of government authorities, their ambiguous status had
coloured their response. What ensued when they intervened was in
direct correlation to their inclusion in the first group, which varied
according to the officer's standing.

Curiously, it was not traditional sectional police who intervened
most often, but other public authorities such as *commissaires civils*
and officers of the peace. Signs of the withdrawal of habitual police
presence are manifest in the police archives. In the Arsenal section, for
example, Commissaire Caillouey arrived one night at the guard post
to requisition the services of the Garde nationale for a nine o'clock
patrol.[39] To his great surprise, the officers and junior officers were
absent, leaving only a few men from the ranks. Caillouey eventually
left on patrol with four members of the civil committee, and later
commandeered a squad of officers from the Garde he happened to
come upon along the way. The 8 July confrontation in the section of
the Amis de la patrie was that of a lone commissaire. On 14 July, in
the rue du Bourg-l'Abbé, it was a group of officers of the peace from
another section entirely who intervened. They, and the municipal
police administrator who was accompanying them, had simply been
passing by on a prisoner transfer, and their involvement had therefore
been incidental. No local civil commissaires had appeared on the
scene. Several members of the sectional revolutionary committee had
even been participating in the festivities. The *soupers*, it would seem,
suspended the customary practice of police activities by including
some of those who would ordinarily be monitoring them.

The police who did intervene considered banquets the civil
committee had organised perfectly legitimate, and appeared to
have acted with goodwill and restraint during events the committee
had approved. In the Arsenal section, Commissaire Caillouey, his
secrétaire-greffier Boulanger and the members of the civil committee
had limited themselves to a single patrol to ensure that the feast

---

39. Le Pré-Saint-Gervais, APP, AA 70, Night Watch report from 27-28 messidor
Year II.

'would not be disturbed'.[40] The most common approach (if indeed it is possible to judge from the few extant sources) was prevention of *abus*, the excesses which might disturb the peace. Police therefore focused their attention on specific outbursts: firearms, firecrackers and other pyrotechnic devices were their most common targets. Caillouey was obsessed with rockets. He even sent out raiding parties to hunt down the perpetrators who fired them, determined to make them stop:

> We observed the incident from afar, being in Port Paul at the time. We saw three rockets fired into the air near the entrance of the shopping esplanade. We then made haste to the shop of Citizen Champagne, a wine merchant in the mall, whence came the shots. We ordered him to cease firing rockets and forbade all persons residing in the house from doing likewise, inviting all citizens residing in the neighbourhood of the quai des Célestins to denounce all who contravened our orders. From a distance, we also saw others being set off, not rockets but firecrackers.

This first attempt at curbing the pyrotechnics failed miserably, and would be followed by many others just as fruitless. Each time the unit perceived rockets in the sky, it proceeded to the area 'with all possible haste, but upon arrival, no one could say from which direction they had come, nor could we uncover the location'. The commissaire then tried a different tack: after a rocket fired over the rue Antoine, he sent his *commissaire civil*, Pierre Mortier, to 'pass by' incognito and identify the shooters. The alleged perpetrators had been drinking in a second-hand clothes shop, and, when Mortier returned, a patrol was dispatched, to no avail. Caillouey was simply unable to make the explosions stop. To add insult to injury, later that night, police administrators sent the commissaire an indignant letter complaining that the rocket fire in his section was in violation of long-standing regulations, and that he was expected to make it cease by any and all legal means at his disposal. The poor commissaire could only appeal to his fellow citizens to attest to the fact that he had indeed done his utmost to execute his duties.

The officers who had intervened in the rue du Bourg-l'Abbé on a previous night had met with more success. They caught rockets, firecrackers and even the little copper canons arranged on tables 'in the act', as the banquet was winding down, and hastened to

---

40. Le Pré-Saint-Gervais, APP, AA 70, Night Watch report from 27-28 messidor Year II.

confiscate them.[41] A young man who had been firing rockets was arrested and brought before the *commissaire civil*, and he confessed he had fired fourteen of them and still had ten more in his possession. However, the commissaire does not appear to have sentenced him to time in prison. The police who arrested him made no mention of fire hazards, nor of the damage that rockets and firecrackers might cause. Their line of reasoning was more implicit, zeroing in on the scandal, the exuberance and the noise the pyrotechnic displays created. The police intervened not because of risky behaviour, but to counter the inherent disorder that setting off flying rockets promoted, jeopardising the dream of virtuous, dignified celebrations. During the Revolution, fireworks were not seen as positive or harmonious ways to celebrate.

Pyrotechnics aside, the police likely grappled with some of the street dances that sprang up as well. Several witness accounts and complaints following a serious incident on the rue du Bourg-l'Abbé attest to this fact. The officers of the peace had become separated in the gathered crowd, and a group of dancing women had assaulted two officers who had allegedly tried to stop them. According to the report,

Citoyenne Albert Vernier, from number 16, rue du Bourg-l'Abbé, presented her testimony next. She declared that an individual unknown to her, but whom she presumed to be an officer of the peace, arrived at the scene and proceeded to disturb the peaceful enjoyments in which she and others had been partaking. She claimed Citoyenne Genois, whom he had also arrested, said some other *citoyennes* had tipped him off. The assembled *citoyennes* then requested the aid of armed forces as they intended to go to the committee to clarify the situation. The citizen presumed to be an officer of the peace had been accompanied by another who told the dancing *citoyens* and *citoyennes* that they were obstructing a public thoroughfare, which put a damper on their peaceful enjoyment. The *citoyens* and *citoyennes* had replied that they were in no way disturbing the peace nor obstructing the street, to which the officer replied, displaying his insignia, that they were to obey him. But the revellers listened no more to him than they had to the first fellow, so the man departed and never returned. The citizen presumed to be an officer of the peace returned immediately afterwards. Signed, the above-mentioned Citoyenne Albert Vernier.

The police officer who made the offensive comments was not identified in the records. Shortly after this incident, however, the

41. Le Pré-Saint-Gervais, APP, AA 49, 26 thermidor Year II.

same women, along with some men who came to their aid, attacked a third officer of the peace named Henri Renard, who alleged he had not taken part in the incident and had arrived upon the scene in the moments afterwards. Renard had refrained from reproaching the women for dancing and 'obstructing the passageway', and the women had not identified him as the author of the remarks. But, as will be discussed below, the remainder of the participants nevertheless viewed the police intrusion as unjustified. Witness accounts all seem to coincide, suggesting that a police officer likely had threatened the women, either verbally or bodily (perhaps in an attempt to push through the crowd), then appears to have backed down. It was an unfortunate colleague who would bear the brunt of the ire the first officer's arrogance had aroused in the partygoers. None of the officer's entourage would stand by their workmate's reasoning, implying that he had walked, and perhaps crossed, the fine line of police prerogative. Overstepped authority is also the catalyst in our final recorded repression of a *souper fraternel*: an isolated incident occurring on 8 July in the courtyard of 55, rue du Ponceau, section of the Amis de la patrie, which put an end to the banquet.[42]

The fallout from these incidents resulted from two conflicting concepts – where legitimate police authority to intervene began, and where the legality of the *soupers fraternels* ended. Untangling the web of details surrounding them will help us understand why they unfolded as they did.

On 8 July, revellers who had assembled in the former cour du Roi François were interrupted towards eleven o'clock in the evening by a trio of armed men: Nicolas Gambette, the section's *commissaire civil*, and two fusiliers from the Garde nationale. They made a show at the gate, likely intending to be intimidating, as the two guards were armed with rifles and bayonets and, so witnesses claimed, Gambette wore a sabre and carried two pistols for good measure.

Gambette, who apparently had held the office of sectional *commissaire civil* since the summer of 1792,[43] instructed the participants to leave the premises. They in turn argued that they had notified the Comité civil of their forthcoming *repas*, but had been 'about to' leave anyway. Instead, they likely tarried, chanting patriotic songs. In an attempt to force their hand, Gambette entered through the gate, repeating his order and threatening to 'double the number of his

42. Le Pré-Saint-Gervais, APP, AA 49, 26 thermidor Year II.
43. Paris, AN, F⁷ 4715 (Gambette).

armed men' should they refuse: 'He told us we had to remove the tables, rudely pushing and jostling us back to our homes, then had the audacity to remove the cutlery that was on the table.'

Some of the men present reacted by calling out the *commissaire civil* who was manhandling them. Pierre Alard, a ribbon weaver and himself a sergeant major in the Garde, demanded (likely for this reason) what right Gambette had to 'disturb a feast which had been authorised by the committee'. As some of the participants moved to intercede, Gambette had his fusiliers advance on the recalcitrant Alard and, curiously, insulted his manhood. 'He had the effrontery to surround me with his armed men and demand by what right I allowed myself to be protected by women', Alard complained. The commissaire then proceeded to make a request, which by then had become routine: he demanded to see Alard's security card, even going so far as to have one of his officers 'fetch pen and ink' to take note of the man's identity. Alard snatched back his card, saying, 'If he wanted a name, he could get it from the military committee.' It was a way of letting Gambette know that Alard did not recognise his authority. The commissaire responded by having the gate and the main door of the courtyard drawn shut, forbidding the revellers from leaving until he had 'seen to' them, and had verified their identities and whatever else was on their persons. This pronouncement sent a shock wave through those gathered, especially since at least one of them did not live in the building and wished to go home, which only further aroused Gambette's wrath. The grievance report records nothing further, but one can assume that the banquet ended with no immediate consequences, the participants all properly identified, since nothing else was mentioned.

Before turning to what followed the encounter, it is worth going over the episode and the verbal standoff which took place in the courtyard. What we infer from the banquet itself is a type of sociability we might characterise as 'interstitial'. In a city where public spaces were increasingly being corseted by police, sociability had begun to infiltrate the few locations that were still free of police control: in this case, the courtyard. We also deduce that the very lawfulness of the festivities was at issue; certainly, it was a motivating factor for Gambette's intervention. There is nothing to suggest that the revellers had neglected to register their intention to organise a banquet with the civil committee of their section, since it was to this same committee that they made their complaints against Gambette. The *souper fraternel* therefore showed every sign of conforming to the law, and none of Gambette's recorded remarks suggests that an infraction had been committed. It was the act of assembling itself – the banquet – which was an intolerable scandal for the commissaire.

To grasp the significance of Gambette's intervention, it is important to understand the man himself. Gambette resided at number 354, rue Saint-Martin, and, though he lived in his section, he was not truly part of it. He held the position of *commissaire civil* – an elected local official – and was responsible for the administration of the section with eleven other citizens in turn. On the date in question, contrary to what certain scholars have claimed, he was neither a police inspector nor a police clerk – meaning he was not an 'active' police agent.[44] Nevertheless, as one of his section's civil commissaires, it was within his authority to assume the additional duties of a *commissaire de police*.[45] Since 1793, civil commissaires had increasingly become involved in their section's police affairs; Gambette is a perfect case in point. His papers testify to his activism in this regard, though his ambitions extended beyond prosecuting petty infractions. Gambette's claim to fame was orchestrating a trap to capture a trafficker of counterfeit *assignats* (a sort of legal tender).[46] While incarcerated during the Thermidorian Reaction, early in Year III, he revealed to his interrogators some biographical details about the previous occupations that had prepared him for police work. At nearly fifty-three years of age, before the Revolution, he had been a ticket controller at the Beaujolais theatre, near the Palais-Royal, and then an inspector in the Bureau de la première réquisition militaire. Now, he was essentially a minor bureaucrat, a product of the Revolution that had converted a former theatre security clerk (a profession from which the police regularly recruited *mouches*) into a middling administrator. Though Gambette was not a career policeman, the expansion of the police domain during the Terror gave him the opportunity to gradually integrate the field for which he manifested talent and zeal. His previous professional activities attest to the latter, but so did his conduct on the night

---

44. Historians have mistakenly identified Gambette as an *inspecteur de police*, a position he did not hold until Year III. See the report for his interrogation before the Comité de sûreté générale. Paris, AN, F⁷ 4715, 5 frimaire Year III (Gambette).

45. The *Loi du 21 mai-27 juin 1790* authorised *commissaires civils* to 'second' *commissaires de police* (title IV, section 1, V). In practice, *commissaires civils* were frequently granted the same powers. See *Lettres patentes du roi sur le décret de l'Assemblée nationale* [...] *concernant la municipalité de Paris* (Paris, n.n., 1790).

46. Le Pré-Saint-Gervais, APP, AA 48, 7 August 1793.

of the banquet: the precautions he took, arming himself with a sabre and two pistols, and the body language he used when dispersing the crowd. Though we cannot presume to make assumptions about his personality, he does not appear to have been a universally accepted figure. His authority was called into question on several occasions in 1793 through complaints and denunciations by other residents of the section, once for having asked a butcher to set aside some meat for him. His experience in law and order, gained intermittently over the preceding year and a half, allowed him to take advantage of a vacancy in the section. It was this new position that gave him the necessary authority to intervene and personally commandeer two guardsmen to put an end to the banquet.

Truth be told, Gambette had little reason to reproach the revellers except for having assembled in the first place – in any event, the Comité civil, of which Gambette himself was a member, had authorised the assembly. He could therefore do no more than attempt to intimidate those who had gathered (through a display of weapons and by inspecting identification) and exhibit a little brutish behaviour (removing the cutlery, some pushing and shoving) to put an end to the party. Even Alard's gesture of defiance, snatching his papers from Gambette's hands, did not lead to an arrest. The incident unfolds as if Gambette were keenly aware he walked a fine line, for no definitive argument was given to disperse the crowd and no action taken beyond threats and the use of force. According to those present, no explanation for Gambette's interruption was provided either, save a vague invocation of the law to justify sealing the gate and detaining them in the courtyard. As one of the guards mentioned in his deposition the following day, Gambette had acted entirely of his own volition and without written authorisation to enlist the help of the Garde nationale.[47] Both Gambette and the banquet goers were navigating a legal 'grey zone', each invoking the legitimacy of their cause: Gambette was vested with police powers, but the revellers had the Comité civil's official sanction.

Gambette temporarily won his gambit through brute force. However, the inhabitants of number 55 quickly switched battlefields. They had undoubtedly already begun lodging their complaints before the committee by the time the officer who had accompanied the *commissaire civil* gave his deposition, setting the tone for what was to follow. The officer reported that, when the citizens were instructed to

---

47. Le Pré-Saint-Gervais, APP, AA 49, statement of Varillier, 23 messidor Year II.

leave, 'though they had been in their own courtyard', they had indeed obeyed.[48] Furthermore, no official orders nor instructions had been issued to requisition the men. In hindsight, this ought to have raised a few eyebrows at the time, but the officer admitted to having obeyed Gambette nonetheless. On the following day, several of the erstwhile revellers formally denounced Gambette's conduct in a collective deposition before *commissaire civil* Auger. Gambette's response, if there is one, is unknown. However, the Comité likely wished to pre-empt blame for Gambette's apparently solitary expedition, and moved quickly to 'disown' him. They shuffled the deposition to the Comité révolutionnaire (also known as the Comité de surveillance) and denounced him to the municipal authorities:

> The civil committee of the section of the Amis de la patrie has forwarded excerpts of the complaint against the aforementioned accused to our colleagues in the Comité de surveillance. As we have come to understand that this citizen has Hébertist leanings, we wish to advise you that on the *agent national de la Commune*'s habitual day [of assembly], the same excerpt will be forwarded to the police administration and to the Comité de discipline militaire.[49]

Accusations of Hébertism had become a typical ploy in the aftermath of the Jacobin attacks, in March, against the Cordeliers and the former *procureur-syndic de la Commune*. Denouncing Gambette for having Hébertist sympathies meant designating him a heretic out of line with current political orthodoxy. It was a rather vague, slanderous allegation used to dispense with an opponent, and all the more ironic that Gambette's attitude and suspicion towards the fraternal banquets foreshadow the Jacobin counteroffensive which occurred only a few days later – sanctioned by none other than *agent national* Payan, Barère and Robespierre himself. In truth, Gambette was perfectly 'in line' with the revolutionary government, but had had the bad manners to act prematurely. It might explain the lack of further action, other than that it occurred only days before Robespierre's fall on July 27. Whether Gambette's expedition had been an isolated act of bravado or executed on the orders of a superior officer who wished to remain discreet – a member of the Comité civil or police administration delegating their dirty work, for example – the affair reveals the turmoil visited on even the most perspicacious of

48. Le Pré-Saint-Gervais, APP, AA 49, statement of Varillier, 23 messidor Year II.
49. Paris, AN, F⁷ 4715 (Gambette).

officers of the peace. The commissaire's alienation during the affair, the lack of written authorisation, and the absence of a partner to second Gambette suggest that his was an independent undertaking. The unfortunate man's subsequent estrangement from the other commissaires further points to the existence of divisions within the Comité over what attitude to adopt towards the *banquets fraternels*.

Proponents of the revolutionary government must have felt they were losing control over the situation. No dignitary presided over the unstructured *repas* – no member of the Convention or political leader would openly commit himself so. This spontaneous, powerful and irresistible new movement rallied Parisians street after street without the least impetus from officials. At first, faced with such a massively popular patriotic initiative brimming with civic virtue, the revolutionary government remained circumspect, even ambivalent. 'The revolutionary government,' Albert Soboul wrote of those July days, 'is walking on thin ice.'[50] Gambette, though relatively low in the pecking order, must also have felt the threat. His own rise and fall parallel the way events unfolded. A by-product of revolutionary bureaucracy, he owed everything to the circumstances which, since 1792, had led him to preside over the destinies of his section, stripped him of anonymity and thrust upon him exciting new duties. He had become a senior officer of law and order in his neighbourhood, bootstrapping his way to power by instilling fear in his fellow citizens and by dint of the events in 1793 that had granted him an increasing hold over them. His awareness of the political situation may explain his brutal attitude and attempted power grab on the night of 8 July. The regime in place in 1793 had given him everything; he stood to lose everything in the wake of developing circumstances. This element is perhaps one of the keys to the July face-off in the former cour du Roi François.

The second of our two incidents, which occurred on 14 July in the rue du Bourg-l'Abbé, also speaks of the conflict surrounding the legitimacy of police intervention, as well as the 'upset' the banquets caused in the police. Henri Renard, another officer of the peace, gave the section's Comité civil the following description of events:

> We broke off once again to put a stop to the rocket fire a little distance away. On my honour, I declare that, from that moment on, I no longer lay eyes on my colleagues. Up ahead, I saw a group of *citoyennes*. It seemed to me that there was something troubling the

50. Cited in Aberdam, 'L'heure des repas', p.249.

peace. A citizen I did not recognise called out that I was to reveal my identity or continue on my way. I responded that I had approached merely to learn the reason for the disturbance. He said, 'You must be a snitch or a police informer.' I told them that we no longer used secret informants and that we one and all kept watch over the public and private affairs of our fellows. He retorted that the dance had only been disturbed an instant by a purported inspector or some other officer of the peace, and that I looked to be part of that lot. I replied that I was a public figure and would never gainsay the claim of an officer of the peace. All at once, two women and a citizen pushed me into the shop of a citizen whose identity the declarant is unable to establish. The citizen was followed in by another. I, an officer of the peace, then saw them recognise the symbol of the law which I wore. The two citizens promptly expressed regret for the contempt they had shown me and said to the women present that I was a public officer of the law and a good citizen. I then proffered words of peace and fraternity, making to leave the shop, when a mass of people involuntarily shoved me out of the shop. The declarant asserts that he heard a voice affirm, 'It is he, the one by the shop!' Two citizens standing near the shop immediately grabbed him by the collar and shook him. They tried to strike him down and ripped apart his clothing. The declarant said to them, 'Peace! I am an officer of the peace!' I drew my baton and said to the citizens, 'Cease and desist, in the name of the law!' My signal was ignored. I was verbally abused. Two young citizens came running at my cries to rally to the law and fought tooth and nail to defend me, but other citizens became involved with those who had first seized me by the collar. These others did likewise to the two who had come to my defence and roughed them up. I did what I could to defend them by attempting to avail myself of the protection of the law, but I was jeered by the citizens who surrounded me. We were brought to the guard post on the rue Denis, section of the Amis de la patrie, where the post commander and the entire Garde made every effort possible to protect my person as well as the two citizens who had accompanied me, one of whom was wearing the uniform of a gunner in the Garde. Two citizens seized me by the collar and tried to strike me down. They knocked me over onto a camp cot. [...] Two citizens of the Garde protected me with their pikes. It seemed to me that they held in respect the symbol of the law suspended on the tricolour ribbon which I wore upon my arm. Meanwhile, the two citizens who had aided me were mistreated. At last, calm was restored. During this interval, the *adjudant* had entered. I declared my rank and station to him and requested his protection, which he immediately pledged to me. I requested to be brought before the Comité civil, that the citizens who had entered the guardhouse should also be brought before the Comité, both those who would bear witness and those who would face accusations and whom I would identify for having disrespected my function and mistreated me. Upon arrival at the Comité civil, the citizens who had mistreated me and brought me to the guardhouse and who had over-run the building told me they would get me for this, that they knew what it meant to be an officer of the peace, that we all got guillotined. They took me aside in an adjacent room, and threatened me harshly, saying where did I think I was? This was the Revolutionary Committee, they told me, and they would sort me out like they had sorted out so many others. I replied that I believed I was safe as the law would protect me. Then the same citizens appeared one by one before the Comité civil, where they said that they would make their own declarations, and they made sure that I appeared last, so there was nobody left to identify to the commissaires who received my complaint.[51]

There are obvious parallels between the incident with Renard and the one discussed previously: a police officer found himself accused, his authority questioned by numerous men and women. Renard had also been roughly treated, repeatedly threatened and then briefly detained. The citizens had been heard before the officer was given leave to make his statement, which was customary at the time. But, adding insult to injury, they had then withdrawn, leaving the unfortunate Renard deprived of his confrontation, to his great chagrin.

Renard's misadventures bring several elements to light. First, the revellers had perceived the police's intervention as an abuse of power and judged the prohibition on their dancing inadmissible. The most striking element in these accounts is the way in which we see Renard denied legitimacy – or indeed, legal authority. Instead, we see him labelled a *mouchard* and a police spy. Though he waved the symbols of his office – his tricolour armband and white baton – at the gathered throng and declaimed his qualifications, he mostly remained unheard. It had not been a simple misunderstanding, however; the event reads as a ploy to exact retribution for outside intervention deemed inappropriate and inconvenient. If so, one man's involvement had been a deciding factor in Renard's treatment: that of Pierre Martin Fortenfant, who had been present near the beginning of the incident and was one of the first to make his statement. He had been

51. For this and the following quotes, see Le Pré-Saint-Gervais, APP, AA 70, Night Watch report from 27-28 messidor Year II.

at a nearby café on the rue du Petit Lion when the incident began, and had in fact been asked for aid. His statement reads as follows:

> Le Tellier, a wallet maker from the rue du Bourg-l'Abbé, came into the aforementioned café to fetch a member of the sectional authorities to stop an unknown citizen from arresting *citoyens* and *citoyennes*, who were celebrating the victories of the Republic (after all, it was 14 July) with dancing and a civic feast decreed by the general assembly of the section. Upon arriving on the scene, the sectional officer was unable to determine the cause of the disturbance, and invited the unknown citizen to come with him, as he was a member of the civil committee. The unknown citizen then produced a baton and said that, in the name of the law, I forbid you to arrest me. I announced to him straightaway that I was a member of the Comité de surveillance of the section of the Amis de la patrie, and I invited him to follow me. Seeing as he resisted, showing his baton, and repeating, 'In the name of the law, I am a police officer!' I seized him by the collar and said to him, 'Since you continue to resist, let us go to the Comité civil of my section, which fulfils the function of the police, and there you will give your explanation. Citoyenne Vardier, a feather dealer, said she would make a complaint against the abovementioned citizen. A citizen gunner of the Gravilliers section seemed to come to his defence though he was ignorant of the events.

Pierre Martin Fortenfant was a milliner and indeed a member of his section's Comité de surveillance. He likely could have intervened and acknowledged Renard's qualifications. Instead, he treated Renard as a vulgar troublemaker.

Le Tellier's account also betrays the doubt cast on Renard's authority as an officer of the peace:

> Citizen Joseph Le Tellier, wallet maker, domiciled at number 73, rue du Bourg-l'Abbé, declares he was taking a walk with his wife when a dispute erupted on the rue du Bourg-l'Abbé. A woman approached and told him that a citizen had shown up and said that they should on no account be dancing, that they obstructed the public road. I replied that I would go find someone from the section with authority who could recognise this citizen.

There were other depositions, such as by a man named Genois, a civil servant in the supply trade, who had been with Fortenfant at the time. His statement and those of other witnesses depict the incident not as a question of miscommunication or of mistaken identity but as a challenge to Renard's authority and a confrontation between

police officers. On many levels, what the affair reveals is how strained
relations within the police force had become: first, in the dispute over
legitimacy between an external officer of the peace and local police
authorities who had authorised, protected and participated in the
banquet; second, in the absence of a mediator to effectively intervene
(a role the *commissaire de police* might have played); and third, in the
division between the citizens themselves, one camp (the officers of
the Garde nationale in particular) in defence of the external officer,
and one opposed. It is intriguing to see several key personalities of
the sectional police force – first among them Fortenfant – standing
shoulder to shoulder with the citizens defying Renard. They had
viewed the unfortunate officer as an imposter and an aggressor,
accused him of being an informant, and hurled insults at him,
dredging up the ages-old mistrust of the 'bourgeois' police force of
old. That police force was associated with the authority of dishonest
men who had troubled the peace of 'honest souls', fuelling episodes of
violence throughout the eighteenth century.[52] There were echoes of
the unrest of the summer of 1750 when Parisians demanded justice
from the commissaires against 'them in the police', and in the way
the angry crowd challenged Renard's identity, then dragged him
before the revolutionary and civil committees. Yet this was not the
only setting in which Parisians contested the legitimacy of police
intervention, and had been doing so for decades. We are aware of
the Gambette affair because of the collective grievance filed by the
banquet participants of the former cour du Roi François, not from the
transcript of the *commissaire civil*.

In a separate incident, it was the celebrating citizens who informed
the police of their violation of the peace and their considerably
unfraternal attitude: Caillouey, our anti-rocket commissaire from
the Arsenal section, questioned a group he suspected of having
fired rockets. 'One citizen in particular,' reads the report, 'briskly
approached me and told me that, on a day such as today, we should
not be seeking discord; he was a public servant, and, like me, he
knew the law, but he did not believe I had the right to trouble the
citizens.'[53] The discussion seems to have been cut short after this,
since the commissaire sought to silence the insolent citizen but was

52. Arlette Farge and Jacques Revel, *The Vanishing children of Paris: rumors and
    politics before the French Revolution* (Cambridge, MA, 1993).
53. Le Pré-Saint-Gervais, APP, AA 70, Night Watch report from 27-28 messidor
    Year II.

unable to stop him because of pressure from the surrounding crowd. We see a new discourse beginning to emerge, characteristic of the Revolution. The pride and indignation in the declarations of the artisans mistreated by Gambette, and the quiet remarks of the man from the cabaret on the rue Antoine to the Arsenal commissaire, make it plain that Parisians were preoccupied with having the police respect their rights, and that the same police force was intent on finding its own novel style of self-determination.

***

Naturally, prudence should be exercised before drawing conclusions based on isolated episodes of the *soupers fraternels* occurring within such a particular political context. Notwithstanding the lacunae in the police archives, there are some observations to be made in contrast with pre-1789 conditions. The *soupers* were occasions on which both the police and Jacobins expressed their visceral mistrust towards exuberant sociability, incompatible as it was with the more sober forms of celebration – austere, structured, edifying – they wished to encourage. Yet their reaction essentially perpetuated the cultural combat that the Church, enlightened thinkers and the Parisian police administration had waged against 'common' customs and traditions, some of which were reproduced in the *soupers fraternels*. What is more, they did not support localised, spontaneous sociability for political reasons, as it might pave the way towards a capacity to self-determine. An unsettling thought: here, the conflict that had been coursing through the country since 1789 – around what form their collectivity should take, pitting partisans of direct democracy against defenders of more representative government – was once again rearing its ugly head. The Jacobins were wary of any faction which might weaken political unity, as embodied by the Convention. While the highest authorities remained silent, non-committal, the police reacted, with apparent moderation, attempting only to contain the movement and repressing what they viewed as the more inconvenient aspects. Outright repression, such as in Gambette's case, was the exception. The police's reticence came more from prudence towards a grassroots movement – especially since they still had deep ties to their sections. There was nothing new in the people's reaction to what they deemed uncalled-for police action – in essence, it was yet another iteration of the time-honoured conflict between Parisians and the police. What is striking is the strength of that resistance and the manner in which it played out: the Gambette affair, in a complaint before the civil committee, and on 14 July, in an articulate debate contesting police intervention that had created discord on a day of fraternal celebration. In the field, the police seem to have been painfully conscious of the line they could not cross. And Parisians, for their part, made sure to remind the police, with novel, unequivocal frankness, where those lines were drawn.

Conclusion: beyond the Parisian experience – Enlightenment, the police and sociability in Geneva

Marco Cicchini

Université de Genève

Translated by Nicole Charley

Paris, modèle des nations étrangères, ou l'Europe française was more than the mere title of a book published in 1776; it was a triumphant assertion which foreshadowed the nostalgia for the lost splendour of French civilisation, that guiding light of the Enlightenment.[1] *L'Europe française*, forged in the eighteenth century by prolific author Louis-Antoine Caraccioli, has served as a model ever since. From the outset, it symbolised the dissemination of the genuine or presumed forms and practices of French sociability throughout Europe.[2] The other European nations of the eighteenth century, Caraccioli maintained, had adopted the fundamentally 'sociable' character of the French, and in particular its spirit (*esprit de société*), which generated polite and pleasant conversation, free from all disagreement or misplaced erudition. The centre of the universe was France, and by France, Caraccioli meant Paris; his was a cultural model fashioned by the spaces, the practices and all the underpinnings of sociability which together had conquered the continent. Social life and all its variations – from the reading of *libelles* (polemical essays) and journals and the frequenting of academies, to the theatre, promenades, companionable

---

1. Louis-Antoine Caraccioli, *Paris, modèle des nations étrangères, ou l'Europe française* (Paris, Chez la veuve Duchesne, 1776); Marc Fumaroli, *Quand l'Europe parlait français* (Paris, 2001). For more on Caraccioli's text, see Martine Jacques, 'Louis-Antoine Caraccioli: une certaine vision de l'Europe française', *Revue d'histoire littéraire de la France* 4 (2014), p.829-42.
2. Pierre-Yves Beaurepaire, *Le Mythe de l'Europe française au XVIIIᵉ siècle: diplomatie, culture et sociabilité au temps des Lumières* (Paris, 2007); Rahul Markovits, *Civiliser l'Europe: politiques du théâtre français au XVIIIᵉ siècle* (Paris, 2014).

dining activities, cafés and, of course, a fondness for gambling and for the arts – were the seeds harvested from the natural inclinations of the Parisian, propagated in every corner of Europe.

While many of the French author's contemporaries who were active in Paris and in Edinburgh[3] offered richly developed philosophical reflections on the sociable nature of men, Caraccioli flippantly described the volatility and materiality of a sociability directly indexed to political and institutional locality. Though the writing is appreciated far more for its striking title than for its riveting argument, the text itself raises a compelling point for historians of culture and society: how are sociability, its spaces and its forms *fashioned*, and how much can we ascribe to the 'French effect' (*l'influence française*), which so enthralled Enlightenment observers?

In this final essay, I will seek to demonstrate the complexity of social dynamics in the eighteenth century as opposed to considering any 'influence' or 'imitation' of predefined forms of sociability issuing from the 'Parisian' experience. I will explore the circulation of social forms and practices, how they were mediated and how they interconnected, through a particular case study.[4] Sociability was far from a product of pure social spontaneity. It manifested in assigned spaces, whether through association, appropriation or transformation, and could not exist outside of the regulatory system which authorised or constrained it.[5] The forms of sociability which circulated on a European scale clashed with the conditions which made their acceptance at the local level – and, most importantly, in cities – possible. It was a twofold movement which took shape as new social spaces were defined, manifesting on the one hand as a surge of social emancipation, an *esprit de société* which sought liberation from the constricting dictates of the corporations, and on the other

---

3. *Sociability and society in eighteenth-century Scotland*, ed. John A. Dwyer and Richard B. Sher (Edinburgh, 1993); Stéphane Van Damme, *Paris, capitale philosophique: de la Fronde à la Révolution* (Paris, 2005).

4. This case study was made possible by funding from the Swiss National Science Foundation (International Short Visit) and the generous welcome of Professor Pascal Bastien (UQAM) in the autumn of 2015, which allowed me to benefit from the stimulating environment of the Groupe de recherche en histoire des sociabilités.

5. Stéphane Van Damme's study on philosophical practices during the Enlightenment is the inspiration for this line of thought. Stéphane Van Damme, *A toutes voiles vers la vérité: une autre histoire de la philosophie* (Paris, 2014), esp. p.127-28.

in the modernisation of law enforcement and the methods of social regulation in cities. In urban centres, traditional sociability authorised – or constrained – by civic or corporative obligations gave way to the principle of voluntary membership to the different forms of aggregating, where the rules were no longer externally imposed.[6] In the aftermath of this emancipation movement, no doubt already a sign of the loosening restrictions, the role of royal, urban and ecclesiastical authority was redefined or restructured, perhaps at the risk of becoming more discreet or covert. This process of creating sociability, founded on mutual adaptations between forms of association and renewed policing practices, was especially active in Paris. From at least the end of the seventeenth century, and with the creation of the police lieutenancy in Paris, the constant reorganisation of policing authority echoed the transformations underway in social life in the capital.[7] But the Parisian situation was far from unique. Paris was not the only 'sociable city' forced to reconcile freedom of association with the imperatives of maintaining order in the city.[8]

Though closely tied to France through language, culture and geography, the republican city-state of Geneva nevertheless differed radically in many aspects: in size, in social structure, in polity and in its religious identity. Yet on the cusp of the eighteenth century, and though the city was heir to a socio-political tradition foreign to the French cultural model – aristocratic and *mondain* – observers were already witnessing the development of many new types of assembling socially in Geneva which were analogous to the cultural and social practices in fashion in Paris. As such, Geneva provides a perfect testing ground to examine the influence of Parisian experiments, and to measure to what extent the constitution of sociability and of public spaces during the Enlightenment – while a continental phenomenon imbued with exchanges, mediations and circulations – was always and ever a struggle for power, a contest of wills, determined on a local scale.

6.   Pierre-Yves Beaurepaire, 'La "fabrique" de la sociabilité', *Dix-huitième siècle* 46 (2014), p.85-105.
7.   Steven Laurence Kaplan and Vincent Milliot, 'La police de Paris, une "révolution permanente"? Du commissaire Lemaire au lieutenant de police Lenoir, les tribulations du *Mémoire sur l'administration de la police* (1770-1792)', in *Réformer la police: les mémoires policiers en Europe au XVIIIᵉ siècle*, ed. Catherine Denys *et al.* (Rennes, 2009), p.69-115.
8.   Dominique Poulot, *Les Lumières* (Paris, 2000), p.167-68.

From 'Protestant Rome' to sociable city

In the eighteenth century, the image of Geneva as the 'Protestant Rome' had waned; the city's role in the dissemination of Calvinist orthodoxy had declined significantly since its affirmation of Cartesianism and of natural theology.[9] Except in a few sarcastic essays, such as those penned by Voltaire, the everyday study and appreciation of Calvin's works were no longer commonplace, neither for foreign observers nor for the Genevese. There were new and growing expectations for this 'little republic' (a term coined in 1714 by Vaudois pastor Abraham Ruchat), which sparked discussions on the state's orientation towards a moral code of simplicity and frugality associated with republican virtues rather than tied to a Calvinist identity.[10] Yet, if the image of a laboriously industrious and educated city prevailed, one in which simplicity reigned, the 'sociable' character of its inhabitants was still under debate.

Embodying sociability

In March 1776, an anonymous *libelle* entitled *Essai sur le pour et le contre relatif à la comédie (On the arguments in favour of, and against, the comedic arts)* appeared in Geneva.[11] It featured an imaginary dialogue between a visiting Frenchman named Ariste, and Philon, a Genevan citizen.[12] Ariste is astonished at the absence of theatre in the city. Philon's reply is simple. In what we shall see was an unexceptional riposte, he pronounced, 'to each country its recreations': theatrical works were deemed unsuitable for the 'republican spirit', especially in a little city-state.[13] Philon's main argument hinged on the catalogue of

---

9. Maria-Cristina Pitassi, *De l'orthodoxie aux Lumières: Genève, 1670-1737* (Geneva, 1992).
10. Corinne Walker, '"Le plus joli joujou de notre globe": l'image de Genève dans les récits de voyage (XVIIᵉ-XVIIIᵉ siècle)', *Traverse* 2 (1994), p.17-31; Michel Porret, 'Genève républicaine au XVIIIᵉ siècle: réalité des représentations et représentations de la réalité', *Mémoires de la Société de physique et d'histoire naturelle* 47 (1994), p.3-17.
11. *Essai sur le pour et le contre relatif à la comédie, ou Dialogue entre Ariste et Philon, recueilli soigneusement par l'auteur* (Geneva, n.n., 1776). According to the *Bibliographie historique du XVIIIᵉ siècle* by Emile Rivoire (Geneva, 1897), it is no.1497.
12. Caraccioli also premised the idea that 'there are different degrees of pleasure; and to each nation its own'. *Paris, modèle des nations étrangères*, p.313.
13. *Essai sur le pour et le contre*, p.5.

other 'amusements' in the city, which he believed bespoke the societal spirit which reigned.

Tellingly, the dialogue is set in a café located in the heart of Geneva. Our citizen begins his inventory by mentioning the circles, where 'daily coteries' of men met in 'convenient and agreeable venues' to play games, read the 'gazettes and announcements [*feuilles d'avis*]', converse and occasionally dine; and by such ways did they 'promote friendship between the members'.[14] Philon then speaks of the 'literary societies', and of their 'reformist spirit'.[15] He includes military games amongst the pleasurable pursuits of Genevese social life, highlighting the various shooting societies, such as bow, arquebus or canon shooting, rather than the military exercises of the bourgeois companies.[16]

Ariste is stunned to see only societies of men in this tableau, when women played such a fundamental role in French sociability, tempering the masculine character, making men more 'polite, honest and affectionate'.[17] Philon does concur with this view and, instead of contrasting republican virility with the refinement – even the feminisation – of morals, a favoured topos of civic humanism, he insists on the benefits of the female presence in societies.[18] But, in this, he follows Hume's example rather than Rousseau's:[19] far from valorising the separation of men and women, he commends the regular concerts given in the city, the balls and the dinner parties where members of

14. *Essai sur le pour et le contre*, p.3.
15. In 1776, the year the *libelle* appeared, and in addition to a reading society created towards the middle of the century (Patrick Pitteloud, 'Une société de lecture bien discrète à Genève au XVIIIe siècle: la Société littéraire, 1760-1792', MA dissertation, Université de Genève, 1979), the Société des arts was established, with some 500 members; for more on this association, see Sylvain Wenger, 'Innovation, industrialisation et institutions du savoir: une perspective genevoise (1750-1850)', doctoral dissertation, Université de Genève, 2016.
16. On military games in the eighteenth century, see Christine Lamarre, 'Les jeux militaires au XVIIIe siècle: une forme de sociabilité urbaine négligée', *Histoire urbaine* 5:1 (2002), p.85-103.
17. *Essai sur le pour et le contre*, p.4. Voltaire had already proposed this argument in the second dedication of *Zaïre*, in 1732; see Markovits, *Civiliser l'Europe*, p.211.
18. John Greville Agard Pocock, *The Machiavellian moment: Florentine political thought and the Atlantic republican tradition* (Princeton, NJ, 1975); Quentin Skinner, *Machiavelli: a very short introduction* (Oxford, 1981); and Jean-Fabien Spitz, *La Liberté politique: essai de généalogie conceptuelle* (Paris, 1995).
19. Van Damme, *A toutes voiles vers la vérité*, p.160-61.

both sexes could mingle.[20] To conclude his catalogue of recreational activities, the Genevese citizen adds that, on warmer days, parties in the country were further opportunities for both men and women to gather and make merry.[21]

The pamphlet explicitly echoes the famous debate on the theatre, which nearly twenty years earlier had pitted Jean D'Alembert against Jean-Jacques Rousseau. In 1757, D'Alembert had authored an article on 'Geneva' in the *Encyclopédie*, in which he argued for the establishment of theatre in the city. Four months later, Rousseau rendered opposing arguments in his *Lettre à D'Alembert sur les spectacles*.[22] As one might expect in a Rousseauian diatribe, the philosopher not only delves into the debate surrounding the theatre, but also examines the distinctiveness of a city like Geneva when confronted with the French cultural model. The *Essai sur le pour et le contre* also references a much older but still well-known and often reprinted text in dialogue form, *Les Entretiens d'Ariste et d'Eugène*. Written in 1671 by the Jesuit Dominique Bouhours, it is a declaration of the superiority of the French language in the context of the occupation of Flanders by French troops. By analogy, our anonymous Genevese pamphlet is suggesting a form of cultural anti-absolutism, making an appeal for the cultural resistance of a peripheral city faced with a Gallic Hercules.[23]

Though well informed, Philon's tableau of Genevan sociability is both biased and incomplete. Biased, because it caricatures to the extreme the level of harmony that reigned in the city; we are led to believe that Geneva was a veritable Temple of Delight, yet it was rife with social and political tension. Incomplete, since many spaces and practices of sociability were passed over. Like Caraccioli, Philon not only ignores the scores of cabarets and basement taprooms which peppered the city, as if to deny they were sites where meetings

20. On the rise of musical life in Geneva, see Corinne Walker, *Musiciens et amateurs: le goût et les pratiques de la musique à Genève aux XVIIe et XVIIIe siècles* (Geneva, 2017).
21. Going out of town is also a way of escaping the repression of sexual misconduct: Loraine Chappuis, *Etreintes paillardes: familles et enfants illégitimes à Genève sous l'Ancien Régime (1670-1794)* (Geneva, 2022), p.65-77.
22. Ourida Mostefai, *Le Citoyen de Genève et la République des Lettres: étude sur la controverse autour de la Lettre à D'Alembert de Jean-Jacques Rousseau* (New York, 2003).
23. Sara E. Melzer posits that, in the eyes of Father Bouhours, the promotion of French amounted to a form of 'soft colonisation': *Colonizer or colonized: the hidden stories of early modern French culture* (Philadelphia, PA, 2012), p.151.

and, potentially, reasoned conversation took place, he also blatantly disregards the Masonic lodges.[24] More significantly still, Philon makes only a passing reference to the fondness of some of the citizens – the 'prosperous partisans' – for the theatre. Yet, since the late 1750s, amateurs of the theatre had been travelling to Carouge or Châtelaine, just outside Genevan territory, to see the plays put on by French theatre companies.[25] He also makes no mention of the short-lived wooden theatre built inside the city walls; it had enjoyed considerable success until it was destroyed by fire in January 1768.[26] Nor does he allude to the private theatricals performed more often in the private apartments of the urban elite, but also by simple bourgeois who enacted works from the standard repertoire.[27]

In emulation of the *Lettre à D'Alembert*, the anonymous author of the pamphlet juxtaposes an egalitarian, republican cultural model against the model of *mondain* aristocracy; there is no place for nuance or resemblances in his discourse, nor for any of the modalities of life in society which were not specifically either French or Genevese. The Genevese citizen incarnated by Philon, imbued with the urban patriotism characteristic of all the European elite in the eighteenth century, portrays an image of the sociability in his city which a historian cannot accept without review.

The republican model of Genevese sociability

By the middle of the eighteenth century, Geneva's urban population was approaching 25,000. The renown and high regard contemporaries showed for Geneva were inversely related to its small size. The city owed its reputation to the role it had played since the middle of the sixteenth century in promoting the Reformation, as well as to geography, which not only placed it in the heart of the European market – as it had in the Middle Ages – but also made it a political,

---

24. Véronique Turian, 'Les caves et les cabarets à Genève et dans la banlieue au milieu du XVIIIᵉ siècle', MA dissertation, Université de Genève, 1984.
25. Ariane Girard, 'Les théâtres de la région genevoise au temps de Voltaire', in *Voltaire chez lui: Genève et Ferney*, ed. Jean-Daniel Candaux and Erica Deuber-Pauli (Geneva, 1994), p.83-104. For more on partisans of the theatre among the Genevese oligarchy, see Markovits, *Civiliser l'Europe*, p.206-208.
26. Markovits, *Civiliser l'Europe*, p.225-38.
27. Barbara Romano, 'L'affaire des "comédies particulières": pratiques d'une sociabilité clandestine genevoise (1702-1782)', MA dissertation, Université de Genève, 2008.

diplomatic and intellectual hub. Indeed, the definitive adoption of the Reformation in 1536 had coincided with Geneva's independence from the prince-bishop and its establishment as a veritable sovereign state, which neighbouring nations had recognised in 1603, and as a true republic.[28]

With its independence and the transition to Protestantism, Geneva had become a city-state, and founded institutions to guarantee its strength and stability. In addition to the fundamental laws passed between 1541 and 1576 (the *Edits civils*, the *Edits politiques* and the *Ordonnances ecclésiastiques*), new police regulations, in continuity with the old medieval laws, were introduced to ensure peace and public order. Institutions charged with enforcing city bylaws on a day-to-day basis were grafted onto the political framework formed by the various councils of the Republic, in particular, the Petit Conseil (Small Council), the Conseil des Deux-Cents (Council of the Two Hundred) and the Conseil général des citoyens et bourgeois (General Council). The religious half of Geneva's political diptych was the Consistoire (the Consistory), an institution created in 1541 to guard the faith and preserve religious discipline. The Consistoire regrouped the city's pastors and twelve representatives of the governing council, but had no regulatory powers and was not an actual tribunal.[29] It could impose religious sanctions, but, when 'ecclesiastical censure' was insufficient, it would refer the 'incorrigibles' to the courts. The Petit Conseil was the executive branch of the government and formed the criminal tribunal in the Republic; in 1529, it conferred judicial functions and law enforcement to the Lieutenant's Court. This body was presided over by the *lieutenant* and, after 1568, comprised six magistrates called *auditeurs*, who were responsible for criminal prosecution, civil litigation in the lower courts, daily law enforcement and enforcing police decrees.[30]

In the course of the seventeenth and eighteenth centuries, other institutions would flesh out the republican apparatus but without altering its foundations. D'Alembert would praise the institutional

---

28. Thomas Maissen, 'Vers la république souveraine: Genève et les confédérés entre le droit public occidental et le droit impérial', *Bulletin de la Société d'histoire et d'archéologie de Genève* 29 (1999), p.3-27.

29. Christian Grosse, *Les Rituels de la Cène: le culte eucharistique réformé à Genève (XVIᵉ-XVIIᵉ siècles)* (Geneva, 2008).

30. Marco Cicchini, *La Police de la République: l'ordre public à Genève au XVIIIᵉ siècle* (Rennes, 2012).

framework of the city-state in the same article in which he denounced the absence of theatre in Geneva, suggesting that it was in the smaller nations that one found 'the perfect model of public administration'.[31]

Genevese republicanism stood out all the more against the backdrop of French absolutism. The two nations shared a border and a language; French had been the official language of the Genevan government since the 1530s. The language took root even more firmly as the first Refuge drew persecuted French printers and preachers to Geneva, to the detriment of the Franco-Provençal dialect. Ties with France were further strengthened as economic, financial, military (through foreign service) and especially diplomatic relations developed, and with the establishment of the sole permanent French legation in 1679. French culture and *mœurs* thus played a preponderant role in defining the 'tastes' of the Genevan elite for art, architecture and literary culture, especially in the context of Louis XIV's repressive policies towards the Protestant minority and the influx of Huguenot refugees at the end of the seventeenth century. Yet historiography has unjustly described Geneva as a 'French protectorate'; the Republic also cultivated relations on several levels with its Protestant allies in the Swiss cantons, the United Provinces and Great Britain, with whom they had a religious affinity.[32] By the end of the seventeenth century, Geneva was an important stop on the Grand Tour the British elite were so partial to. The steady stream of English and Scottish nobility also raised the prestige of the city. This allowed local elites to build networks of common interest with Britain, which were strengthened during the eighteenth century – to the point that Sismondi, in 1814, talked of the city as a 'continental British enclave'.[33]

As a Protestant, republican city-state situated at the heart of a mostly Catholic and monarchical Europe, Geneva was viewed, both abroad and within the city, as an exception or an anomaly, a trait which could be leveraged both in its favour and against. If Genevans' ways of being and living in society crystallised the opinions of those well beyond the borders of the diminutive state, it was because they openly challenged not only cultural models, but also forms of

31. 'Genève', in *Encyclopédie, ou Dictionnaire raisonné des arts, des sciences et des métiers*, ed. Denis Diderot and Jean D'Alembert, 17 vols (Paris, Briasson, 1751-1772), vol.7 (1757), p.578.
32. Fabrice Brandli, *Le Nain et le géant: la République de Genève et la France – cultures politiques et diplomatie* (Rennes, 2012).
33. *Genève: lieu d'Angleterre, 1725-1814*, ed. Valérie Cossy *et al.* (Geneva, 2009).

participation in public life, where the relationship of every member of society with affairs of the state played out.

In quest of the exotic: the establishment of coffee houses

Since the second half of the seventeenth century, cafés had become the emblem of an emerging sociability, deriving their originality from the consumption of the new and exotic beverage which had given its name to the establishment.[34] Cafés were favoured by an urban clientele that was curious, cultured and, initially, wealthy, and they were associated, from the outset, with the art of conversation, the dissemination of information and the shaping of public opinion.[35] The restorative virtues of this drink, which even the medical profession endorsed, were an essential component in its success: in 1764, as Pietro Verri inaugurated his Milanese revue *Il Caffè*, he is said to have snidely remarked that whosoever partook in the consumption of coffee was inevitably 'awakened, and became, for half an hour at least, a reasonable man'.[36] A study of the chronology and geography of the first cafés in Europe reveals that, early on, they had been established in port cities with strong ties to the East (Venice, in 1645, Palermo and Marseille next), in intellectual centres offering Oriental studies (Oxford, 1650), as well as in capital cities (London in 1652, Paris in the 1660s, Berlin and Vienna in the 1670s). Europe freely adopted the new habits of consumption and of sociability, but there was also distrust, even disapproval, of the new custom: in Geneva, the passion for coffee was tempered by governmental concern over poorly policed spaces.

A space for sociability

Coffee had come ashore of Lake Geneva in the second half of the seventeenth century and was much appreciated for its therapeutic virtues. In the 1670s, the product could as readily be found in the pharmacopoeia of Osée Baccuet, a master apothecary in Geneva, as

---

34. Daniel Roche, *A History of everyday things: the birth of consumption in France, 1600-1800* (1997; Cambridge, 2000).
35. Brian Cowan, *The Social life of coffee: the emergence of the British coffeehouse* (New Haven, CT, 2005).
36. *Il Caffè, ossia brevi e varii discorsi*, ed. Pietro Verri, 2 vols (Milan, 1804), June 1764, vol.1, p.9 ('che chiunque lo prova [...], bisogna per necessità si risvegli, e almeno per una mezz'ora diventi uomo raggionevole').

in the medical treatises of Jacob Girard Des Bergeries, a professor of Hebrew in Lausanne.[37] Apothecaries imported and sold coffee from the Yemeni port of Mokha, obtained via Cairo and Marseille, and both officiated over the trade of coffee and acted as health advocates for its curative properties.[38] Though they sold coffee by weight, as experts in the handling of therapeutic substances, they also offered to brew it for their clients. Accordingly, their boutiques were the first to be targeted by the authorities, who worried over the fashionable new gatherings in which men and women intermingled over the comforting, tonic beverages called *ptizanes*.[39] Dedicated coffee houses did not yet exist; the new custom of consuming coffee, tea and hot chocolate initially developed outside of specific regulations, and sometimes in places other than the apothecary.[40]

In 1700, the imperatives of public order, and the need to ensure the prestige of a city in which members of the foreign elite resided, initially persuaded the government to opt for a regime of tolerance. It authorised the operation of six *maisons à café*; the novel designation was a direct translation of the English 'coffee house'. The 'coffee sellers' obtained permits to serve brewed coffee, which included the right to sell tea and chocolate. The authorisation was contingent upon the continuing tolerance of the authorities and could be revoked without warning. Members of the Conseil des Deux-Cents were overly fastidious in matters of urban planning and sought to exploit the vulnerability of these new establishments. As they saw neither necessity nor utility in such enterprises, they proposed prohibiting the coffee houses 'for reasons of propriety, piety and politics'.[41] In 1706, following a political compromise, only four coffee houses were still officially recognised, each regulated by a fixed-term lease. The lease

37. Osée Baccuet, *L'Apotiquaire charitable, ou Extraict, en forme d'abrégé pharma-ceutique, qui traitte des aliments et médicaments les plus usitez à présent dans nos boutiques* (Geneva, J. Stoër, 1679); Jacob Girard Des Bergeries, *Le Gouvernement de la santé* (Geneva, Jean Hermann Widerhold, 1672), p.115.

38. Anne-Marie Piuz and Liliane Mottu, *L'Economie genevoise de la Réforme à la fin de l'Ancien Régime: XVIᵉ-XVIIIᵉ siècles* (Geneva, 1990), p.551. Christine Tourn, 'Aliments et médicaments: perspectives d'apothicaires "charitables" à Genève à la fin du XVIIᵉ siècle', *Histoire des Alpes* (2008), p.195-213 (207-208). After 1569, the practice of pharmacy was regulated in Geneva.

39. Tourn, 'Aliments et médicaments', p.206; Geneva, Archives d'Etat de Genève (AEG), R.C. 172, 4 March 1672, p.91; R.C. 190, 21 April 1690, p.114.

40. In 1697, clients of a billiard hall tell of consuming coffee there for 3 *sols* a cup: Geneva, AEG, Jur. Pén. I2 2, 16 November 1697, p.73.

41. Geneva, AEG, R.C. 204, 19 March 1704, p.164.

agreements were awarded to the highest bidder and exclusively to citizens and bourgeois.[42] They included stipulations which spoke of profound mistrust. To obtain the privilege of selling coffee, tea and chocolate, proprietors were obliged to close shop at 10 o'clock in the evening; the cost of a cup of coffee was fixed at 3 *sols* (the price of a pound of white bread); and, above all, coffee-house owners were under obligation to ensure no illegal gaming (in which one played for stakes) transpired in their establishment.[43] The lease provided for the sale of 'lemonades and other liquid refreshments', which implied that the sale of strong drink, under scrutiny by the government for several years already, was forbidden in the cafés.[44]

The problems these regulations were intended to address did not disappear, however. Café proprietors regularly violated closing hours and were periodically accused of selling strong liquor.[45] Though these 'rules of good conduct' applied equally to wine cellars and cabarets, disturbances in 'cafés' (they had received the designation in 1710) were more worrying to the authorities since they concerned young men of good families who risked 'moral corruption'. The gaming, especially the 'forbidden' card games which took place in the cafés, fuelled their anxiety further still.[46] The Consistoire complained bitterly to the Petit Conseil about 'the intemperance and the excesses committed in cafés

42. Under the *Ancien Régime*, the population of the city-state was divided into unequal socio-legal categories. At the uppermost echelon of this hierarchy were the *citoyens* (citizens) and the *bourgeois*, who were granted political, civic and economic prerogatives. Protestant foreigners who had demonstrated their social integration (through employment and financial resources) acquired the status of *habitant*; any of their direct descendants born in the city were recognised as *natifs*. At the bottom end of the social scale were the *étrangers* or, after 1782, the *domiciliés* (the immigrant population who had obtained temporary permission to work and reside in the city), and the *sujets* (those who hailed from the surrounding villages subject to Geneva).

43. Geneva, AEG, R.C. 206, 24 February 1706, p.93; 13 March 1706, p.125.

44. Geneva, AEG, R.C. 190, 21 April 1690, p.114; Geneva, AEG, R.C. 194, 3 February 1694, p.42; Geneva, AEG, R.C. 201, 18 June 1701, p.278; Geneva, AEG, R.C. 202, 12 May 1702, p.227; Geneva, AEG, Jur. Pén. I2 2, 19 May 1702, p.242.

45. Geneva, AEG, R.C. 209, 16 August 1710, p.198; Geneva, AEG, R.C. 210, 4 March 1711, p.77; Geneva, AEG, R.C. 211, 23 May 1712, p.241; Geneva, AEG, R.C. cop. 212, 1 May 1713, p.193; Geneva, AEG, Jur. Pén. I2 3, 15 March 1710, p.316; Geneva, AEG, Jur. Pén. I2 4, 2 December 1710, p.6; Geneva, AEG, Jur. Pén. I2 4, 30 March 1712, p.48.

46. For more on the repression of gaming in Geneva, see Michel Porret, 'L'"Epée de la justice" contre la "Roue de la fortune": guerre contre le jeu ou anathème

where the well-born of the city and from abroad squandered their fortunes on gambling and other foolish expenses'.[47] In 1717, a man named Maudry, a regular client of cafés, lost an important sum in this way; the stakes wagered were equivalent to '1000 cups of coffee'.[48] The constant complaints and infractions the police magistrates also recorded finally forced the Petit Conseil to prohibit all forms of gambling in cafés.[49] It was a move which avoided banning coffee houses outright, despite the desires of the Consistoire and the former conservative *syndic* Jean-Robert Chouet.[50]

But, in the end, Geneva's obsession with coffee (in domestic settings foremost) should not be mixed up with the creation of public coffee houses as spaces of sociability.[51] Unlike the situation in capital cities such as London or Paris, in Geneva, coffee houses were far from indispensable facets of society life at the start of the eighteenth century. The rapid rise of the café was halted just as quickly. The political troubles which flared up towards 1707 around the Fatio affair, as well as the food shortages of 1709 which followed the Great Frost, created unfavourable conditions for proprietors of cafés, which prompted the Council to reduce the number of official establishments to three.[52] Then, in 1722, when it came time to renew the coffee-house leases, the government decided to retain only two.[53]

---

contre le luxe? Le démantèlement d'un réseau de joueurs à Genève en 1774', *Revue du Vieux Genève* 20 (1990), p.13-23.

47. Geneva, AEG, R.C. 215, 11 March 1716.

48. Geneva, AEG, Consistoire R 76, 4 February 1717, p.23-24. At 3 *sols* per cup, this amounts to 250 florins, the equivalent of five months' wages for a manual worker employed by the state in the 1720s.

49. Geneva, AEG, R.C. 215, 2 March 1716, p.117; Geneva, AEG, R.C. 217, 7 March 1718, p.92; 11 March 1718, p.101; 25 March 1718, p.110.

50. Geneva, AEG, R.C. 215, 11 March 1716, p.129-30; Geneva, AEG, R.C. 220, 3 February 1721, p.74.

51. Piuz and Mottu, *L'Economie genevoise*, p.342-43. David Hiler, 'Permanences et innovations alimentaires: l'évolution de la consommation des Genevois pendant le XVIIIᵉ siècle', *Bulletin de la Société d'histoire et d'archéologie de Genève* (1989), p.23-47 (38-39). The tax on coffee sold retail in the city, set at 3 *sols* per pound, was introduced in 1711 (Geneva, AEG, R.C. 210, 2 and 4 May 1711, p.198 and 201; Geneva, AEG, R. publ. 4, 9 May 1711, p.177). The profit generated from this tax went from 200 florins in 1713 to 6800 florins in 1750, which is the equivalent of 800 pounds of coffee imported in 1713 and 27,200 pounds in 1750 (Geneva, AEG, R.C. 250, December 1750, p.57).

52. Geneva, AEG, R.C. 207, 13 August 1707, p.643; Geneva, AEG, R.C. 209, 30 November 1709, p.417; Geneva, AEG, R.C. 210, 26 April 1710, p.124.

53. Geneva, AEG, R.C. 221, 8 April 1722, p.182.

Controlling sociability

Cafés were governed by ad hoc regulation, which restricted their number and the neighbourhoods in which they were permitted to be established. The locations were allocated by authorities as early as 1706. One café was allotted to the Saint-Gervais quarter (the only one on the right bank of the Rhône), one in the neighbourhood of the Maison de ville (town hall), at the top of the city, and the last two in the lower part of the city, in the commercial streets of Molard and Bel Air. After the demise of the café near the town hall in 1710, followed in 1722 by that of the Saint-Gervais café (located on the island which connected the two riverbanks), only those in Bel Air and on Molard remained. The latter would shortly afterwards be designated a *petit café* and would generate more modest revenues; it would move back and forth between the rues Basses and the place du Molard at the whim of the leaseholders. The Bel Air café – the same which served as the background to the *Dialogue entre Ariste et Philon* – seemed to enjoy more prestige. In 1776, the Petit Conseil considered an ambitious project to relocate the Bel Air establishment to the island, in a building built specifically for the café, but the plan was eventually rejected.[54]

Between 1722 and 1782, there were therefore only two cafés, and increasing that number never became an item on the government's agenda. In Geneva during the age of Enlightenment, the development of cafés was bridled by the regulatory requirements of town councillors who would have them be respectable places of business in compliance with the conditions of public order. The attitude of the government tended to remain ambiguous. Cafés were perceived as a potential source of disorder, yet they offered a welcoming environment for visiting foreigners and a substantial source of revenue which the Republic had no wish to renounce.

In fact, the public revenues generated by the coffee-house leases were a precious addition for the state treasury which, in order to guarantee a regular income, willingly associated the privilege of holding a billiard hall with the lease for the Bel Air café.[55] The guardians of public morality nonetheless held a completely different

---

54. Geneva, AEG, R.C. 277, 18 May, 4 and 22 June 1776, p.217, 239 and 273; Geneva, AEG, Finances A 21, 20 April and 3 May 1776, p.151 and 161.
55. Geneva, AEG, R.C. cop. 235, 8 February 1735, p.96; Geneva, AEG, R.C. 253, 9 February 1753, p.73.

opinion about cafés and billiards. They fretted over the dissipation and libertinage this type of leisurely activity would provoke in 'young men'. When the arguments of the moralists prevailed over those of the Council, billiards were forbidden in cafés; when fiscal and financial motivations carried the day, they were authorised.[56] Ultimately, if the talk which circulated in cafés was but the echo of the murmurs on the streets, it was monitored all the same – though the use of police spies (*mouches*) cannot be confirmed: in 1746, for example, police officers interrogated the leaseholder of the Bel Air café, and his valet, on the subject of *mauvais discours* (malicious gossip) that was alleged to have circulated in the establishment.[57]

Until the final decades of the eighteenth century, public spaces in the Republic did not provide fertile ground for coffee-house sociability. The development of cafés was rapidly impeded by regulatory obstacles and government restrictions. The two official cafés were situated in the tight spaces of the fortified city and under the constant watch of the Consistoire, police magistrates and the entire government. They attracted few customers, which in turn discouraged potential 'keepers of coffee houses'.[58] In 1729-1730, the Molard and Bel Air cafés respectively brought in 5200 and 6100 florins for the state treasury. Between 1750 and 1776, the yearly average for each lease was a mere 2921 florins for the former and 5557 florins for the latter.[59] If the cafés were scarcely profitable, it was because the public shied away from such a tightly restricted form of sociability which left little room for free association.

From circles to 'cyclomania'

Rousseau and D'Alembert were very much at odds with each other in the debate over theatre. In 1758, Rousseau developed his famous argument against scenic representation in which, beyond traditional criticism of the morality of plays and comedians, he placed emphasis

---

56. Geneva, AEG, R.C. 259, 23 January 1759; Geneva, AEG, R.C. cop. 271, 19 June 1770, p.307-308; Geneva, AEG, R.C. 273, 26 February 1772, p.145.
57. Geneva, AEG, P.C. 9318, December 1746.
58. Between 1749 and 1753, no one could be found to take over the café on the place du Molard; the keeper of the coffee house in 1746 and in 1749, the sieur Bousquet, obtained a generous discount on the payment due: Geneva, AEG, R.C. 249, 24 September 1749, p.356; Geneva, AEG, R.C. 254, 8 July 1754, p.485.
59. Geneva, AEG, Finances H1 and H2.

on the uniqueness of Geneva, where a 'simple' and 'innocent' republican sociability prevailed, most notably in the circles.[60] The circle societies separated the sexes and offered an environment conducive to sincere and virile discourse; the theatre, on the contrary, cultivated artifice and gallantry, enfeebling the bodies and dulling the minds of citizens. If Rousseau saw the circles and the theatre as distinct forms of social gathering which might coexist in a 'vast city' such as London, Geneva's small size and republican character prohibited such cohabitations. If the comedic arts were introduced, the public would turn away from the societies, which were the cement of republican values, and they would cease to be. Rousseau's praise of social circles created a stereotyped image of republican 'tradition' which was neither ancient nor universally endorsed.

A thriving art, a flourishing expression

Towards the middle of the eighteenth century, detractors as much as promoters of the meeting places that populated Geneva – the 'circles' – tried diligently to describe just what the term signified. The desire for semantic clarification is easily understood upon perusal of the dictionaries published at the time: until its fourth edition in 1762, the *Dictionnaire de l'Académie française* defined 'circles' as 'assemblies which are held in the private homes of ladies', in the way of coteries of princesses and duchesses which encircled a queen in court. The lexicographers of the French monarchy associated circles with gatherings of women, an expression of salon culture, a curial conception, and never with virile, egalitarian republican culture.[61] Though the term 'circle' (*cercle*) had rapidly been adopted in Geneva, booklets, articles and pamphlets were careful to clarify its meaning

60. For more on the *Lettre à D'Alembert sur les spectacles*, its place in the author's oeuvre and how it was received, see Nathalie Ferrand, 'Jean-Jacques Rousseau: le dernier état de la *Lettre à D'Alembert sur les spectacles* (1758)', *Genesis* 34 (2012), p.135-57; Rahul Markovits, 'Cercles et théâtre à Genève: les enjeux politiques et culturels d'une mutation de sociabilité (1758-1814)', in *Hypothèses 2008: travaux de l'Ecole doctorale d'histoire de l'Université Paris 1 Panthéon-Sorbonne* (Paris, 2009), p.273-83; Lucien Nouis, 'La *Lettre à D'Alembert*, ou l'inscription européenne du républicanisme', *Lumen, Canadian Society for Eighteenth-Century Studies / Société canadienne d'étude du dix-huitième siècle* 30 (2011), p.99-112; Mostefai, *Le Citoyen de Genève*.

61. Antoine Lilti, *Le Monde des salons: sociabilité et mondanité à Paris au XVIIIᵉ siècle* (Paris, 2005), esp. p.10-11.

to potential foreign readers, by using synonyms such as 'coterie' and 'society', or associating it with the English word 'club'.[62]

What was a circle? Whether for or against, the accounts generally give the same definition: circles were societies held, of an evening, in private homes, where a certain number of people assembled to play, drink, eat or discuss recent events. Fifteen or so individuals might also decide to share in the cost of a room or a rented space furnished with all the essentials (such as furniture, dishes and wine). Some circles adopted rules and regulations, and elected a president, treasurer or secretary, though this was by no means an established practice. Societies of women or young girls did exist, but gender separation was the guiding principle. Friendship, social identity or occupation generally connected members as well as circles, which were generally held in the city, or sometimes moved to the countryside in finer weather.[63]

Unlike the *mondain*, aristocratic salons in France, which adhered to the guiding principles of hospitality, and in which a prominent figure *received* the invited guests in a private home, circles were conceived in terms of a relationship between equals, in which members of a society voluntarily *came together* at more or less regular intervals, in a space either open to all or exclusive to subscribers. In Geneva, circles were established as a distinct exercise in sociability, and had been recognised as such since the first third of the eighteenth century, long before the gatherings which spread through southern France at the end of the century, to become the epitome of bourgeois sociability in the beginning of the nineteenth century.[64]

62. In 1781, an anonymous partisan of circles likened them to the 'klobs' in England: *Lettre d'un citoyen de Genève à M.**** (Geneva, n.n., 1781), p.6. On the sociability of clubs and how they differed from coffee houses around 1700, see Valérie Capdeville, *L'Age d'or des clubs londoniens (1730-1784)* (Paris, 2008).

63. Few documents produced by circles remain extant; studies are essentially based on sources of repression, with a few exceptions. See Chantal Starrenberger, 'Etude de la fonction sociale et politique des cercles à Genève au XVIIIᵉ siècle à travers le cas du Cercle de l'artillerie, 1777-1782', MA dissertation, Université de Genève, 1980.

64. Maurice Agulhon, *Pénitents et francs-maçons de l'ancienne Provence: essai sur la sociabilité méridionale* (Paris, 1968) (first edition published in 1966 under the title *La Sociabilité méridionale: confréries et associations dans la vie collective en Provence orientale la fin du 18ᵉ siècle*, 2 vols, Aix-en-Provence); by the same author, *Le Cercle dans la France bourgeoise, 1810-1848: étude d'une mutation de sociabilité* (Paris, 1977).

In government archives, the term *cercle* appears for the first time in 1726. In January of that year, two pastors proposed taking 'measures to obstruct the societies and circles which were increasing in number and were organised around gaming'.[65] The type of assembly subject to hostile scrutiny by the Consistoire was not new, but new terminology came into common use.[66] Later accounts report that the phenomenon itself appeared in Geneva in the 1710s, and this is confirmed in the records. In 1709, for example, the Consistoire enquired into the activities of 'some young men' who had been renting 'a room on the ground floor' in the Saint-Gervais quarter, and who were suspected of providing irregular entertainments.[67] In 1713, the innkeeper of the Cheval-Blanc, also in Saint-Gervais, was called before the Consistoire for having rented a room over several years to individuals who had formed a society with membership rules (*société contractée*) which 'frequently' indulged in gambling activities.[68] The guardians of religious morality fretted over the propagation of games of chance in the city and fulminated against venues conducive to the sociability of gambling. The torrent of obstacles imposed on cafés encouraged the rethinking of recreational practices and the reconfiguration of spaces which more readily escaped government control. If the progression from cafés (for-profit businesses subject to ad hoc regulation) to circles (founded on private initiative and free from the regulatory stranglehold) is not linear, the continuity in the practices of sociability initially endorsed by the socially privileged fringes of the Republic – gambling, commensality and the sharing of opinions – is evident. In 1780, one observer described circles as a 'café or *bureau d'adresse* where one might glean the noteworthy news of a certain political group'.[69] In both cases, the resulting sociability reveals the small fortune in money and time allocated to leisurely activities and entertainment.

In the 1720s, when the passion for card games began to conquer the city, the number of circles also increased spectacularly, though coffee-house clientele stagnated or declined. The Consistoire's resulting distress, which would spiral ever upwards over the subsequent decades,

65. Geneva, AEG, Consistoire R 79,17 January 1726, p.243-44.
66. For more on the use of the term *société* in the eighteenth century, see Lilti, *Le Monde des salons*.
67. Geneva, AEG, Consistoire R 73, 14 February 1709, p.17.
68. Geneva, AEG, Consistoire R 74, 7 December 1713, p.483-85.
69. [Pierre Goudet-Caille], *Réponse au remerciement d'un faux négatif, par un véritable ami de la liberté* (Geneva, n.n., 1780), p.48.

gave rise to a blitz of preaching during the month of March in 1727. For two consecutive Sundays, in every temple in the city, pastors delivered sermons to their flock against the craze for gambling and recreational circles.[70] Ignoring the exhortations of their evangelical ministers, the Genevan population – including some pastors and students of theology – wholeheartedly embraced this form of sociability.[71] The complaints of coffee-house keepers added to the recriminations of the Consistoire: in 1731, for example, the proprietor of the Bel Air lamented the losses he incurred because of the mushrooming number of circles he considered direct competition.[72]

In 1745, the attack against circles reached new heights following the release of a report the Consistoire had been preparing for months and had presented to the Petit Conseil. During their investigation, pastors and elders had recorded between forty and fifty circles which were frequented by people of every description: 'literary and military men, citizens, bourgeois, *habitants* and some foreign residents', merchants, artisans of all sorts (from watch makers to blacksmiths) and even circles of young apprentices.[73] Out of this profusion flowed a series of abuses or dangers to the moral values of the Protestant Republic, which the Consistoire was quick to denounce. Four grievances were identified: circles encouraged idleness and dissipation, and promoted futile activities at the expense of productive work and serious studies;

70. Geneva, AEG, Cp. Past. R 22, 21 February 1727, p.268-69. Jean-Alphonse Turrettini, an eminent pastor and industrious correspondent within the European Republic of Letters, published his *Sermon sur les inconvéniens du jeu, prononcé à Genève, le 9 mars 1727*, in which he remarked that 'the city was full of societies uniquely dedicated to gaming or, at least, for which the principal occupation was gambling' (Geneva, n.n., 1727), p.14. For more on Turrettini, see Martin I. Klauber, *Between Reformed scholasticism and pan-Protestantism: Jean-Alphonse Turretin (1671-1737) and the enlightened orthodoxy at the Academy of Geneva* (Selinsgrove, PA, 1994).

71. Geneva, AEG, Cp. Past. R 22, 21 February 1727, p.269; Geneva, AEG, Consistoire R 80, 16 December 1728, p.191, and 21 September 1730, p.374.

72. Geneva, AEG, Finances A 14, 9 February 1731, f.243. Other heated complaints of unfair competition from the circles would follow: Finances A 16, 24 April 1744, f.206; Finances A 21, 2 July 1773, f.247; Finances A 22, 2 February 1780, f.133, 12 May 1781, f.148, and 4 September 1781, f.160.

73. Geneva, AEG, R.C. 245, 18 June 1745, Annex p.177, 'Représentation du Vénérable Consistoire sur les abus des cercles'. The Consistoire's enquiry is mentioned in Charles Du Bois-Melly's *Mœurs genevoises de 1700 à 1760 d'après les documents officiels*, though the author has taken liberties regarding his sources. Charles Du Bois-Melly, *Les Mœurs genevoises de 1700 à 1760 d'après les documents officiels* (Geneva, 1882), p.123-28.

circles stimulated the appetite for card games, leading to inevitable dependencies; circles promoted overindulgence in food and drink, especially in places where wine flowed; lastly, circles diverted fathers and husbands from their familial obligations, and, most grievously, from their children's education. The tribunal of morals was well aware of the difficulties in forbidding these societies, and thereby 'striking at the root of this evil'. Instead, it proposed a series of regulations to oversee the societies which, until then, had largely escaped police and government control. The Consistoire thus took to equating circles with 'more or less public' spaces, and pressed for a ban on card games in these venues, drawing on the example of the coffee houses. As an extra measure, they demanded circles be allowed to open for a maximum of three hours each day, and never beyond 7 o'clock in the evening. Lastly, they insisted on prohibiting minors from joining the circles. The Petit Conseil made a cursory examination of the three proposals and rejected them forthright, uncertain that the measures could even be applied.

The government's leniency towards these circles is all the more remarkable because, in the previous year, the Petit Conseil had officially hindered the development of Masonic assemblies.[74] An English aristocrat had brought Freemasonry to Geneva in 1736, and it had taken root in the little city-state, issuing from the cosmopolitanism of the British elites who sojourned along the shores of Lake Geneva.[75] The first Masonic lodge in Geneva was linked to the Grand Lodge in London, and had initially received authorisation to continue existing on condition that it refuse membership to local residents. Despite this, the movement gained ground rapidly and, in 1744, police magistrates counted six lodges with several local members. Because the confraternity's characteristic 'oath of secrecy' was contrary 'to good governance, by which all that transpires in the state must be made known to the Magistracy', the Petit Conseil decided to publicly forbid Genevans entry into these societies. The Masonic movement continued to expand anyway, though it operated clandestinely, and grew to such an extent that, in 1769, a Grand Lodge was established to federate the ten local lodges.[76]

74. Geneva, AEG, R.C. 244, 23 June 1744, p.274-75.
75. Pierre-Yves Beaurepaire, *L'Espace des francs-maçons: une sociabilité européenne au XVIIIe siècle* (Rennes, 2003).
76. François Ruchon, *Histoire de la franc-maçonnerie à Genève de 1736 à 1900* (1935; Geneva, 2004).

By mid-century therefore, circles, unlike Masonic lodges, could openly flaunt their existence, and the government paid no heed to this detriment to Genevan morality so decried by the Consistoire. Meanwhile, though the pastors applauded the hostility of the *Lettre à D'Alembert* towards the theatre, they tempered their enthusiasm when it came to the section on circles, which they considered as morally injurious as the comedic arts.[77] The authority of the Consistoire was limited; it focused on the wickedness of the assemblies, deliberately avoiding the political issues. Yet the most decisive attacks on the circles were political.[78]

A space for political sociability

After the violent political turmoil in 1707 and especially in 1734-1738, the mid-century was generally perceived as a period of societal peace in Geneva – until the quarrels which erupted over the 'Rousseau affair'.[79] But, if opposition to the political conservatism of the dominant oligarchy became vigorous in the 1760s, public affairs had fuelled partisanship no less during the two preceding decades. As a series of articles published in the *Journal helvétique* in the autumn of 1752 reveals, circles had played an inconspicuous yet significant role in structuring those opinions.[80]

The *Journal helvétique* was published monthly in the principality of Neuchâtel.[81] An anonymous article published in the September 1752 issue stirred up controversy over the circles. Its author lamented that, in these gatherings, 'one did not establish relationships without loosening the ties that bind us as members of high society'. The writer

---

77. Markovits, *Civiliser l'Europe*, p.215.
78. While preparing their brief in 1745, the Consistoire rejected all considerations concerning the 'political government' (Geneva, AEG, Consistoire R 84, 27 May 1745, p.327), with one exception. The only indication of the pastors' 'political' perturbations is the mention that 'current events were discussed, perhaps too often, in [circles]'. 'Représentation du Vénérable Consistoire sur les abus des cercles'.
79. Political tensions were effectively rekindled with the ban on Rousseau's *Emile* and *The Social contract*, which the Genevese government had orchestrated in 1762: Alfred Dufour, *Histoire de Genève* (Paris, 1997), p.85-86.
80. *Journal helvétique [...] septembre 1752* (Neuchâtel, n.n., 1752), 'Examen de cette question: si dans un Etat bien policé on doit permettre les coteries, ou sociétés particulières', p.265-69.
81. *Lectures du Journal helvétique, 1732-1782*, ed. Séverine Huguenin and Timothée Léchot (Geneva, 2016).

was a veritable moral entrepreneur who espoused the most important points of the argument the Consistoire (of which he was quite probably a representative) had leveraged a few years earlier.[82] All the same, his interest lay far less in the harmful effects of gaming than in the political consequences of the 'coteries' whose 'spirit of intrigue and cabal' he denounced. He accused the gatherings of sowing discord instead of state unity, for it was there, he claimed, that 'party leaders' rallied their partisans, 'instructing them on what they must say, and on what they must do', especially as to the elections which were held twice a year to renew the republican magistratures. The political question was at the heart of the debate on circles and was openly discussed in the articles which appeared in the *Journal helvétique* in the following months. Another Genevan citizen would wield his pen in the controversy, affirming that he frequented many circles in which 'they examined, when the occasion called for it, the nature of government and how to maintain their rights and liberties'. Unlike some who claimed public affairs were the exclusive responsibility of the legally assembled Council, this anonymous citizen pleaded for greater knowledge of state matters and for the right to exchange views on the government in 'societies of ordinary citizens'.[83]

During the 1750s, the controversy over circles shifted focus from morals and public order to the far more complex subject of the constitution and the nature of the republican regime. This debate is a perfect example of how practices of sociability did not uniquely concern entertainment but hinged on all manner of gatherings which might challenge or undermine the foundations of the political and institutional structures of the *Ancien Régime*, even in a republic. The contentious role of circles was seemingly on everyone's mind, fuelled in the 1760s by an obsession for the fascicules (*la manie brochurière*) which had begun to inundate public spaces with *libelles*, letters and

---

82. On the notion of moral entrepreneurs, see Howard S. Becker, *Outsiders: Studies in the Sociology of Deviance* (New York, 1963).

83. *Journal helvétique* [...] *novembre 1752* (Neuchâtel, n.n., 1752), 'A l'auteur de l'examen de cette question', p.503-11. The debate also concerned the problem of *brigues* (cabals), which the government equally opposed; unlike for cabarets, however, frequenting circles on the eve of elections had never been forbidden, despite proposals in support of this action: Geneva, AEG, R.C. 250, 7 December 1750, p.476; R.C. 253, 24 March 1753, p.145. For more on the opposition to cabals in Geneva, see Raphael Barat, *'Les Elections que fait le peuple': République de Genève, vers 1680-1707* (Geneva, 2018).

pamphlets printed in Geneva; between 1765 and 1781, some twenty texts of varying lengths were published on the subject.[84]

Was the politicisation of circles an unintended consequence of the *Règlement de l'illustre médiation* of 1738, which had strengthened the monopoly of the state military, and pushed the bourgeois opposition concentrated in the military companies to gather instead in 'the assemblies of society authorised by civilian life'?[85] Had not the first circles to debate public affairs emanated from the ruling class?[86] If the citizens and bourgeois, endowed with political entitlements, could legitimately form circles, what of the *natifs* who wished to create political circles but were deprived of their rights in this respect?[87] Was it true that the power of circles was such that the items the Conseil général was to vote on were decided beforehand in the private meetings of partisans?[88] Or, on the contrary, were societies first and foremost 'recreational', intended to cultivate the simple pleasures – to play games, to eat, drink and be merry with friends?[89] Should circles not be compared to the British 'clubs' which let honest individuals come together in more civil venues than cabarets?[90]

Behind this proliferation of publicly debated issues lies a remarkable phenomenon which testifies to the vitality of Genevese sociability in the second half of the eighteenth century: the explosion in pamphletary production in Geneva in the 1760s was stimulated by the existence of

84. Rivoire, *Bibliographie historique.*
85. *Règlement de l'illustre médiation* (Geneva, Frères de Tournes, 1738); Marco Cicchini, 'Milices bourgeoises et garde soldée à Genève au XVIIIe siècle: le républicanisme classique à l'épreuve du maintien de l'ordre', *Revue d'histoire moderne et contemporaine* 2 (2014), p.120-49 (131).
86. *Leçon nécessaire à un professeur étranger donnée par un citoyen de Genève* (Geneva, n.n., 1781); *Nouvelle défense apologétique des citoyens et bourgeois représentants de Genève* (Geneva, n.n., 1781), p.46.
87. *Edit de la République de Genève, du 22 février 1770: avec des notes pour servir d'éclair-cissement au présent édit* (Geneva, n.n., 1770), p.8-11 and 22-23. For more on the subject, see Françoise Ansermet, 'La prise d'armes de 1770 et les cercles des natifs', MA dissertation, Université de Genève, 1982.
88. *Dialogues entre un citoyen de Genève et un étranger, à Genève, en mars 1765* (Geneva, n.n., 1765) p.5-6; *Lettre d'un citoyen de Genève à un autre citoyen* (Geneva, n.n., 1768), p.56; *Relation d'un voyage fait aux Indes orientales* (Geneva, n.n., 1777), p.15-21; *Dialogue entre deux citoyens représentants* (Geneva, n.n., 1777), p.10.
89. *Recueil de trois pièces dédiées aux amis de la liberté et de la patrie* (Geneva, n.n., 1768); *Lettre d'un membre du cercle des Bons Ragoûts* (Geneva, n.n., 1779); *Le Pour et le contre sur ce qui s'est passé à Genève en février 1781* (Geneva, n.n., 1781).
90. *Lettre d'un citoyen de Genève à M.***.*

circles in which the texts were not only read and communicated, but at times also prepared and composed.[91]

And yet, though the Consistoire's moralising diatribes had little impact on the circles, the role of these societies in the political troubles, real or imagined, would seal their fate. First, in February 1770, following an armed uprising which resulted in several casualties, the 'political circles' formed by *natifs* were dissolved, and would not be allowed to reform as long as the intent was to discuss 'affairs of the state'.[92] Following the coup d'état in April 1782, in which the bourgeoisie overthrew the reigning oligarchy, which resulted in the military intervention of France, Piedmont and Bern, circles were especially in the line of fire once the former government was restored. That August, René Guillaume Jean Prévost-Dassier, a soon-to-be *auditeur* of the lieutenant's court, produced a lengthy address against circles, which he submitted to the ministers plenipotentiary.[93] For Prévost, who had observed circles 'from a political rather than a moral standpoint', they were a veritable 'government in power' (*imperium in imperio*), as the townspeople had become accustomed to 'politick' there, outside of the legally instituted assemblies which elected magistrates. The Genevan craze for circles, or 'cyclomania' as it was dubbed, had transmuted into a 'cyclocracy'. Convinced that the 'political circles', which caused dissension in the Republic, inevitably developed in the shadows of simple 'society' or recreational circles, Prévost made an impassioned plea for the suppression of all assemblies, whatever their form. In addition to their political noxiousness, he denigrated the circles for their effect on the prevailing social harmony; though he admitted to regularly patronising a circle, he observed that these meetings between men resulted in a pernicious microcosmic inter-relationship, a 'hardening of the morals, the absence of urbanity and sociability'. They were the negation, not the culmination, of sociability, and must therefore be eliminated, replaced by public spaces which would more aptly ensure 'decent liberty'. Prévost prescribed a public purse for the merchants, larger and more serviceable coffee houses, and countryside taverns (*guinguettes*) when

91. Among other accounts, see *Lettre d'un membre du cercle des Bons Ragoûts*; *Tableau de la situation politique de Genève en 1779* (Geneva, n.n. 1779), p.28.

92. *Edit du 22 février 1770*, article 3.

93. Geneva, Bibliothèque de Genève (BGE), SHAG 433, 'Mémoire sur l'abus des cercles à Genève remis aux seigneurs plénipotentiaires', August 1782. See also Franco Venturi, *Pagine repubblicane* (Turin, 2004), p.124.

the weather was fair. And he rejoiced to see the theatre return to Geneva, at long last.

Can sociability be defined by decree?

In 1782, a Conseil général pared of its dissident elements ratified the Edict of Pacification (*Edit de pacification du 21 novembre 1782*), sealing the return of the conservative oligarchy to power. The order also eliminated circles in Geneva, forbade shooting clubs, muzzled the publishing industry, and endorsed policing and military measures which reinforced the government's authority. This proclamation in the form of a fundamental law was adopted while foreign troops occupied the city. Its opponents considered it a violation of individual and collective freedoms. Though the situation in Geneva could never compare to the plight of enslaved people at the time, the new legislation was dubbed the *Code noir*, in reference to the edicts which had defined and regulated slavery in France since the seventeenth century.[94] As it had twice before, in 1738 and in 1766-1767, the foreign military intervention guaranteeing Genevese sovereignty led to the institution of a theatre troupe in the city, in the tradition of 'garrison theatre'.[95] Though the art was not formally integrated into the Edict of Pacification, the intent was to create a permanent institution whose main purpose was to distract the Genevese from political affairs.

These transformations in social life, largely encouraged by French diplomacy, have more recently been interpreted as a sign of a 'mutation of sociability' (*mutation de sociabilité*). Maurice Agulhon's expression originally designated the transition in early-nineteenth-century France from the hierarchical, vertical sociability of the salon to the more horizontal, egalitarian sociability of circles.[96] For Rahul Markovits, the *Edit de pacification* created a threefold displacement in republican sociability: first, it tolerated only gatherings which included

94. Jean-Daniel Candaux, 'La Révolution genevoise de 1782: un état de la question', in *L'Europe et les révolutions (1770-1800)*, vol.7: *Etudes sur le XVIIIe siècle*, ed. Roland Mortier and Hervé Hasquin (Brussels, 1980), p.77-93; Franco Venturi, '"Ubi libertas, ibi patria": la rivoluzione ginevrina del 1782', *Rivista storica italiana* 2 (1982), p.395-434; Venturi, *Pagine repubblicane*; Marc Neuenschwander, 'Les troubles de 1782 à Genève et le temps de l'émigration: en marge du bicentenaire de la naissance du général Guillaume-Henri Dufour', *Bulletin de la Société d'histoire et d'archéologie de Genève* 19 (1989), p.127-88.
95. Ariane Girard, 'Le théâtre des Bastions', *Revue du Vieux Genève* (1992), p.14-21.
96. Agulhon, *Le Cercle dans la France bourgeoise*, p.71.

all townspeople, in preference to the social and partisan segregation of coteries; second, it promoted pure entertainment over political sociability; and third, by forbidding the closed forms of sociability which were inaccessible to urban policing forces, it instituted, under the watchful eye of the magistrates, the continuous surveillance of public spaces.[97] But, if the new legislation concerned the suppression of circles and the promotion of public coffee houses, the 'mutation of sociability' was also directly linked to the establishment of theatre in the city. The new contours of social life, otherwise decried by opponents of the oligarchy in Geneva, were thereafter subject to what Markovits described as French 'cultural imperialism'.[98]

This interpretative framework, and the associated concepts, corroborate the politico-cultural ambitions of the Bourbon monarchy and place the notion of a spontaneous expansion of sociable spaces à la française beyond France's borders in perspective. Yet viewing the official promotion of public cafés and theatres, at the expense of circles, as a head-to-head between clearly determined, opposing modes of association, one 'French' and the other 'Genevan', would be to promote the essentialist viewpoint of cultural practices as the product of a particular nation.[99] Can we come to a conclusion on the practices by looking at the norms, and the arguments used to found or justify them, without also considering the diverse forms in which they were appropriated or adapted?

A particular class of café

On 21 November 1782, the abolition of circles – 'coteries or gentlemen's societies [...] which had degraded into secret political conclaves' – was appended with a series of articles grouped under the title 'Des assemblées de sociétés' ('On society meetings'). This prohibition stipulated the creation of 'public coffee houses':

> Art. III. Public coffee houses shall be established in lieu of circles, both in the city and in the outlying districts; the number of coffee

97. Markovits, *Civiliser l'Europe*, p.238-41. This course of thought was first explored in Markovits, 'Cercles et théâtre à Genève'.
98. Markovits, *Civiliser l'Europe*, p.244-46.
99. After all, many observers noted, the playing of card games, now a primary pursuit in circles, had come to Geneva following the revocation of the Edict of Nantes and the subsequent influx of French refugees.

houses shall not be restricted; their establishment shall be permitted in every quarter of the city [...].

Art. IV. Coffee houses shall be open to all individuals, & there shall be in the coffee houses no room, or chamber, with a closed entrance. Above each coffee house a sign shall be erected bearing the words: Public Coffee House.

Clearly, the public nature of the venues, meant to restrict discussion of affairs of state, was a fundamental element of this new medium of sociability developed between July and November 1782. The transition from 'circle' to 'public coffee house' was intended to convey the reconfiguration of the conditions under which individuals might gather.[100] The new norm ratified by the Edict freed the coffee houses from the regulatory constraints limiting their establishment and expansion in the city, but also sought to prevent political assemblies from forming. Police regulation governing the requirements for obtaining a coffee-house permit was therefore rapidly introduced: the keepers of coffee houses were authorised to open places of business situated only 'on street fronts, at street level', or, in other words, in full view.[101] As for circles, they closed of their own accord or following police enquiries initiated by the *auditeurs* and their agents.[102]

Between 1722 and 1782, two coffee houses had toiled painfully to

---

100. The prohibition on all circles, not only political circles, was a specific demand of the French minister plenipotentiary, the marquis de Jaucourt, to the Petit Conseil, in July 1782 (Geneva, AEG, R.C. 283, 16 July 1782, p.249-50). The first ban on societies by police ordinance, on 20 July, had only concerned 'political circles' (Geneva, AEG, Placard 476). The members of the Genevan commission tasked with drafting the Edict had provided, in the first version submitted to the ministers plenipotentiary, that all existing circles be abolished and replaced instead with daily 'public circles' intended to unite people of all social orders, and under direct control of the government: Geneva, AEG, R.C. 283, Annex 'Analyse de l'ouvrage de la Commission', p.4-5 and 36-39.

101. Geneva, AEG, Placard 495, 'Règlement sur les cafés', 2 December 1782. A number of official posters were torn down from the city walls after they were published by malcontents: Geneva, AEG, R.C. 283, 3 December 1782, p.560. On the sabotage of public information in Geneva, see Marco Cicchini, 'Rituel normatif et légitimité policière: l'exemple de Genève sous l'Ancien Régime', *L'Equinoxe* (2010), special issue: *Rites, hiérarchies*, ed. Françoise Briegel and Sébastien Farré, p.46-58.

102. Geneva, AEG, R.C. 283, 9 December 1782, p.589, and 25 December 1782, p.646; Geneva, AEG, Jur. Pen. I2 12, 10 December 1782, p.63, and 27 December 1782, p.69; Geneva, AEG, P.C. 2nd series 4623.

stay open in Geneva. Yet between November 1782 and December 1788, more than sixty proprietors obtained an operating permit from the Petit Conseil.[103] The explosion in the number of applications to open a café was manifestly due not to the sudden popularity of the exotic beverage, but to the reconfiguration of social habits. The long-lived presence of café owners (*cafetiers*) would seem to suggest that these newfangled coffee houses were, by all appearances, a continuation of the old. Louis-Elie Galline, for example, was a *cafetier* from 1765 to 1785, and Guillaume Vignier, who renewed his licence in December 1782, had run the *petit café* on rue Molard since 1766. In reality, the sociology and geographical distribution of the new public coffee houses reshaped this formerly elitist, unappreciated model of Genevan sociability as much as consumption practices had, transforming cafés into meeting spaces often remarkably similar to circles, and frequented by a regular clientele.

At the beginning of the century, the business of coffee houses had been the sole domain of citizens and bourgeois, a sign of socially determined commercial privilege. After 1782, it was open to the entire community. Among the sixty-odd owners of public coffee houses registered by the state, there were sixteen citizens, three bourgeois, eighteen *natifs*, eleven *habitants*, twelve residents and one *sujet*. It is difficult to paint a picture of typical coffee-house clientele in the absence of sufficient sources, but the profiles of the shop holders suggest that cafés were becoming more democratic. The geography of public coffee houses makes it possible to fine-tune this first observation. Commercial thoroughfares continued to be favoured by *cafetiers*, but public coffee houses could also be found in Saint-Gervais as well as in the streets located in the upper city districts where the ruling families lived. A good quarter of the permits were authorised for cafés in the suburbs, such as in Plainpalais, Eaux-Vives or Pré-l'Evêque, which were open during the fair-weather months. And, though the coffee-house clientele could expect to consume the usual exotic beverages (coffee, tea and chocolate), *cafetiers* could also sell wine if they had registered with the Chambre du vin. As circles had in the past, coffee houses now offered wine drinkers the conditions for voluntary sociability which, though not exclusive, avoided the unpleasantness associated with cabarets and basement taprooms, reviled as veritable

---

103. Sixty-five *cafetiers* have been identified in the registers of the Conseil: Geneva, AEG, R.C. 283 to 292 (1782-1788).

dens of 'excess' and interpersonal violence frequented by the lower classes or garrison soldiers.[104]

Public coffee houses were registered at the Petit Conseil, the state treasury and, eventually, the Chambre du vin, and displayed a signboard which clearly identified them. They spread through the city and the outlying districts under the watchful eye of the government: some forty coffee houses were operating in 1787 alone. The ideal of an open and accessible form of sociability which allowed for police surveillance increasingly solidified. And so, after years of dithering over the necessity of controlling the proliferation of billiard rooms in the city, the Petit Conseil finally resolved to permit the association of the billiards trade with the administration of a public coffee house; 'this way, they would be unable to avoid police vigilance'.[105]

Yet, despite appearances, the enthusiasm for circles, and old habits, had not disappeared completely. Thus it was that, in 1785, the Petit Conseil initiated proceedings against a shop employee who had rented out a private room in the café where he worked. Witness accounts collected by the authorities reveal the rental concerned a group of well-established merchants and traders, citizens, bourgeois and members of the Conseil des Deux-Cents, with perhaps thirty subscribers in all.[106] In one of the many statements collected, Louis Vialat, a seventy-six-year-old retired trader, admitted frankly that, 'when the circles were dissolved, my friends and I continued to frequent the old flat we rented in what is now a coffee house'.[107] In 1785, the Petit Conseil investigated three other cases, each clearly demonstrating the continued relationship between recreational circles and public cafés.[108] On 15 September 1785, at 8 o'clock in the evening, the *auditeur* Bontemps burst into a private house, discovering 'individuals congregating in a ground-floor flat which had formerly housed a circle by the name of *Bons ragoûts*. Twenty-five people were gathered around three game tables, playing either cards or lotto games.'[109] The Chambre du vin issued summonses to appear before them – not as sensational as criminal proceedings, but still – to

104. Michel Porret, 'Violence des "excès" et excès de la violence: aspects du quotidien genevois, 1760-1767', *Revue du Vieux Genève* (1988), p.2-19.

105. Geneva, AEG, R.C. 287, 20 August 1784, p.989-91.

106. Geneva, AEG, P.C. 14527, report of the *auditeur* de La Rive, 27 January 1785.

107. Geneva, AEG, P.C. 14527, deposition of Louis Vialat, 26 January 1785.

108. Geneva, AEG, P.C. 14601, P.C. 14615, P.C. 14712.

109. Geneva, AEG, P.C. 14712, report of the *auditeur* Bontemps, 15 September 1785. For more on this circle, see *Lettre d'un membre du cercle des Bons Ragoûts*.

cafetiers who served beverages 'to private societies in private rooms' or whose 'coffee houses were nothing more than an assembly of ten to twelve individuals'.[110] Neither the Petit Conseil, which, as early as 1785, had relaxed the regulations governing coffee houses and authorised their installation on the second floors of buildings, nor the Chambre du vin, intimately aware of the manoeuvrings of 'societies' which operated 'as so-called coffee houses', was blind to the pretence of the change in sociability as defined by the Edict of 1782.[111] The new coffee houses offered spaces which promoted the continuation of the practices in former recreational circles.

'A theatre erected to distract the people'

The first stone theatre in Geneva was inaugurated on 18 October 1783. The monumental three-storeyed neoclassical construction had a seating capacity of 1200 spectators and was completed at a cost of 92,000 *livres*.[112] It was erected in the bourgeois Bastion, in the very spot where the city militia – dissolved following the Edict of 1782 – used to assemble; and it was the very embodiment of the new direction in which the government wished to steer republican sociability. Yet the construction itself occurred within the larger context of three concurrent transformations. First, it concretised the recurrence of foreign military interventions to pacify the political troubles in Geneva. Indeed, it was the marquis de Jaucourt who had insisted that comedy be introduced into the city; he had been anxious to provide some distraction for his 6000 soldiers come to restore the power of the oligarchy with the support of 6000 more troops from Piedmont and Berne.[113] Second, the size and magnificence of the building

---

110. Geneva, AEG, Chambre du vin, 26 November 1785, p.119; 11 February 1786, p.137; 22 September 1787, p.226; 26 April 1788, p.252.
111. Geneva, AEG, Placard 590, 25 February 1785; Geneva, AEG, R.C. 288, 22 February 1785, p.229-30.
112. The building was designed by Genevan architect Jean-David Matthey. For more on Matthey, see Anastazja Winiger-Labuda's contribution in *Genève, ville forte: les monuments d'art et d'histoire du canton de Genève III*, ed. Matthieu de La Corbière (Berne, 2010), p.292-300. Construction costs, including interior decoration, were equal to one quarter of the Republic's budget for 1780. Geneva, AEG, Ms hist. 215, 'Journal manuscrit de ce qui s'est passé à Genève de 1782 à 1811', 18 [October] 1783, p.76.
113. Geneva, AEG, Ms hist. 215, 'Journal manuscrit de ce qui s'est passé à Genève de 1782 à 1811', vol.1, p.3.

clearly signalled the expectations of such a venue for the international prestige of the city. Since the state had only committed to providing funding in the form of a loan covering 10 per cent of expenses, most of the financing was provided by private investors who had formed a Comité des actionnaires (shareholders' committee); members were for the most part from the wealthy families of the oligarchy in Geneva, who wished to demonstrate their dedication to the dramatic arts.[114] Lastly, the theatre manifested the political domination of an oligarchical class determined to circumscribe the political sphere by confining its expression solely to official council assemblies.[115] The bourgeois opposition had been targeted by this political repression which had banished its leading figures in the wake of the *Edit de pacification*; their response had been to envision a movement of mass emigration to found a New Geneva under friendlier skies. For those who remained or who would return, political engagement was either smothered or else diverted by the theatre.[116]

The distraction of the 'people' was indeed one of the principal objectives of the new edifice; the Comité des actionnaires, charged with administering the theatre, attests to as much in the report it submitted to the Petit Conseil in January 1783: 'It has become clear to us that citizens who are completely absorbed in their own concerns, and who scarcely find distraction but in intense speculation, had need above all of distraction of another sort.'[117] To encourage the success of this recreational enterprise, and if possible reap some benefit from their financial investments, the committee entrusted the artistic direction to two French theatre professionals: Gallier de Saint-Gérand, who was the artistic director from 1782 to 1783 and again from 1788 to 1791; and Jean-Marie Collot d'Herbois, who took up the position in the interim period (1784-1787). Collot d'Herbois would later become a member of the Jacobin Club, a deputy of the Convention nationale and a member of the Comité de salut public in France.[118] Not only

---

114. Markovits, *Civiliser l'Europe*, p.242-43.
115. *Edit de pacification du 21 novembre 1782, imprimé par ordre du gouvernement* (Geneva, n.n., 1782), article 13, 'Des représentations'.
116. Neuenschwander, 'Les troubles de 1782 à Genève'; Venturi, 'Ubi libertas, ibi patria'. [Francis d'Ivernois], *Tableau historique et politique des deux dernières révolutions*, 2 vols (London, n.n., 1789), vol.2, p.277.
117. Geneva, AEG, Finances J 4, bundle 1783, 'Mémoire du 15 janvier 1783', cited in Lia Leveillé Mettral, 'Le théâtre des Bastions (1783-1791): la vie théâtrale à Genève au XVIIIe siècle', MA dissertation, Université de Genève, 2016.
118. For more on d'Herbois, see Michel Biard, 'De la difficulté d'être directeur du

were these two men responsible for the programming, they also recruited the actors and orchestral musicians, inevitably foreigners one and all.[119]

Comedies, tragedies, operas and the occasional pantomime were presented, one after the other, during a theatre season which ran frenetically from autumn to Easter. A vast repertoire of over 600 shows was announced between 1784 and 1791. It included the works of classic playwrights such as Racine, Corneille, Molière and Shakespeare, in addition to those of contemporaries such as Goldoni, Beaumarchais, Marivaux and Voltaire. Even Genevan playwrights were regularly showcased.[120] At times, the Comité des actionnaires seemed to guide programming choices, and the Consistoire did not always hide its displeasure at this. Nonetheless, the artistic director had the final say, though he stayed attentive to public approval: a show's longevity was a measure of its success.[121]

The music of André Grétry, who had sojourned in Geneva during his youth, was regularly performed, in particular his *Zémir et Azor*, composed in 1771 to a libretto by Jean-François Marmontel. Giovanni Paisiello's 1782 operatic adaptation of Beaumarchais's *Barber of Seville* was equally often staged. Did the political message of some of the works resonate with the people? Also regularly headlining in Geneva, between 1785 and 1787, were Michel-Jean Sedaine's *opéra comique* and Louis-Sébastien Mercier's dramatic work, both entitled *Le Déserteur* (and written in 1769 and 1770 respectively). These works were a criticism of the forced recruitment of professional soldiers; their performances coincided precisely with the period in which deserters of the Genevan garrison were being subjected to rigorous punishment following the adoption of the *Edit de pacification*.[122]

The range in admission price suggests that a disparate audience frequented the theatre: between 1 florin and 9 *sols* for the more

---

théâtre de Genève (1784-1787)', *Revue suisse d'histoire* 46:2 (1996), p.185-96.

119. This provision forbidding the hiring of Genevans stemmed from persistent misgivings about the dubious morals of actors.

120. Ulysse Kunz-Aubert, *Spectacles d'autrefois (à Genève au XVIIIe siècle)* (Geneva, 1925).

121. Leveillé Mettral, 'Le théâtre des Bastions', p.61.

122. Jean Chagniot, *Paris et l'armée au XVIIIe siècle: étude politique et sociale* (Paris, 1985); Marco Cicchini, 'Sa Majesté voulant pourvoir d'une manière digne de sa sagesse et de son humanité à la punition des déserteurs', *Crime, histoire & sociétés* 5:1 (2001), p.75-91.

economically priced tickets to more than 6 florins for prime seating (in the boxes), with an average price of 3 florins for floor seats. While few sources containing information on the social identity of spectators remain extant, the relative youthfulness of theatregoers is often mentioned, as is the presence of women in the theatre hall and seated in the stalls, which remained modest despite preferential ticket pricing. Attendance was also unreliable during early weekday performances (5 o'clock) and Sunday matinees (3 o'clock). The pastor Dunant-Martin alludes to turnouts ranging anywhere from 100 to 1000 per performance. He also mentions the charitable balls which graced the hall four times a year; he claimed they were lucrative yet tasteful, which is to say absent of actresses and women of ill repute.[123]

Theatre sociability necessitated the adoption of certain rules of conduct which were far from innate. Several directives were issued prohibiting spectators from making noise or being rowdy during a performance, discarding tickets and programmes or reading them in the theatre, and heckling the theatre director. The new norms seem nevertheless to have been regularly transgressed.[124] The means deployed to police the theatre clearly reflect the challenges posed by this new form of sociability in the city. Within the theatre, several members of the lieutenant's court stood guard to impose order in the hall, and especially in the dozen rows on the floor of the seated parterre. On the outside, garrison soldiers regulated the flow of carriages which crowded the entrance before performances and quelled the disturbances which occurred after the final curtain fell each evening.[125] While the British model seemed to depend on a system of self-regulation which tolerated spectators' disruptive behaviour, both the military and the magistrates of the Republic imposed a system of theatre discipline styled after the French cultural code of silence imposed by police order.[126]

---

123. Geneva, AEG, Ms hist. 215, 'Journal manuscrit de ce qui s'est passé à Genève de 1782 à 1811'.

124. For more on disorderly conduct in theatres in the eighteenth century, see Jeffrey S. Ravel, *The Contested parterre: public theater and French political culture, 1680-1791* (Ithaca, NY, 1999).

125. Cicchini, *La Police de la République*.

126. Martial Poirson, 'De la police des spectacles à la civilisation des mœurs théâtrales: domestication du public et production des affects chez Louis-Sébastien Mercier', *Journal for eighteenth-century studies* 32:4 (2009), p.529-47; Marco Cicchini, '"Une prison gardée à vue"? Le théâtre et son public sous l'œil de la police (Genève, 1780-1830)', *Etudes de lettres* 315 (2021), p.17-40.

Critics of the political regime imposed in 1782 could not help but point out the irony that, from 'a theatre erected to distract the people', there emerged 'a new platform for assembling, from which the first jumbled whispers of public rumour then [escaped]'.[127] On 10 December 1788, the dismissal of a popular actress caused a riot at the theatre; the uproar lasted several nights and forced the troupe to intervene. This spontaneous uprising would afterwards seem like a dress rehearsal for an episode of sedition which, fewer than two months later, would lead the government to abandon its plan for a form of civic sociability based solely on entertainment.

The sociability of the Enlightenment: a continuous adaptation

Between coffee-house customs, the recomposition of circles and the theatre, there is therefore nothing to say that sociability in the Republic was fashioned from imposed cultural practices from abroad. While there were no radical or violent changes in the forms of association and reasoned conversation in Geneva, they did evolve in the flow of daily social interactions. These forms and modes which other foreign societies had experimented with suffused Genevan sociability, but not exclusively, nor were they engendered through elimination or rapid creation. The effect on sociability was gradual and cumulative. This complex process evolved out of a context in which the response of the receivers was never quite homogeneous – for the 'Genevese' were complex and diverse – and in which policing methods indexed on specific institutions evolved, in turn, in the presence of new cultural practices.

Back to Paris

For eighteenth-century observers of public life, it was convenient to represent sociability through an inventory of predefined social configurations. The table of contents in Caraccioli's *Europe française* is symbolic of this narrow conception of urban sociability, which he reduced to a list of forms of association and defined meeting spaces such as 'plays', 'newspapers', 'promenades', 'fine dining', 'songs', 'cafés' and so on.[128] Though a catalogue of occupations would no doubt prove instructive, our publication was conceived more as an entryway into

---

127. [Ivernois], *Tableau historique et politique*, p.277.
128. Caraccioli, *Paris, modèle des nations étrangères*.

the fine mechanics of life in society. Such a perspective underscores the dynamics of the bustling, energetic eighteenth-century city, so much more than a set of prefabricated rules and institutions regulating enlightened sociability. The vitality of the city was expressed as much in the flesh of its inhabitants as in the stone of its buildings.[129] The authors of the essays in this volume are all specialists of Parisian society in the eighteenth century. They have presented a window into the sprawling, expanding city and its polyphonous, cacophonous exchanges, encounters and tensions. Correspondingly, the new ways of living and of policing were far from permanently set; they were like a melody continually revised and rewritten, around which the harmonies of sociability were orchestrated.

The *fluidity of sociable practices* in the fabric of urban life is what makes eighteenth-century Paris so remarkable. The reordering of associations and recreational life resulted at least partly from the influence of police authorities, as the decline of Parisian confraternities after 1760 demonstrates. Unlike the forms of religious sociability such as Freemasonry, Jansenism and Protestantism, whose unorthodoxy had made them the targets of earlier opposition, confraternities were tolerated for some time before secular and religious authorities began to condemn them as 'vectors of superstition'. The reconfiguration of meeting places could also result in more ephemeral, cyclical forms, such as in the spontaneous appropriation of open spaces. The Marché-Neuf had over-run its official, regulated market boundaries, to become a space open to all manner of occupations, from day-time playground to the scene of evening festivities for local inhabitants. The *soupers fraternels* of the summer of 1794, set against the ruins of the *Ancien Régime*, were further expressions of spontaneous and intense neighbourly sociability. But, like a wave in a storm, the phenomenon had swelled suddenly, spreading rapidly from neighbour to neighbour, crested and, a mere ten days later, come crashing down. The outdoor communal banquets, organised in the margins of official revolutionary celebrations, had united thousands of Parisians in the courtyards and passageways of the capital. The police had tolerated the movement, to a limited extent, but, in the end, it was smothered by the revolutionary government. In contrast to social connections such as these, which were openly flaunted, others transpired in unexpected places, out of sight of the prying eyes of urban law-enforcement

129. Richard Sennett, *Flesh and stone: the body and the city in Western civilization* (New York, 1994).

agents. One such space, the carriage interior, figured prominently in the study on the repression of debauchery. Carriages could circulate discreetly through the city streets and were, for the wealthy, a space in which to meet in intimacy, one which escaped all forms of restriction and eavesdropping.

The Parisian police force which braved these urban evolutions was neither a rigid hierarchy nor a homogeneous institution. On the contrary, the essays in this collection show that the police *adapted* to the evolutions in social life, and were *intricately interwoven* into each development. As the forms of voluntary association evolved increasingly beyond the traditional control of the corporations, the police began to reorganise itself around the use of more or less clandestine agents and observers, and to centre on the discreet surveillance of spaces and practices that were on the margins of the law. Social impenetrability both haunted and guided their efforts to adapt, even as they confronted the politicised sociability of Paris on the eve of the Revolution. The vogue for mesmerism in the bourgeois and aristocratic salons of the late 1770s required the subtle intervention of the Parisian police and royal authorities. Their successful campaign to discredit mesmerism was much more than the simple condemnation of a charlatan medical practice; together, the Parisian police and the royal administration had worked to combat a powerful web of influence which had touched the highest levels of the state and the court.

The repertoire of police activity was by no means limited to repression and intimidation. It was enriched by practices which the police adapted to evolutions in sociability, as well as to different social strata. In the last decade of the *Ancien Régime*, the staff of the Ferme générale hunted down counterfeit playing cards in the cafés and taverns, and even in the private homes of the middle class, though they spared the nobility, the upper clergy and bourgeois notables. Even so, in the sociable cities of the Enlightenment, police agents were viewed not as outsiders but as accepted members of society. Indeed, the example of Parisian commissaires has demonstrated that they were familiar faces in their respective quarters, and frequented with predilection certain sociable associations that were perched on the edge of clandestinity, such as the Freemasons.

This book, understandably, presents a paradox: the century that formulated, and later came to demand, human rights and liberties, and promoted a sociability free from religious and political constraints, also saw the birth of modern policing. Paris was at the crux of these closely intertwined – perhaps even interdependent – evolutions. While the efficiency of the Parisian police was extolled and recognised well beyond the borders of the kingdom, the French capital provided fertile ground for the development of urban sociability and the creation of a critical public space. Though the Parisian example figures more prominently in historiography, and indeed had left an impression on contemporaries even then, Paris was no exception or paragon. The city nonetheless gives us a window into the transformations which urban societies underwent in the eighteenth century. Between renewed police practices and the novel expressions of sociability, there was the perpetual give and take of order and disorder, of endlessly enmeshed 'cause and effect'.[130] At the intersection of this social interplay, with its divergent interests and multiple players, a means of regulating 'societal relations' and 'coexistence' emerged. It kept individual liberties in check while encouraging forms of association which, though not directly under the eye of the authorities, were no threat to them. The enlightened city was shaped by the reciprocal adaptations that fused policing and sociability, a melting pot that created the 'society of individuals' Norbert Elias had so prized.

---

130. Simone Delattre, *Les Douze heures noires: la nuit à Paris au XIXe siècle* (Paris, 2000), p.324.

Bibliography

Archival documents and collections

Archives de la Préfecture de police (APP), Le Pré-Saint-Gervais, Fonds antérieurs à 1871 (de l'Ancien Régime au Second Empire) (AA)

Archives de Paris (AP), Paris
Archives départementales (D)
Documents entrés par voie extraordinaire (3AZ)

Archives départementales de la Gironde (ADG), Bordeaux, Administrations provinciales et contrôle des actes avant 1790 (C)

Archives départementales de Seine-Maritime (ADSM), Rouen, Administrations provinciales et contrôle des actes avant 1790 (C)

Archives départementales de Seine-Saint-Denis (ADSSD), Bobigny

Archives d'Etat de Genève (AEG), Geneva

Archives du ministère des Affaires étrangères (AAE), La Courneuve, Contrôle des étrangers (CE)

Archives nationales de France (AN), Paris
Administrations financières et spéciales (G)

Administrations locales et comptabilités générales (H)

Archives imprimées (AD)

Biens des établissements religieux supprimés (S)

Châtelet de Paris (Y)

Fonds Malesherbes (399AP)

Juridictions extraordinaires (W)

Juridictions spéciales et ordinaires (Z)

Maison du roi sous l'Ancien Régime (O¹)

Minutier central des notaires de Paris (MC)

Monuments ecclésiastiques (L)

Monuments ecclésiastiques, registres (LL)

Monuments historiques (K)

Papiers privés tombés dans le domaine public (T)

Parlement de Paris (X)

Police générale (F7)

Archives publiques des Hôpitaux de Paris (APHP), Paris

Bibliothèque Carnegie, Reims

Bibliothèque de Genève (BGE), Geneva

Bibliothèque de l'Académie nationale de médecine, Paris

Bibliothèque de l'Arsenal (Ars.), Paris, Archives de la Bastille (MS Bastille)

Bibliothèque de l'Institut, Paris

Bibliothèque de Port-Royal, Paris, Fonds patrimoniaux

Bibliothèque historique de la ville de Paris (BHVP), Paris

Bibliothèque Mazarine, Paris

Bibliothèque municipale d'Orléans (BmO), Orléans, Fonds ancien

Bibliothèque nationale de France (BnF), Paris

Estampes et photographie

Factums

Fonds Delamare

Fonds Joly de Fleury (JF)

Fonds maçonnique (FM)

Fonds Moreau

Manuscrits français (MS fr.)

Philosophie, histoire et sciences de l'homme (4-Z)

Printed sources and secondary works

Abad, Reynald, *Le Grand Marché: l'approvisionnement alimentaire de Paris sous l'Ancien Régime* (Paris, 2002).

–, 'Les luttes entre les juridictions pour le contrôle de la police de l'approvisionnement à Paris sous le règne de Louis XIV', *Mélanges de l'Ecole française de Rome* 112:2 (2000), p.655-67.

Abdela, Sophie, *La Prison parisienne au XVIIIᵉ siècle: formes et réformes* (Ceyzérieu, 2019).

Aberdam, Serge, 'L'heure des repas de rue (juillet 1794)', in *Les Nuits de la Révolution française*, ed. Philippe Bourdin (Clermont-Ferrand, 2013), p.237-50.

Agulhon, Maurice, *Le Cercle dans la France bourgeoise, 1810-1848: étude d'une mutation de sociabilité* (Paris, 1977).

–, *Pénitents et francs-maçons de l'ancienne Provence: essai sur la sociabilité méridionale* (Paris, 1968).

–, *La Sociabilité méridionale: confréries et associations dans la vie collective en Provence orientale à la* fin du 18ᵉ siècle, 2 vols (Aix-en-Provence, 1966).

Allemagne, Henry-René d', *Les Cartes à jouer du XIVᵉ au XXᵉ siècle*, 2 vols (Paris, 1906).

Almanach spirituel de Paris pour l'année 1737 (Paris, n.n., 1737).

Alpaugh, Micah, *Non-violence and the French Revolution: political demonstrations in Paris, 1789-1794* (Cambridge, 2014).

Alteroche, Bernard d', *L'Officialité de Paris à la fin de l'Ancien Régime (1780-1790)* (Paris, 1994).

Ansermet, Françoise, 'La prise d'armes de 1770 et les cercles des natifs', MA dissertation, Université de Genève, 1982.

Antoine, Michel, *et al.*, *Guide des recherches dans les fonds judiciaires de l'Ancien Régime* (Paris, 1958).

Aprile, Sylvie, and Emmanuelle Retaillaud-Bajac (ed.), *Clandestinités urbaines: les citadins et les territoires du secret (XVIᵉ-XXᵉ siècle)* (Rennes, 2008).

Argenson, René-Louis de Voyer d', *Journal et mémoires du*

marquis d'Argenson, 9 vols (Paris, 1849).

Armando, David, 'Armonie discordi: una rilettura del movimento mesmerista alla fine dell'Antico regime', *Rivista storica italiana* 131:3 (2019), p.847-88.

–, 'Magnetic crises, political convulsions: the mesmerists in the Constituent Assembly', *Annales historiques de la Révolution française* 391:1 (2018), p.129-52.

–, and Bruno Belhoste, 'Mesmerism between the end of the Old Regime and the Revolution: social dynamics and political issues', *Annales historiques de la Révolution française* 391 (2018), p.3-26.

Aubert, Raymond, *Journal d'un bourgeois de Paris sous la Révolution* (Paris, 1974).

Baccuet, Osée, *L'Apotiquaire charitable, ou Extraict, en forme d'abrégé pharmaceutique, qui traitte des aliments et médicaments les plus usitez à présent dans nos boutiques* (Geneva, J. Stoër, 1679).

Bachaumont, Louis Petit de, *Mémoires secrets pour servir à l'histoire de la République des Lettres en France depuis 1762 jusqu'à nos jours, ou Journal d'un observateur*, 36 vols (London, John Adamson, 1771-1789).

Backouche, Isabelle, *La Trace du fleuve: la Seine et Paris (1750-1850)* (Paris, 2000).

–, Boris Bove *et al.* (ed.), *Notre-Dame et l'Hôtel de Ville: incarner Paris du Moyen Age à nos jours* (Paris, 2016).

Backouche, Isabelle, Nicolas Lyon-Caen *et al.* (ed.), *La Ville est à nous! Aménagement urbain et mobilisations sociales depuis le Moyen Age* (Paris, 2018).

Backouche, Isabelle, and Nathalie Montel, 'La fabrique ordinaire de la ville', *Histoire urbaine* 9:2 (2007), p.5-9.

Bailly, Jean-Sylvain, *Exposé des expériences qui ont été faites pour l'examen du magnétisme animal* (Paris, n.n., 1784).

–, *Rapport secret sur le mesmérisme*, in *Le Conservateur, ou Recueil de morceaux inédits d'histoire, de politique, littérature et de philosophie tirés des porte-feuilles de M. François de Neufchâteau de l'Institut national* (Paris, Year VIII), p.146-55.

–, 'Secret report on mesmerism or animal magnetism', *International journal of clinical and experimental hypnosis* 50:4 (2002), p.364-68.

Baker, Keith Michael, 'Enlightenment and the institution of society: notes for a conceptual history', in *Main trends in cultural history*, ed. W. F. B. Melching and W. R. E. Velema (Amsterdam and Atlanta, GA, 1994), p.187-205.

Barat, Raphael, *'Les Elections que fait le peuple': République de Genève, vers 1680-1707* (Geneva, 2018).

Barbier, Edmond-Jean-François, *Chronique de la Régence et du règne de Louis XV, 1718-1763*, 8 vols (Paris, 1857-1866).

Barbier, Frédéric, *et al.*, *Dictionnaire des imprimeurs, libraires et gens du livre à Paris (1701-1789)* (Geneva, 2007).

Barère, Bertrand, *Rapport fait au nom du Comité de salut public [...] sur la suppression des repas civiques et des fêtes sectionnaires: séance du 28 messidor, l'an deuxième de la République française une et indivisible, imprimé par ordre de la Convention* (Paris, n.n., 1794).

Barré, Pierre-Yves, and Jean-Baptiste Radet, *Les Docteurs modernes: comédie-parade en un acte et en vaudevilles, suivie du baquet de santé: Divertissement analogue mêlé de couplets; représentée pour la première fois à Paris par les Comédiens italiens ordinaires du roi, le mardi 16 novembre 1784* (Paris, Brunet, 1784).

Barrie, David G., *Police in the age of improvement: police development and the civic tradition in Scotland, 1775-1865* (Cullompton, 2008).

–, and Susan Broomhall (ed.), *A History of police and masculinities, 1700-2010* (London and New York, 2012).

Bastien, Georges, 'Les prisons de l'Hôtel de ville (1515-1794)', *Seine et Paris: bulletin d'information de l'Association générale des administrateurs de la Préfecture de la Seine* 72 (1974), p.1-15.

Bastien, Pascal, and Simon Macdonald (ed.), *Paris et ses peuples au XVIIIᵉ siècle* (Paris, 2020).

Baudriot, Pierre-Denis, 'Essai sur l'ordure en milieu urbain à l'époque pré-industrielle: boues, immondices et gadoue à Paris au XVIIIᵉ siècle', *Histoire, économie et société* 5:4 (1986), p.515-28.

Beaurepaire, Pierre-Yves, *L'Autre et le frère: l'étranger et la franc-maçonnerie en France au XVIIIᵉ siècle* (Paris, 1998).

–, *L'Espace des francs-maçons: une sociabilité européenne au XVIIIᵉ siècle* (Rennes, 2003).

–, 'La "fabrique" de la sociabilité', *Dix-huitième siècle* 46 (2014), p.85-105.

–, *Le Mythe de l'Europe française au XVIIIᵉ siècle: diplomatie, culture et sociabilité au temps des Lumières* (Paris, 2007).

Beccaria, Cesare, *On crimes and punishments, and other writings*, ed. Richard Bellamy (Cambridge, 1995).

Becker, Carl, *The Heavenly city of the eighteenth-century philosophes* (1932; New Haven, CT, and London, 1966).

Becker, Howard S., *Outsiders: Studies in the Sociology of Deviance* (New York, 1963).

Belhoste, Bruno, 'Mesmer et la diffusion du magnétisme animal à Paris (1778-1803)', in *Mesmer et mesmérismes: le magnétisme animal en contexte*, ed. Bruno Belhoste and Nicole Edelman (Paris, 2015), p.21-61.

–, *Paris savant: parcours et rencontres au temps des Lumières* (Paris, 2011).

Bell, David A., *The Cult of the nation in France: inventing nationalism, 1680-1800* (Cambridge, MA, 2001).

–, *Lawyers and citizens: the making of a political elite in Old Regime France* (New York and Oxford, 1994).

Belleguic, Thierry, and Laurent Turcot (ed.), *Les Histoires de Paris (XVIᵉ-XVIIIᵉ siècles)*, 2 vols (Paris, 2012).

Belmas, Elisabeth, *Jouer autrefois: essai sur le jeu dans la France moderne, XVIᵉ-XVIIIᵉ siècle* (Seyssel, 2006).

Bely, Lucien, *Espions et ambassadeurs au temps de Louis XIV* (Paris, 1990).

Benabou, Erica-Marie, *La Prostitution et la police des mœurs au XVIIIᵉ siècle* (Paris, 1987).

Bennet, Jean, *La Mutualité française des origines à la Révolution de 1789* (Paris, 1981).

Berlière, Jean-Marc, 'Histoire de la police, quelques réflexions sur l'historiographie française: présentation du dossier', *Criminocorpus* (2008), special issue: *Histoire de la police*, http://journals.openedition.org/criminocorpus/73 (last accessed on 22 January 2024).

Berlière, Justine, *Policer Paris au siècle des Lumières: les commissaires du quartier du Louvre dans la seconde moitié du XVIIIᵉ siècle* (Paris, 2012).

Besse, Laurent, *et al.* (ed.), *Voisiner: mutations urbaines et construction de la cité du Moyen Age à nos jours* (Tours, 2018).

Biard, Michel, 'De la difficulté d'être directeur du théâtre de Genève (1784-1787)', *Revue suisse d'histoire* 46:2 (1996), p.185-96.

Birn, Raymond, *Royal censorship of books in eighteenth-century France* (Stanford, CA, 2012).

Blanc-Chaléard, Marie-Claude (ed.), *Police et migrants: France, 1667-1959* (Rennes, 2001).

Boltanski, Ariane, and Marie-Lucie Copete (ed.), *L'Eglise des laïcs, XVIᵉ-XXᵉ siècle* (Madrid, 2021).

Bombelles, Marc-Marie, *Journal du marquis de Bombelles*, ed. Frans Durif and Jean Grassion, 2 vols (Geneva, 1978).

Bonzon, Anne, *et al.* (ed.), *La Paroisse urbaine: du Moyen Age à nos jours* (Paris, 2014).

Boulet-Sautel, Marguerite, 'Police et administration en France à la fin de l'Ancien Régime: observations terminologiques', in *Histoire comparée de l'administration (IVᵉ-XVIIIᵉ siècles)*, ed. Werner Paravicini and Karl Ferdinand Werner (Munich, 1980), p.47-51.

Bourdin, Philippe, and Jean-Luc Chappey (ed.), *Réseaux et sociabilités littéraires en Révolution* (Clermont-Ferrand, 2007).

Brack, Charles-Pierre, *Histoire du magnétisme en France, de son régime et de son influence, pour développer l'idée qu'on doit avoir de la médecine universelle* (Vienna, Chez Boyer, 1784).

–, *Lettre de Figaro au comte Almaviva sur la crise du magnétisme animal* (Madrid, Chez les marchands de nouveautés, 1784).

–, *Testament politique de M. Mesmer, ou la Précaution d'un sage, avec le dénombrement des adeptes, le tout traduit de l'allemand par un Bostonien* (Leipzig and Paris, n.n., 1785).

Brandli, Fabrice, *Le Nain et le géant: la République de Genève et la France – cultures politiques et diplomatie* (Rennes, 2012).

Brennan, Thomas, *Public drinking and popular culture in eighteenth-century Paris* (Princeton, NJ, 1988).

–, 'Taverns and the public sphere in the French Revolution', in *Alcohol: a social and cultural history*, ed. Mack Holt (Oxford and New York, 2006), p.107-20.

Brockliss, Laurence, and Colin Jones, *The Medical world of early modern France* (Oxford, 1997).

Burrows, Simon, *Blackmail, scandal, and revolution: London's French libellists, 1758-1792* (Manchester, 2006).

Burstin, Haim, *Révolutionnaires: pour une anthropologie politique de la Révolution française* (Paris, 2013).

Cabantous, Alain, *Entre fêtes et clochers: profane et sacré dans l'Europe moderne, XVIIᵉ-XVIIIᵉ siècle* (Paris, 2002).

–, *Histoire de la nuit, XVIIᵉ-XVIIIᵉ siècle* (Paris, 2009).

–, 'Le quartier, espace vécu à l'époque moderne', *Histoire, économie et société* 13:3 (1994), p.427-39.

Candaux, Jean-Daniel, 'La Révolution genevoise de 1782: un état de la question', in *L'Europe et les révolutions (1770-1800)*, vol.7: *Etudes sur le XVIIIᵉ siècle*, ed. Roland Mortier and Hervé Hasquin (Brussels, 1980), p.77-93.

Canepari, Eleonora, 'Civic identity, "juvenile status" and gender in sixteenth- and seventeeth-century Italian towns', in *The Routledge history handbook of gender and the urban experience*, ed. Deborah Simonton (London, 2020), p.182-94.

Capdeville, Valérie, *L'Age d'or des clubs londoniens (1730-1784)* (Paris, 2008).

Caraccioli, Louis-Antoine, *Paris, modèle des nations étrangères, ou l'Europe française* (Paris, Chez la veuve Duchesne, 1776).

Carbonnier, Youri, 'Les maisons des ponts parisiens à la fin du XVIIIᵉ siècle: étude d'un phénomène architectural et urbain particulier', *Histoire, économie et société* 17:4 (1998), p.711-23.

Centre historique des Archives nationales, *Châtelet de Paris: répertoire numérique de la série Y*, vol.1: *Les Chambres Y 1 à 10718 et 18603 à 18800* (Paris, 1993).

Chabaud, Gilles, *et al.*, 'La géographie parisienne de l'accueil', in *La Ville promise: mobilité et accueil à Paris (fin XVIIᵉ-début XIXᵉ siècle)*, ed. Daniel Roche (Paris, 2000), p.109-71.

Chagniot, Jean, 'Le guet et la garde de Paris à la fin de l'Ancien Régime', *Revue d'histoire moderne et contemporaine* 20:1 (1973), p.58-71.

–, *Paris et l'armée au XVIIIᵉ siècle: étude politique et sociale* (Paris, 1985).

–, 'Le problème du maintien de l'ordre à Paris au XVIIIᵉ siècle', *Bulletin de la Société d'histoire moderne et contemporaine* 8 (1974), p.32-45.

Chaperon, Sylvie, *et al.*, 'Introduction', *Genre, sexualité & société* 10 (2013), special issue: *Eros parisien*, ed. Sylvie Chaperon *et al.*, https://journals.openedition.org/gss/3039 (last accessed on 25 January 2024).

Chappuis, Loraine, *Etreintes paillardes: familles et enfants illégitimes à Genève sous l'Ancien Régime (1670-1794)* (Geneva, 2022).

Charle, Christophe (ed.), *Le Temps des capitales culturelles, XVIIIᵉ-XXᵉ siècles* (Seyssel, 2009).

Chassaigne, Marc, *La Lieutenance générale de police de Paris* (1906; Paris, 1975).

Chassaignon, Jean-Marie, *Les Nudités, ou les Crimes du peuple* (Paris, n.n., 1792).

Chaunu, Pierre, *et al.*, *Le Basculement religieux de Paris au XVIIIᵉ siècle* (Paris, 1998).

Chevallier, Pierre, *Histoire de la franc-maçonnerie française*, 3 vols (Paris, 1974-1975).

Cicchini, Marco, 'Milices bourgeoises et garde soldée à Genève au XVIIIᵉ siècle: le républicanisme classique à l'épreuve du maintien de l'ordre', *Revue d'histoire moderne et contemporaine* 2 (2014), p.120-49.

–, *La Police de la République: l'ordre public à Genève au XVIIIᵉ siècle* (Rennes, 2012).

–, '"Une prison gardée à vue"? Le théâtre et son public sous l'œil de la police (Genève, 1780-1830)', *Etudes de lettres* 315 (2021), p.17-40.

–, 'Rituel normatif et légitimité policière: l'exemple de Genève sous l'Ancien Régime', *L'Equinoxe* (2010), special issue: *Rites, hiérarchies*, ed. Françoise Briegel and Sébastien Farré, p.46-58.

–, 'Sa Majesté voulant pourvoir d'une manière digne de sa sagesse et de son humanité à la punition des déserteurs', *Crime,*

histoire & sociétés 5:1 (2001), p.75-91.

Claudel, Anne-Claire, 'L'intermédiaire entre la justice et les justiciables: l'huissier de justice dans le duché de Lorraine et de Bar au XVIIIᵉ siècle', in *Entre justice et justiciables: les auxiliaires de la justice du Moyen Age au XXᵉ siècle*, ed. Claire Dolan (Sainte-Foy, 2005), p.227-44.

Cock, Jacques de (ed.), *Marat avant 1789* (Lyon, 2003).

Coleman, Charly, 'Religion', in *The Cambridge companion to the French Enlightenment*, ed. Daniel Brewer (Cambridge, 2014), p.105-21.

–, 'Resacralizing the world: the fate of secularism in Enlightenment historiography', *The Journal of modern history* 82 (2010), p.368-95.

–, 'The spirit of speculation: John Law and economic theology in the age of lights', *French historical studies* 42:2 (2019), p.203-37.

Collin, Nicolas, *Traité des confrairies en général et de quelques-unes en particulier* (Paris, n.n., 1784).

–, *Traité du pain béni [sic], ou l'Eglise catholique justifiée sur l'usage du pain-béni* (Paris, n.n., 1777).

Collins, James B., 'Women and the birth of modern consumer capitalism', in *Women and work in eighteenth-century France*, ed. Daryl M. Hafter and Nina Kushner (Baton Rouge, LA, 2015), p.152-76.

Contat, Nicolas, *Anecdotes typographiques* (Oxford, 1980).

Cossy, Valérie, *et al.* (ed.), *Genève: lieu d'Angleterre, 1725-1814* (Geneva, 2009).

Cottret, Monique, *Jansénismes et*

Lumières: pour un autre XVIIIe siècle (Paris, 1998).

–, and Valérie Guittienne-Murger (ed.), *Une Aventure de presse clandestine au siècle des Lumières (1713-1803)* (Paris, 2016).

Couture, Rachel, '"Inspirer la crainte, le respect et l'amour du public": les inspecteurs de police parisiens, 1740-1789', doctoral dissertation, Université du Québec à Montréal and Université de Caen Basse-Normandie, 2013.

Cowan, Brian, 'English coffeehouses and French salons: rethinking Habermas, gender and sociability in early modern French and British historiography', in *Making space public in early modern Europe: performance, geography, privacy*, ed. Angela Vanhaelen and Joseph P. Ward (London, 2013), p.41-53.

–, 'In public: collectivities and polities', in *A Cultural history of emotion in the Baroque and Enlightenment age (1600-1800)*, ed. Claire Walker *et al.* (London, 2019), p.155-72.

–, *The Social life of coffee: the emergence of the British coffeehouse* (New Haven, CT, 2005).

Croq, Laurence, 'Les années 80 de Siméon-Prosper Hardy: de la mémoire des offenses au triomphe des vaincus', in *Mes loisirs, ou Journal d'événemens tels qu'ils parviennent à ma connoissance (1753-1789)*, ed. Pascal Bastien *et al.*, 11 vols (Paris, 2012-2024), vol.8: *1783-1785* (2022), p.1-27.

–, 'Le déclin de la confrérie Notre-Dame aux prêtres et aux bourgeois de Paris sous l'Ancien Régime', *Paris et Ile-de-France: mémoires* 50 (1999), p.243-89.

–, 'Des "bourgeois de Paris" à la bourgeoisie parisienne (XVIIe-XVIIIe siècles)', in *Les Histoires de Paris (XVIe-XVIIIe siècles)*, ed. Thierry Belleguic and Laurent Turcot, 2 vols (Paris, 2012), vol.1, p.269-83.

–, 'Les édiles, les notables et le pouvoir royal à Paris, histoire de ruptures (XVIIe-XVIIIe siècles)', in *Le Pouvoir municipal en France de la fin du Moyen Age à 1789*, ed. Philippe Hamon and Catherine Laurent (Rennes, 2012), p.223-50.

–, 'L'entrée en religion, entre choix familial et vocation: l'exemple des fils de la bourgeoisie parisienne au XVIIIe siècle', in *L'Eglise des laïcs, XVIe-XXe siècle*, ed. Ariane Boltanski and Marie-Lucie Copete (Madrid, 2021), p.117-35.

–, 'Essai pour la construction de la notabilité comme paradigme socio-politique', in *La Notabilité urbaine Xe-XVIIIe siècles*, ed. Laurence Jean-Marie (Caen, 2007), p.23-38.

–, 'La municipalité parisienne à l'épreuve des absolutismes: démantèlement d'une structure politique et création d'une administration (1660-1789)', in *Le Prince, la ville et le bourgeois (XIVe-XVIIIe siècles)*, ed. Laurence Croq (Paris, 2004), p.175-201.

–, 'Pour ou contre les parlements: genèse des engagements révolutionnaires des bourgeois parisiens', in *Les Pratiques politiques dans les villes françaises d'Ancien Régime: communauté, citoyenneté et localité*, ed. Claire Dolan (Rennes, 2018), p.183-206.

–, (ed.), *Le Prince, la ville et le bourgeois (XIVᵉ-XVIIIᵉ siècles)* (Paris, 2004).

–, and Nicolas Lyon-Caen, 'La notabilité parisienne entre la police et la ville: des définitions aux usages sociaux et politiques au XVIIIᵉ siècle', in *La Notabilité urbaine Xᵉ-XVIIIᵉ siècles*, ed. Laurence Jean-Marie (Caen, 2007), p.125-57.

–, 'Le rang et la fonction: les marguilliers des fabriques parisiennes à l'époque moderne', in *La Paroisse urbaine: du Moyen Age à nos jours*, ed. Anne Bonzon *et al.* (Paris, 2014), p.199-244.

Darnton, Robert, *Censors at work: how states shaped literature* (New York, 2014).

–, *The Devil in the holy water, or the Art of slander from Louis XIV to Napoleon* (Philadelphia, PA, 2010).

–, *Mesmerism and the end of the Enlightenment in France* (Cambridge, MA, 1968).

–, *Pirating and publishing: the book trade in the age of Enlightenment* (Oxford, 2021).

–, *Poetry and the police: communication networks in eighteenth-century Paris* (Cambridge, 2010).

Dehorne, Jacques, *Réponse d'un médecin de Paris à un médecin de province sur le prétendu magnétisme animal de M. Mesmer* (Vienna and Paris, Delalain le jeune, 1780).

Delamare, Nicolas, *Traité de la police*, 2nd edn, 4 vols (Paris, n.n., 1729).

Delattre, Simone, *Les Douze heures noires: la nuit à Paris au XIXᵉ siècle* (Paris, 2000).

Delon, Michel, 'Morale', in *Le Monde des Lumières*, ed. Vincenzo Ferrone and Daniel Roche (Paris, 1993), p.41-48.

Denis, Vincent, 'Les commissaires de police de la chute de la monarchie à la Restauration', in *Le Commissaire de police au XIXᵉ siècle*, ed. Dominique Kalifa and Pierre Karila-Cohen (Paris, 2008), p.27-40.

–, 'L'histoire de la police après Foucault: un parcours historien', *Revue d'histoire moderne et contemporaine* 60:4 (2013), p.139-55.

–, 'The invention of mobility and the history of the state', *French historical studies* 29:3 (2006), p.359-77.

–, 'Les Parisiens, la police et le numérotage des maisons du XVIIIᵉ siècle à l'Empire', *French historical studies* 38:1 (2015), p.83-103.

–, 'Peut-on réformer un "monument de la police"? La réforme de la police de Strasbourg en débat à la fin de l'Ancien Régime, 1782-1788', in *Réformer la police: les mémoires policiers en Europe au XVIIIᵉ siècle*, ed. Catherine Denys *et al.* (Rennes, 2009), p.131-50.

–, *Policiers de Paris: les commissaires de police en Révolution, 1789-1799* (Ceyzérieu, 2022).

–, 'Quand la police a le goût de l'archive: réflexions sur les archives de la police de Paris au XVIIIᵉ siècle', in *Pratiques d'archives à l'époque moderne: Europe, mondes coloniaux*, ed. Maria-Pia Donato and Anne Saada (Paris, 2019), p.183-203.

–, and Vincent Milliot, 'Police et

identification dans la France des Lumières', *Genèses* 54 (2004), p.4-27.

Denys, Catherine, *et al.* (ed.), *Réformer la police: les mémoires policiers en Europe au XVIIIe siècle* (Rennes, 2009).

Depaulis, Thierry, 'Between Germany and France: cardmakers in Landau and Kehl', *The Playing-card* 49:2 (2020), p.50-61.

–, 'Des "figures maussades & révoltantes": Diderot et les cartes à jouer', *Le Vieux Papier* 412 (2014), p.256-64; 413 (2014), p.289-98; 414 (2014), p.342-53; and 415 (2015), p.409-21.

–, 'Le portrait des cartes à Lyon: la Révolution et après', *Le Vieux Papier* 408 (2013), p.49-56 and plates 8 and 9.

Descimon, Robert, 'Les auxiliaires de justice du Châtelet de Paris: aperçus sur l'économie du monde des offices ministériels (XVIe-XVIIIe siècle)', in *Entre justice et justiciables: les auxiliaires de la justice du Moyen Age au XXe siècle*, ed. Claire Dolan (Quebec City, 2005), p.301-25.

–, and Jean Nagle, 'Les quartiers de Paris du Moyen Age au XVIIIe siècle', *Annales. Economies, sociétés, civilisations* 34:5 (1979), p.956-83.

Des confréries érigées en l'honneur des saints: traité moral et historique, dans lequel on s'attache particulièrement à combattre les abus qui y règnent (Avignon, n.n., 1714).

Des Essarts, Nicolas Toussaint Le Moyne, dit, *Dictionnaire universel de police contenant l'origine et les progrès de cette partie importante de l'administration civile en France*, 8 vols (Paris, Moutard, 1786-1790).

Deslon, Charles, *Observations sur le magnétisme animal* (London and Paris, n.n., 1780).

Desmette, Philippe, *Dans le sillage de la Réforme catholique: les confréries religieuses dans le nord du diocèse de Cambrai (1559-1786)* (Brussels, 2010).

Dewerpe, Alain, *Espion: une anthropologie historique du secret d'Etat contemporain* (Paris, 1994).

Dialogue entre deux citoyens représentants (Geneva, n.n., 1777).

Dialogues entre un citoyen de Genève et un étranger, à Genève, en mars 1765 (Geneva, n.n., 1765).

DiCaprio, Lisa, *The Origins of the welfare state: women, work, and the French Revolution* (Champaign, IL, 2007).

Dictionnaire de l'Académie française, 4th edn (Paris, La Veuve de Bernard Brunet, 1762).

Diderot, Denis, *Le Neveu de Rameau*, ed. Roland Desné (Paris, 1972).

–, and Jean D'Alembert (ed.), *Encyclopédie, ou Dictionnaire raisonné des arts, des sciences et des métiers*, 17 vols (Paris, Briasson, 1751-1772).

Dolan, Claire (ed.), *Entre justice et justiciables: les auxiliaires de la justice du Moyen Age au XXe siècle* (Quebec City, 2005).

– (ed.), *Les Pratiques politiques dans les villes françaises d'Ancien Régime: communauté, citoyenneté et localité* (Rennes, 2018).

Donaldson, Iml, 'Antoine de Lavoisier's role in designing a single-blind trial to assess whether "animal magnetism" exists', *Journal of the Royal Society of Medicine* 110:4 (2017), p.163-67.

Dosworth, F. M., 'The idea of police in eighteenth-century England: discipline, reformation, superintendance, c. 1780-1800', *Journal of the history of ideas* 69:4 (2008), p.583-604.

Dreyfus, Ferdinand, 'L'Association de bienfaisance judiciaire (1787-1791)', *La Révolution française* 46 (1904), p.385-411.

Driancourt-Girod, Janine, *Ainsi priaient les luthériens: la vie religieuse, la pratique et la foi des luthériens de Paris au XVIIIe siècle* (Paris, 1992).

–, *L'Insolite Histoire des luthériens de Paris: de Louis XIII à Napoléon* (Paris, 1992).

Du Bois-Melly, Charles, *Les Mœurs genevoises de 1700 à 1760 d'après les documents officiels* (Geneva, 1882).

Dufour, Alfred, *Histoire de Genève* (Paris, 1997).

Dupont-Ferrier, Gustave, *Du Collège de Clermont au Lycée Louis-le-Grand, 1563-1920*, 3 vols (Paris, 1921-1925).

Dupuy, Roger, *La Garde nationale, 1789-1871* (Paris, 2011).

Durand, Yves, *Les Fermiers généraux au XVIIIe siècle* (Paris, 1971).

Durand de Maillane, Pierre-Toussaint, *Dictionnaire de droit canonique et de pratique bénéficiale*, 2 vols (Paris, n.n., 1761).

Dwyer, John A., and Richard B. Sher (ed.), *Sociability and society in eighteenth-century Scotland* (Edinburgh, 1993).

Dyonet, Nicole, 'L'ordre public est-il l'objet de la police dans le *Traité* de Delamare?', in *Ordonner et partager la ville, XVIIe-XIXe siècle*, ed. Gaël Rideau and Pierre Serna (Rennes, 2011), p.47-74.

Echeverria, Durand, *The Maupeou revolution: a study in the history of libertarianism, France, 1770-1774* (Baton Rouge, LA, 1985).

Edit de la République de Genève, du 22 février 1770: avec des notes pour servir d'éclaircissement au présent édit (Geneva, n.n., 1770).

Edit de pacification du 21 novembre 1782, imprimé par ordre du gouvernement (Geneva, n.n., 1782).

Essai sur le pour et le contre relatif à la comédie, ou Dialogue entre Ariste et Philon, recueilli soigneusement par l'auteur (Geneva, n.n., 1776).

Factum pour les maîtres, gouverneurs et administrateurs, tant anciens qu'en charge, de la confrérie du S. Sacrement de l'Autel, première érigée en l'église paroissiale S. Nicolas-des-Champs […] contre maître François Mommignon, […] curé de ladite paroisse (Paris, n.n., 1682).

Farge, Arlette, *Dire et mal dire: l'opinion publique au XVIIIe siècle* (Paris, 1992).

–, *Fragile lives: violence, power, and solidarity in eighteenth-century Paris* (1986; Cambridge, 1993).

–, *Le Vol d'aliments à Paris au XVIIIe siècle* (Paris, 1974).

–, and Michel Foucault, *Disorderly families: infamous letters from the Bastille Archives* (1982), translated by Thomas Scott-Railton (Minneapolis, MN, 2016).

Farge, Arlette, and Jacques Revel,

The Vanishing children of Paris: rumors and politics before the French Revolution (1988; Cambridge, MA, 1993).

Farge, Arlette, and André Zysberg, 'Les théâtres de la violence à Paris au XVIIIe siècle', *Annales. Economie, sociétés, civilisations* 34:5 (1979), p.984-1015.

Ferrand, Nathalie, 'Jean-Jacques Rousseau: le dernier état de la *Lettre à D'Alembert sur les spectacles* (1758)', *Genesis* 34 (2012), p.135-57.

Ferrière, Claude-Joseph, *Dictionnaire de droit et de pratique*, 2 vols (Paris, Chez Brunet, 1749).

Ferrone, Vincenzo, and Daniel Roche (ed.), *Le Monde des Lumières* (Paris, 1993).

Fontaine, Laurence, *Histoire du colportage en Europe* (Paris, 1993).

–, *Vivre pauvre: quelques enseignements tirés de l'Europe des Lumières* (Paris, 2022).

Fosseyeux, Marcel, 'La dévolution des biens de l'hôpital Saint-Jacques-aux-Pèlerins aux XVIIe et XVIIIe siècles', *Bulletin de la Société de l'histoire de Paris et de l'Ile-de-France* 41 (1914), p.117-34.

Foucault, Michel, *Histoire de la folie à l'âge classique* (Paris, 1972).

–, *History of sexuality: an introduction* (1978; New York, 1990).

–, *The Punitive society: lectures at the Collège de France, 1972-1973*, ed. Bernard Harcourt (New York, 2015).

[Fournel, Jean-François], *Mémoire pour Me Charles Louis Varnier, docteur régent de la Faculté de médecine de Paris et membre de la Société royale de médecine, appelant d'un décret de la faculté* (Paris, n.n., 1785).

Franklin, Alfred, *Dictionnaire historique des arts, métiers et professions exercés dans Paris depuis le treizième siècle* (Paris, 1906).

Fréminville, Edme de La Poix de, *Dictionnaire, ou Traité de la police générale des villes, bourgs, paroisses et seigneuries de la campagne* (Paris, n.n., 1771).

Freundlich, Francis, *Le Monde du jeu à Paris, 1715-1800* (Paris, 1995).

Froeschlé-Chopard, Marie-Hélène, *Dieu pour tous et Dieu pour soi: histoire des confréries et de leurs images à l'époque moderne* (Paris, 2006).

Fumaroli, Marc, *Quand l'Europe parlait français* (Paris, 2001).

Funck-Brentano, Frantz, *Les Lettres de cachet à Paris, étude suivie d'une liste des prisonniers de la Bastille (1659-1789)* (Paris, 1903).

Garnier, Bernard, 'Les marchés aux bestiaux: Paris et sa banlieue', *Cahiers d'histoire* 42:3/4 (1997), special issue: *L'Animal domestique, XVIe-XXe siècle*, http://ch.revues.org/310 (last accessed on 19 January 2024).

Garrioch, David, 'Confréries de métier et corporations à Paris (XVIIe-XVIIIe siècle)', *Revue d'histoire moderne et contemporaine* 65 (2018), p.95-117.

–, 'Les confréries religieuses, espace d'autonomie laïque à Paris au XVIIIe siècle', in *La Religion vécue: les laïcs dans l'Europe moderne*, ed. Laurence Croq and

David Garrioch (Rennes, 2013), p.143-63.

–, *The Formation of the Parisian bourgeoisie, 1690-1830* (Cambridge, MA, and London, 1996).

–, *The Huguenots of Paris and the coming of religious freedom, 1685-1789* (Cambridge, 2014).

–, *The Making of revolutionary Paris* (Berkeley, CA, 2002).

–, 'Mutual aid societies in eighteenth-century Paris', *French history and civilization* 4 (2011), p.22-33.

–, *Neighbourhood and community in Paris, 1740-1790* (Cambridge, 1986).

–, 'The paternal government of men: the self-image and action of the Paris police in the eighteenth century', in *A History of police and masculinities, 1700-2010*, ed. David G. Barrie and Susan Broomhall (London and New York, 2012), p.35-54.

–, 'The people of Paris and their police in the eighteenth century: reflections on the introduction of a "modern" police force', *European history quarterly* 24 (1994), p.511-35.

–, 'The police of Paris as enlightened social reformers', *Eighteenth century life* 16:1 (1992), p.43-59.

–, 'La sécularisation précoce de Paris au dix-huitième siècle', *SVEC* 2005:12, p.35-75.

–, 'Why didn't Paris burn in the seventeenth and eighteenth centuries?', *French historical studies* 42:1 (2019), p.35-64.

–, and Michael Sonenscher, 'Compagnonnages, confraternities and associations of journeymen in eighteenth-century Paris', *European history quarterly* 16 (1986), p.25-45.

Gaston, Jean, *Les Images des confréries parisiennes avant la Révolution* (Paris, 1910).

Gauld, Alan, *A History of hypnotism* (Cambridge, 1995).

Gauthier, Aubin, *Histoire du somnambulisme*, 2 vols (Paris, 1842).

Gauvard, Claude, and Jean-Louis Robert (ed.), *Etre Parisien* (Paris, 2004).

Gay, Jean-Lucien, 'L'adminis-tration de la capitale entre 1770 et 1789: la tutelle de la royauté et ses limites', *Mémoires de la Fédération des sociétés historiques et archéologiques de Paris et de l'Ile-de-France* 8:12 (1956-1961), p.299-370.

Gelfand, Toby, *Professionalizing modern medicine: Paris surgeons and medical science and institutions in the 18th century* (London, 1980).

Genequand, Christiane (ed.), *Sociétés et cabinets de lecture entre Lumières et romantisme* (Geneva, 1995).

Genet, Stéphane, *Les Espions des Lumières: actions secrètes et espionnage militaire sous Louis XV* (Paris, 2013).

Gerard, Kent, and Gert Hekma (ed.), *The Pursuit of sodomy: male homosexuality in Renaissance and Enlightenment Europe* (New York and London, 1989).

Girard, Ariane, 'Le théâtre des Bastions', *Revue du Vieux Genève* (1992), p.14-21.

–, 'Les théâtres de la région

genevoise au temps de Voltaire', in *Voltaire chez lui: Genève et Ferney*, ed. Jean-Daniel Candaux and Erica Deuber-Pauli (Geneva, 1994), p.83-104.

Girard Des Bergeries, Jacob, *Le Gouvernement de la santé* (Geneva, Jean Hermann Widerhold, 1672).

Godineau, Dominique, *Les Femmes dans la société française, XVIᵉ-XVIIIᵉ siècle* (Paris, 2003).

Goudet-Caille, Pierre, *Réponse au remerciement d'un faux négatif, par un véritable ami de la liberté* (Geneva, n.n., 1780).

Gouzi, Christine, 'Tapisseries nomades et déplacements de sacralité dans l'espace paroissial parisien au XVIIIᵉ siècle', *Europa moderna: revue d'histoire et d'iconologie* 4 (2014), p.40-57.

Goyau, Georges, *La Pensée religieuse de Joseph de Maistre* (Paris, 1921).

Graham, Lisa Jane, *If the king only knew: seditious speech in the reign of Louis XV* (Charlottesville, VA, 2000).

–, 'Scandal: law, literature and morality in the early Enlightenment', *SVEC* 2005:04, p.232-40.

Gras, Marie-Carmen, 'Les processions en l'honneur de sainte Geneviève à Paris: miroir d'une société (XVᵉ-XVIIIᵉ siècles)', *Histoire urbaine* 3:32 (2011), p.5-30.

Grenier, Jean-Yves, 'Temps de travail et fêtes religieuses au XVIIIᵉ siècle', *Revue historique* 663 (2012), p.609-41.

Gribaudi, Maurizio, *Paris ville ouvrière: une histoire occultée, 1789-1848* (Paris, 2014).

Grimm, F. M., *Correspondance littéraire, philosophique et critique par Grimm, Diderot, Raynal, Meister, etc.*, ed. Maurice Tourneux, 16 vols (Paris, 1877-1882).

Grosse, Christian, *Les Rituels de la Cène: le culte eucharistique réformé à Genève (XVIᵉ-XVIIᵉ siècles)* (Geneva, 2008).

Guyot, Joseph-Nicolas, *Répertoire universel et raisonné de jurisprudence civile, criminelle, canonique et bénéficiale*, 64 vols (Paris, n.n., 1775-1783).

Halévi, Ran, *Les Loges maçonniques dans la France d'Ancien Régime, aux origines de la sociabilité démocratique* (Paris, 1984).

Hamon, Philippe, and Catherine Laurent (ed.), *Le Pouvoir municipal en France de la fin du Moyen Age à 1789* (Rennes, 2012).

Hardwick, Julie, *Sex in an Old Regime city: young workers and intimacy in France, 1660-1789* (Oxford, 2020).

Hardy, Siméon-Prosper, *Mes loisirs, ou Journal d'événemens tels qu'ils parviennent à ma connoissance (1753-1789)*, ed. Pascal Bastien *et al.*, 11 vols (Paris, 2012-2024).

Hensinger, Eliane, 'La prostitution et la police des mœurs au XVIIIᵉ siècle à Paris', *Mappemonde* 2 (1988), p.40-44.

Herlaut, Auguste-Philippe, 'L'éclairage des rues à Paris de la fin du XVIIᵉ au XVIIIᵉ siècle', *Paris et Ile-de-France: mémoire* 43 (1916), p.130-240.

Hiler, David, 'Permanences et innovations alimentaires: l'évolution de la consommation des Genevois pendant le XVIIIᵉ siècle', *Bulletin de la Société d'histoire et d'archéologie de Genève* (1989), p.23-47.

Hillairet, Jacques, *Dictionnaire historique des rues de Paris*, vol.2 (Paris, 1960).

Huguenin, Séverine, and Timothée Léchot (ed.), *Lectures du Journal helvétique, 1732-1782* (Geneva, 2016).

Hunt, Lynn, *The Family romance of the French Revolution* (Berkeley, CA, 1992).

–, 'Révolution française et vie privée', in *Histoire de la vie privée*, ed. Georges Duby and Philippe Ariès, vol.4: *De la Révolution à la Grande Guerre*, ed. Michelle Perrot (Paris, 1985), p.21-52.

Hurtaut, Pierre Thomas, and Claude Drigon de Magny, *Dictionnaire historique de Paris*, 4 vols (Paris, n.n., 1779).

Instructions et prières tirées de l'Ecriture sainte et des Saints Pères, pour la confrérie de Saint Jean Baptiste, érigée en l'église royale de Saint-Victor-lez-Paris (Paris, n.n., 1684).

Isambert, François-André, *et al.*, *Recueil général des anciennes lois françaises, depuis 420 jusqu'à la Révolution de 1789*, 29 vols (Paris, 1821-1833).

[Ivernois, Francis d'], *Tableau historique et politique des deux dernières révolutions*, 2 vols (London, n.n., 1789).

Jacques, Martine, 'Louis-Antoine Caraccioli: une certaine vision de l'Europe française', *Revue d'histoire littéraire de la France* 4 (2014), p.829-42.

Jacquet, Marie-Elisabeth, 'Vie et mort d'un dépôt d'archives: les archives de la Bastille dans les années 1780', *Circé: histoire, savoirs, sociétés* 16:1 (2022), http://www.revue-circe.uvsq.fr/vie-et-mort-dun-depot-darchives-les-archives-de-la-bastille-dans-les-annees-1780/ (last accessed on 16 January 2024).

Jarvis, Katie, *Politics in the marketplace: work, gender, and citizenship in revolutionary France* (Oxford, 2019).

Jean-Marie, Laurence (ed.), *La Notabilité urbaine Xᵉ-XVIIIᵉ siècles* (Caen, 2007).

Jones, Colin, 'The great chain of buying: medical advertisement, the bourgeois public sphere, and the origins of the French Revolution', *American historical review* 101:1 (1996), p.13-40.

Journal helvétique, ou Recueil de pièces fugitives de littérature choisie, 63 vols (Neuchâtel, n.n., 1738-1769).

Julia, Dominique, 'Jansénisme et "déchristianisation"', in *Histoire de la France religieuse*, vol.3: *Du roi très chrétien à la laïcité républicaine*, ed. Philippe Joutard (Paris, 1991), p.249-57.

Juratic, Sabine, and Nicole Pellegrin, 'Femmes, villes et travail en France dans la deuxième moitié du XVIIIᵉ siècle', *Histoire, économie et société* 3 (1994), p.477-500.

Jussieu, Antoine Laurent de, *Rapport de l'un des commissaires chargés par le roi de l'examen du magnétisme animal* (Paris, veuve Hérissant, 1784).

Kale, Steven D., *French salons: high society and political sociability from the Old Regime to the Revolution of 1848* (Baltimore, MD, 2004).

Kalifa, Dominique, and Pierre Karila-Cohen (ed.), *Le Commissaire de police au XIXᵉ siècle* (Paris, 2008).

Kaplan, Steven Laurence, *La Fin des corporations* (Paris, 2001).

–, 'Idéologie, conflits et pratiques politiques dans les corporations parisiennes au XVIIIᵉ siècle', *Revue d'histoire moderne et contemporaine* 49:1 (2002), p.5-55.

–, 'Note sur les commissaires de police de Paris au XVIIIᵉ siècle', *Revue d'histoire moderne et contemporaine* 28:4 (1981), p.669-86.

–, 'The Paris Bread Riot of 1725', *French historical studies* 14:1 (1985), p.23-56.

–, *Raisonner sur les blés: essais sur les Lumières économiques* (Paris, 2017).

–, 'Réflexions sur la police du monde du travail, 1700-1815', *Revue historique* 529 (1979), p.17-77.

–, and Vincent Milliot, 'La police de Paris, une "révolution permanente"? Du commissaire Lemaire au lieutenant de police Lenoir, les tribulations du *Mémoire sur l'administration de la police* (1770-1792)', in *Réformer la police: les mémoires policiers en Europe au XVIIIᵉ siècle*, ed.

Catherine Denys *et al.* (Rennes, 2009), p.69-115.

Kaplow, Jeffry, *The Names of kings: the Parisian laboring poor in the eighteenth century* (New York, 1972).

Kavanagh, Thomas, *Enlightened pleasures: eighteenth-century France and the new Epicureanism* (New Haven, CT, 2010).

Kerien, Goulven, *Pour l'honneur des familles: les enfermements par lettres de cachet à Paris au XVIIIᵉ siècle* (Ceyzérieu, 2023).

Klauber, Martin I., *Between Reformed scholasticism and pan-Protestantism: Jean-Alphonse Turretin (1671-1737) and the enlightened orthodoxy at the Academy of Geneva* (Selinsgrove, PA, 1994).

Koslofsky, Craig, *Evening's empire: a history of the night in early modern Europe* (Cambridge, 2011).

Kreiser, B. Robert, *Miracles, convulsions, and ecclesiastical politics in early eighteenth-century Paris* (Princeton, NJ, 1978).

Kunz-Aubert, Ulysse, *Spectacles d'autrefois (à Genève au XVIIIᵉ siècle)* (Geneva, 1925).

Kushner, Nina, *Erotic exchanges: the world of elite prostitution in eighteenth-century Paris* (Ithaca, NY, 2013).

Kwass, Michael, *Contraband: Louis Mandrin and the making of a global underground* (Cambridge, 2014).

La Corbière, Matthieu de (ed.), *Genève, ville forte: les monuments d'art et d'histoire du canton de Genève III* (Berne, 2010).

Laffont, Jean-Luc, 'Policer la ville: Toulouse, capitale provinciale au siècle des Lumières', doctoral dissertation, Université Toulouse II Le Mirail, 1997, 3 vols.

Lamarre, Christine, 'Les jeux militaires au XVIIIᵉ siècle: une forme de sociabilité urbaine négligée', *Histoire urbaine* 5:1 (2002), p.85-103.

La Pradelle, Michèle de, *Les Vendredis de Carpentras: faire son marché en Provence ou ailleurs* (Paris, 1996).

Laqueur, Thomas, *Solitary sex: a cultural history of masturbation* (New York, 2004).

Lavoisier, Antoine Laurent, *Correspondance*, vol.4: *1784-1786*, ed. Michelle Goupil (Paris, 2012).

–, 'Sur le magnétisme animal', in *Œuvres de Lavoisier*, vol.3 (Paris, 1865), p.499-527.

Le Bihan, Alain, *Francs-maçons et ateliers parisiens de la Grande Loge de France au XVIIIᵉ siècle (1760-1795)* (Paris, 1973).

Le Cler Du Brillet, Anne, *Continuation du Traité de la police*, vol.4: *De la voirie* (Paris, Chez Jean-François Hérissant, 1738).

Leçon nécessaire à un professeur étranger donnée par un citoyen de Genève (Geneva, n.n., 1781).

Légier-Desgranges, Henry, *Du jansénisme à la Révolution: Mme de Moysan et l'extravagante affaire de l'Hôpital général, 1749-1758* (Paris, 1954).

Lemaire, Jean-Baptiste-Charles, 'La police de Paris en 1770: mémoire inédit composé par ordre de G. de Sartine, sur la demande de Marie-Thérèse', ed. André

Gazier, *Mémoires de la Société de l'histoire de Paris* 5 (1879), p.1-131.

Le Roux, Thomas, 'Les effondrements de carrières de Paris: la grande réforme des années 1770', *French historical studies* 36 (2013), p.205-37.

Lettre d'un citoyen de Genève à M.*** (Geneva, n.n., 1781).

Lettre d'un citoyen de Genève à un autre citoyen (Geneva, n.n., 1768).

Lettre d'un membre du cercle des Bons Ragoûts (Geneva, n.n., 1779).

Lettres patentes du roi sur le décret de l'Assemblée nationale […] concernant la municipalité de Paris (Paris, n.n., 1790).

Leuwers, Hervé, 'Pratiques, réseaux et espaces de sociabilité au temps de la Révolution française', in *La Révolution à l'œuvre*, ed. Jean-Clément Martin (Rennes, 2005), p.41-55.

Leveillé Mettral, Lia, 'Le théâtre des Bastions (1783-1791): la vie théâtrale à Genève au XVIIIᵉ siècle', MA dissertation, Université de Genève, 2016.

Lilti, Antoine, *The Invention of celebrity* (2014; New York, 2017).

–, *Le Monde des salons: sociabilité et mondanité à Paris au XVIIIᵉ siècle* (Paris, 2005).

–, *The World of the salons: sociability and worldliness in eighteenth-century Paris* (2005; Oxford, 2015).

Logette, Aline, 'La Régie générale au temps de Necker et de ses successeurs (1777-1786)', *Revue historique de droit français et étranger* 60:3 (1982), p.415-45.

Loiselle, Kenneth, *Brotherly love: Freemasonry and male friendship in*

Enlightenment France (Ithaca, NY, and London, 2014).

Lothe, José, and Agnès Virole, *Images de confréries parisiennes: catalogue des images de confréries (Paris et Ile-de-France) de la collection de M. Louis Ferrand* (Paris, 1992).

Luckett, Thomas M., 'Hunting for spies and whores: a Parisian riot on the eve of the French Revolution', *Past and present* 156 (1997), p.116-43.

Lyon-Caen, Nicolas, *La Boîte à Perrette: le jansénisme parisien au XVIIIᵉ siècle* (Paris, 2010).

–, 'Les marchands du temple: les boutiques du Palais de justice de Paris aux XVIᵉ-XVIIIᵉ siècles', *Revue historique* 674 (2015), p.323-52.

–, 'Un "saint de nouvelle fabrique": le diacre Pâris (1690-1727), le jansénisme et la bonneterie parisienne', *Annales. Histoire, sciences sociales* 65 (2010), p.613-42.

–, 'Territoire paroissial et investissement notabiliaire: Marc-Etienne Quatremère et les limites de Saint-Germain-l'Auxerrois', *Hypothèses* 9 (2005), special issue: *L'Appropriation du territoire par les communautés*, ed. Nicolas Lyon-Caen, p.79-88.

–, and Mathieu Marraud, 'Multiplicité et unité communautaire à Paris: appartenances professionnelles et carrières civiques, XVIIᵉ-XVIIIᵉ siècles', *Histoire urbaine* 40:2 (2014), p.19-35.

–, and Raphaël Morera, *A vos poubelles citoyens! Environnement urbain, salubrité publique et investissement civique (Paris, XVIᵉ-XVIIIᵉ siècle)* (Ceyzérieu, 2020).

–, 'Naissance, réorganisation ou formalisation d'un système d'information? La propreté des rues de Paris, XVIᵉ-XVIIIᵉ siècles', *Flux* 1-2:111-12 (2018), p.44-56.

McHugh, Tim, *Hospital politics in seventeenth-century France: the crown, urban elites and the poor* (Ashgate, 2007).

McMahon, Darrin M., *Happiness: a history* (New York, 2006).

–, 'Writing the history of illumination in the *siècle des Lumières*: Enlightenment narratives of light', in *Let there be Enlightenment: the religious and mystical sources of rationality*, ed. Anton M. Matytsin and Dan Edelstein (Baltimore, MD, 2018), p.103-28.

McManners, John, *Church and society in eighteenth century France*, 2 vols (Oxford, 1998).

Maire, Catherine, *Les Convulsionnaires de Saint-Médard: miracles, convulsions et prophéties à Paris au XVIIIᵉ siècle* (Paris, 1985).

–, *De la cause de Dieu à la cause de la nation: le jansénisme au XVIIIᵉ siècle* (Paris, 1998).

Maissen, Thomas, 'Vers la république souveraine: Genève et les confédérés entre le droit public occidental et le droit impérial', *Bulletin de la Société d'histoire et d'archéologie de Genève* 29 (1999), p.3-27.

Majault, Michel-Joseph, *et al.*, *Rapport des commissaires chargés par le roi de l'examen du magnétisme animal* (Paris, Imprimerie royale, 1784); English translation: Benjamin Franklin *et al.*, 'Report of the commissioners charged by the king with the examination of animal magnetism', *International journal of clinical and experimental hypnosis* 50:4 (2002), p.332-63.

Malandain, Gilles, 'Les mouches de la police et le vol des mots: les gazetins de la police secrète et la surveillance de l'expression à Paris au deuxième quart du XVIIIe siècle', *Revue d'histoire moderne et contemporaine* 42:3 (1995), p.376-404.

Manuel, Pierre, *La Police de Paris dévoilée, par Pierre Manuel, l'un des administrateurs de 1789*, 2 vols (Paris, n.n., 1790).

Marin, Brigitte, 'Administrations policières, réformes et découpages territoriaux (XVIIe-XIXe siècle)', *Mélanges de l'Ecole française de Rome: Italie et Méditerranée* 115:2 (2003), p.745-50.

Markovits, Rahul, 'Cercles et théâtre à Genève: les enjeux politiques et culturels d'une mutation de sociabilité (1758-1814)', in *Hypothèses 2008: travaux de l'Ecole doctorale d'histoire de l'Université Paris 1 Panthéon-Sorbonne* (Paris, 2009), p.273-83.

–, *Civiliser l'Europe: politiques du théâtre français au XVIIIe siècle* (Paris, 2014).

Marraud, Mathieu, 'Le cérémonial urbain à Paris au XVIIIe siècle: représentation et négociation politique', in *Les Histoires de Paris (XVIe-XVIIIe siècle)*, ed. Thierry Belleguic and Laurent Turcot, 2 vols (Paris, 2012), vol.1, p.245-67.

–, 'Communauté conjugale et communauté politique: les usages de la coutume de Paris dans la bourgeoisie corporative, XVIIe-XVIIIe siècles', *Revue d'histoire moderne et contemporaine* 58 (2011), p.96-119.

–, *De la ville à l'Etat: la bourgeoisie parisienne, XVIIe-XVIIIe siècle* (Paris, 2009).

–, *Le Pouvoir marchand: corps et corporatisme à Paris sous l'Ancien Régime* (Ceyzérieu, 2021).

Martin de Saint-Léon, Edme, *Le Compagnonnage* (Paris, 1977).

Mauzi, Robert, *L'Idée du bonheur dans la littérature et la pensée françaises au XVIIIe siècle* (Paris, 1969).

Maza, Sarah, *Private lives and public affairs: the causes célèbres of prerevolutionary France* (Berkeley, CA, 1993).

Mellot, Jean-Dominique, *et al.*, *La Police des métiers du livre à Paris au siècle des Lumières* (Paris, 2017).

Melzer, Sara E., *Colonizer or colonized: the hidden stories of early modern French culture* (Philadelphia, PA, 2012).

Mercier, Louis-Sébastien, *Tableau de Paris* (1781-1788), ed. Jean-Claude Bonnet, 2 vols (Paris, 1994).

Mercier-Faivre, Anne-Marie, 'La science au quotidien: l'affaire Mesmer dans le *Journal de Paris* (1783-84)', in *Metamorfosi dei Lumi*, ed. Simone Messina and Paola Trivero, vol.6 (Turin, 2017), p.148-68.

Merrick, Jeffrey, *The Desacralization of the French monarchy in the eighteenth century* (Baton Rouge, LA, and London, 1990).

–, 'Sodomitical inclinations in early eighteenth-century Paris', *Eighteenth-century studies* 30:3 (1997), p.280-95.

–, 'Sodomitical scandals and subcultures in the 1720s', *Men and masculinities* 1:4 (1999), p.365-84.

Mesmer, Franz Anton, *Le Magnétisme animal: œuvres*, ed. Robert Amadou (Paris, 1971).

–, *Mémoire de F. A. Mesmer, docteur en médecine, sur ses découvertes* (Paris, Fuchs, 1799).

–, *Précis historique des faits relatifs au magnétisme animal jusqu'en avril 1781* (London, n.n., 1781).

Métayer, Christine, *Au tombeau des secrets: les écrivains publics du Paris populaire – cimetière des Saints-Innocents, XVIe-XVIIIe siècle* (Paris, 2000).

Milliot, Vincent, *'L'Admirable Police': tenir Paris au siècle des Lumières* (Ceyzérieu, 2016).

–, 'Aimer et détester la police? Le peuple et les polices au siècle des Lumières', in *Paris et ses peuples au XVIIIe siècle*, ed. Pascal Bastien and Simon Macdonald (Paris, 2020), p.49-64.

–, 'Ecrire pour policer: les "mémoires" policiers, 1750-1850', in *Les Mémoires policiers, 1750-1850: écritures et pratiques policières du siècle des Lumières au Second Empire*, ed. Vincent Milliot (Rennes, 2006), p.15-41.

– (ed.), *Les Mémoires policiers, 1750-1850: écritures et pratiques policières du siècle des Lumières au Second Empire* (Rennes, 2006).

–, 'La police parisienne dans la tourmente: la bousculade de la rue Royale et ses retombées (Paris, 30 mai 1770)', in *Una storia di rigore e di passione: saggi per Livio Antonielli*, ed. Stefano Levati and Simona Mori (Milan, 2018), p.317-40.

–, *Un Policier des Lumières, suivi de Mémoires de J. C. P. Lenoir, ancien lieutenant général de police de Paris, écrits en pays étrangers dans les années 1790 et suivantes* (Seyssel, 2011).

–, 'Réformer les polices urbaines au siècle des Lumières: le révélateur de la mobilité', *Crime, histoire & sociétés* 10:1 (2006), p.25-50.

–, 'Saisir l'espace urbain: mobilité des commissaires et contrôle des quartiers de police à Paris au XVIIIe siècle', *Revue d'histoire moderne et contemporaine* 50:1 (2003), p.54-80.

–, 'La surveillance des migrants et des lieux d'accueil à Paris du XVIe siècle aux années 1830', in *La Ville promise: mobilité et accueil à Paris (fin XVIIe-début XIXe siècle)*, ed. Daniel Roche (Paris, 2000), p.21-76.

Minard, Philippe, *Typographes des Lumières* (Paris, 1989).

Moheau, Jean-Baptiste, *Recherches et considérations sur la population de la France, 1778*, ed. Eric Vilquin (Paris, 1994).

Monod, Paul, *The Power of kings: monarchy and religion in Europe, 1589-1715* (New Haven, CT, 1999).

Mostefai, Ourida, *Le Citoyen de Genève et la République des Lettres: étude sur la controverse autour de la*

Lettre à D'Alembert de Jean-Jacques Rousseau (New York, 2003).

Moulin, Annie, *Les Maçons de la Creuse: les origines du mouvement* (Clermont-Ferrand, 1994).

Muyart de Vouglans, Pierre-François, *Institutes au droit criminel* (Paris, n.n., 1757).

Napoli, Paolo, *Naissance de la police moderne: pouvoirs, normes, société* (Paris, 2003).

Neuenschwander, Marc, 'Les troubles de 1782 à Genève et le temps de l'émigration: en marge du bicentenaire de la naissance du général Guillaume-Henri Dufour', *Bulletin de la Société d'histoire et d'archéologie de Genève* 19 (1989), p.127-88.

Noiriel, Gérard, 'Les pratiques policières d'identification des migrants et leurs enjeux pour l'histoire des relations de pouvoir: contribution à une réflexion en "longue durée"', in *Police et migrants en France, 1667-1939*, ed. Marie-Claude Blanc-Chaléard (Rennes, 2001), p.115-32.

Nougaret, Pierre-Jean-Baptiste, *Tableau mouvant de Paris, ou Variétés amusantes*, 3 vols (London and Paris, n.n., 1787).

Nouis, Lucien, 'La *Lettre à D'Alembert*, ou l'inscription européenne du républicanisme', *Lumen, Canadian Society for Eighteenth-Century Studies / Société canadienne d'étude du dix-huitième siècle* 30 (2011), p.99-112.

Nouvelle défense apologétique des citoyens et bourgeois représentants de Genève (Geneva, n.n., 1781).

Orain, Arnaud, *La Politique du merveilleux: une autre histoire du Système de Law (1695-1795)* (Paris, 2018).

Ozouf, Mona, *Festivals and the French Revolution* (Cambridge, MA, 1991).

Pardailhé-Galabrun, Annik, 'Les déplacements des Parisiens dans la ville aux XVIIe et XVIIIe siècles: un essai de problématique', *Histoire, économie et société* 2 (1983), p.205-53.

Pary, Etienne-Olivier, *Guide des corps des marchands et des communautés des arts et métiers tant de la ville et fauxbourgs de Paris, que du royaume* (Paris, n.n., 1766).

Pastureau, Guillaume, 'L'argent secours sous l'Ancien Régime: le cas du Mont-de-Piété', in *Argent, commerce et échange sous l'Ancien Régime*, ed. Anne-Sophie Fournier-Plamondon and Andrée-Anne Plourde (Paris, 2016), p.27-45.

Pattie, Frank A., *Mesmer and animal magnetism: a chapter in the history of medicine* (Hamilton, NY, 1994).

Paulet, Jean-Jacques, *L'Antimagnétisme, ou Origine, progrès, décadence, renouvellement et réfutation du magnétisme animal* (London, n.n., 1784).

–, *Mesmer justifié* (Constance and Paris, Chez les libraires qui vendent les nouveautés, 1784).

–, 'Les miracles de M. Mesmer', *Gazette de santé* 28 (9 July 1780) and 29 (16 July 1780).

[–], *Réponse à l'auteur des Doutes d'un provincial* (Paris, n.n., 1785).

Peveri, Patrice, '"Cette ville était alors comme un bois…":

criminalité et opinion publique à Paris dans les années qui précèdent l'affaire Cartouche (1715-1721)', *Crime, histoire & sociétés* 1:2 (1997), p.51-73.

–, 'Clandestinité et nouvel ordre policier dans le Paris de la Régence: l'arrestation de Louis-Dominique Cartouche', in *Clandestinités urbaines: les citadins et les territoires du secret (XVIᵉ-XXᵉ siècle)*, ed. Sylvie Aprile and Emmanuelle Retaillaud-Bajac (Rennes, 2008), p.151-70.

Philipon de La Madelaine, Louis, *Vues patriotiques sur l'éducation du peuple, tant des villes que des campagnes* (Lyon, n.n., 1783).

Piasenza, Paolo, 'Juges, lieutenants de police et bourgeois à Paris aux XVIIᵉ et XVIIIᵉ siècles', *Annales. Histoire, sciences sociales* 45:5 (1990), p.1189-1215.

–, 'Opinion publique, identité des institutions, "absolutisme": le problème de la légalité à Paris entre le XVIIᵉ et le XVIIIᵉ siècle', *Revue historique* 587 (1993), p.97-142.

–, *Polizia e città: strategie d'ordine, conflitti e rivolte a Parigi tra sei e settecento* (Bologna, 1990).

–, 'Rapimenti, polizia e rivolta: un conflitto sull'ordine pubblico a Parigi nel 1750', *Quaderni storici* 22:64 (1987), p.129-51.

Pinard, Adolphe, *et al.*, *Commentaires de la Faculté de médecine: 1777 à 1786*, 2 vols (Paris, 1903).

Pinet, Edouard, *La Compagnie des porteurs de la châsse de sainte Geneviève, 1525-1902* (Paris, 1903).

Pitassi, Maria-Cristina, *De l'orthodoxie aux Lumières: Genève, 1670-1737* (Geneva, 1992).

Pitteloud, Patrick, 'Une société de lecture bien discrète à Genève au XVIIIᵉ siècle: la Société littéraire, 1760-1792', BA dissertation, Université de Genève, 1979.

Piuz, Anne-Marie, and Liliane Mottu, *L'Economie genevoise de la Réforme à la fin de l'Ancien Régime: XVIᵉ-XVIIIᵉ siècles* (Geneva, 1990).

Plumauzille, Clyde, 'L'allaitement nourricier des petits Parisiens: naissance d'un service public au XVIIIᵉ siècle', in *Paris et ses peuples au XVIIIᵉ siècle*, ed. Pascal Bastien and Simon Macdonald (Paris, 2020), p.39-48.

–, 'Le "marché aux putains": économies sexuelles et dynamiques spatiales du Palais-Royal dans le Paris révolutionnaire', *Genre, sexualité & société* 10 (2013), special issue: *Eros parisien*, ed. Sylvie Chaperon *et al.*, https://journals.openedition. org/gss/2943 (last accessed on 25 January 2024).

–, *Prostitution et révolution: des femmes publiques dans la cité républicaine, 1789-1804* (Ceyzérieu, 2016).

Pocock, John Greville Agard, *The Machiavellian moment: Florentine political thought and the Atlantic republican tradition* (Princeton, NJ, 1975).

Poirson, Martial, 'De la police des spectacles à la civilisation des mœurs théâtrales: domestication du public et production des affects chez Louis-Sébastien Mercier', *Journal for eighteenth-century studies* 32:4 (2009), p.529-47.

Porret, Michel, 'L'"Epée de la justice" contre la "Roue de la fortune": guerre contre le jeu ou anathème contre le luxe? Le démantèlement d'un réseau de joueurs à Genève en 1774', *Revue du Vieux Genève* 20 (1990), p.13-23.

–, 'Genève républicaine au XVIIIe siècle: réalité des représentations et représentations de la réalité', *Mémoires de la Société de physique et d'histoire naturelle* 47 (1994), p.3-17.

–, 'Violence des "excès" et excès de la violence: aspects du quotidien genevois, 1760-1767', *Revue du Vieux Genève* (1988), p.2-19.

Poulot, Dominique, *Les Lumières* (Paris, 2000).

Le Pour et le contre sur ce qui s'est passé à Genève en février 1781 (Geneva, n.n., 1781).

Preto, Paolo, *I servizi segreti di venezia: spionaggio e controspionaggio ai tempi della Serenissima* (Milan, 2010).

Price, Munro, *The Fall of the French monarchy: Louis XVI, Marie-Antoinette and the baron de Breteuil* (London, 2002).

–, *Preserving the monarchy: the comte de Vergennes, 1774-1787* (Cambridge, 1995).

Puget, Julien, 'From public garden to public city: the controversy over the housing project at the Palais-Royal in 1781', *French history* 31:2 (2017), p.174-93.

Quétel, Claude, *De par le roy: essai sur les lettres de cachet* (Toulouse, 1981).

–, *Une Légende noire: les lettres de cachet* (Paris, 2011).

Rabier, Christelle, 'Le "service public" de la chirurgie: administration des premiers secours et pratiques professionnelles à Paris au XVIIIe siècle', *Revue d'histoire moderne et contemporaine* 58:1 (2011), p.101-27.

Raeff, Martin, *The Well-ordered police state: social and institutional change in the Germanies and Russia, 1600-1800* (London, 1983).

Raffestin, Claude, *Pour une géographie du pouvoir* (Paris, 1980).

Rainhorn, Judith, and Didier Terrier (ed.), *Etranges voisins: altérité et relations de proximité dans la ville depuis le XVIIIe siècle* (Rennes, 2010).

Rau, Suzanne, *Raüme der Stadt: eine Geschichte Lyons 1300-1800* (Frankfurt, 2014).

Ravel, Jeffrey S., *The Contested parterre: public theater and French political culture, 1680-1791* (Ithaca, NY, 1999).

Recueil des titres de la confrérie de Saint-Crespin et Saint-Crespinien (Paris, n.n., 1754).

Recueil de trois pièces dédiées aux amis de la liberté et de la patrie (Geneva, n.n., 1768).

Recueil d'instructions et de prières à l'usage de la confrairie du Saint Sacrement, érigée le 9 août 1690, en la paroisse de Sainte Marguerite, fauxbourg S. Antoine, à Paris (Paris, n.n., 1780).

Reculin, Sophie, 'Le règne de la nuit désormais va finir: l'invention et la diffusion de l'éclairage public dans le royaume de France, 1697-1789', doctoral dissertation, Université Charles de Gaulle – Lille III, 2017.

*Reglemens de la confrérie du
S. Sacrement de l'église paroissiale
de S. Barthelemy, donnez par son
éminence Monseigneur le cardinal de
Noailles* (Paris, n.n., 1708).

*Règlemens en forme de statuts, pour
la confrérie du Très-Saint-Sacrement, érigée en l'église paroissiale
de S. Médard de Paris, pour la
société des boursiers-confrères de
ladite confrérie, sous l'invocation de
S. Pierre* (Paris, n.n., 1783).

Règlement de l'illustre médiation
(Geneva, Frères de Tournes,
1738).

*Règlement des Frères tailleurs établi à
Paris en 1647 suivant le texte ancien
et nouveau, avec des éclaircissements
et des additions faites en l'an 1725*
(Delatour, n.n., 1727).

*Relation d'un voyage fait aux Indes
orientales* (Geneva, n.n., 1777).

Rey, Alain (ed.), *Dictionnaire
historique de la langue française*
(Paris, 1995).

Rey, Michel, 'Police and sodomy
in eighteenth-century Paris: from
sin to disorder', in *The Pursuit
of sodomy: male homosexuality in
Renaissance and Enlightenment
Europe*, ed. Kent Gerard and Gert
Hekma (New York and London,
1989), p.129-46.

Rideau, Gaël, and Pierre Serna
(ed.), *Ordonner et partager la
ville, XVIIᵉ-XIXᵉ siècle* (Rennes,
2011).

Rigogne, Thierry, 'Readers and
reading in cafés, 1660-1800',
French historical studies 41:3 (2018),
p.473-94.

Rivoire, Emile, *Bibliographie
historique du XVIIIᵉ siècle* (Geneva,
1897).

Robertson, Ritchie, *The Enlightenment: the pursuit of happiness,
1680-1790* (New York, 2021).

Robin, Pierre, *La Compagnie des
secrétaires du roi (1351-1791)* (Paris,
1933).

Roche, Daniel, 'Le cabaret parisien
et les manières de vivre du
peuple', in *Habiter la ville, XVᵉ-XXᵉ
siècle*, ed. Maurice Garden
and Yves Lequin (Lyon, 1984),
p.233-51.

–, *The Culture of clothing: dress and
fashion in the Ancien Régime* (1989;
Cambridge, 1997).

–, *France in the Enlightenment* (1993;
Cambridge, MA, 2000).

–, *A History of everyday things: the birth
of consumption in France, 1600-1800*
(1997; Cambridge, 2000).

– (ed.), *Jacques-Louis Ménétra: Journal
de ma vie, compagnon vitrier
au XVIIIᵉ siècle* (Paris, 1982).

–, *The People of Paris: an essay in
popular culture in the 18th century*
(1981; Berkeley, CA, 1987).

–, *Les Républicains des Lettres: gens de
culture et Lumières au XVIIIᵉ siècle*
(Paris, 1988).

–, *Le Siècle des Lumières en province:
académies et académiciens
provinciaux, 1680-1789*, 2 vols
(Paris, 1989).

– (ed.), *La Ville promise:
mobilité et accueil à Paris
(fin XVIIᵉ-début XIXᵉ siècle)* (Paris,
2000).

Rochon, Elisabeth, 'Le marché aux
chevaux de Paris (1662-1789): un
espace, des usages, une police',
doctoral dissertation, Université
du Québec à Montréal and
Université Paris 1, Panthéon-
Sorbonne, 2023.

Romano, Barbara, 'L'affaire des "comédies particulières": pratiques d'une sociabilité clandestine genevoise (1702-1782)', MA dissertation, Université de Genève, 2008.

Romon, Christian, 'L'affaire des "enlèvements d'enfants" dans les archives du Châtelet (1749-1750)', *Revue historique* 547 (1983), p.55-95.

–, 'Mendiants et policiers à Paris au XVIIIᵉ siècle', *Histoire, économie et société* 1:2 (1982), p.259-95.

Rousseau, Jean-Jacques, *Emile, or On education*, ed. Allan Bloom (Chicago, IL, 1979).

Roy, Jean-Michel, 'Les marchés alimentaires parisiens et l'espace urbain du XVIIᵉ au XIXᵉ siècle', *Histoire, économie et société* 17:4 (1998), p.693-710.

Royer, Jean-Pierre, *Histoire de la justice en France* (Paris, 1996).

Ruchon, François, *Histoire de la franc-maçonnerie à Genève de 1736 à 1900* (1935; Geneva, 2004).

Sack, Robert D., 'Human territoriality: a theory', *Annals of the Association of American Geographers* 73:1 (1983), p.55-74.

Sauval, Henri, *Histoire et recherches des antiquités de la ville de Paris*, vol.1 (Paris, C. Moette, 1724).

Sennett, Richard, *Flesh and stone: the body and the city in Western civilization* (New York, 1994).

Seppel, Marten, and Keith Tribe (ed.), *Cameralism in practice: state administration and economy in early modern Europe* (Cambridge, 2017).

Simiz, Stefano, *Confréries urbaines et dévotion en Champagne (1450-1830)* (Paris, 2002).

Singham, Shanti Marie, '"A conspiracy of twenty million Frenchmen": public opinion, patriotism, and the assault on absolutism during the Maupeou years, 1770-1775', doctoral dissertation, Princeton University, 1991.

Skinner, Quentin, *Machiavelli: a very short introduction* (Oxford, 1981).

La Solide Dévotion à la passion de Notre Seigneur Jésus-Christ, à l'usage des confrères et sœurs de la confrérie royale de la Passion du Sauveur et de Notre-Dame de Pitié (Paris, n.n., 1782).

Sonenscher, Michael, *Work and wages: natural law, politics and the eighteenth-century French trades* (New York, 1989).

Soulavie, Jean-Louis, *Mémoires politiques et historiques du règne de Louis XVI*, 6 vols (Paris, 1801).

Spitz, Jean-Fabien, *La Liberté politique: essai de généalogie conceptuelle* (Paris, 1995).

Starrenberger, Chantal, 'Etude de la fonction sociale et politique des cercles à Genève au XVIIIᵉ siècle à travers le cas du Cercle de l'artillerie, 1777-1782', MA dissertation, Université de Genève, 1980.

Strayer, Brian E., *Lettres de cachet and social control in the Ancien Régime, 1659-1789* (New York, 1992).

Swann, Julian, *Exile, imprisonment, or death: the politics of disgrace in Bourbon France, 1610-1789* (Oxford, 2017).

Tableau de l'Archiconfrairie royale du Saint-Sépulcre de Jérusalem [Paris, n.n., 1790].

Tableau de la situation politique de Genève en 1779 (Geneva, n.n. 1779).

Terpstra, Nicholas (ed.), *The Politics of ritual kinship: confraternities and social order in early modern Italy* (Cambridge, 2000).

Thiéry, Luc-Vincent, *Le Voyageur à Paris, extrait du Guide des amateurs & des étrangers voyageurs à Paris*, vol.2 (Paris, Chez Gattey, 1790).

Thouret, Michel-Augustin, *Recherches et doutes sur le magnétisme animal* (Paris, Prault, 1784).

Tilly, Charles, *The Contentious French* (Cambridge, MA, 1986).

Tourn, Christine, 'Aliments et médicaments: perspectives d'apothicaires "charitables" à Genève à la fin du XVIIe siècle', *Histoire des Alpes* (2008), p.195-213.

Touzery, Mireille, *L'Invention de l'impôt sur le revenu: la taille tarifée 1715-1789* (Paris, 1994).

Tricoire, Damien, *Die Aufklärung* (Cologne, 2023).

Turian, Véronique, 'Les caves et les cabarets à Genève et dans la banlieue au milieu du XVIIIe siècle', MA dissertation, Université de Genève, 1984.

Turrettini, Jean-Alphonse, *Sermon sur les inconvéniens du jeu, prononcé à Genève, le 9 mars 1727* (Geneva, n.n., 1727).

Vacher, Marc, 'Au bonheur de voisiner: sociabilités et solidarités dans les immeubles lyonnais au XVIIIe siècle', in *Etranges voisins: altérité et relations de proximité dans la ville depuis le XVIIIe siècle*, ed. Judith Rainhorn and Didier Terrier (Rennes, 2010), p.67-93.

–, *Voisins, voisines, voisinage: les cultures du face-à-face à Lyon à la veille de la Révolution* (Lyon, 2007).

Valade, Pauline, *Le Goût de la joie: réjouissances monarchiques et joie publique à Paris au XVIIIe siècle* (Ceyzérieu, 2021).

Van Damme, Stéphane, *A toutes voiles vers la vérité: une autre histoire de la philosophie* (Paris, 2014).

–, 'Farewell Habermas? Deux décennies d'études sur l'espace public', in *L'Espace public au Moyen Age: débat autour de Jürgen Habermas*, ed. Patrick Boucheron and Nicolas Offenstadt (Paris, 2015), p.43-61.

–, *Paris, capitale philosophique: de la Fronde à la Révolution* (Paris, 2005).

Vandenkoornhuyse-Davet, Isabelle, 'Policer Paris par la lumière (1667-1769)', MA dissertation, Université Paris Nanterre, 2018.

Van Kley, Dale K., *The Damiens affair and the unraveling of the Ancien Régime, 1750-1770* (Princeton, NJ, 1984).

–, *The Jansenists and the expulsion of the Jesuits from France, 1757-1765* (New Haven, CT, 1975).

–, *The Religious origins of the French Revolution: from Calvin to the Civil Constitution, 1560-1791* (New Haven, CT, 1996).

Venard, Marc, 'Si on parlait des confréries de métiers…', in *Sacralités, culture et dévotion: bouquet offert à Marie-Hélène Froeschlé-Chopard*, ed. Marc

Venard and Dominique Julia (Marseille, 2005), p.221-38.

Venturi, Franco, *Pagine repubblicane* (Turin, 2004).

–, '"Ubi libertas, ibi patria": la rivoluzione ginevrina del 1782', *Rivista storica italiana* 2 (1982), p.395-434.

Verri, Pietro (ed.), *Il Caffè, ossia brevi e varii discorsi*, 2 vols (Milan, 1804).

Vidoni, Nicolas, *La Police des Lumières, XVIIᵉ-XVIIIᵉ siècles* (Paris, 2018).

–, 'Une "police des Lumières"? La "violence" des agents de police à Paris au milieu du XVIIIᵉ siècle', *Rives méditerranéennes* 40 (2011), p.43-66.

Vilevault, Louis-Guillaume, and Louis-Georges de Bréquigny, *Ordonnances des rois de France de la troisième race*, vol.10 (Paris, Imprimerie royale, 1763).

Voltaire, *Essai sur les mœurs* (1756), 2 vols (Paris, 1829).

Vovelle, Michel, *Les Métamorphoses de la fête en Provence, 1750-1820* (Paris, 1976).

Walker, Corinne, *Musiciens et amateurs: le goût et les pratiques de la musique à Genève aux XVIIᵉ et XVIIIᵉ siècles* (Geneva, 2017).

–, '"Le plus joli joujou de notre globe": l'image de Genève dans les récits de voyage (XVIIᵉ-XVIIIᵉ siècle)', *Traverse* 2 (1994), p.17-31.

Wanegffelen, Thierry, 'D'une dévotion à l'autre? L'évolution de la pratique du pain bénit mise en rapport avec le processus de "sortie de la religion"', *Histoire des dévotions* (2000), https://hal. archives-ouvertes.fr/hal-00285123 (last accessed on 23 January 2024).

Watts, Sydney, 'Boucherie et hygiène à Paris au XVIIIᵉ siècle', *Revue d'histoire moderne et contemporaine* 51:3 (2004), p.79-103.

Wenger, Sylvain, 'Innovation, industrialisation et institutions du savoir: une perspective genevoise (1750-1850)', doctoral dissertation, Université de Genève, 2016.

Williams, Alan, 'The police and public welfare in eighteenth-century Paris', *Social science quarterly* 56:3 (1975), p.398-409.

–, 'The police and the administration of eighteenth-century Paris', *Journal of urban history* 4:2 (1978), p.157-82.

–, *The Police of Paris, 1718-1789* (Baton Rouge, LA, 1979).

Wolodkiewicz, Witold, 'L'Association de bienfaisance judiciaire: les philosophes des Lumières à la veille de la Révolution', *Revue historique de droit français et étranger* 68 (1990), p.363-74.

Zeller, Olivier, 'Espace privé, espace public et cohabitation: Lyon à l'époque moderne', in *La Société des voisins: partager un habitat collectif*, ed. Bernard Haumont and Alain Morel (Paris, 2005), p.187-207.

Index

Printed in the USA
CPSIA information can be obtained
at www.ICGtesting.com
CBHW050332221024
16210CB00005B/262